THE POST-BROADCASTING AGE: NEW TECHNOLOGIES, NEW COMMUNITIES

Papers from the 25th and 26th University of Manchester Broadcasting Symposia

Editors:

Nod Miller
Department of Innovation Studies
University of East London
(Symposium Director)

Rod Allen
PSInet Ltd

THE POST-BROADCASTING AGE: NEW TECHNOLOGIES, NEW COMMUNITIES

Papers from the 25th and 26th University of Manchester Broadcasting Symposia

Edited by

Nod Miller
Department of Innovation Studies, University of East London

Rod Allen
PSInet Ltd

Published with the generous support of Channel 4 Television

Current Debates in Broadcasting: 4/5

UNIVERSITY
of
LUTON PRESS

E00049I5I99001.

British Library Cataloguing in Publication Data

A catalogue record for this book is available from the British Library

ISBN: 0 86020 502 X
ISSN: 0963-6544

Published by

John Libbey Media
Faculty of Humanities
University of Luton
75 Castle Street
Luton
Bedfordshire LU1 3AJ
United Kingdom
Telephone: +44 (0) 1582 743297; Fax: +44 (0) 1582 743298

Typeset in Palatino and designed by THL Typesetting, London NW6
Printed by Gemini Press Ltd, Shoreham-by-Sea, West Sussex BN43 6NZ

Contents

Sponsors and committee

One of the objectives of the Symposium Steering Committee is to keep the cost of attending the event as low as possible. It is greatly assisted in achieving this objective by the generosity of its long-term supporters and sponsors. The Committee would like to express its gratitude to its 1994 and 1995 supporters and sponsors, who were:

Independent Television Commission   **Channel 4 Television**
BBC North   **Granada Television**
Carlton Television   **Action Time**
Border Television

In organising the Broadcasting Symposium, the School of Education of the University of Manchester was advised by a Steering Committee, the members of which were:

Colin Shaw, CBE, Broadcasting Standards Council (chair)
John Gray, independent consultant (honorary president)

Nod Miller, University of Manchester (director)
Marjorie Burton, University of Manchester (administrator)
Margaret Crawford, University of Manchester (administrator)

1994 committee:
Rod Allen, HarperCollins Interactive
Liz Ashton Hill, College of St Mark & St
    John, Plymouth
Helen Baehr, University of Westminster
Steven Barnett, Henley Centre/Goldsmiths'
    College
Genevieve Clarke, Independent
    Television Commission
Luke Crawley, BECTU
Andrew Curry, Videotron
Phillip Drummond, University of London
Lynne Fredlund, independent producer
Fred Hasson, PACT
Jerome Kuehl, Open Media
Roy Lockett, BECTU
Shivaun Meehan, BSC
Pam Mills, consultant
Kim Peat, Channel 4 Television
Roy Saatchi, BBC North
Brook Sinclair, Adcomm
Mike Spencer, Granada Television
Veronica Taylor, British Film Institute

1995 committee:
Rod Allen, HarperCollins Interactive
Liz Ashton Hill, College of St Mark & St
    John, Plymouth
Helen Baehr, University of Westminster
Sue Caro, Channel 4 Television
Phillip Drummond, University of London
Lynne Fredlund, independent producer
Allan Jewhurst, Chameleon Television
Jerome Kuehl, Open Media
Roy Lockett, BECTU
Pam Mills, consultant
Kim Peat, BBC Television
Ruth Pitt, Real Life Productions
Roy Saatchi, BBC North
Brook Sinclair, Adcomm
Nick Smith, Independent Television
    Commission
Mike Spencer, Granada Television
Veronica Taylor, British Film Institute

Transcriptions by Francesca Garcià-Quismondo
Audio recordings by David Griffiths, Terry McMylor and Stephen Glasgow

The post-broadcasting age: passing painfully into the postmodern

Nod Miller
Department of Innovation Studies, University of East London (Symposium Director)

Rod Allen
PSInet Limited

IN this book we offer papers and discussion from both the twenty-fifth and the twenty-sixth University of Manchester Broadcasting Symposia. These events brought together academics, broadcasting practitioners and those concerned with public policy and the regulation of broadcasting. Both conferences looked forward to a new age in mass media — one in which, thanks to digital technology, bandwidth scarcity has been replaced by bandwidth multiplicity, and one in which all the existing paradigms for the management of radio and television service provision, based on the allocation of limited resources in the public interest, have been made utterly obsolescent. The technological changes which have to be contemplated, and their implications, are described and discussed thoroughly by Helen Cunningham, Pam Mills and Alan Morris in their session on 'The technological rollercoaster'. The concerns addressed at both Symposia were those of an industry and a community passing, with some pain, from one epoch to another — a movement which many would recognise as a passage from the modern to the postmodern age, but which we have characterised in this volume as the passage towards the post-broadcasting age. However, it is important to remember, as Hassan (1987) points out, that

> Modernism and postmodernism are not separated by an Iron Curtain or a
> Chinese wall; for history is a palimpsest, and culture is permeable to time past,
> time present and time future. We are all, I suspect, a little Victorian, Modern
> and Postmodern, at once. (p87)

In this context, the discourse of many of those who are thinking beyond the broadcasting age reflects the constraints of earlier systems and technologies. Many of the sessions of the Symposia addressed issues which, while related more to the old paradigms, are still to be resolved and which will remain highly relevant into the digital future; among these are the arguments about regionality, community and diversity which take up much of the second part of the book.

Gillian Reynolds describes in her contribution the way that broadcast coverage has historically been arranged for the most part on a subnational, or regional, basis, because of the nature of analogue transmitter technology. Thus the original BBC radio transmitters served the West of England, the Northern region, or Scotland; and the television areas enshrined in the Independent Television Commision's

1991 ITV licences are still based on the coverage of the obsolete 405-line VHF transmitters which went out of service during the 1970s. (Why else would a single licensee serve the chalk and cheese of Wales and the West of England?) Around these artificial territories have grown up generations of broadcasters who are united by their non-metropolitan location, and who have laid historical claim to a share of resources for 'the regions'. The future for the strong tradition of regional programme-making in Britain is discussed by Paul Bonner, Duncan Dallas and John Whiston in their contributions to the session on 'New regions for old'. While Paul Bonner, who served his apprenticeship on the old BBC West of England Home Service, is pessimistic for the future of regional programming in an increasingly competitive world of network broadcasting, John Whiston, who works for the BBC in Manchester, makes a robust case for his region's ability to reach parts of the audience that the metropolis cannot.

Yet digital transmissions, especially those delivered by cable or Internet technologies, are in no way constrained by geography or national borders, which makes redefinition of the 'regions' or 'communities' served by broadcasters all the more important. Because of an accident of technological history, some would say that geographical communities have to date been exceptionally well served by broadcasting: the technological advance now presents the opportunity to serve communities of interest, the members of whom do not necessarily live in proximity to one another. The corollary, however, is that the difficult issues of reallocating resources (and jobs, and skills, and the other human elements affected by major structural changes) to serving these newly accessible communities must now be faced.

At the same time, there is a postmodern paradox which must be taken into account. Many of the contributors to the session entitled 'Is commerce the enemy of diversity and creativity?' address with fear or contempt the increasing dominance of transnational organisations like News Corporation, Time Warner and Turner Broadcasting; and the positive and negative influences of the European Union are mentioned by contributors including Colin Fletcher, Phillip Whitehead and Gillian Reynolds. The paradox is the parallel development of transnational communities and alliances alongside the growth of fierce local and regional loyalties. As Hassan *(op. cit.)* puts it, 'our earth seems caught in the process of planetization, transhumanization, even as it breaks up into sects, tribes, factions of every kind.' (p96). Those who operate the mass media are facing the need to accommodate the structural globalisation of the industrial enterprises which distribute and deliver channels while at the same time creating and funding content which addresses fragmented audiences in terms both of geographical area and of narrowing areas of common interest. Judith Mackay, who manages the content of Birmingham Cable, describes how she has grappled with this problem in her contribution to 'Democracy down the tube'.

Concern about globalisation of media ownership is expressed in many of the contributions to this volume. The fear is that national identities and regional cultural interests will be eradicated by the economic power wielded by large international media owners putting commercial considerations before the political or cultural interests of their users, or customers. The session on 'Home Shopping' painted a somewhat bleak picture of channels devoted entirely to the sale of goods, without the intervention of programmes to alleviate the advertising, which for some represented the inevitable outcome of the growth of the transnationals. But home shopping channels in fact only occupy a small portion of the bandwidth available to the viewer. Many argue that control over the distribution of content is more important than questions of the content itself. A previous Symposium contributor, Nicholas Garnham (1986), has pointed out that:

> It is cultural distribution, not cultural production, that is the key locus of power and profit. It is access to distribution which is the key to cultural plurality. (p31-2)

This view is graphically illuminated by an exchange in 'Face the Symposium' between Bob Phillis, deputy director-general of the BBC, and Granville Williams, of the Campaign for Press and Broadcasting Freedom. Phillis describes News Corporation's decision to remove BBC World Service Television from its satellite covering the People's Republic of China so as not to offend the Chinese government, and admits the BBC had to bow to commercial realities in this case.

Yet the commercial interests of the transnational are most often best served by recognising the local and particular needs and interests of the audiences they reach, whether they are communities of interest, such as those served by MTV or the sports channels, or geographical communities, such as those addressed by Judith Mackay's Birmingham Cable. The importance of local and regional news, which is unlikely to decline as channels multiply, is emphasised in the session on 'Whose News?', which featured a lively debate on the purpose and functions of regional news programmes like Yorkshire TV's *Calendar*; Steve Morrison, of LWT, interviewed for 'Face the Symposium' by Rod Allen, described his company's regionally-based response to the increased competition for audiences in the early evening time slots which have in the past been protected for regional factual programmes by regulation.

However, some theorists of the postmodern, like Baudrillard (1985), are entranced by the removal of geographical boundaries implied by satellite and cable-delivered services, even though they are of necessity operated by large international entities. Baudrillard writes, in an essay enthusiastically entitled 'The ecstasy of communication', of a media-induced world of 'absolute proximity, the total instantaneity of things, the feeling of no defence, no retreat.' (1985: 133). More practically, though with equal enthusiasm, the response to the 'hunger for community' imagined by Howard Rheingold (1994) is described by Robins (1996) in the following way:

> the virtual community of the network is the focus for a grand project of social vitalisation and renewal. Under conditions of virtual existence, it seems possible to recover the values and ideals that have been lost to the real world. Through this new medium ... we shall be able to construct new sorts of community, linked by commonality of interest and affinity rather than by accidents of location. (pp18-19)

An optimistic reading of the potential power of network technology leads to a vision of new possibilities of interaction and affirmation through new-style communities whose members are widely dispersed in space and time. But these are not necessarily substitutes for traditional communities based on geography, and proponents of computer-based communications believe that these technologies can regenerate and animate groups characterised by physical proximity and face-to-face communication. Phil Wood and Steve Avery describe in their contribution to the Symposium session called 'Does regional culture matter?' the way in which geographical communities like their own in Kirklees, West Yorkshire, are exploring the potential of pro-active local cultural policy to generate both economic activity and social action. One important effect of the development of new channels is, of course, the creation of new opportunities, both creative and economic, for the makers of cultural products. Chris Griffin, a 'traditional' independent programme maker, Sheila Rodgers, whose company makes electronic publications for distribution on CD-ROM, and Brian Harper Lewis, a former TV producer who is exploring the opportunities of 'interactive television' for the cable operator Videotron, described some of these opportunities in a session called 'What price independence?', and warned that it would be a tough struggle for small, imaginative producers to survive outside the world of the multinational production and distribution entities like News Corporation. Professor Colin Young, in his session, reminded the Symposium of the importance of training for these new opportunities.

One striking feature of the movement into the post-broadcasting age is the fact that institutions whose objective is to regulate and, as some would say, censor media output seem to be multiplying. Yet the underpinnings of institutional regulation can be argued to be withering away as the moral foundations of the modern age are stripped away. Bauman (1987) suggests that one of the characteristics of postmodernism is the demise of moral certainties:

> It is perhaps debateable whether the philosophers of the modern era ever articulated to everybody's satisfaction the foundations of the objective superiority of Western rationality, logic, morality, aesthetics, cultural precepts, etc. The fact is, however, that they never stopped looking for such an articulation ... The postmodern period is distinguished by abandoning the search itself, having convinced itself of its futility. (p117).

The modern age was greatly concerned with the identification of moral precepts which could be used as a foundation for law and regulation, whereas postmodernity celebrates the impossibility of establishing such absolutes. Yet it is clear that the regulators are not going to give up without a fight. In his paper 'The Future of Regulation', which was commissioned for this book, Colin Shaw makes a spirited stand for both the technical practicality and the social need to regulate new channels; others, including Jane Vizard and Michael Redley in the session entitled 'Testing the Boundaries', echo his call for the benign influence of regulation for the public good. The argument for the beneficial outcome of regulation was cogently argued in a previous Symposium by Anthony Smith (1991), who said:

> the more perfectly deregulation is imposed upon broadcasting, the more we lose of what viewers and legislators actually value — and that is the production of

programmes which encompass a wide range of society's needs and interests. (p.9)

Smith's position is that regulation, by creating a scarcity of channels, makes it possible to demand the production of particular kinds of programme in return for the right to use the scarce national asset of broadcast spectrum. Yet it remains likely that as spectrum capacity becomes virtually infinite, television transmission merges imperceptibly with world-wide network systems, and the distinctions between broadcasting, publishing, common-carrier operations and point-to-point communication slowly disappear, both the need for and the feasibility of regulation will also diminish to the point of disappearance. The FBI has already (February 1996) declined to enforce the American Congress's Telecommunications Act, which seeks to eliminate 'indecent material' from the Internet, on the grounds that it is not only likely to be found unconstitutional by the courts, but that it is also effectively unworkable. In any case, many would argue that in the postmodern age it has become difficult to make clear statements about what is and what is not fit to be transmitted. Bauman *(op. cit.)* says that the postmodern period:

> tries to reconcile itself to a life under conditions of permanent and incurable uncertainty; a life in the presence of an unlimited quantity of competing forms of life, unable to prove their claims to be grounded in anything more solid and binding than their own historically shaped conventions. (p117)

This implies that the inability to settle the arguments over what should be regulated, and how it should be regulated, is likely to render the regulators powerless; the debate itself becomes part of the subject matter of the media and by constantly questioning the underpinning assumptions of the regulators neutralises them.

None of this is to say that the role of government, and the public interest, in the media sphere is over. On the contrary, it can be argued that government has been derelict in its duty to pay attention to communications issues. In his keynote presentation for the 1994 Symposium, Professor Roger Silverstone, of the University of Sussex, makes an important plea for the effective creation of public policy capable of dealing with the profound changes through which the media are passing. He recalls one of the key characteristics of the model of public service broadcasting, universal provision; and he notes that to the extent that current public communications policy is discernible, no concept of universal provision of the new communications services, such as the Internet, is to be found. Silverstone reminds us that to exclude people (meaning, inevitably, those who are unable to pay for a multiplicity of channel choices) from access to the means of two-way communication of ideas in the post-broadcasting age is likely to result in social deprivation and disharmony at least as damaging as that which can result from excluding people from housing, welfare, medical care or employment.

The University of Manchester Broadcasting Symposium is designed as an experiential event, and every year a participatory exercise takes place in the hope that it will help those attending to come to grips with one of the key issues being discussed through taking part in a hypothetical or a role-play. John Gray and Mike Davis contribute reviews of the experiential learning that took place in both

Symposia, though of course it is in the nature of such exercises that the only way to get their true flavour is to be there on the day.

Nod Miller
Rod Allen

References
Baudrillard, J. (1985), 'The ecstasy of communication' in Foster, H. (ed.), *Postmodern culture*. London: Pluto.
Bauman, Z. (1987), *Legislators and Interpreters*. Oxford: Basil Blackwell.
Garnham, N. (1986), 'Concepts of culture: public policy and the cultural industries' in *Cultural Studies* 1(1), pp. 23-38.
Hassan, I. (1987), *The Postmodern Turn*. Columbus: Ohio State University Press.
Rheingold, H. (1994), *The Virtual Community: finding connection in a computerized world*. London: Secker and Warburg.
Robins, K. (1996), 'Cyberspace and the World We Live In' in Dovey, J. (ed), *Fractal Dreams: new media in social context*. London: Lawrence and Wishart.
Smith, A. (1991), 'Public service broadcasting meets the social market' in Miller, N. and Allen, R. (eds), *And Now For the BBC*. London: John Libbey.

Part 1

Nintendo Millennium

The 1994 Symposium: Keynote address

Future imperfect: media, information and the millennium

Professor Roger Silverstone
School of Cultural and Community Studies
University of Sussex

IT is a commonplace to observe that things are changing in our media world. New technologies, new delivery systems, new industrial alliances are being announced almost daily. The rhetoric is apocalyptic and breathless. It is a familiar but insistent rhetoric both of revolution and crisis. It is a rhetoric of competing utopian or dystopian visions, fought out in and on the very media who are its subject. It is a rhetoric deeply engrained in the militaristic and sexual metaphors of strategic advance and big bangs. In a recent television documentary on these issues (*Me TV*, BBC-2, 25 September 1993) Diane von Furstenburg, a close friend and associate of Barry Diller, formerly head of Paramount, then head of Richard Murdoch's Fox Broadcasting and now running QVC, the biggest interactive home shopping company in the US, recounted how she had suggested that he see the new interactive television technology for himself. "He came", she said with a smile, "and the rest was history".

Yet there is no doubting these changes. They have already begun in earnest. Take for example the effect of the presence of satellite or cable as well as video in today's households. The average share of weekly viewing gained by BBC 1 in all homes last year was 32.7%. In homes with satellite or cable this fell to 24.4%. For BBC2 the fall was from 10.2% to 6.5%. For ITV 40% to 30.5%. And for C4/S4C 11% to 7.2% (*Screen Digest*, March, 1994). Take for example the fact that the computer games market world-wide is now bigger than that of recorded music — a market incidentally dominated in both hardware and software by two companies (Nintendo and Sega) who between them took 96% of the US market. Take for example the sudden take-off in the sales of mobile phones, a market which is currently increasing at the rate of 25% per year.

The selection of these examples is significant not just on their own account, but because it draws attention to the fact that our media world is not any more one of isolated technologies or monopoly delivery systems. It is a world of converging technologies and intense competition. It is also a world which is no longer shared or so easily shareable. New and alternative delivery systems — broadcast, narrowcast, terrestrial, satellite, cable as well as the rapidly increasing range of software and programme choices — allow consumers to express their own individual tastes much more intensely and consistently. At the same time it is a world in which the internationalisation of culture begun by Hollywood is being equally intensified as huge new multi-nationals fight to integrate hardware and software production, and to extend the distribution of programme content, content which they themselves increasingly own, across media and across continents.

In this lecture I want to explore some of the issues raised by all of this — by what is increasingly being called the 'multi-media revolution'. But I want to do so with one main aim in view. It is to question the coherence of the revolutionary vision, to question it from the point of view of its inevitability, from the point of view of its uniformity and from the point of view of its consequences. I will argue that it is not technology that creates social change but how we use that technology. And I will argue that use is no simple matter. It depends on access, competence, desire. It is inflected by gender and age, class and culture. In pursuing this argument I will draw on some of our own ongoing research at Sussex into the way in which media and information technologies, both old and new, are adopted by today's households, and I will try to offer an account of the 'multi-media revolution' which takes seriously the realities of technological change but offers other visions of the future: visions that are grounded in the mundane but still complex realities of everyday life. I think it is important to register that our media and information future is a difficult and contradictory thing — much like, indeed, the present. So future is, or ought to be, plural, and these futures are social futures — the futures of individuals, families and households as well as the futures of technologies and industries.

What are, or should be, our concerns in all of this? I have touched on some of them already. First, perhaps, is the issue of control, and the question of the increasing dominance and power of media and information industries on the one hand, and the greater freedom of action that consumers and users may have on the other. This is a huge issue that touches both surveillance, for example in the increasing possibilities of data gathering and data integration consequent upon the introduction of home based multi-media interactivity, and freedom or even subversion, for example in the almost entirely unpoliced (and possibly unpoliceable) Internet — the rapidly expanding international computer network which as a result of its free and open access lets a thousand and one interest groups communicate with each other from keyboards in offices and homes all across the US and internationally. The second concerns access to this insistent media culture, and especially the denial or restriction of access to groups and individuals who do not have the resources to participate in an increasingly market dominated system. This has significant implications for the quality of our social, cultural as well as our political life. And the third issue is that of choice — embodied perhaps in what is currently being called 'Me-TV'. Me-TV refers to the increasing capacity of television to change from being the end of the line of a broadcast signal to a domestic communication and information hub, through which individuals and families can command information and media products (at a price) but at the touch of a button. Me-TV refers to my ability to determine what I want from my screen.

Each of these inter-related concerns — control, access and choice — are both released and intensified not just by the relentless march of technology but by the particular ways those technologies are themselves being developed and, more or less, regulated. But these concerns are also being articulated through the consumption and use of these technologies, as new and old machines and services jostle for position in the endless to-ing and fro-ing of our everyday lives. Indeed it is here, I shall argue, within our domestic rituals and resistances, that the battles for our media and information futures will be won or lost.

So let me open out this discussion by telling three separate but related stories. The first is the technological story. The second is the industrial story. And the third is the domestic story: The domestic story involves brief accounts of two very different contemporary lives with technology — one, that of a high-tech teleworking household, and the other, that of a desperately low-tech lone parent one. Each offers a different perspective on our media and information futures, and in trying to make sense of what those futures might be, none of these stories, I suggest, can be ignored.

The Technological Story
First, then, the technological story. It is, it must be said, difficult to penetrate the smog of claims and counter-claims. But at least two things are clear. The hype itself both signals, as it attempts to mask, a high level of anxiety in the industry, as major players invest massive resources in a technological game in which there are going to be — by most accounts — some very big winners and some cataclysmic losers.

But the second thing that is absolutely clear is that the technology is changing, and changing very quickly. One thing above all is making this possible — digitisation. This conversion of continuous — analogue — information into bits, offering more accurate and precise reproduction of sound and image, as well as accurate and rapid transmission of data, is well established already in music audio and in electronic publishing. What makes it so significant right now is a technical advance that allows the digitised information to be compressed — squashed into a smaller delivery channel or storage space. This compression, which depends on a complex mathematical and technical process of eliminating redundancy in parts of a continuous image, allows as much as one hundred times more information to be stored or transmitted in a given space. This is the miracle which releases the techno-genie from the lamp. For with this degree of compression a number of things become possible. In terms of transmission, and in terms of cable — especially fibre-optic cable, but also apparently the old twisted copper wire — it becomes possible to generate interactive signals enabling a two-way communication in real time to be conducted through the television screen. It also becomes possible to transmit many more discrete channels of high quality video down a single cable or in principle also within a given hitherto limited and tightly controlled radio spectrum. In terms of storage, it becomes possible — it already is — to fit 72 minutes of full motion video and stereo sound onto a single CD, as well as to store, as we already know, thousands of pages of printed material on the same CD.

Digital compression in turn enhances and reinforces a technological change in which the previously discrete media and information technologies — television, telephone, computer — are converging. Once upon a time the telephone was a telephone and the television a television, and no-one had heard of computers. Perhaps we have barely noticed that the computer game is already a hybrid, as indeed was Prestel, a not much lamented and almost entirely unsuccessful tel-ephone- and screen-based home information service. The term *Multi-media* sig-nals a convergence and an intensification of this process, in which either within a single piece of hardware, like Philips' CD-I, or within a cable based network it becomes quite possible to integrate image, sound and data within a single system and for the user-consumer to interact with a complex of materials: gaining access, making entertainment choices, responding to, or initiating, requests for informa-tion. It is the capacity of this new generation of convergent technologies to release this kind of interactivity that is seen as being its main, and most exciting, conse-quence.

Technological convergence is underpinned and reinforced by two further fac-tors. The first is the emergence of agreed world standards for the storage and trans-mission of the digital coding of moving pictures and sound. A group of engineers (the Motion Picture Experts Group or MPEG) has been working since 1986 to pro-duce a common language to enable different producers in the various and increas-ingly interrelated industries of telecommunications, computing and television (as well as their customers) to be confident that such advance will not be hampered by the babel of incompatible voices. The second factor is interconnectivity. Vice-President Al Gore talks of an information super-highway. What this Algore-ithm indicates is the perceived need to develop a communication network — available both for commercial and private use — which will massively increase both the speed and efficiency as well as the power of the system as a whole. Systems are always greater than the sum of their parts. This is never more true than of a system that depends on the transmission and storage — in the widest sense of the word — of information.

Those who see in this scenario a vivid new technological future also see a number of quantum leaps in what we can expect from what was once a plain old TV set. The first is, surprise surprise, home shopping. The second is a conversion of exist-ing broadcasting culture into a publishing culture in which consumers will be able to select what to watch when they want to watch it (or indeed in some versions of the vision in which a smart TV set does the job of selection for you). This will have consequences both for the scheduling of media content — it will become redun-dant — and universal provision. Audiences will become consumers, fragmented both in time and space. And the third is the quality of the image and sound. Digitisation, compressed or uncompressed, produces high fidelity (to use a curi-ously old-fashioned term) images within existing PAL or SECAM TV systems. This, it is argued, makes HDTV (High Definition Television), in which improved picture quality is being sought by increasing the number of lines on the screen, obsolete at a stroke. HDTV has become a kind of media equivalent of Concorde — expensive, beautiful but probably unnecessary.

So far, perhaps, so good. Yet perhaps like so much else that has its origins or base in California, visible integrities mask profound uncertainties.

The first uncertainty concerns the ways in which such interactive multi-media products and services will be delivered. The MPEG standard requires complex encoding technologies that send the signal, but relatively less complex (and therefore cheaper) technologies to receive and decode it. This means a set-top box that receives the digitally compressed signals either by cable, satellite or terrestrial transmission (and therein lies the rub) and turns the dumb television set into a smart computer-video terminal. The race is on to develop the box. But the competition is also on between alternative delivery systems, in which cable and satellite are the principle — but not the only — contenders. Existing terrestrial transmission — the radio spectrum — has less capacity, and commentators believe that terrestrial television transmission will not be best suited for digital TV. Running alongside these network-based systems, and likely to have an early advantage, are those technologies — more strictly multimedia — which embody within a self-contained unit — an integrated video, computer and CD player — the capacity to access and interact with images, sounds and data. The problem here is the lack of an agreed standard for CD-based interactive multimedia machines. The problem is also that cable or satellite based systems will soon be able to do all that the standalone CD player can do and more.

The other uncertainties are not strictly technological and indeed they are much more profound. Of course these machines and systems will deliver — one way or another. The potential is there, and massive investment will ensure that this potential will be realised — sooner or later. No, the real uncertainties, as ever, relate to issues of control, to issues of content and to issues of consumption. In short we can ask how this new (or indeed maybe not so new) media and information environment is to be controlled and regulated, and by whom; we can ask whether such a radical enhancement in the number of delivery channels (500 and more cable channels are being talked about in the US) can possibly be supported; and we can ask does anybody really want or need any of it?

Such questions — which, of course, I cannot hope to answer conclusively, lead me however to my next story: the industrial story.

The Industrial Story

I have already introduced the idea of convergence in relation to technology. It re-emerges here too as a crucial dimension of the reconstruction of the media and information industry world-wide. The driving force behind this convergence — a convergence which involves the coming together of major companies which have previously confined their attentions to a single sector: telecommunications, film production, hardware manufacture, software development, distribution systems — is the perceived need to control the integrative potential of the emerging lattice of technology. If I understand this process correctly, the key prizes are content — films, television programming and computer software production on the one hand, and control over the distribution networks, especially cable, on the other.

Ownership of content is crucial. The talent to produce new materials for new media will always be at a premium, and so too will be the rights to existing software — be it in the form of films, television programmes or computer games.

There is only one *Gone with the Wind, M*A *S*H* or, perhaps mercifully, *Jurassic Park* or *Super Mario,* and the he or she who owns them earns from them. Equally the ownership of the distribution networks is crucial. In a world in which principles of common carriage are disappearing like water in the sand, in that ownership lies the ability to charge others for access to the consumer and to charge consumers for access to content. Those who can control both content production and rights as well as distribution, so the argument goes, will find themselves on a gravy train of unprecedented proportions. It is fair to say, though, that others (e.g. Bowen, 1994) argue such consolidation and vertical integration will be counterproductive, denying organisations flexibility in a constantly changing technological and commercial environment.

So the results have been seen in purchases of Hollywood studios by Japanese hardware producers (Sony bought Columbia in 1989; Matsushita bought Universal in 1990), but also by Newspaper publishing groups (Murdoch's News Corporation bought 20th Century-Fox in the late 1980s). And most recently, in February 1994, after a huge take-over battle, the last independent major Hollywood studio, Paramount Pictures was bought for a billion dollars by the cable and film distribution company Viacom (which had only a few months earlier taken over Blockbuster Entertainment) and which had co-opted one of the largest of the US 'Baby-Bell' telecommunications companies (Nynex) into the deal.

Meanwhile on the other side of Wall Street other Baby Bells with high cash reserves and faced with increasing competition in their traditional telephone markets have been investing heavily outside their familiar domains. US West put $2.5bn into Time-Warner (owner of a huge portfolio of film and television programmes as well as already being the second biggest US cable company), and Bell Atlantic and TCI (the biggest US cable company) narrowly failed to consummate a merger, preferring instead, given what they felt was an unstable regulatory environment, the prospect of living in comfortable but less compromising commercial sin.

Meanwhile, on the other side of the Atlantic, Bertelsmann, the German media conglomerate, is joining forces with Deutches Telekom, and British Telecom, with its recently announced video-on-demand project (and despite existing government regulations), is associated with a whole range of British television production companies including, apparently, the BBC.

At the same time hardware competitors Matsushita, Philips and Sony are combining in a software consortium called General Magic, and Bill Gates of Microsoft is investing $100m a year in smart-TV software development with the computer chip manufacturer Intel. And this is just the tip of the iceberg, or the froth on the sea, depending on your judgement of the temperature and the quality of the water.

Perhaps all of this is more in hope than in certainty, but whatever the detailed outcome and whoever the winners or losers it does look as though the industrial map is changing. What are the implications? Indeed, what are the implications of the combined effects of the technological and industrial convergences which I have so briefly outlined?

It is possible to point to a number of different possible consequences and problems. The first seems reasonably clear. There will be more television — or, more strictly, more screen-based products and services. And quantity really does turn into quality (in the non-evaluative sense) for such expansion must involve a more focused and a more fragmented media environment, with distinct programmes, software or services being directed to distinct bodies of consumers. It must also involve a *de facto* shift in the dominant ethos of our media world: from broadcasting to publishing.

Secondly and consequentially there looms the question of access and accessibility. Public service broadcasting, in Europe at least, seeks to provide a universal service within a national culture. It cannot hope to survive in its present forms, but the question of a universally available service equally cannot be left to the depredations of the market-place. Equally, the media market-place itself is unlikely to produce even a marginally disinterested publisher unless some principles of common carriage — that is allowing content producers, programme makers, service providers and the rest access to the cable networks — are implemented. Every deregulation, as Graham Murdock once pointed out, is, and requires, at the same time a reregulation. There is precious little room for optimism if cable network owners (who are, as I have just noted, also increasingly owners of content) are allowed complete freedom to control the price of entry to their networks. Choice under such circumstances becomes a chimera, and access to those without the necessary resources an impossibility.

Thirdly is the issue of programme hybridity. I have already pointed out that the screen is increasingly likely to become the site of a multi-media culture in which telecommunications, computing and video intertwine. But there is a further dimension of possible hybridisation to be considered. This concerns the discrete presence of advertising — up to now the main motor of the television industry. What will make consumers watch ads when they have so much else to choose from? Two things perhaps. The first is when they are not particularly aware that that is indeed what they are watching, so one might expect an increasing development of what could be called 'advo-tainment' and 'advo-mation' — developments which will make designer shows like *Miami Vice*, pop-ad video channels like MTV or Accurist's sponsorship of BT's speaking clock seem like the media equivalent of *Noddy in Toyland*. The second is when the advertising itself is customised. Remember that interactive home shopping (and even, increasingly, real shopping in real shops) provides the retailing organisation with an opportunity to gain important customer information: information about financial and other dimensions of status as well as a map of individual or household consumer choices, both of media content and consumer products. It does not take much to imagine much more focused, indeed almost personalised ad-appeals, as a result.

I began this lecture by pointing out that claims for the ubiquity and the intensity of the multimedia revolution must be understood not simply on their own terms. It is as easy to be seduced by the rhetoric of technological change as it is easy to be dismayed by it. However as I have also pointed out there is another reality to be considered, one which might be seen to contain or constrain that revolution, as well as possibly diverting it or interrupting it. This is the reality — complex certainly, diverse, perverse — of the everyday life of those who live in and with the present generation of media and information technologies, and who will have to come to terms — some kind of terms — with their future.

To say as much is to say that the multi-media revolution is neither simply nor exclusively a technological nor an industrial phenomenon: and that its logic — the logic of innovation as well as the logic of its effects — is neither assured nor clear-cut. The multi-media revolution, if it is to be understood at all, and indeed if it is to be steered at all, needs to be understood in a social context. It will be worked out at the interface, as Raymond Williams once noted, of new technologies and old social forms.

This brings me to my last story: the domestic story.

The Domestic Story
Our domesticity is a product of a number of interrelated social and cultural processes in which increasingly media and information technologies have been involved. Historically the overall shape of that domesticity has been associated with the rise of industrialisation: with the urbanisation and suburbanisation of populations, with the rise of mass education, and with changing patterns and structures of work. Throughout the twentieth century communication and information technologies (including literally such communication technologies as the tram, the commuter bus and train and the motor car, but also of course radio and television) have enabled the dispersal of populations away from the face-to-face intensities of both inner cities and rural villages. This dispersal has involved increasing mobility (we can move around) and reach (we can communicate with, and learn from, others without moving around) as well as increasing privatisation.

Many commentators see in the present and future generations of media and information technologies a major accelerator of these tendencies, with consequential implications for the quality of our everyday lives, for our sense of belonging, for our sense of security, and for our capacity to participate in the wider society. As ever there are competing visions and competing critiques. There are those who argue that these technologies have contributed to an undermining of a sense of home, creating a new kind of rootlessness, since they have the capacity to unlock, disconnent and decathect individuals from their dependence on place — a rootlessness which results in increasing social isolation and cultural fragmentation. Others have suggested the reverse: that such technologies — telephone, television, computer and now multi-media — have already begun, and will continue, to liberate our domesticity from its dependence on physical location, and at the same time enhance our social and cultural freedoms, enabling us — as active consumers and users — to create our own distinct and meaningful cultural identities.

These debates are important. They go to the heart of the essential tensions that lie at the centre of our domestic and everyday lives and which new technologies throw into sharp relief These are the tensions between security and insecurity, between participation and isolation, and between freedom and control, and they are the defining tensions which any analysis of the role of media and information technologies in our everyday lives must confront. Yet they are not resolvable merely by an examination of the technology. For as the American scholar Ithiel de Sola Pool once noted in his discussion of the telephone, our media and information technologies have double lives: they both connect and disconnect; liberate and constrain, and they do both, or can do both, simultaneously and contradictorily. The particular balance that is struck between these opposite poles is a product, I would suggest, both of the ways in which they are regulated, and the ways in which they are consumed; or in the terms which we adopt in our study — in the ways in which they are domesticated.

The domestication of new media and information technologies involves, quite literally, a taming of the wild and a cultivation of the tame. In this process new technologies and services, albeit already packaged and marketed as user-friendly but nevertheless still unfamiliar, exciting but also threatening, are brought (or not) under control by domestic users. They are bought or subscribed to, understood or misunderstood, used or rejected. And in their ownership and in their appropriation into the culture of family or household and into the routines of everyday life, they are at the same time cultivated. They become familiar and they are moulded and shaped to fit the expectations and values of the household. At the same time, and in that very moulding and shaping, the cultivator is also changed, as is his or her culture.

This process of domestication takes place in complex social and cultural environments: in the pre-existing and necessarily conservative cultures of families and households. New technologies have to be found a place, literally, in the home. They have to be fitted into a pattern of domestic time. They have, in short, to be valued. Such domestication is of course complicated by the social dynamics and politics of families and households. There are conflicts over use and location; over ownership and control; over rights to access. These are conflicts that are played out across the differences between both generation and gender, as adults seek to control the media activities of their children, and boys and girls vie for control over the latest machine. There are anxieties to be dealt with: anxieties about the disruption a new technology might create for the security of familiar routines and rituals, to the challenges it might present to an individual's competence or skill, or to the threat it might pose to the moral values of the family. And the pressures to accept or reject, as well as modify, the meaning of a new technology or service are not generated only by the politics of domestic life, but come too from the conflicts between domestic and public values; from, for example, the competing claims of parents or peer groups, or the incompatible demands of family and work responsibilities.

It is in this sense that our 'multi-media revolution' in all its contradictions has also to be seen, albeit on a different scale and within a different time frame, as a 'domestic revolution'. It is in this sense too that what goes on in the everyday lives of all of us is a necessary pan of the story. It follows that both the present status and impact of new media and information technologies is dependent, to greater or lesser degree, on the social and cultural circumstances of their introduction and use. We might well ask therefore, borrowing but distorting a famous nineteenth century question: who mediates the media? And the answer lies as much in the soil of everyday life as it does in the laboratories of the engineers, the studios of the advertisers and the programme makers, or the offices of the regulators.

Let me dig a little more deeply into that soil by presenting two brief case studies from our current research in the hope that some of the questions, particularly those around access, control and participation can be addressed more precisely. I will then conclude by discussing what I think are the main issues raised by the juxtaposition of these three technological, industrial and domestic stories.

The first comes from our study of teleworking households. Amongst a population within the study of extremely diverse — professional and clerical, employed, self-employed and underemployed, male and female — teleworkers, the Townsends were perhaps the most successful and most deeply embedded in their high technology culture. Jonathan and Emma live in a large house in two acres of rural Oxfordshire. Both have science or engineering degrees. They have two children, Geoffrey, aged 18 and Susan, 15. Jonathan works from home as a managing director with operations both in this country and the US. Emma works from home designing computer software. Their combined income is over £100,000. They both vote (or did at the time of study) Conservative.

They have three separate telephone lines: one for domestic calls, one for business calls and one for the fax, and both fixed and cordless receivers, but no mobile. They have an answerphone, but no photocopier. They have three computers, two printers (one colour), and a modem for work use but no e-mail because of the amount of junk mail Jonathan worries about receiving. Their son, Geoffrey, has the old Amstrad in his bedroom, despite the fact that it was bought originally as a Christmas present for all the family — typical of the presents they buy themselves in so far as it was expected to extend, and extend to, them all. Geoffrey, a computer buff since the age of 7, has been promised a £5,000 Unix workstation if he gets a place to read computing at Oxford. Their daughter, Susan, plays the odd game on the Amstrad. They have two televisions and a video recorder (for bought rather than time shifted videos) and television sockets in most rooms. But the main, teletext, television is a small one, so that it can be 'tucked away', and the old one in the bedroom is too fuzzy to use. These are supplemented by a handsized portable which daughter Susan received as a gift. There is talk of distributed video around the house and getting stereo sound, but they watch television relatively infrequently so do not express much enthusiasm either for satellite or cable (except, suggest the parents, insofar as the foreign programmes would help Susan with her languages). Yet the prospect of home shopping and video on demand was appealing. Television was only really embraced when it involved activity and offered the opportunity to extend their control.

This is a household dominated by a work ethic and by self-confessed technophilia. Jonathan is, by his own admission, a workaholic and his arrival in the home four years earlier as a teleworker, together with the equally committed involvement of his wife, has more dramatically than in any other of our households — transfixed the culture of the family. Their children are paid for the jobs they do around the house. Jonathan sets his wife deadlines for the tasks he asks her to fulfil. His life is dominated by the need to control his environment, and his more or less unsuccessful attempts to hold the boundaries between home and work, especially the temporal boundaries. His domestic life is fractured and disturbed by international telephone calls both made and received at unsocial hours. His wife's is suffused by the deadlines set both by her husband and herself to complete programming tasks. Family television watching involves, often, a shared critique, informed by the family's reading of Robert Thouless' *Straight and Crooked Thinking*, of the rhetoric and argumentation presented on the programmes. Jonathan sees his media and information technologies as a kind of therapeutic drug. "I use technology", he says, "to try and stay sane". The telephone and fax offer a modicum of managerial comfort in an otherwise intolerably frustrating working day. The television offers a degree of relaxation at the end of it.

But while their technology connects them both to a distant world and to some extent to each other, it provides a route neither to their community nor to their children. Both are fighting what they recognise is the increasing isolation from neighbours and friends which their teleworking promotes. And Jonathan in particular bewails his technologically intensified absence in the lives of his children. Meanwhile equivalent technological skills and equivalent commitment to work (though unequal earning capacity) have not affected the domestic division of labour. Susan is still responsible for almost all the household tasks.

I present the Townsend case as neither exemplary nor representative. Nor is it meant to be a moral tale. But it is illustrative, I think, in a number of different ways. Firstly it reveals the power of a family culture to define the character of media and information use. It reveals dramatically, but not exceptionally, how important the capacity to control the flow of information and images into and out of a household has become and how important it is for a family such as this one to be in control — period. It reveals how teleworking can undermine familial closeness without to any significant degree altering the basic gender and age based structures of the household. And, I think above all, it offers a dramatic example of the double life of technology, multiply expressed in the paradox of connective-disconnection. This is not an example of the new media technologies determining family culture, or in any direct sense transforming it. It is however an example of the way in which a particular accommodation is reached between particular expressions of social and technological change.

Let me turn now to a second, but very different, case study. Jackie Berry is a thirty seven year old lone parent living with her ten year old son, Mark, in a two-room basement flat in Brighton. Her income from her part-time job as a school assistant is less than £5,000, though she receives family credit and housing benefit. She does not buy any newspapers. She supports the Liberal Democrats.

Jackie is one of a number of lone parents in our study who are living on an income close to £5,000 a year. She represents the most significant group within it, and as such she also represents the experience of a large proportion of lone parents in the UK. It is, however, important to point out that our study, as indeed the population of lone parents as a whole, includes others with different levels of economic resource and financial independence.

Jackie's poverty is constraining in a number of ways which have a direct bearing both on her use of media and information technologies and the consequences of that use. She is profoundly conscious of her financial situation. She has the sole responsibility for her 10-year-old, who is beginning to make increasing demands on her resources. Her involvement with advanced technology is nil. While Mark has an old no longer used Spectrum computer and a more recently purchased Sega games console (a Christmas present from his mother from savings made during her first year back at work), the basic telephone is rented, and the televisions — one colour, one black and white, which Mark has in his room — are second hand. Second hand too is the stereo. Both have Walkmans, but Jackie rarely uses hers. They do not have a video.

Their relationship to these various media is very largely determined by their limited spatial resources. The main television has been found a place close to the dining table (the kitchen was too cramped) and is therefore on — reluctantly as far as Jackie is concerned — during meal times. Mark has his old black and white in his room so that his mother will not be disturbed too early on a weekend morning — though they will watch the main set together in the evenings. Television is too — certainly for Jackie — a comfort and a companion. The impossibility of finding a baby-sitter, together with the cost of going out, make her something of prisoner in the evenings and in this enforced isolation, the occasional telephone calls and the continuous flow of the television provide company. But even this is the source of anxiety, since Jackie is constantly aware — she can hear the "tick tick tick" of the meter — of how much their involvement with the screen is costing. And since she feels she must get her money's worth from her licence fee, she tries to watch as much BBC as she can. Television is seen as both a problem and a resource — though a resource of which she is still not always able to take full advantage. The problem surfaces in her ambivalence about, and difficulty in managing, Mark's television watching. It is a resource, for she acknowledges how viewing is a facilitator of social interaction both inside and outside the home. Yet the cooling of her night storage heaters and once again her concern about costs force her to go to bed early during the winter with a book instead of the TV, and she feels excluded as a result from the conversation at Gingerbread, her local lone parent support group. Equally she discourages Mark from exchanging computer games at school because of the risk of loss or damage to someone else's game. Mark in any case, as she points out, seems more interested in the computer games magazines than the games themselves, an indication perhaps of his being pushed by economic pressure to take comfort in a secondary discourse as a way of maintaining contact with his peers.

The telephone is seen as essential, as a lifeline and a source of security, especially when she is ill. She makes few calls, though admits that her use increases when she feels bored and lonely. So far Mark is not a significant user, but she expects that will change. She has no desire for anything more sophisticated, and the suggestion of an answerphone is appalling: "Everybody will know if I'm out if there's an answerphone", she says. "Somebody might burgle me".

She does not have a computer but muses about buying a old BBC Micro from the school now that they have upgraded, both for Mark and perhaps for her own use (she talks of writing letters and stories). But Mark is not that keen. He would much rather have one of the new Acorns.

Once again I make no claims for Jackie's case to be representative in any strict methodological sense. On the other hand her circumstances are far from unique — and they are not confined to the circumstances of lone-parenthood. Her life with new media technologies is a life, as it were, without them. What she does have offers her a minimal way of keeping contact with the world beyond her front door, but lack of resources as well as lack of confidence (what the French sociologist Pierre Bourdieu would say was a lack of economic and cultural capital), powerfully limit her participation in a wider social and cultural life. In this case the telephone and the television are technologies of survival. And it would not be hard to make the case that in an increasingly multi-media universe, her disadvantage and isolation is likely to become even more extreme.

These examples serve, I hope, a number of purposes. Together they mark some of the limits of the social and cultural territory across which the multi-media juggernaut must pass. Our everyday lives with media and information technologies in the present is not one simply of bland, inevitable or uniform acceptance. Nor will it, can it, be so in the future. Their benefits are unevenly spread and often contradictory. Their challenges more or less easily met. Their effects constantly mediated by the social and cultural circumstances of their use.

Conclusion

I began this discussion by claiming that I wished to challenge the integrity of the vision of the multi-media revolution and to challenge this integrity both by offering an analysis of multiple futures instead of one, as well as by offering an account of the ways which we use and might to continue to use our media and information technologies. By way of conclusion I would like to return to this and to go even further by pointing to instabilities and uncertainties even within those alternative futures.

There is clearly a enormous degree of uncertainty when it comes to the technological future. Engineers and hardware producers are very fond of telling us that the technology of the future is available now, but its arrival is often a disappointment and is, just as often, premature. Videodiscs, videophones, teleshopping and the rest have all been around before. Technological realities do not always match the dreams. Indeed the introduction of new technologies does not guarantee that they will be used in ways which their makers intended The more complex a system is the more vulnerable it tends to become. And indeed the promise of interactivity is a promise of genuine appropriation — consider the possibilities for otherwise passive consumers to send not only their own home videos but any videos down the videophone lines. Consumers in any event are going to have to be persuaded that they need what the new media will offer. We have seen that even a high-tech family like the Townsends has rejected both e-mail and the mobile phone. Needs in late capitalist society are not God given — they have to be created and sustained.

So perhaps we can be forgiven if we adopt a certain amount of scepticism. There is no doubt what the new technologies can do technically, but we must be careful not to read off an automatic set of social consequences from such potential. And further, we would need to consider how specific applications of new technologies can, or will be, made to fit into our everyday lives. Will not home shopping work better if it is accompanied by a local delivery system? New technologies today are sold with a multitude of features, yet we only ever use a tiny proportion of them. Is that going to change, and how will it affect a multi-choice service? Old social habits die hard and there is no doubt that new technologies and services will be transformed in their consumption.

These uncertainties clearly intrude into the industrial story. The major players are playing for very high stakes. In some ways it does not really matter which of the big multinationals wins or loses — at least not to us, the consumers. Two things do matter however. The first is the amount of media and cultural space that is made available for local, alternative or individual access and use. The second is the effect of the dominance of the mass media market in our overall media environment. This has consequences for broadcasting's traditional role as a provider of the social cement in a nation's culture, and of course for the continued survival of some form of public service provision. On might perhaps suggest that the BBC's future is going to depend as much or more on its success in a world market place for English language television or radio programmes as anything that can be achieved by a renewal of the charter or the maintenance of the licence fee.

One conclusion of these various observations seems clear. It is that both technological convergence, industrial convergence, and the convergence that appears in our use of media and information technologies and services in everyday life require one final level of convergence to be considered: a political convergence in the shape of an integrated national media and information policy. This is profoundly lacking in the UK at the present time. Instead, even as I speak, we have a number of discrete and to all intents and purposes disconnected reviews and debates each focusing more or less exclusively on one particular policy question and on one particular segment of the media environment: the regulation of cross-media ownership; the monopoly control of the computer games industry; the future of the BBC; British Telecom's bid to transmit video on demand; the continuing requirement for BT (as well as other PTTs) to provide a universal telephone service; and the censorship of video.

An integrated media policy would have to confront the interdependence of all of these, but it would have to do more. It would have to take the social dimensions of media and information change profoundly into account. At their core these social dimensions must focus on the issues of universal service and public interest. For while media change in an increasingly market-led world will almost certainly offer greater choice, it will be choice at a price and only for those who can afford it. Those who are, for one or reason or another, systematically denied access to the media and information technologies and services which will increasingly provide the infrastructure of our society are going to be systematically denied a chance to participate — to participate politically as well as socially — in that society. Of course media and information technologies, by themselves, can not eradicate social ills (though they are often used as a way of escaping from their most immediate effects) any more than interactive computer voting, by it-self, can remove the endemic weaknesses in the democratic system. But their absence can substantially reinforce those ills and weaknesses while their presence can at least offer a resource which can be used to change things for the better.

This seems to me, at least, to be the baseline challenge which the Nintendo Millennium poses for us. I hope that I have in this talk provided some stimulus for the next two days of discussions.

Session produced by Colin Shaw

The technological rollercoaster: will we enjoy the ride?

Chair: **Steven Barnett**
Goldsmiths' College & Henley Centre

Helen Cunningham
University of Derby

Pam Mills
Consultant

Alan Morris
Communications and Information Technology Research

STEVEN **Barnett:** I am delighted to introduce Alan Morris, who is co-founder and media advisor at CIT Research Ltd, the well-known international telecommunications and media strategic consultants. He is past chairman of the UK Market Research Society and technical director of JICTAR. He was managing director of SelecTV plc and ran cable stations, developed satellite systems and pioneered a new channel. He also set up Europe's first chain of media independents as managing director of Initiative Media International and helped bring large scale barter and sponsored co-production to Europe.

I did actually ask the panellists — to add a little human touch — what their favourite television programmes were because I thought you might like to know a little about their secret lives, and Alan told me that his was *Between The Lines*.

I think you all know Pam Mills, freelance consultant. Her clients include BBC World Service Television, Channel Four, South Bank Business School, and the independent television companies. She was head of special projects at the BBC Research Department where she once turned me down for a job. She has had a spell in the BBC Secretariat and Television Planning, and she was Head of Research at the Central Office Of Information, with a background essentially in market research. She says she is very good at programming the VCR and operating the washing machine but otherwise she has low technological competence. She refused to answer my question about favourite television programmes, saying it was a meaningless question. Never ask a market researcher a question like that!

Helen Cunningham, lecturer in television and popular culture at the University of Derby, did a postgraduate course at the Manchester Institute for Popular Culture, where she was researching satellite and cable channels, and the question of whether they were down-market television or not. She was at Manchester Poly where she studied sociology and politics. She was born in Wigan but went to school in Liverpool. Her favourite programme — you are not going to believe this — is

This Morning With Richard and Judy, but that is not the end of the story. She likes it so much that she actually tapes it.

Alan Morris: I just want to go through some of what I believe are the key issues in the way in which the technologies might affect what happens to broadcasting. What I want to see are the critical points; I want to draw out some scenarios about what could happen. It is so complex, as our keynote speaker said, with so many variables, that I do not want to delve into any of them. I will touch on some of the technologies, but I do not want to be driven by the technology here. I am more concerned about what people out there actually do and what they view.

I want to see what the year 2000 means for broadcasters. Let us have a quick look and see how UK broadcasters stack up against the bigger companies, such as the telephone companies (telcos). Broadcasting's turnover was about one hundred and fifty six billion pounds last year. T telecoms is much, much larger. If you look at the largest telecoms company, NTT, its annual turnover is greater than the ten largest audio-visual companies in the world — $48bn against $40bn. These are big companies and there are not that many of them, so each one is very large. They have long time scales, and they have massive strategic research departments. They have got the energy and the time and the need to invest a lot of money. And they will do it anyway! They do not care what we say and they care less about the issues that are very important to us in broadcasting. It is not because they are nasty, it is just that they are big and ugly. There is nobody from the telcos here, is there? The importance of looking at the telcos is that TV and telecommunications are coming together. I am not going to be too interested in the tricky stuff in the middle, interactive services. They will be very important to many people, they will provide revenues in the niche markets for many people, but they will not make the earth move. They are the things that provide marginal services. I want to look at the things that make the earth move.

I do not understand the word "multi-media". A lot of people do, but I do not quite understand it. What it means to me is a lot of things about telephony, games, computing, coming into the home through a lot of delivery methods, terrestrial, cable, DTH — lots of different ways of delivering a lot of different types of signal.

The thing I want to bear in mind is that somebody has got to watch the signal. These are some of the things that we can say have relatively strong rules about them. What do people do? What do they like viewing? I have drawn upon a lot of experience over the last twenty or thirty years in the UK, looked at what happened in the States, and seen what happens when people are exposed to a lot of choice. One of the things that happens when people are exposed to a lot of choice is they do not view for hours and hours and hours. Once it gets up to a reasonable sort of level of availability — I am not talking about countries that have very little television, I am talking about developed countries — then viewing levels will settle down, by and large, at about twenty-five hours. So we are not looking at an elastic market. If we look at money as well, we are not looking at a totally elastic market either. What tends to happen by and large is substitution. Pay TV substitutes for video, and video on demand substitutes for Pay TV. If you look at leisure spending as a function of gross domestic product there is a pretty reasonable correlation; it goes down in recession, but by and large it stays the same. If you look at the audio-visual component of that, it does not fluctuate a great deal either. So the amount of time and the amount of money to be spent on watching entertainment programming is not highly elastic. If you are a niche programmer and you have got some very nice programming there is a margin there and you can make some money out of it, I am not denying that for a moment, but I am trying to look at the main forces.

There are an awful lot of people involved. Look at the names around here: Sega, NBC, the American telcos , all the major computer companies, Microsoft, Bill Gates, all putting energies in. Now that worries me a little bit, because there is a massive amount of energy coming in to a market which is relatively small and stable. So what one tends to say is that they are doing it for other reasons — they are doing it for reasons other than broadcasting. The implication of that is that broadcasting will be kicked around a little bit.

Let us look at video on demand. I hope everyone is comfortable with what video on demand is. There is some form of interactivity in which in real time a programme, (normally a premium-priced programme) is delivered to you. It has been highlypublished by British Telecom at the moment. British Telecom is a marvellous publicist; it is a big corporation with lots of very strong, powerful friends. It is making so much fuss about video on demand that it is unbelievable. And bear in mind that British Telecom is a carrier, it is not a programme provider. So why is it making all this fuss? It is not going to be running services; it is not going to be a Blockbuster Video. Also bear in mind that the monies that come from video on demand will tend to come from pay-per-view and will come from video rental. It is reasonably well established.

When you talk about video on demand, going through twisted wires, you are talking about a technology that will not reach all the population, whatever BT says, because there are problems if you are sending it down twisted pairs; a lot of the twisted pair telephone wires in this country are not very well shielded. The run is too long from the home to the point where you can put the transmission equipment. Even allowing for that, they will say it is about ninety-five per cent, whereas we say it is about sixty per cent of the homes they can reach. Sixty per cent of homes is enough to run a national channel, and my contention will be that video on demand is not of itself an issue for broadcasting. Video on demand is about premium price programming, selling at a finite level. It sounds about the same price as pay-per-view and video and it will substitute from that. My contention is that it is a Trojan horse; I will develop that in a moment.

So we will assume that there is a technology called video on demand which will be introduced for various reasons, some of them political, relatively soon in test. We will assume, also, that there is another technology called digital TV which is simply the compression of signals so that more use can be made of the available bandwidth. The question was asked this morning about the likely levels of penetration of digital television and the FCC estimate of full penetration by 2017 was mentioned. I think, when looking at the uptake, of these technologies, the key thing is what they are carrying. Because if you look back at the mofe from monochrome to colour then you get one set of relationships because colour represents an advantage. If you look at 625 lines versus 405, the advantage was marginal. So what happens is that as people replace their sets, they will trade up to the new one, and sets get traded up about every seven years or so. If, however, at the same time as you introduce the new technology, you introduce a substantial consumer benefit, say a range of new programming or some other goody, then your uptake gets enhanced. If you look at VCRs in the second or third year of their off-take in most countries, they increase in penetration ten per cent a year because they give a real consumer. But if all you are doing is enhancing the picture, is that a real benefit? Is that going to cause people to fork up real money? The answer tends to be 'less likely.'

So I am going to look at digital TV as something which will inevitably happen and it will interest me only if it happens early and it happens for other reasons than simply just to enhance technology, to enhance the picture. There is a very strong argument to say that digital technology will be overtaken in terms of its advantage on the screen by other things anyway. There was a nice little bit of fuss yesterday when the BBC was quoted, falsely I gather, that it will be introducing digital technology in 1997. I suspect that there might be tests. The key is is standards. When those come into place transmission can start. But if you are transmitting digital TV and the reason you are doing it is to get more channels, to free up the frequencies, the problem is that you do not want to disenfranchise existing punters, so you have got to have a period of time where you run PAL and digital together. It must be about seven years because that is the turn-over rate of television sets. So in terms of hitting people's lives, digital television takes a while to happen. It does not happen very fast — unless something else goes in there as well, some driving reason. And digital television as far as satellite transmission is concerned has one issue and that really is unless Mr Murdoch has an overriding need to do something, there is not going to be that much momentum behind it. The new SES (Astra) satellites will have digital capability but in order to get people to invest in large numbers of decoders there must be a very strong reason.

Let's go into some hypotheses. Let us say viewers will still favour scheduled viewing for another decade. The evidence is there, people want quality and relevance. If you look at cable homes, it plateaus out after thirty per cent but you are really only filling the gaps in what people do not like. So it is scheduled programming, good quality programming that tends to matter, I will call it scheduled, as it is the only word that I can think of. If you have got forty-five per cent national coverage you can find a new scheduled channel. We could get it together in this room. Give us a bag of money, we can set up a channel. The new franchise holders did it. They got together in a room and set up a new channel. What is so difficult about that? So it can happen relatively quickly. Advertising will tend to follow big audiences for a while. There will be inter-active verbalities on local channels and they are important in their own issues but, by and large, the money goes there. Viewing hours per viewer will not increase significantly. They are not going to spend hours and hours at home. There is a good relationship between public service broadcasting licence fee and its share of audience by and large. And spending on the video end of leisure does not increase significantly. By that I mean that the money that comes out of people's pockets stays about the same for audio visual services.

The worst case for broadcasters is that video on demand is introduced by British Telecom in 1997-1998. British Telecom puts pressure on the Government, but does it through the EEC. 1998 brings a relaxation of its rules allowing it to carry video signals. I am not talking about video on demand here but audio-visual signals. The pressure comes because cable companies tend to grow best when their pass rate goes up higher. You pass a lot of homes, you get good penetration of those homes. It grows because of telephony. Telephony is the thing that brings the money in which allows them to build out past more homes, and as they build out past more homes they get better penetration. So they are forced to compete with British Telecom for telephony. The services that do best as they get better are basic services. Basic services will have much better programming then they do now, as they do in the States. They tend to become like terrestrial programming. So British Telecom is forced to compete. British Telecom does not want to run programming; British Telecom wants to sell capacity. So you get a scenario where out of the sixty per cent of homes that could be connected through video on demand, a significant proportion actually are connected. If you look at the year 2000 you have got penetration rates for cable and satellite that meas about thirty per cent in total. You have got somewhere between about 10 and 50 per cent of homes can be reached by wire, and in addition to those, you have all of a sudden got enough wires and cables going into homes to supply a new channel without any regulation. We could do one, we could put it in the homes. Suddenly without even digital television, you have removed the limitation of terrestrial broadcasting which is bandwidth.

The conclusion could be that something like the lack of terrestrial frequencies at the moment is the only barrier to entry, along with regulation. If BT can deliver TV to millions of homes and there is no difference between cable television and Telecom's networks, it will be impossible to keep BT out. So advertiser-supported TV channels could reach fifty per cent of TV households by 2000 at least. SuperChannel was too much too early. It did not have a big enough reach. Even if this doesn't happen digital television will remove all the barriers. So the only thing that is holding back is going to be regulation — but that will be very hard to sustain.

Let us look at one of the worst cases. Let us say that we can go along to British Telecom and say, 'I want to pump out a new channel and you have got to let me do it. We will call it the Alan Morris Channel.' We will pump that out. It does not matter what share it gains because cable is going up. What happens is the audience drops dramatically. The implication is that one of these two existing second channels — BBC2 or Channel 4 — disappears because it cannot sustain the audience. One of these two starts to go. And if licence fee stays the same it will not be BBC. And everybody ends up at the same sort of level which I would propose is not a high enough level of audience share to sustain enough revenue to produce good programming. So there is a general decrease in programming quality. That is my Domesday scenario. I do not think it will happen because there will be reasons why technology will not move so quickly, and by that time somehow things will happen from a regulatory and commercial point of view to stop it happening. But there is absolutely no technical reason why that could not happen.

Pam Mills: I am not going to talk about technology. What I am going to try and do is communicate some enthusiasm about the opportunities that the new technology might bring to us as consumers and also to put to you some of the evidence that comes mainly from America about how it is going to work and why it is going to work.

I was lucky enough to go in December to the Western Cable Show in Los Angeles where I picked up quite a lot of information about different channels. I am going to try to communicate to you some of the enthusiasm that I picked up there

Currently we have a limited supply for most homes; eighty-odd per cent of homes just have the four terrestrial channels. We are dependent on the supply of assumptions, the supply of culture, the supply of programming formats, and, on occasions, similar sorts of programmes on several channels at the same time. But even with these limited four terrestrial channels — make no mistake about it — we are infinitely segmented. Each of us is watching our own unique Me-TV now. Me-TV is not something that is going to happen when we have five hundred channels. Each and every person in this room has watched a completely different pattern of television over the past week. I do not think that because of that we actually do have these universal shared experiences that were talked about in the background to this conference because we are all consuming programmes that we like and we process them in ways that suit us. The majority of homes have VCRs, the majority of homes with children have video games and the minority, as you know, but an increasing minority, do have access to extra programming.

But let us get onto the roller coaster. You do not go onto a roller coaster for a smooth ride. You go on a roller coaster for the fun and the excitement and, let us face it, given all the opportunities that we have been hearing about and there are just a few of them, you are going to be hit from one or other of these directions over the next few years. Everything from the fun end of the spectrum with video games entertainment right down to the other end, education, learning and, possibly even, polling or political and other functions.

What we are going to have to do is get used to a completely different way of looking at television. We are going to have to accustom ourselves to different metaphors and new perspectives. The consumer, the viewer, the receiver will be king. There will be a huge emphasis on the orientation towards understanding consumers and giving them what they want in simpler and simpler forms, rather than just supplying. There is emphasis on giving them the experiencse that they want to have, rather than providing them with a system, such as television, computers or multi-media. The scale will be, increasingly international rather than national. The emphasis is on marketing. It will be to do with added-value, niche markets, diversity and personalisation rather than things that our directly substitutable mass markets can do, offering us similar sorts of experience across four terrestrial channels. And this does involve new models and new ways of thinking about television supply. Alan talked a lot about blockbusters and the mass money but we are really going to have get used to the notion that there are ways, and fine ways, of making small profitable — that 0.5 per cent as a rating or as a reach is OK. It is OK if it is of the 50 odd million in the UK but, of course, it is even more OK and more profitable if you can look at it on a global scale.

There is a demand for more television. I know this is debated, but I think it is indubitable. First of all, the terrestrial channels are not providing people with enough of what they want to watch. Satellite and cable can offer people more choice of channels. People who have access to satellite television express more satisfaction with television as a whole than those who do not. It offers different targets and programming for different targets, and particularly programming at different times of day. For example in the States Court TV gets a 0.8 rating during the day, but bombs out at prime time.

Pay-per-view in the States is reaching around 21 million homes, is worth $300-400 million, and has quite a good growth rate. People value pay-per-view. On marks out of ten, the music pay-per-view programming that they were buying scored nine. The wrestling scored nine, boxing scored eight. People will pay for what they want to watch and so that they will pay $29.95 for a big fight. And one that I liked particularly was the New Year Special from Howard Stern at $39.95 which promised us a video version of the outrageous radio programme that led to Stern's $700,000 dollar FCC fine. Can you imagine that translated that to television? And it was estimated that they would be selling about 400,000 of these which actually adds up to $16 million. Quite nice for minority appeal.

Pay-per-view provides sports, events, movies — and people will pay more for how they want it to be. In the States there is a lot of research evidence to show that people are very willing to pay a premium for flexibility. The suppliers want them to order up-front in advance but they want to leave their order until the last minute because they actually want to make a decision then and there about what they are going to watch — and they are prepared to pay a premium in order to do that.

We have heard a lot about video on demand, or nearly on demand. Movies, favourite programmes, the episode that you missed of *Coronation Street* or *EastEnders*, and, again, people want to do this at the shortest possible notice. In some experiments there had to be a two hour gap before you could see the video movie you ordered. If they decreased this to a half an hour wait time, orders rose 40 per cent, if they decreased it again to a quarter of an hour wait time, orders increased 80 per cent. So it's just like going through the channels — people are continuing their normal behaviour. The more similar you can get it to that, the more immediate the satisfaction, the more likely people are to shell out money to get what they see as a very convenient service that offers them a lot of choice. And they really like not having to rewind and return the video to the shop afterwards.

And there is a demand for other sorts of these services as well. There are the channels from abroad. We tend to think of us sending programming out but there is a lot of interest in the States, and here of course, in keeping in touch with your roots, wherever they are from, watching channels from your home country. Also — I get this in research on BBC World Service Television and other international news channels — there's interest in keeping in touch with a different sort of point of view, seeing the world through different spectacles. There is also an argument that we are going back to the early days of television, with people inviting the neighbours round so that they can watch pay- per-view events. Indeed, in America, for boxing pay-per-view seventy-seven per cent of the homes had guests for pay-per-view events, for wrestling it was sixty-one per cent, for music getting on for fifty per cent. So, again, people are making an event of it and contrary to this image of people separating into their own infinite segments, you have here a different vision of people coming together to share experiences through the television. Of course, too, you have all the interactive fun, the instant replays of sports events, the goal again, the exciting gold medal again. Game shows in America are already experimenting with viewers participating; *The Price Is Right, Wheel of Fortune, Trivial Pursuit* — these sorts of things bring people into television and help them interact with it. And one thing that really appeals to me, is the idea of a personalised two-page text-based news which excludes lots of the news that I am not interested in and gives me the sort of news that I want, possibly even on Sunday good news rather than bad news. Weather for your area — do you have to take your umbrella today or can you leave it at home? Sports — information about your team, not about everybody else's team.

And, of course, people need the sort of wonderfully customised information about what is on television because it is estimated not only that with five hundred channels it would take you something like forty-five minutes to flick through them all but the programme guide would look something rather like the Bible.

It will happen. The stakes are high, the opportunities are compelling, the guys are big, the money is there, they are prepared to stick in there feeding us these opportunities, and making a mistake it will actually feel good, I believe for quite a lot of the time for quite a lot of the people because it will only work, it can only work, if they really try every damn way to tempt us with the choice, the range, the best of the products, tailored to the way we live, trying to simplify, to optimise, to provide on the spot instant satisfaction and give us lot of promotions and deals so that the whole thing becomes much more attractive.

But it will not be the end of life as we know it. Existing services will continue. Most people will still continue to spend most of their time watching existing terrestrial and other channels and, of course, we will still go shopping, we will still watch videos. It took fifty years in the States for cable to reach 60 per cent of homes. Nearly 40 per cent of homes in the States still do not have cable. So, of course, we are talking about a very, very long lead time, providing, of course, that we do not have all these restrictions and restrictive regulations, that the technology works, and that the equipment looks good. All these sorts of things that are part of the marketing mix in terms of presenting us with a package that will make it all acceptable to us.

It is true that not all will benefit. Not all have cable in the States, not all have everything here. There is a hierarchy of access with less freedom and choice for the poor. In the States there are differences to the order of two or three times the access to video on demand for the more advanced interactive technology. But that, as Roger Silverstone said, is not a problem to do with media, it is a problem to do with society.

I really am not sure, however, that this is what it is all about because the bit in this that really gets me excited (and I know it is exciting a lot of people in America) is to do with education and the community. This is something that kept being said at the Cable Conference in Los Angeles from the top guy to the very smallest guy, that the main impact of all these developments will be at these levels. It would spread the benefits of the new technology through the whole of the community rather than limiting it to the rich. And it would affect us all.

In some communities, for example, the people are combining with the big guys, spending their own money buying bonds to invest in their own community to link up all the homes and all the schools with interactive cable networks. So they are integrating the community, using distance learning so that everybody has access to the same resources and they are sharing. They have created a sort of personal knowledge factory. In some places in some experimental work this has improved the teaching and the support systems within the community and this has had a dramatic effect on, for example, the drop-out rate in schools because the teaching is better, the effort is better, the community is coming together. In one community drop-out went down from twenty-five per cent to ten per cent and unemployment went down because the kids were coming out that bit better equipped for jobs. And they recouped the costs that they had invested in the community in wiring themselves up in lower welfare payments. Whether this was because of the technology or because of the community involvement is not clear, but it does not matter because the two were working together.

This seems to me to be about connecting, about local neighbourhoods, about the possibility of real public access to the media and using it in a very constructive way for local democracy. For example we were told about some schools where they put the whole of the Clinton health package in special ways to the children and to the wider community and they had a reasonably informed debate at a local level about how it would affect them. So instead of being given these sorts of debates by the traditional suppliers with arguments between people whom we are not interested in, it is helping people to get involved in those sorts of processes.

So where does this end leave us? Superhighway or dead-end? Well, I hope it is the superhighway and I can see that through this not only would we benefit from all the things that we associate with television in terms of entertainment and information, that there are ways through this, if we can think constructively about it, to build new communities. And one new central community and new involvement — will there be more couch potatoes or mashed potatoes? Well, perhaps, it is even proper people who are having some fun on this super highway and on this new technological roller-coaster. So I am feeling pretty up-beat about all this. I can see that there are opportunities there, providing we can take advantage of them but they are probably not going to happen by the millennium.

Helen Cunningham: What I would like to do in this presentation is to expand upon one of the points raised by Professor Roger Silverstone — the gendered use of domestic technologies. Studies of leisure technologies such as the video cassette recorder and the home computer have suggested that it is the men in the households who use and understand these technologies the most.[1] I have recently been undertaking research into one of the new home leisure technologies, which I believe is showing a different pattern of usage — the computer games console. When you talk to young children technology and computers are not seen by them as boring machines understood only by 'boffins' or 'swots', (which is the image of computers which I grew up with). Computers are now the source of fun and what's more this fun is being had by girls as well as boys. I believe that with the new generation of computer games consoles something has altered and computer game-girls are now just as common as computer game-boys.

In the early 1980s, when the video game was just beginning to emerge as part of the television home entertainment system, most of the research undertaken suggested that playing video games was a predominantly male leisure pursuit.[2] In the late 70s and early 80s, when this research was carried out, video game playing was not a home based activity. Arcades were the place where game playing took place and these arcades were populated by adolescent males.[3]

A decade later in the early 1990s the second wave of game playing has occurred primarily through the purchase of dedicated games consoles which are plugged into the home television set. The main companies in the console industry are Sega and Nintendo. This domestication of computer games has increased access to them. Firstly access has opened up for a lower age group who previously could not play video games in arcades (the minimum age to play legally in arcades being 16) and secondly as the context of games playing has changed female participation in games culture has increased. Young girls can now be found huddled around Gameboy handhelds in the playground and girls as well as boys now talk of 'Sonic' (Sega's trademark), and 'Super Mario' (Nintendo's). There are over 9.4 million computer game consoles in use in the UK and the vast majority of these are used by children aged between seven and fifteen. Computer games are the new children's medium of the 90s. The main focus of interest has been over the feared addictive nature of game-playing and their violent content. Within these discussions of computer games both the computer games industry, journalists and also many academics have portrayed game playing as a predominantly male preserve. My research suggests that this is no longer true and that the gendered nature of games playing is changing. To begin to assess the nature of girls involvement in computer games cultures I interviewed a group of girls aged between 10 and 11 who attended a primary school in a Liverpool suburb. All but one of the girls in their class played and enjoyed computer games. Female participation in games culture has significantly increased since computer game play moved out of the arcades and into the home. This increase in girls' participation with computer games is encouraging.

The Computer Game Industry

In 1991 Sega and Nintendo began their big push for computer game console sales to children in Britain. Prior to 1990 these two firms were unheard of in British homes, but three years on 60% of children own a computer games machine and 80% of children are said to play computer games regularly.

Sega and Nintendo are the brand leaders who dominate the market internationally. Nintendo is the largest of the two world-wide but in the UK Sega holds the largest share of the market. In 1989 the computer games market was worth £78 million, but by 1993 sales of games, consoles, magazines and accessories totalled £1.1 billion.

The games industry and other areas of the entertainment industry are joining forces. Computer games are often more profitable than movies. One game, *Super Mario Brothers 3,* has sold 14 million copies and has generated more money than the movie *ET.* Nintendo now makes greater profits than all of the American movie studios combined. Sega and Nintendo have licensing deals with film companies in order to use animated characters including Disney cartoon characters. Many computer games are based on successful films: *RoboCop, The Terminator, Jurassic Park,* and *Aladdin* are just some of the texts which have transferred from the big screen to the games console. This cross-media licensing has not all been one way. The film *Super Mario Brothers* was released last year and both *Super Mario* and *Sonic the Hedgehog* have their own cartoons, broadcast on Sunday morning children's TV in the UK. The advertising industry has also expressed an interest in computer games as a medium for product placement. In December 1993 the game *Snapperazz'* was launched having been devised by *The Sun* newspaper and sponsored by the pizza delivery chain *Domino's Pizza* and the Leaf UK brand *Fizzy Chewits*. In the USA sponsored games have featured 'Spot', the character in 7 Up's advertising. Sponsorship and product placement within computer game software will probably increase as at present in Britain there is no regulation of such practices within computer games.

It is not only the entertainment industry which has been affected by the rise of the computer games industry. Over the past five years Nintendo has made bigger profits than many of the international computer giants. The microprocessor within computer game consoles is similar to that used in many personal computers. When the chief executive officer of Apple Computer was asked what computer company he feared most in the nineties, his reply — "Nintendo" — was not altogether surprising. These games consoles, which at present are primarily used for games playing, are 8-bit and 16-bit computers, which with the addition of other pieces of hardware are capable of becoming more than just toys for playing games on. Sega and Nintendo can be seen to have had great success at getting children involved in computer technology. These two companies have put computers in the homes of 60% of households with children. This entertainment led technological revolution has been achieved not by cable TV or by any of the leading computer manufacturers — but by a blue hedgehog and a plumber in red dungarees.

Computer games were initially welcomed by many parents. Any childhood contact with computers was seen as educational. If parents had worries over their children playing computer games they were concerned over the cost of the cartridges more than over the content — *Sonic* and *Super Mario Brothers* appeared harmless.

As most children's first experience of computers is through computer games in the home many of the parents I interviewed bought computer game consoles for their children believing an active enthusiasm for computer games to be the first step into computer literacy, hoping that once the interest in game playing wanes

27

the enthusiasm for computers and new technology will remain. Early contact and familiarity with computers was seen as important for young children. This view was expressed particularly in relation to daughters. The parents I talked to were very aware of the need to actively encourage their daughters to be involved with new technologies.

Nintendo is increasingly marketing itself as an educational gaming console which can be used for both entertainment and educational functions. *Edutainment* is the word used in their promotional leaflets to parents. The interactive and co-operative nature of computer game playing provides the potential for computer games as a tool in children's early learning.

However this may be an optimistic viewpoint because at present the main use these machines are being put to is games playing. and none of the edutainment games appears near the top of the game charts. The computer games industry is driven by commercial imperatives and the genres of games currently being produced are very profitable.

The industry is not likely to attempt to push consoles or software in any other direction until the market for entertainment games is saturated in the UK. Computer games have become part of 'youth culture' and the iconography of the games has been used in advertising, 'Youth TV' programmes, and within club cultures. Computer games have been appropriated by young people and have been marketed to them as anarchic, rebellious and anti-establishment. Neither young people or the games manufacturers want to lose their street credibility by being seen as too educational.

As most children's first experience of computers is through computer games it is vital that girls are included in these arenas where familiarity with new technology is established.

Gender and game play

My research suggests that girls do play computer games, (although the console may have been bought for her brother) but game cultures are still thought of as being a boys' preserve. Angela McRobbie in her work on youth cultures posed the question of why girls are invisible in many accounts of youth cultures. She suggests that female invisibility is due in part to the media's concentration on violent aspects of the youth culture.[4] This can be seen to be true within games culture. The girls I spoke to all mentioned platform games as being their current favourite game, rather than the more violent genre of 'Beat 'em ups'. Media concern has concentrated on 'Beat 'em ups' and the aggressive nature of boys' play rather than that of girls. However this is not to suggest that girls do not enjoy playing some of the more violent games as Sarah expressed, "I like violent games...especially the one where you kill and blood comes out" The 'Beat 'em up' game 'Mortal Komba' to which I presumed Sarah was referring had only just been released a few days earlier amongst a barrage of media publicity and all the girls were keen to play it. This popularity of 'gore' genres spread over into other media as every girl I interviewed preferred horror books as their favourite type of reading.

Gender stereotyping within computer games is an issue that has been raised by

many critics.[5] When human female characters are present they are often represented as the 'quest' to be saved by the male hero. This gender stereotyping has to
be acknowledged as a problem within the design of the games, even though it has
to be stressed that these games are still very popular amongst female games players. In the 'Beat 'em up' genre female characters are increasingly appearing and
are not always weaker than their male rivals. 'Blaze' in *Streets of Rage,* 'Chun Li' in
StreetFighter 2 and 'Sonya Blade' in *Mortal Kombat* are all formidable females who
are often chosen for their special moves. Patricia Marks Greenfield acknowledges
the importance of involving girls in computer game play as an "entry point into
the world of computers" and so she suggests "...there is an urgent need for widely
available video games that make a firm contact with the fantasy life of the typical
girl as with that of the typical boy."[6] The vast majority of games designers are male
and perhaps game design reflects this. Nintendo have attempted to engage with
'the fantasy life of young girls' and marketed a *Barbie* game. This is a platform
game in which Barbie travels through Mall World and Soda Shop World in her
search for 'Magical fantasy accessories' and ball gowns. This game has not been
well received by the young female games players I interviewed. Julie claimed "I'd
never buy that Barbie game it's stupid", her friend Sarah was in agreement , "No
way ... I'd rather play violent games any day."

The games most popular with the girls I interviewed were: *Sonic, Sonic 2, Super
Mario Brothers, Super Mario Brothers 3, Mickey Mouse in Castle of Illusion., Streets of
Rage,* and *Street Fighter 2*. Although these games could all be described as action
and adventure (and in some case they are violent 'Beat 'em up' games), the playing of them can not be seen as gendered. Hopefully as more female games designers enter the industry a wider range of genres will develop and more female
characters will be available within the existing genres as well as more gender neu-
tral characters such as 'Sonic the Hedgehog'. Platform games appear to be the
favourite choice amongst young children, both male and female. The girls also
enjoyed 'Beat 'em ups' and found pleasure in the violence of these games enjoying
being able to fight and win when playing against brothers or male peers.

The girls enjoyed the chance to express themselves in a violent and aggressive
manner through the violence of these games. In most areas of society this violent
and aggressive side of a girl/woman's nature has to be repressed due to socially
expected norms of what is feminine and acceptable behaviour. Playing violent
games gives female players the chance to express this aggression in a safe context.
My future research on computer games will concentrate on the experience of playing these violent games and how 'pleasures' are created.

To conclude, Sega and Nintendo's success at getting consoles into children's
homes has changed the nature of female participation with games technology.
Computer games as a medium have a great potential for involving girls in new
technology. The moving of computer games play from the arcades into bedrooms
and shopping centres has significantly changed the experience of game playing.
This changing context of computer games has to be recognised in any account of
computer game cultures. The experience of playing games has been transformed
since the days of *PacMan* and *Ms PacMan*. Gillian Skirrow's claim 'the pleasure of

computer games is gender specific ... women do not play them'[7] is no longer true. As games playing has become an activity of public concern and interest the continuing portrayal of computer games as an activity only of boys is very worrying. Computer games are a relatively new medium and as such it is difficult to predict how their popularity amongst the girls I interviewed will be maintained as they grow older and develop new interests. Hopefully these girls who 'play' with technology in 1994 will have grown up with an openness to new technology and the gendered use of home leisure technology will slowly be eradicated. But perhaps I am too much of an optimist!

Discussion

Liz Ashton-Hill (College of St Mark & St John, Plymouth): My question is to Helen. It is interesting what you say about the gender differences. Research that I have seen suggests that the remote control in the TV home is very much a male preserve. Do you think that this is going to change with girls using the home computer much more? Do you think that they will actually start to become more proactive in using the remote control of the TV set?

Helen Cunningham: Well, I would like to say yes and I hope yes, but the problem is that the girls I am interviewing are ten and eleven; they don't yet have to spend time in the kitchen washing up, cooking, cleaning, whatever. And that is the main problem in terms of female use of leisure technologies. But once these girls grow up and if things do not change and they are involved in traditional gender roles, most women do not have time to sit and watch television to the extent that men do, do they? And that is why I think that the remote control is controlled by the men. In most households it is the men who have more leisure time to watch these programmes.

Steven Barnett: But there is a technology issue there as well, isn't there? It is well known that men are more comfortable using VCRs than women are. So there is a technology barrier as well.

Pam Mills: And children more than men.

Helen Cunningham: But then children now do know how to program the VCR. Quite often in the household it is children that set the timer for their mothers and fathers. That is what I am hoping, that because females are gaining confidence with technology through computer games, I am hoping that this will spread over into other technologies as they grow older. But I hope to go back in years to come and interview the same people.

Brian Harper-Lewis (Videotron): You began by saying the parents perceived the assistance in getting a good introduction, any kind of introduction into the world of computing. Have you extrapolated that at all? I am only doing this from memory, but I heard a piece on Radio Four last week conducted by a professor of psychology at the University of Greenwich who showed that in 1989 twenty-seven per cent of girls went on into computer studies, whereas in 1993 only six percent. If this is success, then we are on an evolutionary blind alley. I worry for our future. They may have wonderful thumb muscles, but that does not necessarily mean that they know about the operating system or whatever.

Bernard Sharratt (University of Kent): This question to Helen might ricochet on to the two other members of the panel. Can you tell us more about Nintendo's plans for a Nintendo Channel? I gather that there are trials in Canada precisely along those lines.

Helen Cunningham: I do not know very much about it, but there are hopes for cable channels in Britain which just relay games down the channel and rather than having to go out and buy your games, you just play them from the TV set.

Pam Mills: Can I say something about the Sega channel? I was interested in going to ask Helen because I read that their target is young boys, even though a third of their machines are owned by men aged twenty-four or over. I was interested in what research there might be from America to indicate how widely girls use the games they own because this suggests that the market is defined almost exclusively in male terms.

Alan Morris: I think we have to make a distinction between the shoot 'em up games, as you call them and other things. For example, there is a programme for Games World that we have been working in partnership with. We make it interactive by adding a quiz thing which gets a fantastic response. There are some games that come up which are just more of the same. All of the time you are just seeing the same thing dressed up in the Emperor's new clothes. But along comes one thing that particularly stands out, a thing like *Sim City* and, frankly, if I was running a class for trainee town planners, it would be compulsory that they go and play *Sim City* to find out where to put the nuclear power plant, i.e. not at all. Those kind of things, I think, do have a future.

Brian Kelly (Open Campus Television): We had the Pollyanna viewpoint from Pam and the Domesday one from Alan. But if you are going to have digital channels, you are going to have five hundred of them. Where is all the programming, in your viewpoint, going to come from? It still takes time to produce television. Who is going to make them?

Alan Morris: The reason that I call it Domesday is that people watch good programming. And if there is no good programming around, they will watch something else. The thing that worries me is that there is a finite amount of money around and we know it costs money to make good programming. You cannot put crap out. You do not get audiences. And if you look at these small channels, they get small audiences. I did some work recently with 195,000 hours of programming put out in the UK of which only about 12,000 was original programming. There are massive amounts of programming put out and a lot of that is either repeated or recycled American programming. So your point is very valid that in order to preserve audiences, and preserve audiences for advertising and to keep the whole thing going, there needs to be quality programming. A lot of the content of the channels will be low-cost repeated material etc. and people will browse through those channels but they will not be the main staple of their viewing diet. They cannot be because, as you say, there ain't the money to do it.

Brian Kelly: It is the same kind of question to you, Pam. You said that 0.5% is a good figure, or should be viewed as a good figure. How is that going to help in terms of production? How can you make a decent production if you have those kind of figures coming in?

Pam Mills: Well, it depends how you are funding it. If you are actually getting $39.95 from a person who is tuning into something, then you can actually produce something really worthwhile. I do not believe that this is all going to be funded by advertising; there just is not the revenue. You are talking about subscription; you are actually then talking about viewers' willingness to pay for what they actually want to watch. And there is a lot of evidence from here, and from the States, and from the rest of the world, that television has been very underpriced historically and that people are prepared to pay more to get the programming they want. But another answer to your question is, of course, that some channels, I mean loads of channels, can be really cheap because you are talking about simple weather channels that just recycle themselves, that do not cost much to do. And, you know a lot of people actually tune in to UK Gold and watch *EastEnders* from ten years ago at six thirty and then watch *EastEnders* from today at seven thirty.

Alan Morris: I think one of the things that we are missing and we will not have time to cover now are the cultural implications of this kind of demassification, because it comes back to the kinds of people that can afford and who cannot afford to pay $39.95 for a programme and what happens when you lose the ten to twelve million people who watch so-called 'free' television.

Pam Mills: Mind you, if you share between say ten people watching a boxing match, then it is not so much.

Alan Morris: Then if you talk about a shared national culture ...

Pam Mills: Ah, yes, but I do not believe in such things. *Most* people do not watch anything.

Brian Kelly: But if you pay a licence fee, you get to see Manchester United play Oldham in the semi-final tonight or if you watch Sky you will get to see it, and you get to see feature films and so forth. You were saying that people are going to pay forty dollars or forty quid every time they want to watch a programme?

Pam Mills: No, no. Just occasionally. Occasionally they will do that and that will fund the programming. That will fund that particular sort of programming.

Brian Kelly: We are not all that rich.

Steven Barnett: This whole question is a session in its own right.

Granville Williams (Campaign for Press and Broadcasting Freedom): I really would value some of the information you have given me on the experience on education and community initiatives in America. Because the symbolic example for me of the invasion into education is, of course, Channel 1 in America where you get the equipment in the schools, where the big corporate advertisers pay $129,000 or something, for thirty seconds, to advertise Clearasil, or fast foods and so on. The important point for me is that to the extent that you evacuate the availability to those who are unable to afford pay-per-view subscription, you start to raise the spectre of a disenfranchised, poverty-stricken, unplugged society. And it is that that should be the concern of people who care about the potential for broadcasting. It is not to say that there should not be a range of choices but I think the important point is this: what is raised by this notion that there is a whole range of programmes that can be provided through pay-per-view subscription to the extent that those seem to be developing in the States, is that they are not about providing education without a number of other bolt-on things like advertising. I think that raises enormous implications about the space within which people can develop and grow and understand about society.

Pam Mills: I do not understand why you have to have advertising. I mean if you have got a community and all the skills are interlinked together, you can say, 'OK, we have got a slot for Spanish,' and you have the best Spanish teacher and it goes out to all the schools. That is not a programme — that is an interactive capability.

Granville Williams: Right. The work that I looked at was about Channel One and the evidence there suggested that the schools that took up the equipment were the ones with the least funding; they saw it as a way of getting the equipment. The evidence suggests that the quality of the news programmes was of very little educational benefit so it raises issues that are fundamental to this debate about advertising sponsored, commercial sponsored, pay-per-view future for broadcasting versus one which looks at other criteria which are quite central, in my view.

Alan Morris: It links in with the point that Helen was making which I think is absolutely crucial and she is absolutely right when she says what is happening in terms of product placement and sponsorship, that advertisers who want to aim themselves at the youth market are seeing computer games as a wonderful area to get into and get over the kind of interactivity of people who flick through advertising.

Ted Mercer (Allison & Humphreys): At the moment Nintendo and Sega voluntarily regulate the content of their programs. Should they be statutorily content-controlled by the ITC or will voluntary regulation be all right until something goes wrong?

Helen Cunningham: Sticky question. I am probably going to be shouted at in a minute because I think I am a bit away from the majority of opinion on this. I do not see a problem with the violence of the games. I think that children are not stupid. What is the difference between cartoons like Tom and Jerry and the violence in them, where people are hit over the head with frying pans and get up and walk away, and violence in a computer game where you kick someone or your pull their throat out and they die and they get up and they live again? Children know that it is fiction; children do not think that it is real. I think it is patronising to children to think that they actually think that this is real life. And therefore I do not see the violence as the problem that other people in the media have focused. I disagree with that completely. So maybe I am not the right person to ask because I do not have a problem with the violence.

Ted Mercer: But computer games are just one facet of a whole series of interactive services that might come in the future. Funnily enough somebody asked me today 'Would the Department of National Heritage be bright enough to consider whether or not, for example, video on demand where that involves not true video on demand but interactive video on demand, be brought within the spectrum of control?' I think that it might be an issue that also Europe is beginning to get attached to as well.

Brian Harper-Lewis: Do you think we are likely to see something like some of the US PBS (Public Broadcasting Service) stations appearing in the UK where you have got a mother or a dignified grandpa telling you they need $40, or $400 or $4,000 because the station cannot survive and we have got a biggie for you tonight but we are not going to run it until you, the community, cough up? Is that going to happen in the UK?

Alan Morris: I sincerely hope not. I do not see things like that happening for various reasons. I see PBS working in Europe in a different way from it does in the States. I wanted to say one more thing about the games channels. There is a commercial imperative about Sega and Nintendo and the other s going onto cable and that is that if you look at the results of the last year, sales are down, of course, because first year buyers become second and third year buyers and the purchase per buyer of games drops down. So you need something else; you need CD-I or you need a games channel because you need constant changes, significant changes, not just little cosmetic ones, to keep the market going. And they have been wanting to do this for years. I tested virtually-on-demand games services in the States in 1983/84, so they have been waiting for cable operators like you to give them access to sufficient homes. That is the commercial imperative to drive it along.

References

[1] For an account of the gendered use of the VCR see Anne Gray (1992) *Video playtime: The gendering of a leisure technology*, London: Routledge, and for a study of the use of home computers see Jane Wheelock (1992) *Personal computers, gender and an institutional model of the household* in Roger Silverstone & Eric Hirsch (eds) *Consuming technologies: Media and information in domestic spaces*, London: Routledge.

[2] For accounts of video games which put forward this view see Gillian Skirrow (1986) 'Hellivision: an analysis of video games' in Colin McCabe (ed) *High Theory/Low Culture: Analysing Popular Television and Film*, Manchester: Manchester University Press, and also Leslie Haddon (1988) 'Electronic and Computer Games: The history of an interactive medium' in *Screen* vol. 29 no 2.

[3] The most extensive research on the gendered nature of arcade game playing is S Kaplan (1983) 'The Image of Amusement Arcades and the difference in male and female video game playing,' in *Journal of Popular Culture* vol. 17 no 1 pp 93–98.

[4] Angela McRobbie (1991) *Feminism and Youth Cultures*, London: Macmillan.

[5] See Eugene F Provenzo Jr (1991) *Video Kids: Making Sense of Nintendo*, Cambridge, MA: Harvard University Press, and Marsha Kinder (1992) 'Playing with Power on Saturday Morning Television and on Home Video Games' in *Quarterly Review of Film and Video*, vol 14 pp 29-59.

[6] Patricia Marks Greenfield (1984) '*Mind and Media: the effects of television, video games and computers* London: Fontana.

[7] Gillian Skirrow, *op. cit*, p115.

Session produced by Pam Mills

Democracy down the tube: can the fractured small screen play a role in the democratic process?

Chair: **Suzanne Franks**
CCT Productions

Professor James Fishkin
University of Texas

Judith Mackay
Birmingham Cable

Phillip Whitehead
Brook Productions

S UZANNE Franks: This morning's session is all about the role that televi sion performs in the democratic process. Our concern is with the viewer as *citizen*, not merely as passive watcher. And the question is whether the multi-channel television of the future can, by empowering the citizen, help inform the democratic process.

The three panellists all have a very different perspective on this subject as academic, TV producer and politician. My own involvement is in many ways from within the engine-room of political television at Westminster, where I am responsible for the televising of Parliament. When the Commons after thirty years of deliberations decided to allow in the cameras they chose do this through an independent producer rather than one of the two established broadcasters, although during the early experimental phase ITN was responsible for televising the Lords.

Since October 1991 when televising has been a permanent feature in Parliament, CCT Productions has covered over 6,000 hours of proceedings, including the Commons, Lords and the various committees. The terrestrial broadcasters have for obvious reasons dipped in and out, but the overwhelming majority of the output has been transmitted to a select band of viewers via the Parliamentary Channel which provides a fairly basic service of unedited Parliamentary proceedings to cable subscribers. MPs were emphatic that when televising became permanent there must be some dedicated service which broadcast their complete and unedited deliberations. Interestingly, arcane parliamentary authorities have decided that MPs themselves are not allowed to see this continuous feed in their offices within the Palace of Westminster. Presumably they fear that idle Members would choose to watch proceedings on the box and not bother to attend in the Chamber.

Now that the televising of Parliament has become an established fact the question is whether it has had any effect upon the democratic process. Earlier this year Michael Portillo made a widely reported speech about the decline in authority and respect for British institutions. He blamed the television cameras for undermining the authority and respect for Parliament. Some of my colleagues were alarmed by this pronouncement from one of the Prime Minister's heirs apparent. Yet in many ways the speech says more about Portillo and his positioning within the Conservative party. Any lowering in respect is more likely to have come from the public exposure to the strange ways in which Parliament chooses to organise itself, whether that be yelling and shouting or throwing top hats around the Chamber.

My personal feeling is that simply by being there the cameras can only have enhanced democracy. At the very least the opening up of Westminster in this way has reduced the steady decline in the relevance and meaning of Parliament. Perhaps I can just share with you two contrasting vignettes on this.

One was presented by the ebullient Lord Healey who recently bounced into the TV control room at the Commons. He was there to record some material for a programme in the forthcoming Channel 4 democracy season, *Bite the Ballot*. According to Lord Healey the televising of Parliament had in some ways brought about a return to Athenian democracy. Now for the first time in over two thousand years all the citizens of a democracy can observe the legislature in action. After hearing this I basked in a warm glow.

Unfortunately soon afterwards came a correspondingly cold chill. The BBC conducted some research on the viewers of the *6 o'clock News*, seeking their views on how politics is covered on television. The results showed that viewers hate the sight of the green benches, because it represents yah-boo politics. This image apparently communicates to them a feeling of powerlessness and alienation from the charade which is contemporary adversarial politics.

Professor James Fishkin, from the University of Texas, has his own very special response to overcoming the sterile nature of political debate and returning to Athenian ideals or possibly the American town meeting of the last century. He is seeking to empower citizens through television by the use of deliberative polling. Here in Manchester Channel 4 and Granada TV are to mount the first ever large scale demonstration of deliberative polling this coming weekend. The results will also feature in the Channel 4 *Democracy* season next month. I will now invite Professor Fishkin to outline the concept of the deliberative poll.

Professor Fishkin: I have a particular diagnosis of what I think of the problem that I am addressing and it has to do with the combination of television and opinion polling. Then I have got this, I will not say solution, but constructive remedy which will be taking place tomorrow here in Manchester at the Granada Television studio over the entire weekend. It is interesting that we just had Athenian democracy invoked because the last time anybody tried to do what we are doing tomorrow was, I believe, twenty-four hundred years ago in ancient Athens and that is not the assembly dimension of Athenium democracy that you mentioned but another dimension which was quite distinctive. It was the use of juries and legislative commissions chosen by lot, and what is a lottery but a random sample, to form deliberative microcosms of the entire citizenry who would think carefully about an issue and, in fact, by the fourth century in Athens, make the final decisions on new legislation. In my view this is a distinctively different kind of democracy, and with my political sciencist hat on, it is just worth noting that democracy was thought to be a kind of curiosity until the latter part of the eighteenth century because it could not be adapted to the large scale. It was thought you had to have a monarchy or some other form of government, but it was only adapted through the innovation of elected representatives, elected representation. But there was this other solution sitting there on the desk of history.

My proposal is for what I call a deliberative opinion poll. An ordinary opinion poll models what the public thinks, given how little it thinks, how little it knows, how little it may be paying attention; it gives just a snap-shot of public opinion as it is. I will come back to the reasons why public opinion may be a mistake. But a deliberative poll models what the public would think if it actually had a better chance to think about it. So the idea is very simple. Take a national random sample and variable age population. Move them into a single place which tomorrow will be the Granada Television studio. Steep them in the issues. Allow them to work through their key concerns, in small group deliberation with trained moderators. Allow them to debate, discuss the issues with experts, competing experts, because for ordinary citizens deference is a very important factor so you do not want there to be some single anointed solution, so you have competing experts who disagree. Allow them to question key politicians, always with the issues or concerns that they have worked through from small group interaction and debate so that then individuals are not just speaking and asking questions off the top of their head, but rather the questions that really concern them and that really concern their groups. Tape all of this or broadcast it live. And insert that into the political process. A survey research organisation in London has selected a national random sample from 40 polling districts randomly chosen, and those people will show up tomorrow and they will be gathered together for a weekend. The topic is rising crime and what to do about it. We had to get a topic that would concern ordinary citizens. If it was a dry academic subject, we would not get them to show up any better than students in my university show up to their classes. This is a joint undertaking of Channel 4, Granada Television and *The Independent*. And *The Independent* newspaper, working with SCPR, developed from focus groups, has produced briefing materials on the issues that are very carefully balanced and speak to alternatives that we turned up in the focus groups that occurred to the public. So instead of the inital debate being a kind of a technical debate, it is one that ordinary citizens should be engaged by right from the beginning.

Another detail of what we did is we did interviews with every citizen who was approached face-to-face in their homes. We did interviews about their attitudes. Of course we knew their demographics, and then we invited them only after the interview, so we had the data to determine exactly how representative our statistical microcosm is both on demographic grounds, and on attitudinal grounds. I am happy to say that the first look at the data last night on the people who say they are definitely showing up was that they are, indeed, a microcosm in every way; there is no ideological distortion, class distortion, regional distortion; we did not get people who were more knowledgeable; we did not get people who were more educated. The two samples are virtually indistinguishable. At least that was our first look. Of course we will not really know until we know who shows up tomorrow.

Now the problem this speaks to is that ordinary citizens suffer from rational ignorance and ordinary opnion polls report non-attitudes to a considerable extent. By rational ignorance I mean the idea that if I have got one vote in millions, why should I spend a lot of time and effort thinking through complicated issues? I will not have any effect on their outcome but I can better use my time by things that affect my life more directly. I do not mean to be cynical, but it is in that sense rational for a citizen not to invest a lot of time in information, thinking through complex problems and, to that extent, to be ignorant.

That is a terrible disability for democracy. But notice that in this deliberative poll there will be a strong incentive for those citizens to overcome rational ignorance. If I have one vote in several *hundred* and I am going to be on national television, I am going to want to think through the issues very carefully. In fact, from the standpoint of conventional polling, the reason this is completely crazy is that from the moment these citizens are asked to come to Manchester, they begin to become unrepresentative in the conventional sense. Why? They begin to think. They begin to discuss the issues with their friends and family. They will begin to listen to the media and read the media more carefully. In short they will begin to behave as ideal citizens. Now, just imagine what this society would be like if everyone magically were transformed to behave like ideal citizens. They would all be watching the parliamentary channel all the time but they would also not just be watching, they would be debating face-to-face with each other.

Now, unfortunately for the parliamentary channel and unfortunately for democracy, that is virtually impossible. Or extremely unlikely; there may be some special moments of national crisis when the public is engaged in that way but they are very rare indeed. But we can do the experiment. We can take this statistical microcosm, subject them to this experience and determine, in a sense, what the public would come to if it were engaged, as ideal citizens, on some particular issue. And we can then broadcast the results and insert that into the policy debate process. You see, what we are doing tomorrow in Manchester is, in a way, in another sense, completely crazy because what we have done is take an actual sample from a hypothetical society, the hypothetically more deliberative and thoughtful society that we do not have. And this is not specific to Britain, we do not have in that any of the developed countries around the world.

Now this also refers to the second major defect in opinion polling, which is that it reports non-attitudes. Non-attitudes show up when people do not actually have a well-formed opinion on some subject but they are asked a question by an opinion pollster and they do not want to appear stupid so they say something which does not reflect any stable well-formed opinion. We know that because repeated studies show that these opinions are not stable; they are just top of the head reactions. But very often those non-attitudes are in control of public policy. In my own country you see now that Clinton has order air-strikes in Bosnia. Well, last summer he had decided, according to the *Washington Post* and others, to order air-strikes in Bosnia but the Gallup Poll came out three to one against the plan, and they got scared and held up on the air-strikes. Now what do ordinary American citizens know about Bosnia? What does anybody know about Bosnia? Soon after George Gallup invented the opinion poll for political purposes, he gave a lecture in 1938 where he said it would restore the democracy of the New England town meeting to the large scale nation-state. He did not have the term opinion poll then; he called it the sampling referendum. His argument was that the radio and newspapers (no television in those days) would send out the opinions of political leaders and, as if everyone were in one room, the public would transmit back, through the sampling referendum, its views. Just like the New England town meeting where everyone was in one room, they discussed the issues, there was some conclusion. In a way he was right and in a way he was wrong. There was an extraordinarily successful innovation with unattended consequences. The difficulty is everyone is in one great room but the room is so large that no individual can conclude that he has much effect on the debate and people tune out. So you have one room where the bouncing back is what some political scientists have compared to an echo chamber. It is a rather hollow effect and this interaction of television and opinion polls does not lead to any democracy of active citizens, it leads to a democracy of inattentive, inactive citizens.

But the deliberative poll would actually do what Gallup envisaged if it works. The deliberative poll with the statistical microcosm based on this old Athenian notion of choosing a deliberative microcosm by lottery would bring power to the people under conditions where the people can think which is the theme of this little book which I have written called *Democracy and Deliberation* which promotes the idea.

A couple of years ago I managed to talk PBS in the United States into committing itself to doing this at the beginning of the presidential selection season. They announced it with great fanfare for the '92 election but they did not raise enough money and so it was cancelled. Last year I was on sabbatical at Cambridge where I had been a student twenty-seven years ago and I managed to talk Channel 4 and Granada and *The Independent* into doing this, being the first. And since then I have got McNeil Lehrer Productions who will be sending a team over tomorrow to Manchester to observe, committed once again to try the American version at the beginning of the presidential selection season before the Iowa congress or the New Hampshire primary where it could have a big effect on the inital momentum of candidates.

And so if the experiment in Manchester tomorrow works it could set an example for democracy in all kinds of places. There is also a team from Canada that will be coming over and there are some other countries where there is quite a lot of interest. There is even a Bulgarian translation of this book and in Bulgaria the Centre for Democracy is proposing to do one of these things in Bulgaria. But the British will be first. If it does not work they will be last. I mean if it does not work, this idea will not be heard from again for another twenty-four hundred years. But we will see.

Prof Fishkin's remarks were discussed before the other contributions were heard.

Bernard Sharratt (University of Kent): I have a specific question but within a wider context: Did you look at how many of your sample have served on juries before? Because one of the interesting things about what you are proposing is that if I remember my Greek history right, one of the things at stake in the assembly and in the large juries was that they were not obliged to observe any previous legislation; the notion of *autonomia* meant that each case was decided in fact on its own merit. And what you seem to be proposing is a curious mixture of that. You have the citizens but you are asking them to make, as it were, legislative proposals of a kind that the Athenian democracy did not really believe in because it did not think that you could make those kind of laws, if you like, in the sense that which we now understand it. So the specific question is, how many of the people that you are looking at will have served on juries and is that proved to be relevant? And, secondly, can you say a bit more about the brief they are given as to the kind of recommendation or the kind or proposal they would come out with?

Professor Fishkin: Well, modern jury service is not anything like the Athenian juries which, as you say, had a very special mandate. I cannot remember if we have a question in this vast questionnaire about jury service. But I would point out to you but by the fourth century Athens the legislative commissions chosen by lot were making legislation. The deliberative microcosm developed and increased its role from the fifth century to the fourth century. The Athenian jury system had an additional advantage which is compulsion in getting their sample. In our project we have to attract the people to come so we have got a whole spiel about, you know, you will be on television, this is important, you will be on the set of *Coronation Street*, you will be on the set of the Sherlock Holmes production, we will pay them £50, we will pay all their expenses, put them up in what I think, with rhetorical flourish, has been said to be a four-star hotel, they will have a wonderful time. So far we have had a quite reasonable response rate but we cannot force them to come.

Steve Barnett (Goldsmiths' College and Henley Centre): I am particularly interested because at Goldsmiths we have just started a course on political communication, which is one of the very few in the country. And I want to pursue this idea of the model of Athenian democracy, although I think we can possibly take it too far, which is that one of the defining characteristics of that era was that there was a duty of citizenship. It was part of the culture of ancient Athens that people should participate in the policies that were being developed for the future of the nation state. Now it seems to me what you are doing, which I find absolutely fascinating because I think it does overcome the problems of the simplistic polling that we are saturated with, is that you are doing this within a protective bubble, this experiment, but you are then sending people back into the same kind of political culture, the same kind of community that they came from, which is essentially one, and this is not peculiar to Britain, which is anti-democratic. I do not mean that in the sense that there is not the same kind of sense of duty as citizen. People do not generally take much notice about the political world around them but what they do do is they get their information and they develop their political attitudes second-hand through the media that they are surrounded with the whole time. So we will still be reading the tabloid newspapers, watching the TV, listening to the sound bites and developing our opinions and political attitudes on that basis much as we were before, apart from the thousand people that you have chosen for your experiment. So is it anything other than just a very interesting experiment; does it have any wider resonance?

Professor Fishkin: One of the important things is that this experiment tomorrow is a dry run for something which Channel 4 and *The Independent* have committed themselves to at the launch of this in public which is to do it in the next general election here in Britain, whenever this is. Now if this is done in the general election the soundbite will have an effect. But in addition to the soundbite, and just as important as the soundbite, if it is good television it will dramatise the arguments and considerations on either side of each part of the issue. It will bring the issues to life in a way that speaks to the concerns of ordinary citizens because it is the people speaking, not news commentators or politicians or people in the Houses of Parliament yelling at each other but it is the people speaking, a statistical microcosm of a country speaking under thoughtful conditions. And that should have a recommending force and that could have a recommending force in the denouement of an election. It would certainly have a big effect at the beginning of the American Primary season; ideally it would be the kind of thing you would do right before a referendum.

Helen Baehr (University of Westminster): Most of the research about the role of the media shows that the media are actually part of the formation of people's language about what a problem is. And I think are you calling yours,'How to solve rising crime?'

Professor Fishkin: Channel 4 is calling it something like that.

Helen Baehr: Yes, well, that is straight out of the way in which the media pose a problematic, isn't it? I would have thought one of the interesting things to do in the study you are doing is to see how the language that people bring actually is formulated by media constructs already. Are you going to be bringing that into any of the research?

Professor Fishkin: Before we got a team together to do the briefing materials, we did focus groups with ordinary citizens to see on this issue of crime how they formulated the issue. And we took those formulations as the basis for the alternatives for which conflicting arguments were offered. We think we are speaking to the people in their terms. I mean, we will know tomorrow. But the programme is very much structured so it is the people's agenda that is brought to the experts and politicians rather than the other way around. For example, before there is any contact with the experts or politicians they will have three and a half hours of small group discussion based upon the briefing materials, determining the key concerns, the key questions that they want to raise in sessions with experts and with politicians later. So it is structured so that their agenda is brought to the elites rather than the other way around.

Helen Baehr: I do not want to pursue this but what worries me is you are already using a media agenda by having ordinary people, experts, politicians. It just seems a missed opportunity not to deconstruct that language when you have actually got these people together in the way they are going to debate it.

Birgit Thiel-Weidinger (*Suddeutsche Zeitung*): If this good example is going to be continued, who else could you think would finance it because it seems to be quite expensive to get all the people together, to prepare them, to pay them? You have two different channels, you have the newspaper so, ideally, would you then make another try for another kind of programme on the screen? Or would you think of other institutions which should then be financing it? How would it work?

Professor Fishkin: Well, my hope for this is that it will work and then it will be tried over and over. There have been lots of propositions to do it in the United States, for example, at the State level where it might be less expensive. The travel costs would be less. And as I say Channel 4 and *The Independent* are committed to the General Election. There have been proposals in the Swedish press for doing it as part of the education efforts for the Swedish referendum on joining the European Union, for example. There have been proposals in Australia. I do not know. We will see.

Unidentified questioner: Isn't there a vast danger that though we may provide information, truly democratic information, the political masters will dismiss it as purely another form of entertainment? The other side of that coin is, how much does it entertain? You began with a caveat that said that these people are coming because of *Coronation Street*, because of Sherlock Holmes, because of £50 and a four-star hotel; what happens when that is eliminated, when you can sit in your own home and watch it if you want to, like your parliamentary channel? What are the viewing figures on the parliamentary channel versus *Coronation Street*? I do not know the answer to that and I am frightened for it.

Professor Fishkin: Let me just make one thing clear. The interactive model in the home is not part of my proposal. It might some day be useful but the desiderata for my proposition is that the deliberative poll has to be two things. It has to be representative and it has to be deliberative. To be representative you cannot have a self-selected sample. I have to have a proper sample but it also has to be deliberative. Now the best way to be deliberative, I think, is to bring all the people to one place and have them debate face-to-face over an extended period of time. Now, some day, there may be ways of modelling that on a computer. I met Monday morning with the chief scientist at Xerox PARC, who is very up on all of these developments. He, to my relief, reassured me when he said, 'You are doing exactly the right thing. We don't have the technology now. Someday we will but we don't have the technology now to structure the kind of interactive thoughtful debate that you want. And so you are absolutely right to have real people seeing each other over a few days. You will get much better results. Someday the technology will catch up but it is not there yet. You would be a fool to go down the other path.' It also works better for television in that it will be an event if all the people are there in one place. It will be like a political convention or something. So it has that merit. It is much easier for television to make a programme out of it. But I think that after a while the people will hopefully forget that the television cameras are there and they will interact with each other in a reasonably natural way, or at least as in this phrase that I have been using, as ideal citizens would over three days. But it is very important that the sample be representative and that the process be deliberative.

Suzanne Franks: Judith Mackay is herself part of the new multi-channel future. She is head of programming and production services at Birmingham City Cable which is known as Network 021 City Cablevision. The franchise was awarded in 1989 and is now the largest in Europe with 450,000 homes. Birmingham Cable began broadcasting last July. Judith has a passion for sport; she was on the Sports Council, part of the Birmingham Olympic bid and Chair of the National Coaching Foundation. She is also interested in exploring the possibilities for cable in local politics. Hers was the first cable channel to cover a local by-election and she is hoping the channel can be involved in the forthcoming local elections in May. I would like to ask Judith to explore the notion that cable television can have a role in informing the democratic process.

Judith Mackay: Good morning, everyone. I am quite impressed how debate can get started so quickly at nine o'clock in the morning, especially if you have got somebody to provoke you.

Now, clearly, at this time of the morning I do not want to speak for too long. But I am also aware that the most important principles can be very briefly expressed For instance, The Lord's Prayer has got fifty-six words in it. The Ten Commandments has 297 in it; the American Declaration of Independence, with which I have some affinity, has 300; but an EEC directive on the import of caramel and caramel products requires 26,911.

Unusually for me, I have not really prepared a detailed script — partly because the experience of cable and the democratic process, in this country, does not really exist yet. In fact you could argue that the industry does not exist yet; it is still on a knife edge. No-one, including the investors, really knows if it is going to succeed or not. So what I am going to say now is, in many ways, a reaction to what Jim Fishkin has said and a personal view from me and not one that expresses the industry view. But I think it is probably important that we all start from a common base. Looking through the particpants' list I see that you come from a variety of backgrounds. So I beg your indulgence just to spend a couple of minutes talking about the cable industry and what it really is today in the United Kingdom.

Cable is a very expensive industry. It is probably worthwhile remembering that there are still well under a million cable customers so, in terms of a sample or representation of a national audience, it does not exist yet. Cable franchises were awarded in almost all of the urban areas in the country but not all of them so there are still some up for grabs.

In the early days, people put together the money to make the bid and did not have the money to build the franchise. This is the only country in the world where you can build a telecommunications fibre network down the same channel as you lay your cable television fibre network, but with the change in capital gains legislation, with the onset of the duopoly review, with the Broadcasting Act of 1990 there has been a total dearth of UK investment in the cable industry. So the American telephone companies and cable operators have moved in in a substantial way. I do not know the exact statistics; I suppose something like 95% of the investment in cable in the UK is transatlantic money. The French are also there, in some degree, as well.

The significance of this is really quite enormous. It is going to cost something in the order of £300 million pounds to build Birmingham Cable's network. It is going to take us something like seven years to do that. It is expensive because it has to be trenched; it has to go underground, not on poles the way it is in the States. That is serious money. The cable industry is worth billions of pounds. The legislation in the States at the moment means that you cannot operate a telephone company and a cable teleivision company as one unit. But that is quickly changing. As the edges are crumbling on the modified final judgement [in the Bell case which broke up the telephone monopolies in the USA—*Eds.*], American investors are over here in Europe looking for new opportunities and gaining experience of how to run television and telephones together. And there is no doubt in my mind that they will take the experience here and eventually they will go back to the States and use it there. I will make a sweeping statement here: the States is, by and large, an isolationist country and it is the experience here that they will take back to the States that is really of importance to them, I mean as well as making a few dollars on the way.

I think that Parliament got the legislation right on the programming side as carried out by the Cable Authority and now implemented by the ITC. Local cable in the States exists in towns and cities where in a city the size of Birmingham there are four or five competitors. It is a very crowded media scene. The difference here is that there is no local television whatsoever but there are other differences as well.

So, if we look at the American scene, you will find a national affiliate station, you will find an independent network with a local station, you will certainly find the cable operator at least putting out some sort of news service but you will also find the public access channels. Now, as I understand it, the intention when the cable legislation was written and developed was that public access, the right to freedom of speech according to the first amendment of the Constitution, would be enshrined in the cable legislation and therefore there was the right by law for any group or individual to have their opinion aired on a cable network. It means that you get a diversity of programming ranging on the one hand from Manhattan Cable and, on the other hand, to the Ku Klux Klan. And where public access works in the States, it works very well and where it does not work, it is horrid.

The other difference in geographic terms is that the United States and Canada are actually nothing more than an enormous collection of small towns, many of them separated by large distances from other small towns all of whom have, at least, one cable network. And there is no national press. So you look to your local cable, your local news operation for different reasons than you do here where you have a national press and you have a national television network which carries regional and local news.

But the legislation here, I think, interprets public access correctly for what you can do in this country. I do not think you will get the awful excesses of Manhattan

Cable, although there is a school of thought and there are people who would like to see true public access come into being here as well. And if that happens that would be interesting indeed because it would be a manifestation of the democratic process that I do not think has worked particularly well in the States.

But there is an obligation in everyone's franchise licence from the ITC to provide a local programming service to allow the community access to a cable channel. And there is an annual agreement which is undertaken in discussion with the cable operator to make sure that they fulfil their promises. So you could say if this happens with all 130 we are very close to the fifth channel already.

In the early days there were some experiments with local cable programming. I have to say that Granada's Waddington experiment put back the cause of local programming by at least a decade. And viewers' habits have changed. No longer are people content to sit and watch a programme from the beginning to the end. Research has shows that the average viewing time, without flicking the remote, is three minutes. So when you look at how you make the democratic process work, I think you need to be aware of the world in which we live in and the way people really behave, not the way that you think that they are going to behave. I do have some concerns with samples and polling because I am only too aware, as I am sure you are, of the statistician who drowned in the lake with an average depth of six inches.

I run Network 021, City Cablevision. We put out between an hour and a half and three hours' programming a day, rolled over four times, seven days a week. I believe the secret to making a success of that will be that the channel looks live, although it is not at the moment, that it has an immediacy about it and it fills a niche that is not filled by the regional broadcasters. Therefore we concentrate on news, current affairs, sport and music. There is an audience. I think there are a number of people now working in local programming who have demonstrated that there is an audience. We have done some simple work on an election but I have my doubts as to whether or not we will be able to take it much further.

Whatever you feel about television and whatever you feel about the moral tone of cable, and we put out forty-two channels, my belief is that down the road the cable industry will be driven by telephones and telecommunications and that that is where the attention of the investors will go. Cable television is now at a plateau from which, if it does move, will simply mean more channels with the same kind of content and not a new breakthrough and I do not believe this is going to drive the business at all.

I think you need to think of a cable operator as a delivery mechanism and not as an initiator. If someone has a product the cable operator will carry it if it will provide viewers; if it will not provide viewers the cable operator is not going to be interested.

Cable has two unique qualities. One, it can be interactive and two, it can be local and it can be addressed set top by set top. So I should think it is a pollster's dream. I should think they would love to get hold of our appliance, they would love to see our customers and they would love to count them in ever increasing numbers. But there is, fortunately, some very good legislation which prevents them doing that too thoroughly.

I think what I would like to do, though, to perhaps demonstrate the difference. I have brought a tape which has its origins in Maclean Hunter who are a Canadian cable operator. It is about thirty-two generations away from the original so the quality is extremely poor. But it will show you what happens in small town local public-access television in Canada and this is an excerpt from a very much longer tape.

Extract is shown

I think examples are a legion from towns where there is a commitment to the community, but I would like to finish with perhaps one or two personal thoughts. My roots are in New England. And when I go back to Cape Cod in the summer my mother tells me what has been happening at the town meetings where there is no town council, where every citizen has a voice. The turnout is no greater than it is for a local election here. The by-election that we covered in Birmingham recently had a turn-out which is considered high of thirty-nine per cent. I do not think that interest in local politics is any greater in the States than it is here.

I would stress again that in England and Great Britain generally you have a much stronger national press, a much stronger media presence than you do in the States, and that to me is a significant difference. Television is a one-to-one relationship. I believe that tomorrow morning's experiment with Granada is not television in itself; it is not interactivity, it is Granada making a television programme and the success of it will depend on how good it is as entertainment. I think there is a real issue about the impartiality of broadcasting. The legislation is really quite clear; there are undue prominence and impartiality rules. I think you play with those at your peril.

I want to make one last point. To me democracy is not a right. It is a privilege, and you have to earn privileges. They are not given to you. I do not think that you deserve to be in a democratic society unless you work at it, and to work at it you have to be well informed, and if you are going to be well informed you have to make an effort. Simply to choose a topic in which the citizenry is interested is not sufficient in my view to actually change the way in which television is delivered. But I will leave you with one final thought, just to be provocative, and perhaps totally take apart what I have just said. There is an old saying that goes "Tell me and I forget; show me and I remember; involve me and I understand."

Suzanne Franks: Phillip Whitehead is part of a very select band who have been at the heart of the democratic process as well as a distinguished TV producer, informing audiences about the nature of political power. In fact Phillip is posed to return very shortly to active politics as an MEP. Until 1979 he was MP for Derby North but he is now seeking to join Edwina Currie on the road from Westminster to Strasbourg. Phillip, despite his direct interest in seeking ways to empower citizens and involve voters in political debate, tells me he has come here to perform the function of house cynic.

Phillip Whitehead: I think that if I were to follow Edwina Currie there, or anywhere, the journey would not be worth making. Statistically it is unlikely that we would both get to that place. I am billed in the programme this morning as a veteran, I see, for the first time. One of the characteristics of a veteran is about this time of day your war wounds start hurting. Listening to the speakers this morning, and trying to address the subject before you, it does seem to me that some old war wounds are hurting.

I was on the Annan Committee in the 1970s when cable was already established here, though very much in its infancy and we described it then, in one of Noel Annan's more colourful phrases, as a ravenous parasite. I am now a subscriber to London Cable, I get my thirty-eight channels, I watch them and I still think it is a ravenous parasite.

Nevertheless it may be, in its way, a useful piece of added value to our domestic lives. This session is about is the degree to which it is going to enhance our democracy, is doing now, may do in the future. And I have my doubts about that. I have my doubts for a variety of reasons. We look at the democratic process today, and we are all part of it, not just those of us who, from time to time, run for office. Meeting voters on the doorstep, listening to the way that they do interact with politicians, one thinks about the famous confrontation about the *Belgrano* between Mrs Thatcher and a housewife from Bristol and one remembers who came off better in that exchange. There is a level at which the voters interconnect when they get their opportunity with the political process. And our levels of turnout in general elections, at least, in percentages of the high 70s and low 80s, suggest that that process is still working for all its imperfections and for all of the problems with the mass media.

The question is whether the media are giving us better tools for the enhancement of democracy or are they, in some ways, subverting that process itself? The problem is that the processes of subversion through the mass media, are at least as far advanced as any notions of enhancement, and we are seeing this in Europe and in the United States. I do not think that the experiment that Jim Fishkin was talking about can really be seen as anything more than another television programme. These four hundred people are being told to think for England. They are being told to go up there and allow the processes and the agonies of their decision making to serve in some representative way for the whole *polis*. This may be some new science which I suppose we could call demiotics, but it does not seem to me to be an advance, necessarily, in democracy because democracy has to be about allowing everyone to sort through the jumble of ideas, prejudices, half-remembered principles and matters of immediate concern which together make up the package which determines how they vote at elections and how they think as citizens for the whole time. And that is a very different process. Why, oh, why did they choose the rise in crime as the subject for this deliberative assembly? Why? Well, we know perfectly well why and I think Helen Baehr was right to point out that the language in which the media frame discussions of this sort seems to have shaped already the way in which that assembly is coming together. So I have my doubts. I also have my doubts, because of the cost involved in this very expensive exercise, that it could ever be used at a local level where it might be possible, if we write the rules correctly, for local stations, cable stations, interactive systems to be engaged in an exercise of this kind.

The cost of this operation would prove to you that at the end of the day four hundred people can be brought together as a wholly representative sample from all over the country, can be taken through this process, paid their money, put on after *Sherlock Holmes*, and can be sent home again at the end of the process having informed and entertained the citizen body. But, by the same token, you can, if you spend enough money, put eight human beings in a biosphere in the middle of the desert and prove that they can live in entirely artificial conditions for a whole year. It does not prove much about the way the rest of us are living out there in the smog. And the rest of us have to have our being out there and it is the out-thereness of out there that I want to address, in terms of the way the citizen is informed.

Now, how am I informed, as a citizen, by London Cable for which I pay ten pounds a month? I am given a vast number of new channels — not quite the number that Rod Allen and his colleagues have informatively put in their list of five hundred, although the list of five hundred does seem to cover some of Professor Fishkin's notions since I see, you have got a channel called 'Dead White Males' and another channel called 'Hellenic,' and I suppose if you put those two together you would get something like Athenian democracy. We should not, in our idealisation of the Athenian marketplace, forget that the excludees far outnumbered those who participated as, indeed, they are going to in these television experiments.

I look at these channels and I think to myself, 'Well, the common-carrier rules give me what I would have had anyway and what I pay for, anyway. They gave me some parts of Sky but not all the things that Sky thinks it can charge me more for. They give me programmes in a variety of foreign languages. And they give me about ten different ways of being interactive with pop videos, so that I could, if I wanted, get the video of my choice played here or there. And I also learn lots of other things. I learn that the French have a higher proportion of serious discussion programmes than anyone else, that American movies dub better in Italian than they do in German, but if you want really solid pornography, you have to wait for the German channel at 1.00am in the morning.' Now these are all things that as a citizen I may wish to know. They have not, any of them, affected me along my road of preferences and if we extend the number from 38 through 42 or maybe even up to 100 or 200 or 500, that proliferation of choice is not, necessarily, giving me additional information. It may be leaving me in the hinterland between the zappers on the one hand and the prisoners, as I would call them, on the other — that is, those who flick through the channels and those who get themselves so stuck in the Hindi films or the Hellenic music show, or whatever it may be, because that is their thing, that is something that they can have over and above anything that they get anywhere else on the system. For them it really is genuinely added value. But it is not allowing, and it is not necessarily helping people, to talk or debate or argue with each other. As this proliferation increases and these various bits of programming — something borrowed something blue coming from here and there — come into the home, I wonder what it is actually doing in terms of allowing the viewer to weigh deliberative choices. I think the answer to that is not a lot. And as I sit there with my hundred channels, it reminds me a bit of a joke now current in Russia which says 'All leaders have their problems. For example, Mr Clinton has a hundred bodyguards; one of them is a KGB agent but he does not know which one. Monsieur Mitterand has a hundred mistresses; one of them has a social disease but he does not know which one. And President Yeltsin has a hundred economic advisers; one of *them* is right but he does not know which one.' One of these channels may be helping me but I do not know which one. I do not quite know the way in which these processes would do that without a greater insistence on public participation than we have been able to write into the legislation, or to insist on, thus far with cable in this country.

I was on the Parliamentary committee on the legislation which brought in the present cable system and the regulatory authority and I am glad we have got the regulatory authority. I am glad the cable we have in this country is trying as hard as it is. But I have two caveats about it. One Judith touched on: the investment is overwhelmingly from overseas, and its insistence will be first and foremost on a return. There is not likely to be for some time to come the money to invest even on a modest scale in the kind of experiments, the interaction between the town hall and the citizen, which cable could do. Someone mentioned Columbus, Ohio, and the wiring up with modern interactive systems of cities like that was the subject of immense enthusiasm at seminars like this some ten or fifteen years ago, as, in its early days, was Manhattan Cable and its devotees used to come here before enough of us had been to New York to watch it, to tell us that this, too, was the democratic future. It has not quite turned out like that.

The problem for cable in this country is not that the will is not there — there are sincere people who would wish to make it so — but that the particular economics of cable in this country are unlikely to create the resources on the margin that would allow it to be so. Cable here has not grown in the way that it has in the United States and Canada for all sorts of reasons that we all know about like the fact that there it overcomes the tyranny of distance, it gives you better reception whereas here, of course, we have always had fewer channels better received than was the case in the States. So it has taken off more slowly and it has had the misfortune of being leapfrogged now by satellite.

I will come on to satellite in just a moment. But why should I knock the people who are running satellite? My wife works for UK Living and there she sits in Teddington Studios with a budget of two thousand pounds an hour for the whole show, putting it on the air, family entertainment it is called and it is the wave of the future and it is slowly but surely eating into the national advertising pool of revenue and it is beginning to make its small impact. I am very fascinated to see what they are doing; I am fascinated to see what the satellite system is doing in general. But I do not believe, with the fast growth of the Murdoch empire and everything else that is coming to us via Astra out of the skies at the moment, that cable coming along on its own, doing its own thing in the localities, is going to have the spare cash to produce citizens' programming of the sort that I would like to see.

This brings me to one other thought which is that while we sit here, locked in our small worlds reached and encapsulated in the cable, large things are happening in the world. And we might be like the people in that famous E.M. Forster story 'The Machine Stops,' watching our world crumble around us on our small screens without knowing the larger movements, quite threatening to democracy, that are taking place meanwhile. Here we are talking here today about how the proliferation of the small screen can aid democracy. Not so far away, inside the EU, with representatives going to Brussels and Strasbourg and all of that, is what has happened in Italy in which a political party run by a TV mogul has seized power within a couple of months of its formal foundation. Berlusconi took control of all three private channels of Italian television — Rod Allen knows far more about this than I do — but it is worth thinking about the rules in the private sector of Italian television that were intended to maintain a plurality of ownership and a diversity and how Berlusconi got round it and built a vast empire which now has fifty per cent of the media outlets in Italy, then took over a football team, took the slogan of the football team to the name of the political party. Now he has marched on Rome in much the same way, using the methods of the 1990s, that Mussolini's blackshirts used in the 1920s. Mussolini was a newspaper editor; he knew about the presentation of style, opinion, strength, vigour, novelty, in those days. Berlusconi is simply doing the same thing with the softer images of the mass media age and he is doing it successfully. And in the great State of Texas from which the professor comes, an eccentric millionaire and control freak called Ross Perot managed to buy his way on to national television, to exploit the easy access to the chat shows of the Larry King variety, used an enormous fortune on so-called infotainment programmes and got himself going on for twenty per cent of the poll in the American presidential election. These things are happening here and now. They are influences in the political process, interventions in it, which seem to me to be far more threatening than the positive elements of small scale changes here and there, can we get the town meeting on television and so on, are those nice Canadians the wave of the future? This is, perhaps, what we were asked to discuss today.

I am rather reminded, looking at this gathering today, of the scene from antiquity, since we are talking about the 2,500 years of democracy, with which V.S. Naipaul ends one of his books. You may remember the scene. The Athenians are in the theatre, the performance is on, it is one of the great classics, they are happy and together, they are looking inwards. At the end of the performance they look outwards, they see the Scythian bowmen around the amphitheatre, and their bowstrings are drawn. Now I think we are quite close to that point here and I am alarmed by what is going on in terms of how major influences are beginning to subvert the independence of the television media as we know them. It seems to me that that is a dangerous threat which moves into this microcosmic area as well because the power that can buy up all those television stations in Italy is only one or two steps, not one or two light years, or even one or two light entertainment years, away from buying its influence, or forcing its influence, into our politics, too.

Discussion

John Gray (independent consultant): If I can pick up from Phillip Whitehead and get back to the fundamental questions that head this session of democracy and the means of communication, there is a saying to the effect that societies are conditioned by the means of communication at their disposal.

Now we have had five hundred years in which the means of communication for thought and entertainment has largely been the written word or the printed word. And our institutions, parliaments, the legal system, the educational sytems have been founded on this which is the idealisation of the rational man, and the rational man, according to Professor Fishkin, can take rational decisions for the common good. But we are not using that medium. We are using a medium where ritual and reaction come first. It is, in Nicholas Garnham's phrase, the era of the new priesthood. And I think very much that whilst it *seems* that the media today are bolstering up "democracy," the existing democratic systems, particularly the political ones, in fact, by their very existence they are destroying them. This does not mean to say that we cannot have a democratic society which is using the media as they now exist, but we are a democratic society with entirely different institutions and, as a result of that, the users of the media which are Nicholas Garnham's priesthood will have to be made very much more responsible than they are. And there is an antithesis within our present industry derived largely from the nineteeth-century journalism by which the practitioners of the media like to think of themselves as free to criticise, and to some extent, undermine the existing institutions. I think they undermine them by their very existence and we have to evolve a new democracy with new institutions to support it.

Phillip Whitehead: Obviously I agree with some of that. I think that at the moment public cynicism about politics is much more to do with the practice of the politicians than the practice of those who comment on it. You have only to look at some of the procedures currently under way, like the Scott enquiry. It used to be said that good government flourishes in the dark (I think that was a sort of mushroom theory of Rab Butler) and governments hate to have the media expose the full range of their transactions. I think that is true of all political parties. What I think the media have been able to do in this country in terms of interventions in the electoral process is, occasionally, to spatchcock back into it what the ordinary citizen says and thinks. I think radio and television and local television have played a major part in confronting politicians with the views of the ordinary citizen, and if Birmingham Cable, come the next election, can put the local MPs and political leaders on the spot through the interactive process with the viewer from home, not sitting there passively but actually saying, 'Hang on. How much did it cost to build the conference centre?' (or whatever it may be), then I think that really is added value in the system. Inevitably in the age of the sound bite and the PR tease and the rose instead of the rosette, we are going to get a good deal of manipulation by political parties who will deeply resent anything that they say or present to the voters being challenged at all.

Phillip Reevell (Mersey Television): I am just wondering if Judith could say what kind of audience, presuming it does get an audience, do you get for that two hour programme and how do the different repeats fare by day part; in other words is there a better audience in the evening or during the day?

You also mentioned Channel 5. You said there were 130 cable franchises, five or six owners and therefore you are effectively doing the fifth channel. That is not quite what I understood the fifth channel potentially to be. I understood that to be a national network with some option for local programming or local players. I wonder if you could go on to explain a little bit more how you think cable represents the fifth channel?

And, finally, it is a very interesting point that Phillip makes about the Italians. It sort of raised the issue of whether plurality of ownership is an alternative or as important issue. I wonder how far you think current broadcasting policy and regulation reflects plurality of ownership in this country and whether that is an issue that ought to be taken further?

Judith Mackay: Can I deal with the fifth channel first? Perhaps I did not make it particularly clear. Yes, the ITC have advertised Channel 5 and are now considering whether or not and how to advertise it again, not having awarded it the first time. The point that I was making is that *de facto* there is going to be another network in place before another Channel 5 is advertised. The ITC are here so they can speak better than I can. The fifth channel does not have to be city-based and it may not be, but one of the options they are looking at is whether or not to franchise a number of cities to run a separate channel. The point that I am making is that with local cable operations now springing up throughout the country there will be, through networking and negotiation, a fifth channel which has a rather unique combination of very local programming and programming that will transfer and travel.

On the news side. I am not aware that anyone is regularly doing what I would call hard news on a local cable operation. By and large they tend to be magazine programmes or soft features. If I just take an American example again, simply because there is no template here, Channel 5 on Long Island has continuous news all day long, and they up date it every two hours. They operate from a position that I try to duplicate in Birmingham which is you have got a combination of very local news which is only of interest to people who are going to say, 'Hey look, it's mom on telly ...' With a city the size of Birmingham, which has a national and international role to play, that you can bring a different dimension to it. I am not sure that that would work in York or in Bournemouth. I think that there are different disciplines that would affect news coverage there but in a city the size of Birmingham with four main conurbations surrounding it, I think there is quite a unique opportunity to put out news that is of interest to all of Birmingham as well of being of interest to the people in Acocks Green and Edgbaston.

Phillip Whitehead: I would just like to say one word about Channel 5, because I very much support the idea of a Channel 5 and I believe that it ought to be a federation of local stations and it ought to be funded by subscription. That way it would have a more discrete source of revenue than if it were just dipping into the advertising pool like everyone else. There is a good deal of argument about whether this is the case or not. I personally regret the fact that the Channel 5 option was withdrawn by the ITC or whatever it was then called a couple of years ago, and I hope we will return to it this time. But I think there may be a way in which a national Channel 5 could both link into and strengthen and, in some cases, rejuvenate local cable systems as well. That is the only reason why they should not operate in harmony.

On your question about plurality of ownership, of course that is the heart of the matter. How do we maintain plurality of ownership when the investors are small in number and even smaller in their ambitions, in where they want the system to go? I am a great believer in anti-trust laws and we do not really have them in this country to the extent that they have them in the United States. One of the reasons that I am intersted in the European Parliament — and this is not a party point at all — is that it is only at the European level that you can tackle the international regulation of broadcasting or the international control of pollution and matters of that sort. Like it or not, we have got to deal with that internationally or we are going to wake up here one day and find Forza Italiana or Murdoch or something as the new political force in this country.

Unidentified speaker: On a question that Phillip touched on, which is the conduct of public and political life, I wonder whether we forget that, to some extent, there is a lot of concern about the degradation of political life because the people going into politics are of a lower calibre and lower quality than they used to be. That may be what the proliferation of media is doing, by casting the spotlight on the real qualities of the people who are our elected representatives. If you go back again to the Athenian model the citizens were the policy makers. Here we have citizens having to elect policy makers and perhaps the people that they are electing are not up to the job any more, or less than they used to be.

Phillip Whitehead: That may be true. I think one of the problems is that they are much more of a muchness than they used to be. It is hard to see here in the symbiotic relationship between television and politics which comes first. But in the confrontation between smooth, glib polytechnic lecturers, if I can throw the insult back at the audience, and smooth, glib market research and PR men on the other side which you now have between the Labour and Conservative how do you reduce the number of unclassifiable people who came in from other backgrounds, without having been professional politicians all their lives? I mean there are not many modern equivalents of Joseph Chamberlain, say, who was a successful screw manufacturer, a great radical agitator, Lord Mayor of Birmingham and then, at the age of forty something, came into Parliament with a big career behind him. There are not many people like that any more. So, maybe, that is what has happened but very few politicians would agree with that.

Granville Williams (Campaign for Press and Broadcasting Freedom): Just two very quick observations on Europe. On behalf of the Campaign I have twice gone to give evidence at Council of Europe hearings on journalistic freedoms and human rights and on the other issue of media concentration. There is a very important green paper on pluralism and media concentration. What really worries me is the effort and the energy and the money which the big media corporations are putting in to destabilise and derail very basic initiatives and demands to guarantee pluralism and to guarantee journalistic freedoms to be able to report without pressures from commercial advertising and other sources. But that is also paralleled, it seems to me, at a national level and when you mentioned your cable channel in London what is quite clear from the research we have been doing in the Campaign for a new publication is that the news provider for the cable networks in London is Associated Press, the *Daily Mail,* and you see the cross pattern of ownership now extending so that in London *the Daily Mail* is, with the *Evening Standard,* a very important powerful paper and the news provider through cable. The cross-media ownership patterns are already there very strongly and yet we are now seeing this very strong lobby to lift these restrictions between press, broadcasting and other media interests.

Michael Redley (Independent Television Commission): The ITC issued a document about two months ago now which is a contribution to this interministerial enquiry into cross-media ownership. I do not think anybody knows quite why they wanted the information so quickly but I think the assumption must be that they have in mind some sort of legislative possibility, at least. I think the pressure is in the direction of relaxations, but I think it has to be said that the restrictions were put together at a considerable speed in the Broadbcasting Act of 1990 and it may well be that there are things that have to be taken out and re-examined and put back again in a slightly different way to make the thing work. And that is really where I think the ITC's view of it comes in. The ITC has had the experience of trying to work the ownership rules of 1990 and it has not been an altogether happy one. And so the thought is that some of this detail has to be looked at again.

You have in the European context the concepts of internal pluralism and external pluralism and they interact, to a degree, which I think is quite an interesting question in itself. Internal pluralism is the concept that within any channel, or perhaps even any programme, there has to be a degree of balance and internal political integrity, on the one hand. And external pluralism is the concept that across the media as a whole you have to have a multiplicity of owners and that if you shrink below a certain level, an alarm bell rings so if you have maybe four conglomerates, as it were, well, that is all right but if it shrinks to three, then you are in trouble.

There is an interesting inter-reaction because in a sense if you have got a really solid base of internal pluralism, you have to ask yourself whether you need external pluralism. If each channel is preserving a proper discipline of internal pluralism, then do you need to worry about who owns services? The ITC's reaction to that is that you do. You do need both. You cannot rely on only one. You have to have the back-up. It is partly belt and braces, it is partly discipline, looking at the system as a possibility, as Phillip Whitehead was talking about in Italy, where the situation can just be rolled over by pressure. You need as much defence in the system, at as many different levels, as you can.

Having said that the other side of it, though — and this is the issue that we are discussing round here — is that of whether convergence and new technology and all the rest of it is, in some sense, fundamentally changing things; whether print is on the way out and must seek an alternative vocation in electronic media. One can see how that can be a self-serving argument on the part of those who put it but I think it does need a serious appraisal on the level at which it is put.

Session produced by Helen Baehr, Steve Barnett and Kim Peat

Testing the boundaries: will the old regulatory system survive?

Chair: **Russell Twisk**
Reader's Digest Association

Ted Mercer
Allison and Humphreys, Solicitors

Michael Redley
Independent Television Commission

Jane Vizard
BBC

RUSSELL Twisk: This has been a wonderful week for regulators. Communicopia might well have meant the death for regulators, defeated by new technology and the sheer number and variety of opportunities offered to avoid the stern eye of those who seek to uphold standards. Suddenly regulation has found a new life after all. Just take yesterday's headlines. "Video nasties to be outlawed for children,' 'Now Chuckie can't come out to play,' 'Video crack-down,' 'New war on video horrors.' Regulation is very much alive and kicking. But can it cope with the proliferation of media? When a child can dial on his modem into a notice board, perhaps in another country, probably the United States, and receive straight into his computer the most explicit pornography; when satellite, with enormous footprints, can trample over the most cunning and carefully worked out regulations? As broadcasting makes way for ever more narrow casting, can the regulators, who sometimes struggle to cope with a dozen channels, possibly handle five hundred channels?

Who will pay for it if they can? And how will it be policed? And how much of the regulators' very survival is wrapped up in the future of the BBC Charter? And if a new law can be bounced along by a group of back-benchers this week, how easy would it be for the same group of back-benchers, anti-BBC back-benchers for instance, to bounce along a privatisation of the BBC before the Charter is safely tucked away? The BBC itself, senior management, seem vastly to overlook this possibility.

How, above all, will the regulators keep up with the new technology? It was Nikita Khruschev who when he was at the United Nations and was talking about intercontinental ballistic missiles once said, 'Oh, you expect it through the door, and then it comes through the window.' And that is one of the things that is happening to us with the new technology and the proliferation of television stations.

We have got the 'A' team of regulators here.

I am going to introduce them each individually and Ted has volunteered to go first. He went to the school in Birmingham which was the same place that brought us Sir Michael Checkland and afterwards he went to Trinity, Cambridge, where he became a Cambridge freshman and Open English University Debating Champion, a fact that rather startled one of his fellow panellists when I broke that to him. After a spell in local government, where he finished up as Legal Officer in a Lancashire borough, he became secretary of the newly founded Cable Authority where he stayed until 1988. He probably then decided that he could use some money, and he has been in private practice with the firm of Allison and Humphreys specialising in telecommunications and broadcasting regulation. He is a churchwarden in his home town of Sussex, Lewes in Sussex and he has made a life-long study, he says, of the use of malt and hops in fermenting processes.

Ted Mercer: It is not often that the oppressed minority like me, that is to say a lawyer in private practice, gets the chance to go first, so here goes. Let me set you two scenarios: the first in ten years' time and the second in twenty years' time.

In the first scenario, digital transmission terrestrially speaking has been going for about five years. There is also the beginning of digital compression techniques being used heavily on satellites. Video-on-demand is available in outlying rural areas by courtesy of BT and in urban areas by courtesy of BT and broadband cable systems. Significant difficulties over rights for such slots, what one can describe as 'one-to-one video services', or programmes being sent on individual demand, have been overcome to some degree but only through use of European Community competition law. Mr Average in the community in urban areas has connection to a cable system or a dish he has been given by his brother-in-law who has connected to cable. His viewing range or pattern is over 30 channels per week but he still spends most of his time watching BBC or Channel 3, for he is a creature of habit. Channel 3 licensees had their licences renewed about six years ago under the terms of the now repealed 1990 Act. They are paying about a third PQR and cash-bid payments that they were. ITV viewers seem to have got used to *News at 8.30 p.m.* although it has never had the ring of *News at Ten*. Channel 3 and Channel 4 and Pearson Media (a.k.a. Channel 5) do still have public TV positive obligations on them although these were considerably eroded by the last Broadcasting Act in the year 2000. There is still a distinct division of the ITC whose job it is to monitor this — all two of them. Independent Scheduling Limited, the consortium company that now provides ITV Channel 3 core hours, complains bitterly that it does not get first choice of programming from programme makers within its ranks and in particular is very upset about LWT's new contract to provide programming to Sky which is now, as well as being on satellite, a digital terrestrial channel for which it paid the Radiocommunications Agency a considerable amount of money to gain the necessary spectrum space.

The ITC is now combined with the Broadcasting Complaints Commission and the Broadcasting Standards Council and spends most of its time being reactive to complaints in respect of most channels it regulates. As I said only two or three people are still interested in making sure that Channel 3 lives up to its public service obligations. All in all people are surprised that the new bursts of technology promised since the mid-1990s have not taken root and are doing so only slowly. Programming is still dominated by sequential sets of programming sent by a scheduler or packager and video-on-demand and other services are used merely as an adjunct for normal viewing much in the way as a visit to a video shop was in the late 1980s. James Ferman and the Video Control Boards stood out alone for a long time but have now been merged with the ITC who spend a lot of their time in the Courts following the third David Alton amendment to the Video Control Bill of 1998. No one has ever quite worked out the 'works of artistic merit and taste' exception and are not letting anything through that might affect junior in any way, possibly in line with Mr Alton's legislation — you can only get copies of Dennis Potter's works in sex shops. Things went particularly wrong when Michael Grade was accidentally named Chairman of the ITC's Video Classification Sub-Committee on his retirement from Channel 4. There are still regulators, they are still hammering out the same consumer controls relating to good taste and decency, prevention of harm to junior and no nasty adverts.

In twenty years' time, in my second scenario, there is still a ban on subliminal imaging and the Programme Classification Board work of the ITC is its main task. It no longer has any channels under its control which have a positive content remit. Most channels work on a pay-per-view basis with perhaps yearly subscriptions to sport and your favourite News Channel. All programmes have either to submit to the ITC's Classification Committee or a rating which determines when they may be made available to the public or if they can be made available at all. All programme makers can self-certify on risk of penalty if they fail to certify under a category into which later on appeal following complaint the ITC put the programme.

There are very few sequential channels in the traditional sense apart from the seven 24 hours a day news channels. They are still subject to codes and guidelines (impartiality, taste, decency, incitement, etc.) and some of the channels have been fined several times in the last few months when in respect of complaints investigations have led to it being shown that they have breached the guidelines. Apart from the film classification work, most of the time the ITC and their lawyers are dealing with the formality of classification enforcement. Most control is self-control by programme makers. There is also a DTI department that deals with quotas and our European obligations and some means of delivery have had some difficulty in keeping to the 51 per cent European hours shown formula. There is a much greater relationship between the regulators and the individual programme makers looking for classification and most programme makers have at least one member of staff who have successfully passed the ITC's certification course.

But wait. What has happened to the BBC in all of this? During the first ten years it chugged on quite merrily, following licence and charter renewal. Some time later it was made subject to the same content controls as everybody else and is now actually content controlled by the ITC at 20 years out, except that the Governors are still responsible for its positive programming remit. It is still watched by a surprising minority of people, most of whom have degrees in the liberal arts. Its transmitter arm was privatised some years ago and was thereafter merged with

NTL. Still a premium programme maker, it makes a lot of money out of its archives which it sells widely using the money to finance the making of new programming. It is regarded as the best programming training machine in the country, if not the world. It now concentrates on making programmes and buys in very little and surprisingly is still subject to a yearly levy payable by all who have a television set. Its radio arm is still heavily into providing programmes for car users and digital high-quality music and data. Jenny Abramsky retired as Director-General only two years ago and the new one is … oh dear, my crystal ball fades. It must be time to hand over to Michael Redley of the ITC.

Russell Twisk: Michael Redley is a Cambridge man, too, where he got a PhD in history, followed by a Master's in economics at the LSE. He has worked in the Ministry of Defence as well as the Treasury. He joined the staff of the IBA from the Treasury in 1989 and became chief assistant to the Director-General. He is now Secretary to the ITC. His responsibilities have covered all aspects of the Broadcasting Bill, preparation for licensing and an international interest in broadcasting.

Michael Redley: Listening to Gypsy Ted's millennarian musings, one is left wondering a bit whether there is not a public interest element in all this. I mean, basically, should we not band together to at least try to shape the future so that quality and choice in broadcasting are real options and not a sort of residual that may come out of all this technological express train process?

Shaping, of course, can mean a number of different things. The idea of a broadcasting authority exercising the authority of the State on its behalf to manage commercial broadcasting is the sort of thing that the IBA did. It was still doing it when I first joined it in the late 1980s. That is clearly not an option. Nor, I suppose, is public ownership isolated entirely from commercial pressure. But facilitating, tying the ends together, organising a framework, taking the viewer's side, the side of the small guy where there is an issue about small versus large, defining vocations for commercial broadcasters in ways which allow a virtuous rather than a vicious circle to inform what happens, working with the grain of the creativity out of which good television occurs rather than against it — all of that seems to be the sort of regulation we can sensibly talk about. And, I hope, envisage continuing in one form or another for the indefinite future.

What I want to try to do is examine the case for this. Neville Chamberlain, who is not a man noted for his wit, said actually rather wittily of trying to understand the programme of his political opponents that it was 'like looking in a dark cupboard for a black hat that is not there.' I feel this a bit about the digital superhighway, about convergence, about the whole bag of tricks offered by technology. The issue is not whether the thing works on the laboratory bench (quite a lot of it does, although a surprisingly large amount on closer examination does not yet) but the old one of evolution or revolution. Does the change conform to the established patterns or does it overthrow them?

I did some economic forecasting in the Treasury. And a lot of the discussion that one hears about this rather conforms to the problem that occurs in forecasting where you divide the economy into sectors and each sector concentrates on its own problems, and some extraordinarily bizarre blooms flourish in the isolation that this organisational problem establishes. It is only when you put the whole thing together that you see the picture. I think I am very much concerned that that overall perspective should prevail.

Another point, again of an introductory nature, is that the technologies may converge but perhaps we can still, and may indeed want, to concern ourselves with a particular segment within that convergence and apply regulation to that rather than, as it were, giving up because the whole thing is swimming around in a large and rather difficult-to-manage sea of indifference.

So can we just first of all stand back and ask why we have the regulation of television to start with? The reason is bluntly is that broadcasting is seen partly, but not only for political reasons, as an absolutely vital thing for society. Broadcasting is, if you like, a sort of central nervous system. You will find broadcasting described, interestingly enough, about 150 years before it ever existed in the political thought of Coleridge who defined the concept of a clerisy. He perceived a need arising out of a set of social circumstances. A clerisy was a body of people with the means to facilitate communication within society. The need it was addressing, in his view, was the need of a complex, fragmented, pluralist society that came out of the industrial revolution and the French Revolution and the changes of the time. It had not been needed before. There was an organic society which worked in a different way now for the first time. There was this new problem. And into the void broadcasting, you could argue, developed.

I would like to go on to develop the implications of this sort of perspective for regulation. But let us consider some of the points sometimes made against the continuation of regulation. It is sometimes said, for example, that regulation is a matter of spectrum shortage and that as spectrum shortage erodes, it ceases to be practicable to regulate, or that there ceases to be a point. Just to flesh that out a bit: if you have only two channels, what you have to do is so organise them that they meet all the needs of all the members of society; so you need an organ of central management to achieve that. I think the spectrum management argument was always used as a justification for regulation for other purposes. I think that is beginning to become more apparent as multiplicity develops and new causes and purposes in regulation are still being devised and applied. The economic case in terms of this spectrum shortage argument was always a weak one. So I would put that on one side.

It is sometimes said that the United States comparison is one we ought to look at. There we have essentially an unregulated market. It has flourished; it is producing diversity and so on. However, the US comparison is flawed because of the First Amendment to the Constitution which established the independence of the press and the judgements of the Supreme Court extended it to television. Attempts are continually made in America to regulate television, whether for political partiality, serving local interests, violence, children. But they have always foundered on the First Amendment. I am not so sure that they would have foundered without the First Amendment. If you look at the historical pattern, the pendulum has swung backwards and forwards over time in the United States and there has been a continuing political desire to push the pendulum out and then it swings back again. The US networks have codes of their own. They are being applied all the time. Advertisers and moral fervour in American audiences, which is a sort of phenomenon with which we are not so acquainted here, also impose disciplines of various kinds. So it seems to me that the United States is a *sui generis* situation.

Another point that is frequently made, and one that has been made a number of times today, is that you cannot regulate in cirumstances of narrowcasting, or you cannot regulate in the cirumstances of specialised channels. And, anyway, how do you regulate when you have got so much to regulate? Well, you cannot regulate in the way you have regulated in the past. That is certainly true. There are lots of difficulties that have arisen in the European context of regulation out of adopting the model of a generalist channel and attempting to regulate specialist channels by the same method. But there are methods of doing it. It is possible to apply a more selective form of regulation or to address the particular issue raised by that specialist channel, and attempt to tailor regulation to it. How do you do it? Well, a whistle blower is the term that is sometimes used in this general way. The audience tells you if things are going wrong. To back that up you can dipstick monitor, as it is called. You do not look in a blanket fashion, but you do the thing selectively.

So the fact that the broadcasting scene is changing in the way that it obviously is does not mean that regulation is outmoded, or has no practical capability of application.

Now let us just look very briefly at what regulation is today, and ask ourselves how much of it we might want to see continue anyway. First of all is the concern with the viewer as a consumer. The Broadcasting Act of 1990 created a basic standard of consumer protection to be applied to all licensed services regardless of how they are delivered, by cable, by satellite, by terrestrial means or whatever. There are the phrases that have occurred in Broadcasting Acts successively back to the beginning and which occur again: offence against good taste and decency; incitement to crime or leading to disorder; offence to public feeling; due impartiality in respect of political or industrial controversy or related to current public policy; respect for religious susceptibilities; no editorialising; protection of children and young people and subliminal images. They keep coming back.

A range of regulatory prescriptions, into which I will not go, applies to advertising and sponsorship. In the same way the Commission must do all it can to ensure that these principles are applied. It does this through codes. Now these can and must change to reflect changes in public attitude, but the principle of having a public watchdog doing this sort of thing and applying these principles is the British way of doing it. There are many different ways, as one discovers looking across Europe, in the way this can be done but the concept of a consumer, the concept of a common minimum standard, seems to me basically a very sensible one. It is the one that is now finding its way into the European method of regulation of trans-frontier signals; it is gaining an extra purchase there. I think in a sense if it had not existed, it would have had to be invented. I cannot see the political pressures which we have seen swirling about in the past two or three years being coped with in any other way.

The consumer protection angle on regulation deserves to be distinguished from what, in the trade, is called positive programme regulation, referring to strands of programmes of particular quality which must be part of a service. These apply to Channel 3 and Channel 4 and would apply to Channel 5 . If you imagine it like a tabletop on which stand bottles of different sizes, the tabletop is the common standard of consumer protection regulation and then, on top of that, you have positive requirements which apply differently to different channels depending on the cirumstances of those channels. And the circumstances really are the issues of revenue and the degree of economic monopoly. The principle can be summarised best as regulation following revenue. The so-called Channel 3 auction took out benefit for the public interest in kind, that is to say requirements for types of programmes at a standard which might not otherwise have appeared, as well as in cash. It was a mixture of cash and kind. As long as there is an element of monopoly profit being earned then there is something to tax in this way and something for regulation to bite upon as it has in the past.

Economic regulation is also important. Some go so far as to say it will supercede regulation entirely. I think that it is worth bearing in mind that we already have requirements as to fair and effective competition in the regulation as it is applied now. Obviously the issue of access to a superhighway is an immensely important one, not just as an anti-monopoly measure but also to ensure pluralism. But it is not, I think, enough in itself. We still need the disciplines of internal pluralism. There also remains a concern about agenda-setting. Even if you have services that are internally plural, you have to worry about whether they are all internally plural in the same way or whether there is a diversity and whether agenda-setting is occurring in some general way despite the fact that you have got a great plethora of regulation designed to prevent concentration and designed to prevent concentration of the sources of information which somehow just misses the point.

I think that the superhighway is coming along quickly. Will regulation continue? Yes. Consumer protection regulation seems to me an inevitability, a sort of *sine qua non*, of the development of all this. Among the main traffic on the superhighway will be television programmes. I mean to put it no higher. They may not be the driver, they may not be the main feature, but they will certainly be there. And the appeal of the superhighway is that it is a better form of this clerisy idea which I mentioned at the beginning. It is not an entirely different way of looking at the world. It is about better inter-communication and I do not, therefore, see that inherent in the development is the demise of regulation. Even positive requirements may have a longer life than people think. Ted suggested that there would be just two people engaged in regulating even ten years out. Well, I am not so sure. I think it depends on the extent to which generalist channels survive with a very substantial command of a core audience. There are reasons to think that this may not be a disappearing situation in the way that people think. For one thing the generalist channels command substantial resources. They can fight back. They have got the means to take action to develop their unique selling proposition against specialist channels. Quality is good for them. It is attractive to advertisers. They have got the means, at the present time, to deliver that quality if they deploy it correctly and, by that means, to sustain their audiences against channels which have very little resource to devote per hour to programming.

There is a distinction developing in the UK between free TV and subscription television. This has been present in the United States for a long time. It has been the subject of political campaigns in the television area but, with the onset of satellite services paid for by subscription, the concept of free TV is coming into focus. It seems to me that free TV will tend to be generalist TV and there will be a tendency for campaigning to focus on this point and, therefore, for there to be some will for the generalist channel to survive. And even in the US experience, where niche channels have been around for a long time and are undoubtedly eroding core audiences, it is happening at a slower pace than some people thought it would. The networks still have a substantial amount of the audience and there is still value placed on the generalist channel. The general point here is that there may be, somewhere down the track, a new equilibrium to be found between niche and generalist channels. We are still in the transition phase where niche channels appear very attractive, and they are developing very fast. They are finding their own vocation. They are developing it. But is there some point at which the diet in the audience for a mixture of the two will actually stop the erosion and cause a levelling out?

I know that people in Whitehall have studied with great fascination the speech that Al Gore delivered in January [1994] in Los Angeles about the superhighway. The speech does have a passage right at the back on regulation. It is often overlooked. He prefers adaptive regulation, in other words the concept that one does not want regulation to stop change, one wants regulation to keep up with change in the public interest not to interrupt change or development but to keep in the public interest what is desired and required. Adaptive regulation perhaps ought to be the keyword to the way one thinks about these things at the moment.

Russell Twisk: Now we come to Jane Vizard, who was called to the Bar in 1977, joined the Independent Television Companies Association in 1979 and became the ITCA's legal adviser in 1980. While at the ITCA she represented ITV on the legal committee of the European Broadcasting Union. She left in 1988 to join Yorkshire Television Enterprises for a spell and then in 1989 she became assistant legal adviser of the BBC. The following year she became head of statutory and commercial legal affairs where she advises on constitutional, corporate and contractual matters for the Corporation. She has written a number of articles on European broadcasting law.

Jane Vizard: It is tempting to open *Broadcast* nowadays and read an ever-increasing number of articles about alliances, mergers, takeovers, multimedia explosions and conclude that the emergence of the new technologies defies regulation.

Even if it doesn't, what's the point? Surely viewers or listeners will be offered such a dazzling array of services that they can be their own schedulers and the arbiters of what they see and when? Surely regulation is a thing of the past. Instead of receiving a variety of programming from a few, highly regulated sources, the consumer will receive a hugely varied diet of programming of all kinds, from an infinite number of suppliers whose only obligations will be to adhere to the most minimal of regulations. The old justification for regulation was predicated on the assumption that in an environment of spectrum scarcity, the entrance fee for access to that spectrum, where there were few purveyors of broadcast services, was to comply with the Reithian trinity of informing, educating and entertaining. Now, with an estimated 180 channels in Europe by the mid-1990s and 3,500 by the beginning of the next century, that trinity will be delivered in a more diffuse way — choice follows as an axiom of availability. 'The market will provide'. But will it? And does it matter if it doesn't? I doubt that it will and I rather think that it does matter.

The difficulty of finding a mechanism to offer real choice is that it doesn't happen by chance, and the conundrum is how to match up the right to freedom of expression (a.k.a. market entry) with a pluralistic broadcasting structure which guarantees the delivery to the consumer of a real choice. The underlying question which legislators will have to address is: is there a role for public service broadcasting in the Nintendo age?

It is interesting to note that in the 'Austrian radio' case (24 November 1993), the European Court of Human Rights (ECHR) held that pluralism is a constitutional objective of fundamental importance within the mass media. Article 10 of the European Charter of Human Rights imposes on states a positive obligation to further pluralism. The ECHR held that freedom of expression can be realised only if grounded in the principle of pluralism, of which the state is the ultimate guarantor.

There is no sign that member states are considering abandoning the dual public service and commercial broadcasting system which has existed for years. The German constitutional court (22 February 1994) held that consistent with constitutional principles, the very existence of commercial broadcasting is only acceptable in the presence of a strong public service broadcasting system, and that funding must always be sufficient for public service broadcasting to thrive and implement independently reached editorial decisions.

The end of spectrum scarcity will have several consequences:

1. The massive expansion in broadcast channels will intensify competition for audiences and revenue:
   — fragmentation of broadcasting supply: more and more channels, a trend that will be reinforced by the introduction of digital compression;
   — fragmentation of broadcasting consumption: people increasingly choosing from a widening menu of services;
   — segmentation of the broadcasting market: more channels targeted at specialist audiences, often accessible only to those who can afford them.
2. Growth in direct spending on broadcasting, enabling rapid take up of new services:
   — redistribution of audience share: new services growing at the expense of older-established services;
   — shift in the relative importance of revenue sources, from advertising to subscription.

This brings with it an inherent tension between commercial pressure to maximise audiences and the needs of pluralism. Diversity of ownership is not the same thing as diversity of voices. More likely, there will be a convergence in programming content as a greater number of channels compete for the attention of the most lucrative sections of the audience.

The danger is that if you are not attractive to advertisers and can't afford to pay for tiered packages, your choice may well diminish. The much-vaunted choice offered by satellite and cable is prone to limit the choice to those who can afford to pay. It is interesting to note in passing that when the FCC re-regulated the pricing structure applicable to cable in February, certain highly- publicised mergers were called off (the most notable of which was between Southwestern Bell and Cox Communications). Apparently, there was considerable disgruntlement on the part of the cable operators about a stop-go policy by the regulators — which sounded familiar echoes of government policy on cable in the UK in the early 1980s. But it is a salutary lesson about how the regulator (even a reputedly light-touch one like the FCC) is not satisfied that the market can be left to its own devices if the consumer is to be properly protected.

With so many channels available, what will fill them? Broadcasting throughout Europe will have moved from a position of spectrum scarcity to product scarcity. There is a need to preserve a strong audiovisual production sector in the community. That will not be achieved by the commercial sector alone. It is likely that as the number of new channels grows, demand will shift from commissioned production to acquired. Acquired programming from the US is cheap, though it is getting less so, because the costs have already been amortised across the home market. BBC estimates show that terrestrial television in the UK spends an average of £100,000 per hour on programming whereas UK satellite is spending £9,000 per hour. The trade deficit in EU programming is growing: in 1992, the EU spent $3.7 billion on US films and TV programming — thirteen times more than the US spent on acquisitions from the EU. In the commercial sector, the need to generate returns to shareholders limits the proportion of revenue which can be spent on original production — or indeed on other people costs such as training and generation of creative works and talent.

But this comes at a price because as we all know programme production is extremely expensive. All this argues for secure funding to enable public service broadcasting to flourish alongside the commercial broadcast sector.

Public service broadcasting (PSB) has to be preserved as part of the structure of choice. PSB is a public good and a lively, adequately funded public service broadcaster is a mark of a civilised society. Those trying to regulate should look not only at the issue of corporate control. Internal pluralism (that is to say, the remit of the broadcaster in question) is as important. One can envisage in a system which is regulated to prevent concentration of power in the hands of a few, that system could none the less produce programming which does little for the democratic process. Broadcasting is first and foremost a cultural activity providing freedom of expression across the range of human activity as:

— the source of news and information which informs political debate;
— the guardian of cultural heritage in drama and music and instigator of new work; and

— the mirror of regional and linguistic diversity of society.

Most important of all it is and must remain, universally available.

Is there an argument to say that territorial boundaries are obsolescent, and given the rapid expansion in technology, there should be one set of minimum regulations across the world? This is the superstate writ large: even if such a system could be devised, it would probably be impractical because of broadcasting being seen as predominantly a cultural matter — and something in which national governments would have strong views, varying greatly as to what matrix of services their peoples should receive and the standards that should be applied. One only has to look at the recent debate over content quotas in the GATT negotiationsto be discouraged from thinking that consensus could be reached. The EU sees it as a matter of the European Union against the USA, so it is probably not feasible.

It is tempting to look towards the European Commission as the solution to the problem of how to regulate broadcasting throughout the Community. However, the broadcasting directive, which was incorporated into national law two years ago, raises a fundamental contradiction: it was designed as a mechanism for one-stop regulatory shopping. Broadcasting was seen as a service forming one of the pillars of the internal market and the idea was that once a broadcaster had been licensed in one member state, it should be able to broadcast without hindrance throughout the rest of the community. But this 'one-stop' approach means that the mores of one particular society (the primary market for the channel in question) are then imposed on the people of the secondary markets. The cultural standards of the two may be very different. The example of Red Hot Dutch is a case in point.

The Commission's green paper on pluralism last year canvassed the idea of trans-European regulation of media ownership. But even on that limited scale, agreement is likely to be elusive. The current diversity in regulation reflects a real diversity in needs. The appropriate solution for one member state will not necessarily work for another. It is interesting — but probably no more than that — to see the recent events surrounding Silvio Berlusconi and the use he made of being a multi-media proprietor for political ends. The fact of the matter is that it happened in Italy, but it couldn't happen here. The way in which member states regulate broadcasting as a whole and cross media ownership in particular is largely a matter of political will.

The definition and maintenance of a pluralistic structure in broadcasting is bound up with the particular democratic and cultural traditions of each member state. The principle of subsidiarity suggests that for the time being at least the prime responsibility for protecting pluralism should continue to lie with individual member states. The federalists might like the idea, but the pragmatists would argue that there is no evidence that lack of harmonisation of ownership rules is impeding the internal market. If they do legislate then there are strong arguments in favour of excluding public service broadcasting from such a measure.

As far as existing regulation is concerned, with separate regulators in the form of the ITC and the BBC, while it is not without its critics, it would seem sensible to leave the present system intact because the convergence of the media is in such a state of rapid change that whatever were done now would probably be out of date by the time it came into force.

In conclusion:

1. Regulation is a means to an end and it is the end which matters.
2. While it is interesting to examine the different regulatory structures which might apply at the Nintendo Millennium, the fundamental question is that of what kind of broadcasting we want. Only then can an informed view be taken as to the best way of regulating to ensure delivery of that broadcasting.
3. To deliver real choice to the viewer or listener there has to be public service broadcasting as a guarantor of a generalist channel, not only making, commissioning and delivering the kinds of programming which the commercial sector is unlikely to deliver, but also serving society as a whole — with an impartial news service and a wide range of programming available to all, regardless of their purchasing power.

Discussion

Graham Thompson (Yorkshire Tyne Tees Television): I would like to endorse what Jane has said about not leaving it to the market. I think it would be horrific if the Domesday scenario that we heard about yesterday came about, where you have five or six channels which are so marginalised that they cannot have economic audiences, and not all of them are free anyway. They are cable or satellite that you have to pay for which means the end of the sort of quality programming which, through public service broadcasting by both the commercial sector and the BBC, have become world renowned. It would be disastrous if this Domesday scenario occurred because no-one would be able to afford to make the sort of programmes which people like to watch. And I think it would be a disaster if we got into a de-regulated state where we get hung up about ownership and the rest of it.

Ted Mercer: This Domesday scenario that we hear about so often is that the market cannot get it right, the market would never get it right, broadcasting is something which defeats the market, which is outside of the market, which cannot be governed by normal market rules. I have never heard a convincing argument as to why that should be the case. We are dealing here with a product and a service. We might have made the same argument, I suppose, for radio. We might make a lesser argument for it now than in the 1930s. You might make the same argument for newspapers, and say they are something special so we should not let the market regulate them. In fact we still have the vestiges of control of newspapers left in our system as there are particular rules on mergers of newspapers left. But we worry a lot less about that these days. It is simply that because we have a popular service medium, it does not mean that we have something which in economic terms works a great deal differently. Yes, you have got to be careful. You cannot afford to make mistakes in this area. But the market does not do a bad job if it is left to do it properly. It is sometimes thought that television is some kind of special product that requires a special care, that if you breathe on it too hard the whole edifice will fall away. I think it is a more robust business than that. I think it is a very robust business that has all kinds of new ways to express itself, that has new ways to deliver, new ways to provide services to the public. And I think if you provide quality product and if the regulators provide a means for the delivery of that quality product, then people will still watch it. They may have to pay for it or they may pay for it in a different way but they will still take it. I think you should trust people, or trust the market more, or at least trust the market to find what it wants.

Steve Barnett (Henley Centre and Goldsmiths College): I think what you said just now is not just wrong but dangerously wrong. Why is broadcasting different? There are a number of reasons. The arguments have been rehearsed over the years but I think it comes back to what Jane was saying at the end, which is that we are not just talking about consumerism, we are talking about citizenship. We are talking about something which is about the creation of meaning and actually adds to, enhances, in some ways produces the kind of cultural and social environment in which we live. And in that sense it is different.

There is no such thing, and there never has been any such thing, as a free market. The free market is a nonsense. It is a myth. It is the essence of every competitor in a marketplace to become a monopoly provider; that is the essence of capitalism. And the point about people involved in the media business is that it is their job and their duty to their shareholders to expand and to try and become monopoly providers within the bounds of industrial and commercial law. That is why you get media monoliths and we will continue to get media monoliths. What your point fails to address is the way in which large media corporations are involved in the creation of certain kinds of meaning which have nothing to do with providing choice or with citizenship but have a lot to do with making things that a few people will pay a lot of money for or which a few people who are valuable to advertisers will be prepared to watch in large numbers. The problem is that the kind of things that I am saying now are not part of the current political conventional wisdoms, it is not a popular thing to say when talk about the free market and market forces is the way in which the current political wisdom works.

The ITC's position is one, I believe, that is absolutely vital for the protection of the citizen in democracy as opposed to the consumer. What it needs to do to establish itself, I am quite sure, is to do some research on the way in which the creative process can somehow become undermined when it becomes too commercialised, when it is left entirely to the private sector without any kind of positive forces.

Can I just give one last example about the way in which market forces are inimical to the wider citizenship which is to do with sporting events? We have had a situation for thirty or forty years where the great sporting events have been available to every single person in this country who has a television set. For the cost of the licence fee you could see the FA Cup Final, you can see Wimbledon and so on. Gradually these things are eroding, because their value to a single satellite provider is enormous. And I am quite sure it will not be long before we will be stuck with the highlights on the BBC or, possibly, ITV; it will be pay-per-view or if it is not allowed to be pay-per- view it will certainly be subscription TV for the rest of us who want to see the cricket or the rugby or the tennis.That is the free market.

Ted Mercer: Well, I think we are back to Athens here. We are back to looking at things in terms of Plato's guardians and the rest and people setting themselves up and saying, 'Well, we see something and we must guard it for the others. They don't know what a jewel they have got and we must keep it for them.'

I quite agree with you that market forces are totally imperfect. In this country we desperately need a better anti-trust law system to cope with the international conglomerations which will be produced as superhighways and technology develops. But the market does have a part to play. You cannot ignore that the market has a part to play, that somehow the operation of the market defeats choice. It gives people what they want. What they want may not be good for them. It may be bad for them but that must be their choice. Must we always provide for them?

Steve Barnett: In the cultural world people do not know what they want. People did not know that they wanted *Minder,* which had to have two series before it got off the ground. You cannot go out with a clipboard and ask people about whether they want to see sketches about dead parrots. People do not know what kind of comedy or drama or soap opera or current affairs they want to see. It evolves, and the framework within which it evolves is a framework which we have a structure to provide whether it is regulatory or public service or commercial.

Roger Wilson (Learning Television): Surely the issue is actually about rigged markets, not free markets, because we are actually operating at the moment in a rigged market. And it is how we free it up that is going to be the way we resolve these issues of pluralism and access. Just to give an example, Granville Williams, in the session before coffee, mentioned the London News service which is going to be run by Associated Newspapers. Well, that contract was granted by the cable companies in London and it was granted quite openly as far as they are concerned on the basis that the overlap of audience with the *Evening Standard*'s readership is likely to attract people to their telephony products. It had nothing to do, in that context, with being a television service. And what we are seeing in the context of cable, and indeed with British Telecom as well with its video-on-demand, is that if you want to be a programme provider or a channel provider in that environment, you have no *right* of access. These people are absolute gateways. This tallies with Steve's final point, because the nature of these organisations, these large corporations, is always to play safe. It is to play down the known line. They are not going to be ready to experiment and they are certainly not going to be ready to experiment in local markets as has been well evidenced by the failure of the cable industry generally to grasp what I regard as a very strong local television opportunity.

Granville Williams (Campaign for Press and Broadcasting Freedom): At a session last year Charles Tremayne from *World in Action* spoke. *World in Action* is one of the relics (that sounds a bit harsh) of a system that used to exist where we had two prime time current affairs programmes. Now my question really is to the ITC. It is about what happens when a programme like *World in Action* is relegated with an uncertain future. Last time we had a furore about *News At Ten* and something was done to keep it in its spot; whether that is a permanent thing I do not know. It is really a question of clarifying what does the ITC do about the franchise commitments that were made by Granada when now we are seeing the erosion of a system which actually was about programmes. You competed for programmes, not ratings, which is what we have got now with the demise of *World in Action.*

That is a question. Secondly, just a comment. I really do wish these comparisons with newspapers and the way that they have done well for the market were knocked on the head. In the area where I live the last two independent newspapers, *The Halifax Courier and The Huddersfield Examiner,* have just been taken over by two big groups. The elimination of choice in terms of the incorporation of local and regional newspapers into the four or five big companies, cross-media companies like Pearson, goes on apace; it does not provide local news, current affairs reporting — less and less. The criteria that drive it are market criteria rather than consumer and news views from the locality. It is a wrong analogy.

Liz Ashton Hill (College of St Mark and St John, Plymouth): I would like to take the discussion further back to basics and look at the importance of the technological infrastructure and how important it is to have a pluralistic system. My question to Jane is: should the BBC fight to maintain its transmission system or should it become privatised and would the BBC give it up? What importance does it attach to having that system? And my question either to Michael or Ted is to do with the conditional access system that Sky has developed. There has been no mention of whether we ought to regulate (perhaps I did not hear it) to have a pluralist system or whether we can continue to have a monopolist system and what implications that has.

Jane Vizard: Dealing with Liz's question first, with a typical lawyer's caveat, I am a lawyer not a policymaker but I think that the common sense view about transmission probably is that when it is part of the BBC it is a means by which we can undertake research and development. One of the most important things that is going to emerge over the next few years is who is going to have (a) the inclination and (b) the resources to invest in R&D? If transmission were not part of the BBC, it would not (I am not saying it is impossible) but it would not be the same kind of ethos. And the second thing is that to be honest, I cannot really see the point of BBC transmission being hived off because it simply means that one buys back the same services one needs to be able to broadcast and, inevitably, there will be a profit margin that will be built in, and it will end up being more expensive and therefore the licence fee will go less far.

In terms of the delicate orchid, I think that broadcasting is more important than that. I do not think that one can take the risk that is implicit in Ted's answer. It is very easy to dismantle things; it is not nearly as easy to build them up again. I like the adjective that Michael used about adaptive regulation. I think that one simply has to try and match the change in regulation with the timing of the change in technology so that one does not simply throw up one's hands and say, 'Oh, it is all going to change. There is no more need for any kind of regulation or it is just going to be impossible,' and abandon the things that are important about broadcasting.

I also believe that if you leave it to the market then in a sense you hand over responsibility for broadcasting. I think that it has to have more care taken of it. It is a means by which people form a community and I do not think that it should be dismantled in anticipation of the great upsurge. But I certainly think that as part of any kind of broadcasting structure there ought to be a part which is independent both of the market and of the state. I do think it is rather a delicate thing and I think that it is something that is abandoned at the peril of society. It sounds frightfully pompous but I do believe that quite strongly.

Michael Redley: On the *World in Action* point: the applicants for licences had to propose programming that they were going to do in a number of specific areas which reflected the statutory position. Parliament decided that news and current affairs were both to have a degree of special protection cast around them and they are mentioned in the statute, so they have to be provided. The proposals were made and obviously the licensee is committed to providing a certain amount of programming in those categories.

Now the issue of scheduling is a very difficult area. As it happens Parliament provided the protection in the Act for news that there had to be at least one news programme in peak time. Much of the debate that there might have been around the *News at Ten* issue I think was short-circuited by that fact. It is a fact that it has to be in peak time so it then falls, the issue then turns into a definition of what peak is. So let us distinguish that then from the situation which the ITC, or the IBA as it then was, tried to get established that scheduling generally should be an issue in which it could take an interest. The government of the time did not accept that argument. So there are various elements (one of them is Gaelic television) which have to be in peak time but other than that there is very little reference to scheduling or very little reference that you can derive from the Act to scheduling. But there are commitments made by the licensees, particularly in a regional area where they can directly discharge them themselves, where it is clear that they are committed.

To go on to the conditional access point, I suppose I am with Ted on this general area of the place of the market. There is obviously a problem about attracting people to put up very large sums of money for huge capital projects if they know they are going to be regulated and about regulating them subsequently when they did not know they were going to be regulated to start with. And one has to say that these vast projects are actually very much part of this hyperspace highway thing at the moment. Where is it coming from? Well, it is coming from the investment of capital and the Sky system has pioneered a very significant innovation in this country in the marginal programming supplied by the Sky services. Of course, at a certain point, one must regulate conditional access systems because they are absolutely vitally part of the drift of this superhighway concept. You are letting people on using a particular technology which is a proprietary product and the use of that proprietary product, the way in which people can exploit it, is fundamental to the total effect you achieve. I do think, though, that competition law is quite an effective way of doing this. Ted talks about the need to strengthen it. I think that is right. I think one will see developments and changes in this area as time goes on because it is a problem that is bound to come back in various shapes and forms. But if the owner of these proprietary products, perhaps under the implied threat of the application of competition law, makes them available in a fair way to those who would wish to use them, have we not, in a way, achieved the best of both worlds? Have we not got that thing which we might not have had otherwise? And also have we not got it used in a way which is to the benefit of society and the development of broadcasting generally?

Ted Mercer: On transmission systems, I do not think it is necessary for the BBC to have its own tranmission sytem because terrestrial transmission systems may well be *passé* anyway. What is more important for the consumer is what the Director General of Telecommunications has been asking for recently which is to have two or three competitive local loops, two or three competitive hard wires up to the home, one from BT, one from a cable operator, one from somebody else, coming into the home to provide a plurality of superhighways. I think that, in the long run, will do the consumers more good .

On conditional access I am a bit more worried about the present position of conditional access than I think Michael is. I am concerned that a well known operator has sewn up a particular European stand in the market and stands at the gateway of introduction of new channels. That worries me. And I hope very much that the EC will look very carefully at one or two agreements that have had to have been passed by them recently. I also would say, again, that we need a better, more developed competition law generally in this country which would help in the broadcasting sphere. And as far as *World in Action* scheduling is concerned I took a very careful note of what Mr Redley said for future court actions involving my clients.

As far as choice is concerned, I may be particularly thick about this, but choice of what? Choice of very good programmes? Yes, we know that we have had the least worst public service broadcasting in the world for very many years. We have a tremendous choice of programmes on four channels. Will we not get that choice elsewhere? I fail to think that all goodness and all originality and all innovation disappears because you change from an existing four-channel terrestrial system of which you have had the basis since 1956. Is it so fragile a flower that it disappears because you tamper with that? I do not think it is. I really do not. I think we seize on individual programmes and things like *News at Ten*, which I personally find most inconvenient and would far prefer to have *News at Eight*. And yet we have utter furore about that. Nobody asked the consumer whether they find ten more convenient in the first place. I would prefer to find out first from the consumer whether ten is more convenient or whether they would like another time. And that, I suppose, is my view of broadcasting.

Russell Twisk: I suppose many of us have lain in hotel bedrooms in New York flicking through 96 channels and not finding a single thing to engage our interest about nine-thirty at night. It is one of the reasons that you get on Saturday morning fifteen cartoons against each other without not hearing how the hostages are getting on in Washington. That is the sort of problem that you can get with so many channels — many, many channels with nothing that you want to watch.

Birgit Thiel-Weidinger (*Suddeutsche Zeitung*): Don't you think that the fear of all these many channels is in a way a little exaggerated? Because how many channels can people watch? We have in Germany the two public channels which are also partially commercially funded, we have RTL, we have Sat 1, we have Pro7, and whatever. These are about six, and people then have their regional programmes, so they have up to 24 programmes if they are in a kind of situation where they can get all these programmes. So they even now ask when shall we watch all that. They even have Arte which is the minority programme *par excellence* because it is the best you can get for minorities. So who is going to watch all these programmes, and when? And who is going to make good programmes? In a way the market, I think, regulates itself by not giving in to all the fears the public television chains have because they think the private ones will devour the viewers they have. If they continue making good quality programming, sell it in a kind of modern way, why should they not exist and then why should the future be as bleak as it seems to be on this highway?

Michael Redley: Well, I think that is what I was saying in a way. There is an inherited situation; we do not start with a clean sheet of paper. It would be interesting to ask what we would do if we did. But we do not and we start in Germany with up to four channels in most parts of the country now supplied on cable along with many others. But we start with this inherited position where a great deal of the resources are concentrated in an area where they are likely to continue to be concentrated because providing the essential services and allowing the quality that money can provide to continue to be provided will ensure the continuation of the audiences. What has happened, and it is a very interesting and valuable development surely, is the creation at the margin of an opportunity to view in a different way with specialist services. That surely is the key to it. These are much cheaper services to provide so it is possible to imagine them being provided. Who is going to watch? The answer is very, very few people but that does not matter. They are very satisfied customers because they are seeing things that they want to watch, presented in way that they want to have it presented i.e. in a continuous stream of sport or whatever it is. And that seems to me to be an enhancement, to use a word that has cropped up a couple of times. It is a net enhancement. It seems to me there is an inherent stability in this situation. It is not one which necessarily will run away with us but, at the same time, it has got some very positive and beneficial sides to it.

George Cole (*The Times Educational Supplement*): How will this new age of broadcasting affect schools television and education? Is there still a place for it?

Michael Redley: Schools broadcasting is another of these protected categories under the Broadcasting Act. On commercial television Channel 4 is now doing the schools broadcasting that was being done previously by ITV. It seems to be working really rather well, I think, or so the first year's impression of it goes. A tremendous transition has been made within the commercial sector in the conduct of schools broadcasting without the appearance of change, which in terms of providing services to schools is a very good thing. There is quite a lot of resource going into it. There is a lot of support material provided out of the system and I have not got the number of hours of broadcasting at the tips of my fingers but it is really quite a substantial amount and it is winning prizes which is always a good thing. That sounds a bit complacent, doesn't it?

Russell Twisk: I am going to ask the panel to give a minute or two to a summation of their feelings and perhaps what they have learned during this hour.

Ted Mercer: Firstly just a couple of seconds about the answer to the last question. In the interactive superhighway era there is going to be a tremendous place for education. We spent during the 1980s something between £5 and £7 million out of the DTI developing interactive video disks for schools. Now why the DTI did it I have no idea, but they did. What is the trouble with those sytems? The readers are so expenisve you need to network them but you cannot network them until you have a broadband system, *i.e.* fibre getting pretty close to the kerb or pretty close to the school so that schools can share resources. Well, we will get fibre close to the home, close to the school. There are tremendous numbers of interactive services waiting there to be adopted by schools, interactive learning, testing, a lot of things that cannot be used at the moment because we do not have a broadband network to take them round all the schools in the country.

I suppose I feel a bit like the outcast really because I believe in the market. I do not *really* believe in the market, but it is a nice concept. It seems to me that it is a lot easier to believe in than to take the view that broadcasters always know what is good for everybody else and what should be broadcast. And that is a fundamental concept I have always, as a viewer and a regulator, had a little bit of difficulty with. I think we are going to see substantial changes, but the only thing that will stay the same is content control because of the innate conservatism in consumer standards in this country relating to what goes in to our programming. I think we are going to have a lot more difficulty than has come out this morning with cross-European and cross-frontier broadcasting. I think we are going to have a plethora of channels and I think that technology is going to take a lot longer to catch on than some people imagine. I think we are looking at an existing Channel 3 remit through the next Broadcasting Act which will be about the year 2000. I think Michael Grade [chief executive of Channel Four] has got a job probably until retirement, if he plays his cards right and doesn't cheat David Glencross [chief executive of the Independent Television Commission] too much. I think that British broadcasting will retain very many more of its elements, and is more robust than some of you think. And its elements of quality and good programme-making will follow it through to an era where there will be no scheduling and packaging of channels as we know it now, where most of the services will be self-scheduled through a video on demand service. And that will place a greater relationship between the individual and the programme makers, through branding, than there is now. And I have every confidence that the quality of British programming will continue through.

Michael Redley: I occasionally go to schools and give a presentation on regulation to schoolchildren. It is very clear that the basic naïve questions of why do you regulate?, what right have you to come between me and my telly?, it is good stuff and I have got lots of innate appetites which television can satisfy, why on earth do you stop me from enjoying it? are very good questions. Without wanting to appear too sychophantic to Ted, I find myself in a way much more on his side. I think the point I would make in response to him, just to reiterate it, is that it may be terribly unfortunate that television is a regulated sector but it is because society wants it so and I think, having got to that point, you are already then saying to yourself, 'How shall we do it?' because it is better to do it in a sensible way than in an unsensible way.

Behind a lot of the discussion, I think, is the implied analogy with print and to me, as a regulator, a terribly interesting moment arose during the passage of the Broadcasting Act where Parliament had to decide whether Teletext was television or print. They started out by assuming it was print and, therefore, you did not regulate it, therefore in the great tradition of the British press, press freedom was an absolute right and, since it was print, it had to be free. But, blow me, in the course of the debate they came round to concluding that because it came out of a television set it should be regulated so that we now have a public teletext service today. It was a very interesting discussion and I did not know at the start which way it was going to go. It does seem to me there is a significance in that sort of perception which I feel has deep roots and a continuing existence.

Jane Vizard: Picking up the point about schools, I would it to be thought that the BBC was going to disappear from schools. For as long as the BBC is in existence it will be trying better to serve the needs of its audiences and I think sees schools and pupils increasingly as audiences in exactly the same way and rather than making programmes for programme makers, it is making programmes for the pupils and the teachers as a useful additional resource.

In terms of the future, I think that the key is coexistence, trying to find a coexistence between broadcasters or information providers who have two different agendas.

Session produced by Genevieve Clarke and Colin Shaw

Home shopping: when the going gets tough, the tough stay home?

Chair: **Rod Allen**
HarperCollins Interactive

Peter van Gelder
Teletext Limited

Garrett O'Leary
Home shopping consultant

Peter Wenban
Quantum International

ROD Allen: My name is Rod Allen. I am currently Media Adviser to HarperCollins Publishing, which is News Corporation's book publishing company. Remember all that stuff you heard yesterday about Rupert Murdoch taking over the world? Well, I am helping him do it.

We are going to talk now about the marketing dimension of the multi-channel revolution, — home shopping by television. Home shopping by television is not actually new in this country. John Gray and I at least, and perhaps some others of you, remember programmes like *Jim's Inn*, which tried to sell goods and services off the screen in the 50s and 60s. The then ITA put an end to admags, as they were called, in the 1960s; I cannot quite remember what their reasoning was. They probably thought such things were distressingly popular.

The end of spectrum scarcity has made it easier for new uses for television channels to be discovered and tried out. And it is not surprising that as soon as capacity on the European satellites like Astra started to become available, the extraordinarily successful American concept of dedicated home shopping channels started to appear on European screens, both in the segmented kind of services that Quantum International offer and on the twenty-four hour a day QVC in which the company that owns the company that I work for has an interest.

What seems to be happening, as times change and telecommunications and broadcasting technologies continue to converge, is that it has become easier to conceive of the television screen in the home as a direct marketing channel. And it is this particular changing use of the television screen that we want to explore this afternoon. We want to look at it in terms of its impact on the television ecology, what impact it is having on other services, pre-existing and new, its impact (if it has an impact) on the social environment, what happens when you start buying things at home instead of on the High Street, and its effect on the marketing environment — how does it change the business of selling things to people?

76

Today we have with us three practitioners, not people who have just thought about it, people actually doing it, involved in home shopping. Garrett O'Leary was educated in the United States and the United Kingdom at the University of Sussex. Garrett has worked in television and radio and is the author of a book about decision-making in British broadcasting called *Questions of Broadcasting*. He is presently working in advertising as the acting chief executive of CSC Electronic Marketing, which is part of the Chris Still Communications Group. Garrett is working with advertisers and advertising agencies on direct selling in television and interactive media.

Peter Wenban is Corporate Affairs Manager of Quantum International. Quantum is Europe's leading home shopping infomercial broadcaster — it is not the first time you have heard that word in this hall and it certainly will not be the last. Peter is responsible for Quantum's public and industry positioning and he represents the company's interests on British and Continental European industry committees. He deals with aspects of EU commercial communications in the electronic media and direct marketing industries. His previous experience as an international marketing consultant includes advertising, duty-free marketing and interactive shopping.

Peter van Gelder, although born a Canadian, came to this country and took his degree at Aston University at Birmingham in science. He has been a political correspondent for BBC Radio Leeds. He has worked on *Newsnight* for BBC2; he was a reporter, then a producer, then Managing Editor at TV-am. Now he has got a proper job as managing director of Teletext. Teletext, he does not know I am going to say, is one of the great success stories of the decade so far because of the enormous growth in a very short time that it has enjoyed in attracting advertising revenue to its direct off-the-screen selling service.

Garrett O'Leary: I am going to show you some clips from a cross section of TV home shopping. And as I hope you will come to realise, there are more than just one or two categories of TV home shopping.

Some are presently in use like the themed houred programming you see on QVC, which represents a $2.5 billion industry in the United States and it is less than nine years old.

Others are still emerging due to the convergence of telecommunications and compression technology. There are five clips I am about to show you. They will help you to see the diversity of the programming that presently exists or is emerging that we can use to shop from home by the television.

Clip one is a trailer from a well-known actress called Victoria Secret and her health and beauty programme that features on QVC in the United States. Clip two is also from QVC in the States. It is the summary about the Nordic Track exercise equipment. Please listen for the number of Nordic Tracks sold during this hour-long programme. Clip three is a segment from a Philips USA CD-I infomercial. Clip four is from Procter and Gamble Records in the UK. Yes, Procter and Gamble is now in the record industry and I will explain that later; it represents a move away from traditional brand building with a potential for a direct response mechanism. Clip five is from IC TV in the United States and represents a good snapshot of interactive retailing and is a potentially strong challenger to Time Warner's full service network.

Video clips are shown

We have just seen a themed hour programme on QVC. We have just seen the Philips CD-I infomercial and infomercials are quite long so I could only take a snippet of it. The music videomercial (it is a term that I sort of put together) is something that Procter and Gamble is looking at. Teletext, Peter will tell you lots about it. Massive success story, yes it is and it is also a form of shopping. On line and CD-ROM shopping, yes, those two. Video on demand, that is something we have all heard about recently, isn't it? We have heard from BT that is going to represent a third of their profits in the future. Well, we will see. But what really is video on demand? It is solicited advertising. You, the consumer, are soliciting either a movie or a piece of information. And then a full service TV home shopping network. I have just showed you an example of that. I do not know whether you found it interesting. When I saw it I found it pretty interesting. We will see.

In 1993 the television advertising spend in the UK was £2.19 billion. The bottom line is that above-the-line pays for commercial television programming. It does not obviously pay for the BBC, the BBC has a licence fee, but it does pay for Channel 4 and ITV. That money, that $2.19bn, paid for all those programmes you see. Now some of them are obviously original and some of them bought in but still it gives the TV company the ability to go and physically buy or make those programmes.

Advertising is changing. Now the bottom line here is a distinction which is above- and below-the-line. Can I just have a quick show of hands? How many people work in advertising or in marketing? Anybody who works in marketing or advertising raise your hands. Not that many. OK. There is a distinction which is that above-the-line spend is primarily TV but also includes cinema, outdoor and press, and below-the-line is, as it were, mail, also print. But the key distinction between the two is that one has a direct response mechanism, so let us look at this.

Traditional advertising is above-the-line, as we know. Above-the-line, historically, does not have a response mechanism. The result here is that more and more money is being spent through the line and below the line rather than predominantly above the line.

Now, what do I mean by that? Does that not just sound like, 'Oh, God, he is just talking jargon. That is horrible, that is really boring.' Well, if you think about it, it makes sense because audiences are changing. There are more channels; we have success in Sky.

Take the example of Heinz. They are saying: We don't know where to go and spend above-the-line any more. What we want is to freeze our twelve million pounds that we spend on TV advertising above the line. Freeze it. We are not going to stop it, we are just not going to increase it. But out of the rabbit's hat they pull £10 million. £10 million, to me at least, is a lot of money. They said, 'We have got £10 million here and we have asked BMP and BSB Dorling to come up with a below-the-line campaign. Why? Because we are cutting all of our brands. We are just going to have one brand. It is going to be called Heinz. There is not going to be Heinz soup or Heinz baby food or anything like that. It is one brand. There is no distinction, no building of our brands.' Unilever has done the same thing. They have cut 20 per cent of their brands. The number one FMCG [fast moving consumer goods—*Eds*] producer has decided 'Hey, brands are becoming irrelevant. We need to cut the ones that are not making us money.' So they cut 20 per cent. Heinz has taken a very radical approach.

So if we look at this combination of what the effect is, it is basically through the line. What is the result to us as viewers and you as programme producers? Well, it is very simple.

This is home shopping. What is it going to do to us? Slightly radical. Home shopping's effect on programming: less money going from the advertiser to TV companies. Again, what is the result? Less money going to TV producers. Themed TV home shopping programmes in the US have revenues of $2.5 billion in nine years. Not bad. Paul Kagan, a very well known analyst in the United States, estimates that by the end of the decade, just before the year 2000, that industry will be an $8.25 billion industry. Substantial growth.

Now the question I have for you — I do not know the answer — is, how big will the UK market be? I know that I applaud the ITC and their position and what they have done to allow QVC into the market-place, how they have looked at the EC directive [on the regulation of television advertising—*Eds*]. That is a real problem for all advertisers, because it is really how you view programming. I do not want to get into that, I am just saying that there are some big issues and I am taking a position saying there is going to be less money from advertisers going to TV companies, and it is going to have a knock-on effect. Thank you very much for your time.

Peter van Gelder: You have all been talking expertly about the future at a time when I find myself trying to get my head round Quarter 3 1994. I am here to tell you about a feature of the future which is already here and flourishing — broadcast home shopping as it actually works in this country as a mass market — on Teletext. Common themes and buzz words emerge on discussions about the future: information and entertainment on demand delivered digitally in an interactive multimedia format. The question to be asked is how big the market will be.

Anyone involved in teletext is likely to view this vision in the way eloquently summed up by one American commentator 'it is just like *déjà vu* all over again'. Teletext is entertainment and information on demand. It is interactive, delivered digitally, and it is also multimedia with the telephone used to obtain extra information and to purchase advertised goods and services. It is the information and entertainment on demand of the present and the future and it is available to a mass market. Almost everyone has a telephone; half the homes in the country have teletext. The market is huge, both for the editorial product and for the goods being sold.

Now a bit of history. Teletext as a technology is almost 20 years old. The first service was delivered by Ceefax on the BBC and Oracle on ITV in 1976. It grew quietly, subsidised by the enthusiasm of boffins, and so the growth in audience and thus commercial viability took some time to build. Oracle started taking ads in the 1980s and by 1990 had grown into a business owned jointly by the ITV broadcasters with a turnover of about £10m. Then in 1990 with the introduction of the Broadcasting Act along came Teletext Ltd backed by Associated Newspapers, Philips (who invented Teletext) and Media Ventures International. The teletext licence was advertised in much the same way as other ITV franchises and the Teletext consortium bid £8.2m per annum to win the right to run the service. This means that Teletext pays the Treasury in one day what STV or Central will pay during their entire 10-year licence period.

Was it worth it? Yes it was. In bidding for the licence we bid for access to a mass market which has been built up for us in a medium with unique properties. It is broadcast, it is non-linear and non-ephemeral. Teletext is available in 50% of UK homes and is a standard feature of most new TVs. 150,000 teletext TVs are sold or rented in the UK each month.

Touch the text button on your TV and up comes the front page of a service used by 16m viewers every week, 8.4m every day. Only the *Sun* newspaper has a larger readership. Viewers typically watch 2–3 times a day for a total average of 17 minutes. So there's a tip for those wishing to become involved in home shopping — buy into a medium with lots of viewers. Our viewers get 3,200 pages of information specifically for their region updated up to 50,000 times a day. It is like having a rack of magazines. I took a look at the 500-channel future of cable channels, as envisaged in 'Spoilt for Choice'. I found that Teletext carried information contained in 25 of those channels, and that was only scanning from A to D. 800,000 adults a day play our games on Channel 4. About 3m adults a day get their news, weather and sport from Teletext, and 5m a day check the TV listings. And they watch the ads which finance the service. All the ads are direct response home shopping, and Teletext works. Our advertisers judge the effectiveness of our service on cost per conversion, a far stiffer test than that applied to display ads on TV and other media where the adage goes 'I know that half my advertising spend is working but I don't know which half'. Usage by advertisers on Teletext is up by 50% in the past year.

What can you advertise on Teletext? Anything, but it is best suited to products which do not require illustration. Our biggest market is holidays. We estimate that Teletext sells 50% of all non-brochure holidays and 15% of all holidays booked by people in the United Kingdom.

Teletext is different from TV home shopping. Television is linear, ephemeral and subject to the restrictions of continuity. Teletext is random access, non-ephemeral and can be instantly updated. This is a USP which works as well for ads as it does for news, sport and other information. This easy access to the lowest prices means that Teletext is known as the place to get the latest cheapest fare, but our mass market generates other business not so reliant on this property. We attract display advertising from companies such as Peugeot, Buitoni, Coke, Lucozade, banks and building societies and, with great success, Nintendo.

So what of the future? For Teletext the future looks very bright. Terrestrial ITV and the text service on it will continue to thrive because both types of broadcaster have the critical mass to invest in quality domestic product. The digital superhighway in Britain at present is a bit of a B-road yet already cable and satellite have gobbled up all the programming. These channels are likely to stay small scale. Teletext in the future will have higher level graphics and we believe that it is increasingly becoming regarded as a channel on its own. But the digital future of a myriad fractured channels will require a non-linear, non-ephemeral interactive navigation aid. In fact digital is probably the greatest opportunity for Teletext, which will be able to provide a service with all the properties of teletext as well as sound and vision, ideally suited for new advertisers. As for home shopping, I am sure that in the future it will become part of the market, but people will still want non-virtual shopping so that they can socialise and feel the goods.

Peter Wenban: It is true that we promote products on television, but we are not an advertiser, nor are we QVC. Nor are we in the business of direct response television. Let me take each of these markets in turn, and show you why.

I think we all know the elements of traditional advertising, so I will start with direct response television, or DRTV as it is more commonly referred to. DRTV sells a product by stimulating an immediate response from the viewer. In effect, it is a sixty-second hard-sell advertisement. Given the limited amount of time to stimulate a response, products tend to fall into the lower price range, usually below thirty pounds. They are backed by mass market retailing, and have a very high eight to ten times multiple of direct material cost to selling price, in order to cover advertising and produce contribution.

The second category is twenty-four hour home shopping, a phenomenon which was launched in the US, although recently the American market leader QVC, Quality Value and Convenience, has started broadcasting in the UK in a joint venture with BSkyB. QVC's twenty-four hour rolling programme format is divided into themed hours, such as jewellery, or health and fitness hours. During each hour approximately six products are demonstrated live to the viewer by presenters. Throughout the hour viewers see an on-screen record of how many units can be purchased, the sizes available, the recommended retail price and the QVC cost. A catalogue number and telephone order number is also shown. This is also considered a hard sell as viewers are incentivised by beneficial prices. Like DRTV, QVC-style home shopping relies on an immediate response from the viewer.

Quantum chose to develop its European foothold via the infomercial business. Let me talk about the home shopping infomercial for a moment. An infomercial is a twenty-five minute programme which promotes a product by fully demonstrating its capabilities in a tried and tested television format. It could be an outside broadcast or a coffee table programme hosted by a growing number of well-known personalities. Or it could be even a documentary-style programme such as Ford is beginning to develop on terrestrial television here. A twenty-five minute programme allows great freedom to demonstrate the product and its benefits creatively by interaction between a host, a demonstrator and often an audience. Most infomercials are broadcast at the same time every night and generate interest over a period of time. In fact their following is very similar to that of a television series. People surf over the airwaves, find infomercials and stay on. Quantum currently broadcast four branded channels, the Quantum Channel, Sellavision, What's In Store and Amazing Discoveries. Here is a brief extract from our series.

Video extract is shown

Products shown on our infomercials are nearly always unique to us, and always innovative. They are products which cannot be found in shops, and they are owned by us. There is now increasing interest from branded goods manufacturers who are interested in putting together products to offer through our sort of channel.

So you are probably asking yourselves what are the benefits of this form of broadcasting. The benefits are two-fold — to business and to the consumer. Firstly, let us look at the business benefits of the infomercial. We broadcast almost two hundred hours of home shopping infomercials a week to a potential audience of over 30 million homes in Greater Europe alone. Our operational recorded revenues are in the region of $37 million in 1993 and that is with 18 people in the company. Today Quantum's infomercials are a global phenomenon. We broadcast in Australia, New Zealand, Mexico, Brazil, Peru, Singapore and Japan. We are also in discussion with broadcasters in India, Indonesia, Abu Dhabi and Saudi Arabia. Broadcasters in these countries are realising that more channels and different advertising formats such as programme sponsorship are fighting for limited advertising budgets. Broadcasters are looking for alternative methods of revenue generation. For example last year Sky established its package of encrypted channels to which viewers have to subscribe, paying a monthly fee. This is also why broadcasters are looking to infomercials for revenue generation during hours when they would not normally broadcast. However infomercials are a strategic decision for the channel, a decision which must be based on current and future programming schedules and whether the concept fits in with the overall character of the channel. After all the infomercial broadcaster essentially takes over the station .

With no BARB ratings, the quiet or dark hours between 12.00am and 8.00 am officially have no viewers, and a home shopping contract based on traditional advertising becomes irrelevant. Quantum operates by drawing up a contract based on product sales and percentage profit providing a guaranteed fee for a minimum level of sales. So the broadcaster is receiving a regular income from time which would usually be dark, the broadcaster has the additional benefit of on-going programming so viewers stay tuned to that station instead of tuning elsewhere. The potential revenue for channel owners is enormous. Some of our partners can earn as much as two or three million pounds a year from our programming.

Like broadcasters, marketeers are realising that home shopping is a viable alternative to traditional advertising. In Europe at the moment most of our programmes are produced in the US with a cost anywhere between $50,000 and $750,000, but a successful infomercial is not a matter of money but of technique. Quantum has now started producing European infomercials tailored to the European market in order to meet EU quotas. The programmes have a similar format to their US counterparts; however European tastes mean extensive product demonstration and a factual approach to the programme. We expect to be producing 10 to 15 programmes this next year in Europe, using European production companies and talent.

So it is obvious that infomercials make sound business sense both to broadcasters and to marketeers, but we must also consider the benefits of home shopping for the viewers. For the viewer the main benefit of home shopping is the convenience of viewing goods out of hours, at leisure, and seeing products being demonstrated thoroughly by experts or respected personalities. Home shopping also has obvious advantages for those with little time to spare or for elderly people or those with disabilities who may find going to the shops difficult or impossible. But for people who can get to the shops the attraction of home shopping is often the products. As I mentioned earlier, the products sold via infomercials are unique. Viewers can see innovative cooking appliances, health and beauty aids, automotive care packages which they cannot buy in the stores. But for viewers the overriding benefit is that the programmes actually are fun to watch. Many of our viewers watch our programmes for entertainment and not necessarily to purchase product. It is very difficult to estimate how many people watch our programmes because, as I mentioned earlier, there are no BARB ratings during the time we broadcast.

Our programmes are broadcast right across Europe on Vox, Eurosport and Super Channel. We know that the market out there is large yet, to some extent, we have a niche business because sometimes only 80,000 to 100,000 people across the whole of Europe watch our programmes. The footprint for Super Channel goes across the top of Scandinavia, down the west coast of Russia, along the North African coast and up back over Iceland.

Even in the US home shopping is a niche business. QVC's turnover in the US is around $1.4 billion and compare this to K-Mart which turns over in excess of $25 billion. We have gained an advantage by being first on the international scene and, to a certain extent, developing all available air time. However the giants back in the US are beginning to stir. NIMA, which is the National Infomercial Marketing Association, has established a UK headquarters from which they hope to handle the interests of future infomercial business in Europe. But we do not perceive the big US corporations as a threat because we have the European experience. We have European staff, European partners in broadcasting and fulfilment, European programming and, mostly importantly, the recognition from the European broadcasting industry and European viewers that we are a credible and professional company with which to do business. I think that this code of practice that we have established will shape both the future of both Quantum and, to a certain extent, home shopping infomercials in Europe. As a UK based and licensed broadcaster, we must work closely with the Independent Television Commission and the Department of National Heritage. As marketeers, home shopping companies must consult and inform the various consumer associations and councils. We must ensure that we set the pattern of best practice and high standards for the future of the industry.

So how do we see the future of the industry? The possibilities for new product development are endless. However we are finding that there is great interest in instructional and academic courses. One of our most successful academic courses is *Super Times Table*, a video and audio cassette package which teaches children their times tables through pop music and pop videos. We developed the programme with mathematician and TV personality Carol Vorderman who also appeared in the infomercial to demonstrate the product. Take a look at this clip from that programme.

Video extract is shown

We are also looking to extend this concept further by developing infomercials for consumer services. We feel that our future lies in owning different channels which offer different programme formats and are associated with different host stations. This maintains continual but varied on-air exposure and sustained demand; it also creates in-built competition. This strategy is consistent with the way in which broadcasting in general is developing. You are probably already aware of the Travel Channel which launched earlier this year on Astra. Home shopping infomercials could bring additional revenue to the travel channels through a travel-related home shopping infomercial service, offering holiday services and travel-related products. We are offering a new medium for informing the viewing public through entertaining programmes that can promote a wide diversity of products and services. The growth of themed and speciality channels will be enhanced further by cable, and the emergence of video on demand. With video on demand viewers will be able to call up a range of home shopping services.

So we are monitoring these new thematic channels and interactive technologies closely, but at the end of the day, unlike DRTV or twenty-four hour home shopping, infomercials are about entertaining the viewers, ensuring they enjoy the shopping experience. Thank you very much.

Eve Simon (Independent Television Commission): As I am sure a lot of the gentlemen up there know, Europe has recently issued a challenge to the ITC on its licensing of home shopping and suggesting that maybe the ITC got it wrong, and it misinterpreted the broadcasting legislation, and in fact suggested that home shopping should not be licensed. I am wondering if you could comment on that.

Garrett O'Leary: It is a grey area right now, but I think that you should stand firm, because I do not think the Germans have it right, and that it is silly to have a multi-channel environment and not have the ability to have a lot of channels. And a lot of channels means shopping as well as entertainment. The view that the ITC took was that it had to be done within very specific guidelines which were very expensive. I mean QVC was not just like setting up in the States; they had to own the product physically. They had to warehouse it, and so it was much more complex than in the United States. But I think that it was the right move, and I do hope that you do not back down, because the pressure is immense. But, we are with you.

Peter Wenban: We are particularly affected by this, because we are running long-form programming, and in blocks of very long time, and to get get two hundred hours such as we have per week means that we are not advertising, we are deemed to be programme-makers, and putting on programming. And it hinges on two aspects of the directive. We own our products, and we own our air-time. We are broadcasters on our own time, and at a recent conference Jon Davey, who is the

ITC's Director of Cable and Satellite, came out very clearly that, as he says here, 'It so happens that we of the ITC believe on good legal advice that services such as QVC and Quantum Home Shopping are not caught by the directive's limitation.' And that means that the directive is saying that advertising should only be for so many minutes per hour. The interpretation given by the ITC of that directive is that by the nature of the way we operate we fall outside that directive's coverage. It is a very tricky area. The Germans have taken the opposite view. They see what we do as advertising they think it is limited to so many minutes per hour, we have had our broadcasts in Germany affected by this, in that the Länder, which control the cable operators which feed out the signal from the satellite, are now contesting our right to do so, and are putting time locks on our broadcast so that they are not fed out. This is in contravention of the European *Television Without Frontiers* document. So a confrontation is building up between the view of the German authorities and the French authorities who are along in this as well with the British authority interpretation. And at some point in time it has got to be resolved.

Helen Cunningham (University of Derby): I just want to ask a question about Teletext. I was interested in what you said that in most households that have Teletext it is actually watched about three or four times a day for fifteen minutes …

Peter van Gelder: Two or three times a day for seventeen minutes.

Helen Cunningham: Well, in my household it is watched about eight times a day. Quite often the Teletext is on, there is a CD playing, and the Teletext just runs and runs and runs round and round and round for half an hour or whatever. But I have never bought anything from Teletext. I am a very heavy user of the service for the information; *Bamboozle*, the man with the long chin from the computer game pages, is excellent and everyone should read him. I can see with holidays that people use it as a service, they buy the holidays; I have often done that for last minute bargains. But, other than that, I cannot really see myself ever 'phoning up and buying any products that are advertised. I just wondered whether you had any figures as to what percentage of your readers, or viewers, or whatever they are called, actually do buy.

Peter van Gelder: I cannot really relate it in terms of the percentage of people who do buy. All I do know is the figures that I gave you about the holiday market itself; fifteen percent of all the holidays that anybody buys come through Teletext. I will tell you how we get the figures through. We do research by NOP that interviews twenty thousand people a year about each page, the demographics of each page, how people are using it and all that kind of thing. We also use NRS, which is the statistic about readership that is used by all magazines and newspapers, and that is something to do with the direct competition. That is how we know, but we know more directly than that, too. It is direct response. Let's say you are an advertiser, and you put an ad up on Teletext. You will start getting 'phone calls, or you will not start getting 'phone calls. If you do not start getting 'phone calls then you want to know why. You will come in and speak to the advertising department. It is evidenced by the fact that they do come back, they judge it by those really really harsh criteria. Not how much it costs for an ad per somebody ringing up, but actually how much it costs per ad for somebody buying the product. That is the way they judge it. And they come back for more in their masses. So all I can say is that it does work, and I do not have the figures to tell you how many people actually do it. It is enough if you are watching it, you know. That is OK.

Rod Allen: Peter, can you say what other kinds of products, apart from holidays, are particularly successful on Teletext?

Peter van Gelder: As I was saying before, financial products. We are trying to develop all of these things as well. We do not have a lot of computer ads on, so we are looking to have that. That is the kind of thing which is a high value good, so it is worthwhile spending the money to advertise it on telly, either nationally or regionally. It is something you can imagine. You know what an IBM PS/1 looks like. You just really want to know what the price is. Looking at cars is very good. University courses is something else which is sold. Financial products, because it is all about something with rates changing every so often. I could go on. But also, Nintendo is an interesting case history. What they did was to use it in conjunction with television. So they had a commercial and they put up the page number; that is easier to remember. A Teletext page number is easier to remember than a 'phone number — three digits. Look at page 137, and if you look at page 137 you will see all the direct response details, and they are up there; it is not just there while you have got the TV programme on; it is not just there while you have got the commercial on, it is there all the time. Nintendo launched a game called Starwing, which I am sure everybody in this room has and plays regularly. They launched it last year, and what they did before the game was launched, they raised interest in it by referring to a page number through you could see your local stockist in your area, because Teletext is all regionalised. After it was launched they used the page as a scoreboard, so that you could see how children around the country were betting each up on the amount of score they had made. So Johnny in Derby has made fifty-five thousand aliens, and Freddie in Leicester has made ninety-seven thousand. And it was a very good way of adding interest and adding that feedback as well, all that interactivity as well.

Justin Cook (Manchester University): I just wondered if there were any guidelines that restrict the amount of advertising space you have on Teletext. Also I would like to know what the most successful home shopping product has ever been.

Peter van Gelder: Television companies have seven minutes an hour. We are not a thing which depends on time, we are allowed to have thiry-five percent of our source pages made up of advertising, and that is a page number which counts as an ad if it has got advertising on it. If it is a page which combines advertising and editorial product, or if it is a full page ad, then it is counted as a proportion of an advertising page. Those little fractionals, the signposts across the bottom, you are allowed to have as many of them as you want.

Rod Allen: I bet you did not think it was going to be as complicated an answer as that. What is the most successful home shopping product, Peter, that you know of?

Peter Wenban: Well, we have a portfolio running at any time of about thirty-six products, which we promote variously, some are seasonal, some are not. I think probably that one of the most successful certainly, is a product called Europainter which is a kit of paint pads, that essentially describes it. Instead of brushing paint onto a surface you spread paint onto a surface with a paint pad, and it is much more economical and more efficient in covering, and much quicker. And I think that has been, for as long as I can remember, a continuous steady seller, and very successful from that point of view.

Garrett O'Leary: Peter, would you not say that probably the most successful home shopping product that has ever been bought off TV has got to be the Abdomeniser, I would think.

Peter Wenban: Are we talking money, or volume?

Garrett O'Leary: I would say both, actually.

Peter Wenban: I think that that has been a consistent seller, I do not know that it has been the most successful seller.

Garrett O'Leary: I think that at the high volume end I think it has probably got to be the Nordic Track. Does anyone remember how many units were sold? Four thousand. That is not bad in an hour's programme, is it?

Rod Allen: Does anybody in here own one? A Nordic Track?

(a few hands go up)

Garrett O'Leary: It simulates cross-country skiing. It loses your tummy, and it will do wonders for your buttocks.

Rod Allen: Put a 'phone number out in front here!

Pauline McElhatton (Reuters Television): I thought the programming for education was really good, with the counting and multiplication tables. As an aunt, I have several nephews and I would really love to buy it. But as a selective viewer, I do have multi-channels, but I have not seen your channel. So, if I miss your channel, is there any chance that I can see the same information on Teletext?

Peter Wenban: It is a good idea. An interesting idea. The answer is no at the present time, but we have begun to focus on ways of notifying the channel numbers that people can find our programmes on. This may well be one. You may have seen history in the making.

Nick Smith (Independent Television Commission): I would like to ask a bit of a gloomy question. I suppose the panel at the moment thinks this just complements traditional shopping habits. Given the millions of people who will eventually subscribe to these services, what are the implications in terms of local economies, on local retailers and smaller shops who are at the moment feeling very vulnerable with the pressure of hyper and supermarkets? What do you think the effect on retailing is going to be?

Garrett O'Leary: I think the bottom line is it is going to affect them dramatically. It is affecting them in the States. We will look at the US because it is a developed market. In the US, the home shopping market is a $2.5 billion market. Then you have the infomercial market which is another $1 billion.

Then you have mail-order which is an $80 billion market. That is nothing compared to the $1.2 trillion consumer market in the US, excluding car sales. But it does have an effect and it is all based on margins. If you look at QVC, it is operating in a developed market place but their gross margin is forty-three to forty-six per cent. That is not a bad business, is it? Tell me what small retailer can operate with those kind of margins. I do not know many. So, it will have an effect, but I do not know how much and when.

Peter Wenban: Our products are not available on the open market, so really we are not taking away, we are adding another dimension, in fact.

Peter van Gelder: I do not really know about the whole breadth of home shopping, but it might actually happen that way. I still maintain the fact that we are still social people, we are still the same people that we were fifty years ago, we have stayed the same people that we were a million years ago, practically. And we want to socialise, we want to go out, we want to feel the goods. I think that in the same way as terrestrial television has to make room for cable, you have got to make room for home shopping. I cannot see that annihilating things. There are worries about small travel agents with Teletext, because of the amount we take in the holiday market. But it is still quite a big business, and I think still people will want to go into the shop and buy.

Garrett O'Leary: I would like to add one thing to that. There is a trend, and I have seen it particularly with multi-national retailers and European mail-order houses, that with interactive they have decided that it is like if you cannot beat them, join them I think that what you will see is not, 'Oh my God, this small guy is losing;' in business, people lose and people win. But I think what you will see is a trend to 'This is going to be just another form of distribution to our customers. We will still do our catalogue; we will do things slightly differently, but we will use our same brand in an electronic retailing format.'

Alexander Fraser (University of Manchester): When we use Teletext in my household, if we are watching ITV or Channel Four, and we want to find out information about the evening's TV, we will switch to BBC, because it is fast and we do not have to suffer adverts holding up the next page and the next page, and I wonder if that is a problem.

Peter van Gelder: Can you leave the room immediately? No. We have higher viewer figures than Ceefax and we are trying to make the access time as quick as we can. This is a technical issue; Oracle used to have twelve VBI lines to transmit on. We have a lot of material, and we only have seven, seven and a half lines. So it is a play-off between having stuff there for people and having the ability to update, if that is what you are talking about, the pages changing in a subset. The most complaints that we get are that the change-overs are too slow, the second highest complaint that we get is that they are too fast. Keep watching.

Rod Allen: I am very grateful. I see that there is a threat to our traditional broadcasting from these new channels, but I have also always understood that advertising has an accelerator effect on the economy, and in fact one of the things that might happen is that rather than this kind of thing simply replacing other kinds of business, it would increase the total amount of economic activity. However, it is something that we are all going to have to watch very carefully.

Session produced by Rod Allen and Veronica Taylor

What price independence?

Chair: **Jerome Kuehl**
Open Media

Chris Griffin
Independent producer

Sheila Rodgers
3T Productions

Brian Harper-Lewis
Videotron

JERRY Kuehl: This morning is the session which actually brings producers into the Symposium. We have talked about delivery systems, about regulators, and a certain amount about what audiences expect, but we have not, so far, formally been able to hear from the people who will be making the programmes or the audio-visual entities which we will be seeing in five years' time.

Chris Griffin is an independent BBC producer — that is an animal of which there used to be quite a lot. I remember when I first went to work for Thames Television I was on an astonishing juridical device called a rolling contract; the very, very ancient amongst you may remember what they were and you will no doubt regret their passing because they had fiscal advantages of an unprecedented sort and Mrs Thatcher's government simply put a stop to that.

We have Sheila Rodgers who is Managing Director of 3T Productions, a multimedia production company, and we have Brian Harper-Lewis who will be speaking not on behalf of Videotron, his company, but he will be talking about interactive programming from the point of view of someone who is doing it.

Brian Harper-Lewis: Good morning. I would love to have told you about the masterful achievements of Videotron, not only the exciting future of interactive television but the present which some of you may have already had the misfortune to discover at some length is pretty enervating too.

I would have been positively delighted to point out while Messrs Clinton and Gore talked about the future of super highways, Britain has gone ahead with a vast collection of super by-ways and, perhaps inadvertently, leads the world in the deployment of fibre optics.

I would have been proud to tell you that thanks to the courageous inflow of Canadian capital London now has the second largest interactive net on the face of the planet and that as a result of a recently concluded agreement Videotron will be providing a further 200,000 interactive boxes in the London area alone.

I would have imparted the joyful news that Videotron will shortly implement the reverse path to almost all its London viewers and shared the enthusiasm I feel and you would, too, if you knew about the astounding projects soon to be delivered, not as a test but as a functioning fully operational system to 34,000 homes in the Sanguinet area of Quebec.

However I fear I must attempt to be succinct in the extreme which, for those of you who know me of old, means upsetting the habits of a lifetime.

When we first spoke concerning this morning the only edict graved in tablets of stone by the inimitable Jerry was that I should check my guns at the door, which in time-honoured fashion of two nations divided by a common language I have duly done. Yup, I have checked them and they are working just fine. Now let us examine the brief.

The media giants are starting to prepare for the multi-media age, but small independent producers are already active. What battles lie ahead? 'Starting', what is this word 'starting'? Sixteen years ago one of those media giants specified in your programme, albeit slightly less conglomeratised at the time, chucked a whole pile of money at a brave experiment in the American town of Columbus, Ohio, and to the best of my knowledge the world got its first real taste of interactive television. If that was them starting their run-up I sure as hell hope whoever is at the crease has not only an extremely large bat but a neat line in Kevlar underwear. As a participant I am reminded of Douglas Adam's splendid advice [in his radio series *The Hitch Hiker's Guide to the Galaxy* — Eds] re attending a Hotblack Desiato concert, and had I a tiny fraction of the resources at the disposal of our eleven o'clock speaker, I would have played you the clip where the dulcet tones of Peter Jones taught the audience how the best way to view it was from a concrete bunker several feet below the surface of another planet.

As some of us might recall, the Hotblack subsequently took a year off dead for tax reasons, a course of action which might recommend itself to independent producers who have not yet managed to crack the riddle of development costs and *tranche* cash flow. With certain notable exceptions — stand up Channel 4 and be counted — these remain glaringly obvious hurdles in the marathon of the truly independent producer. And if he or she has not yet got a well-established name, forget it. The only way out for you is the umbrella deal or the equally iniquitous privileges of bed-and-breakfasting [where an independent producer is obliged by its customer to make a programme in association with a larger, more established company — Eds]. Having spoken to a number of still determined but disgruntled producers, it is amazing just how many beds appear to have bugs in them or how many breakfasts of thin gruel seem to have been charged for. With a possible exception of a company in Store Street, the imagination is not yet at a premium and for the 450 programmes it commissioned last year, Channel 4, with its laudable commitment to ideas, distributed less than £10,000 each to 350 of them. Is imagination in such short supply? Was Einstein really the originator of that old chestnut about success being one per cent inspiration and ninety-nine per cent perspiration? Despite recent progress I bet even a seriously sweaty chap like him would have struggled with the demons of overheads and timely financing.

At Edinburgh a while ago Sir John Harvey-Jones publicly offered his finely tuned trouble shooter's nose to any takers and was nearly trampled in the rush.

Bernard Clark, hardly an example of one still damp behind the ears, offered his kit-bag of aims, accomplishments, advantages; and what did the great guru tell him? Get rid of everything as soon as possible and operate from a back bedroom. This is progress?

Faced with the prospect of projecting the future for independent producers I undertook some empirical research, being careful about my statistical technique. Well, all right. I rang a few friends. But the consensus was remarkable. How do we prosper in a multi-media age? The answer seems to be be like that of the guerilla. Hide in the hills and live off nuts and berries. When you see the convoy coming, surreptitiously scurry down, find yourself a comfortable gulley and when it rounds the corner bang off the clip, two at the most and then get the hell out quickly. You can capitalise on your position back in the safety of the hills or you could take up market gardening and pray that they need your produce. Perhaps you will think, why did I run? Should I have stayed put? What could they have done? Well, perhaps nothing, perhaps they would have lumbered on by not even noticing you. Or if you had appeared unarmed, save for a couple of cabbages, perhaps they would have thrown you a crust or even stopped to exchange your efforts for a delicious mug of anti-freeze? And, metaphorically at least, you would have been away. Heels clipping, somersaulting with intoxicated delight of not having been shot at for once. Ready for anything. The world as your own personal oyster. Not only have you had your precious wares accepted but you have begun to develop a taste for anti-freeze. It is really not so bad after all and it does get cold waiting in those hills. It is usually at this point you tread on a mine. Received wisdom has it that the equation runs: talent produces distribution. We seem to have overlooked the small matter of rights. Let us try to hang on to them and see what happens.

In this rapidly advancing multi-media age we are told to expect the liberating concepts that computers were supposed to bring a decade ago. How liberated did Professor Silverstone's Townsend family sound? Alan Morris' excellent presentation raised another key question. Who is going to make these programmes? We were told that of the 195,000 programme hours used in the UK last year, a mere 12,000 were home-grown. Maybe the French do have something to offer with their funny ideas about cultural protectionism and libraries in which you can look up programme data. But it is not all gloom and doom. Despite the ever-increasing inroads being made on high quality terrestrial broadcasting, we are told that it should last, well, at least until the turn of the century. That is six years away. But never mind. There is a whole new, wonderful horizon opening up as our $37 million colleague told us yesterday. Infomercials are about entertaining and informing the viewers and they have got fifteen whole exciting new programmes 'til late next year. That is about the most macabre use of the word entertaining I have ever heard. Perhaps we could get Michael Winner to do something for them or perhaps our spoilt for choice excercise should have contained a whole new set of channels. The 'Sad Suite.' Go on, prove me wrong, please. But now you must excuse me; I have to rush home and see if the postman has delivered my Abdominator.

Sheila Rodgers: My name is Sheila Rodgers and I am managing director of a multi-media production company, so I am coming at it from a slightly different angle. We do not produce television programmes, but we do make multi-media programs.

Now, although that is not interactive television as you may have come to understand it, the fact is that some figures have been produced recently about people who actually have interactive multi-media products that they plug into their televisions. Whereas the average television watcher might watch the television for twenty-seven hours a week, if they are actually interacting with multi-media on, for example, CD-I, they can spend up to thirteen hours of those twenty-seven hours interacting with multi-media on the main television set.

Now how accurate these figures are I do not know, but I have had them from two different sources. It means that the interactive multi-media part is having a significant impact on television viewing.

I will give you a little bit of background about 3T Productions, and then I will explain how we got to where we are and how we feel it is not all doom and gloom by any stretch of the imagination. We started off as a software company producing mainly educational titles that were sold directly into schools. But we were approached by a number of television companies who were very interested in linking up their television programmes for schools through the schools broadcasting system with software. So it was not really interactive multi-media; the schoolchildren were watching part of a television programme, then they were stopping, then they were doing some work on a computer that helped with what they were doing in terms of the television programme, and then they went back to the television programme, and so on. In a sense it was an early form of multi-media, although it was on a number of different platforms at the same time. It became clear to us, rather later than to some other people in this room I am sure, that it made a lot of sense to link all these together and to start producing interactive video, as it was then, and putting the television programmes on video disks and linking them in with software so that the two things ran side by side.

However, the television companies were not particularly interested in this, for very good reasons. The market in interactive video, particularly in schools, was not as good as everybody hoped it was going to be, and it was fairly expensive. But we decided we would do it anyway and we developed interactive video for training purposes. And that is the background of how we got into multi-media through interactive video.

In about 1990 we decided that as things seemed to be going very well for us in terms of the products that we were producing, and they were being very well received, we would try to get to the consumer. We still worked closely with television companies, and we worked very closely with a lot of independent producers who had left television companies like Granada Television, for example, just up the road; quite a lot of these people were very keen on getting involved in interactive multi-media.

So we started to look at a number of options available to us. One option was that of taking existing material, stuff that had been produced for television, that perhaps could be reused in multi-media. There are not that many programmes that can be reused in that way without the actual multi-media and the interactive link being a bit nebulous, to say the least. But we came up with a number of possibilities. We are currently working with Granada Television on their *Disappearing World* archive. *Disappearing World* is one of the biggest anthropological archives available in the world and we are making this into a multi-media title. It looks at existing material in a completely different way. The way it works is that you get a series of one hour programmes and each one hour programme focuses on one society somewhere in the world and you watch that for one hour. We have taken a number of different societies, and a number of different topics within those societies, so that you can cross-link them and you can compare. We did a prototype of this and we selected one topic as the role of women. It proved to be a fascinating topic. There were some wonderful lines in there. For example in one society in a fishing boat, the man has to have his head higher than the woman's because the man is considered high but vulnerable whilst the woman is low but dangerously powerful. I thought that was rather a nice line. There are a lot of different sections like that to compare. Taking the role of women as an example, you can compare with different societies to see how in different societies men and women react together.

That is one example of something we are doing with television companies taking existing material. We are also working with Anglia Television on *Survival* footage — that is the wildlife programme, as you probably know. But we came up with another idea because we had done a lot of interactive video work based on drama where you can really interact with the drama and you can control what happens when and where. We decided that this was a concept that we would like to continue. It took us two and a half years, but we finally managed to negotiate a contract for *Cluedo,* the board game, and to make that into an interactive drama where you, the user, can really play the detective. As I say it took two and a half years for the owners to agree, partly because they had not heard of multi-media two and a half years ago or three years ago as it is now, and partly because once they did know, they then suddenly started to think 'Hang on a minute, there might be something more in this for us than we have first perceived', so it took a long time.

But now we have actually produced *Cluedo* on CD-I. What I have got here is the VHS which shows some of the drama sequences. Now they will not make any sense at all, because when you actually play the game you do not see them in any set order. The problems with devising an interactive drama for multi-media are exactly related to that. You have to assume that people are not going to see things in any set order. I imagine that a fair percentage of you have played *Cluedo* the board game, at least I hope so, and, as you are probably aware, when you play the board game you can go into different rooms by throwing the dice. The same thing happens on the interactive multi-media version of *Cluedo*. You play this on your television set; you go into a room, and when you go into that room you then can, if you wish to, see a flashback of something that happened in that room prior to the murder. What you have to do is try to piece the evidence together. There is a lot of other information in there. There are a lot of stills, a lot of voice-over, you can examine the room, you can find weapons, you can find a knife, see whose fingerprints are on it, find a gun, see how many times it has been fired, ask people for their alibis and so on.

But in scripting something like this you have got to remember that people will not necessarily see the scenes in the order that they happened. So when you are writing a scene for something like this, you cannot assume that they have any prior knowledge of what has happened.

Video extract is shown

That just gives you an idea. All those things happen in different sequences; you have to try to piece it together in your own mind without any prior assumptions. And that, to us, is what we should be doing, as a company, in terms of creating interactive television. We do not do it as broadcast television, we do it by creating compact discs that people can play on their televisions at home, but hopefully incorporating some of the best of television values, while at the same time putting the user in control. We see that we have got a great future doing that.

Jerry Kuehl: Chris, with your long track record is this the sort of thing that you are going to be doing in five years' time; is this the sort of thing that you are doing now, is this your day job?

Chris Griffin: No, but it is the one side of the future of television that I do find fascinating. Great fun to do work. Get into interactive drama, change the plot, kill the hero, make the baddie win, you know, depending on the mood. Change a happy ending into a sad ending. I think it has got a lot of fun going for it.

I am, as Jerry said, an independent producer. Over the past fifteen years I have produced about twenty films. I have worked mainly in the independent sector, but in 1991 I went back to the BBC after an absence of nearly twelve years. Now as independent programme makers, particularly in the drama field, we rely almost entirely on the survival and well-being of the major broadcasting companies to buy and fund the products.

So, what price independence in the post-broadcasting age? I am not sure I fully understand what that means exactly — the 'post'-broadcasting age. Anyhow, I was told that generally we would be crystal ball-gazing, and I thought initially that sounded fun. But after a while I was actually not so sure; I got a bit depressed about it and I got rather emotional about it. The thought of five hundred television channels brings a whole new meaning to channel-hopping, and ratings wars. What will happen to drama? Will there be room for it? Will we ever see a single play again? How will the broadcasting companies change? Will advertisers take over? And more worrying particularly to me at the moment, and I think to all of you, should be considered what might happen to Auntie? That is Auntie BBC.

Back in 1985, a bunch of us made a little movie called *Max Headroom*. At that time it was a sort of tongue-in-cheek look at television, as we coined the phrase, 'twenty minutes into the future.' If you would just like to look at a few frames of it.

Video extract is shown

Right. That was a blip-vert, part of my look twenty minutes into the future nine years ago. But I think that we are getting ironically closer to Channel 23. We have had a number of Zip-Zap corporations for many years, and there are certainly powerful forces for moving towards that ultimate power base. So, are blip-verts so ridiculous? Will there be a broadcasting authority big enough to control the standards? Closer to home, having never planned my future more than two, at the most three years, ahead, when looking into the future I found myself reflecting on the past, looking back thirty years since the start of BBC 2. Now, what have we had in those thirty years? Colour in 1967, satellite via Goonhilly Down, I think that was even earlier. Channel 4, some cable, high definition, not yet in wide use, tremendous advances in technical quality of presentation, and although we have had satellite technology for years, its full exploitation has been held up by the lawyers, and only recently has Mr Murdoch's Sky Channel started on its road possibly to monopolise the world of sport.

So, for the past thirty years it has been a relatively steady state of development. What is being promised now could change that steady state into a Big Bang, and I find that rather disturbing. How will the broadcasting companies meet the challenge, and in particular, broadcasting corporations like the BBC? Our future as independents depends on their survival. I have a great affection for Auntie BBC. She has taught me a lot of my craft. And between 1967 and 1978, a period when drama really thrived, the single play featured on both ITV and BBC, *Armchair Theatre, Wednesday Play, Play of the Month, Saturday Night Theatre, Thirty Minute Theatre, Second City Firsts, The Sunday Afternoon Classic Serial*, and many fine series and serials. I remember when every studio in Television Centre was packed with actors and scenery seven days a week; the place buzzed. Stages at Ealing were booked weeks ahead.

I left the BBC in 1978. When I returned in 1991, I walked around the Television Centre again. And it was a bit like the *Marie Celeste*. Thesingle play has declined to, I think, non-existence on ITV, other than Channel 4, of course, whose champions were Jeremy Isaacs and David Rose, and which did an enormous amount to lift the depression of the British film industry. But most of their plays were on film now; there was very little studio work. The BBC still features a season of single plays, though again on film, on both BBC 1 and BBC 2. But I think we will have to ask ourselves for how long they are really safe. If broadcasting's future becomes entirely embroiled in the growing ratings battle as it appears to be starting to be, my fear is that it could be the end of the BBC as we have known it. Now the BBC has always vigorously defended its artistic integrity and independence, and I do not think that we should forget that it is the only truly independent broadcasting company in the world. That is why the politicians do not like it. It maintains the *status quo* brilliantly.

But what will become of Auntie by the year 2000? Not long ago, the wise men ordered an investigation to find out what was wrong. Teams of grey-suited consultants filled the corridors and studios, replacing the actors and cameras. Accountants, visionary men, wielding their scalpels, sorry, their calculators. And after months of economic surgery, they balanced the books. The operation was a complete success. But, sadly, it is touch and go whether the patient will live. How strong will Auntie be to face the challenge ahead? For the independent programme maker, and particularly, quality British drama to survive and thrive into the next century, I believe the BBC should get a cracking good PR company to re-create its image. It will have to do more than shout in its own front room to sell itself to the punters. It will have to get out there. The independents depend on your survival, Auntie.

The BBC is currently bidding, I read, for two new channels, Four and Five, digital channels. I am not a great technologist; I am not quite sure what digital means, other than that it is an improvement in the standard of broadcasting presentation. But perhaps these could be the aspirin for the schedulers. Could it be suggested that if Four and Five become news and current affairs, One and Two could be pure entertainment? I think within a ratings battle those sort of things have to be seriously considered.

On a more positive note, as I said I love the idea of the interactive drama, where you can change the plot to suit your mood. And although drama is one of the most expensive products on TV, it is a very saleable commodity. It has been the major earner for the American economy since movies started to be made. And I think that we should be encouraged by our government to compete, but whether we will be able to in ten year's time, whether we will be making dramas like we were making twenty-five years ago, or whether we will be on a diet of American culture morning, noon and night, is something that should be addressed. Or perhaps we should just look twenty minutes into the future, and not worry too much about the post-broadcasting age. And I find that very difficult.

Peter van Gelder (Teletext): It is really a question for the lady involved in multi-media. I am just wondering how jou are finding the markets developing. Are there lots of CD-Is being sold? Is there an interest, how do you see it in the future? You said it was very bright, but I just wondered if you would give a bit more detail on it.

Sheila Rodgers: Not specifically CD-I. I would not say that the future for CD-I was specifically the bright spot. There are lots of different forms of multi-media. Philips claim to have sold three hundred thousand CD-I players worldwide. Fifty percent of those were sold in the States, fifty percent in Europe, and of the fifty percent in Europe, thirty percent were sold in the UK. Now, personally I would not develop a title for a UK market only, unless it was extremely cheap to develop, and *Cluedo* was not. So *Cluedo* had to be developed for a world market. But, wherever possible, we are aiming to do cross-platform development so we will develop a title that works on CD-ROM or on CD-I, and particularly now that there are boards available that give you the same quality video that you can get on CD-I machines, although they are not standard on allmachines. So the CD-ROM market, and the multi-media market as a whole, I am very confident will become a huge market in the future. But the format that will be the winning format is one that I would not want to predict

Roger Wilson (Learning Television): I have been following and working in the multi-media market as well as in broadcasting as well as in cable during the last twelve years. It has seemed a very fractioned existence at times, although it is quite clearly all coming together, as we have seen over the last three days. Watching the multi-media market, and seeing the analyses that come out from various market reports, I think the one thing that stands out is that the accuracy of market predictions for multi-media is probably under five per cent in the last fifteen years. Every prediction has been missed by massive amounts, and I think that is leading everyone to be very cautious about predicting the future, though because we are seeing a much greater stability now of the actual multi-media platforms, there is lot more confidence than there even was three or four years ago, when it looked as if there would be about seven or eight platforms going into the consumer market. Now it seems fairly clear that there will only be two survivors, each with a different mode of use — one based on the personal computer, and one based on the home television.

Sheila Rodgers: What Roger just said was absolutely right in that they have different modes of use, and therefore even if you wanted to do cross-platform development and titles, we would not necessarily develop them so that they looked identical, because if you are using something like a CD-I machine you are traditionally using that in your sitting room with the television; you have got a hand controller and you are sitting back and watching it whereas if you are using a CD-ROM, the CD-ROM is on your computer screen, and what you want to use it for and what it ought to look like on the screen will be very different but the basic concept of the programme can be the same. Does that make sense?

Chris Griffin: In the structure of these dramas, there are a couple of things that interest me. You are making them yourself or you are sort of farming out the dramas?

Sheila Rodgers: We use independent producers and directors, people whom we have known for a long time and the same is true of facilities, editors and so on. It is extremely difficult to find people who understand the concept of interactivity, particularly when they are editing. They want to edit it together like a television drama so that for example sound spills over from the end of one scene into the beginning of another, and in interactive terms that does not work. I can remember years ago doing a video disk for the education centre at Windsor Safari Park, and we had a section on monkeys which was then followed by a section on whales. The editor could not get to grips with cutting the sound straight between one and the other so at the beginning of the whale sequence we had chimpanzees. But, of course, because it is being used in an interactive way the user may have gone to it and thought, 'Let's have a look at the whales,' so clicked to see whales — and they get beautiful pictures of whales that we got from *Survival*, with chimpanzee sounds for about the first two seconds. So finding the right people to produce anything that it is going to be interactive, whether it be drama or whether it be documentary, is quite difficult.

Chris Griffin: But with the structure of a drama, even like *Cluedo*, you can still only give so many options of choice. The choice is never going to be endless, is it? So that the viewer cannot actually, truly, manipulate the plot lines and the story lines to suit themselves exactly, not actually make it up as they go along.

Sheila Rodgers: *Cluedo* is a bit of an oddball because it has to establish certain facts, so it is not like an interactive drama where you determine how the situation goes. I think in developing an interactive drama traditionally as people did that for, maybe, interactive video training it was just a branching flowchart really, but it did not need to be and they could be developed so that things crossed backwards and forwards; so every time you went through this process, when you made decisions, there were knock-on effects.

If I can give you an example, I have seen interactive videos produced for training where you see a bit of drama. It stops and says, 'What do you think you should do now?' It gives you three multiple options on the screen. You chose one and it says, 'No, that is not right. Try C,' which is really impressive and there were an awful lot of those about. We produced a drama for the Post Office which was based on the procedural agreement for unions, I mean such a terrible subject. But, basically, we actually put control in the hands of the person who was running the Post Office and the drama did not stop at all. What happened was you ran the drama and when you thought that this chap should do something you interrupted and you were then faced with his office. And you had the filing cabinet, you had the telephone, you could call somebody into the room. And when you did something you did not necessarily see the result of your action because in real life that does not happen. And so the whole thing weaved in and out and if you actually made a series of wrong decisions, nothing happened until everybody walked out on strike and you did not know which in particular of those actions it was until you went through the story afterwards. So, yes, there is a finite number of routes that you can take but if you actually put enough thought into the development process, you can cross those over and interlink them so that there are a whole variety of different routes through.

Chris Griffin: About seven years ago we attempted to do an interactive video about learning to drive and it went totally out of control. I mean it started as quite a neat little package, but it turned into very funny scenes. It was a comedy at the end of the day with sort of tragic results. It just got bigger and bigger and bigger and we did not know actually how to stop it. Do you know how to stop it now?

Sheila Rodgers: Each programme is different so it is very difficult to answer that. *Cluedo* is, as I say, very specific; but with *Cluedo* we have reused the scenes and we have used a lot of additional voice-over and still images so that we can take the same basic storyline and have completely different outcomes by just having different evidence which is done by stills and voice-over because there is a limited amount of drama on the disk. In *Cluedo* there will be three different dramas on each of two disks, and each of the three dramas has four possible outcomes. So it is containable, but whether successfully or not I could not say really.

Naomi Sargent (VLV): I wonder whether you could just give us an idea of one or two of the titles that you have been making that have been particularly successful and/or interesting? But, more prosaically, I wanted to ask Brian as well as you, if one is using existing material which is clearly very sensible and may be absolutely necessary, you do then get into enormous problems about copyright and ownership of previous materials. That will happen more in materials that one wants to use for educational applications whether for home learners or for institutions and I just wonder whether you have yet learned anything that is worth sharing with us, because I think this is really under-thought about.

Brian Harper-Lewis: The rights issue is a minefield. I had a discussion with somebody who calculated that the rights for one particular program would, if they had sourced it in the normal way, have been in excess of five hundred thousand pounds. Very few independent producers can afford to take those sort of risks on board. And that was in respect of an educational title. Who is going to pay for these programs? I think that it needs to be addressed on an industry-wide basis.

When we get to educational materials where we have to buy from such a wide range of sources, it becomes a minefield. Looking at programmes I have handled, for example a production that went to the Museum of Mankind in Taiwan, we found ourselves some years ago in exactly this minefield where material that we wanted to use became prohibitively expensive because the rights holder saw a gravy train and jumped on it. And when we tried to point out, 'Hey, look, this is for five year olds or post-grad students, please help us,' we basically got the traditional landlord approach, 'You stay, you pay.' Not all companies have done that. With *Survival*, how did you clear the material, or was it simple because it was *Survival*-owned?

Sheila Rodgers: *Survival* is an odd one out in a sense because they thought very well ahead at Survival Anglia and they have got all the rights to use the material in any way that they want. However, we are only allowed to use the material that was not broadcast because various other people have got the rights to the material that has actually been broadcast, but because their shooting ratios are so high, there is not going to be any shortage of material there at all. And, of course, because it is animals it is not a major problem.

With *Disappearing World*, again, that is another odd one out because most of the people who have actually been filmed are unlikely to be seeing CD-I in the near future, but they have got the rights as well. What we tend to do, wherever possible, is originate the material ourselves because although it sounds horrendously expensive it is much cheaper to send a photographer out to get the photographs than it is to actually buy the photographs as they exist already. Some photographic libraries are charging £100 for one image or a part of an image and when you think of how many you can get on multi-media title, it does actually end up being extremely expensive.

We have the music specially written, wherever possible, as well, particularly for things like *Cluedo*. So, wherever possible, we do source the material ourselves and we have it produced ourselves. If we are working with existing footage, as with Granada or with Survival Anglia, we negotiate directly with the television company and it is their responsibility to make sure that they have all the rights; obviously the contracts involved in these things are horrendous. They are huge — forty pages long. And what we do is we tend to pay royalties to the people who own the rights, rather than paying them a flat fee because a flat fee puts up the production costs and does not do wonders for your cash flow whereas if it is a percentage, a reasonable percentage, then it works out much better. Does that answer your question?

Jerry Kuehl: We still want to know some of your exciting titles.

Sheila Rodgers: We all like *Cluedo* the best because it is such good fun. We have only been developing in the consumer area for about eighteen months. We developed a title for teenage girls for Philips which is quite good fun if you are a teen-age girl; basically, it is all to do with beauty and make-up. It does not use moving footage at all, but you can build a face. You can choose eyes, nose, mouth, face shape, eyebrows and because the CD-I technology will allow you to do this, we have developed techniques that blend the features together so you can choose any eyes, any nose, any mouth. We photographed four hundred girls and selected individual features from these. And you can build two million different faces and each of those two million faces can be made up in twelve different ways. You can go up from natural sporty to the wild party look. You can take one face and apply all these different make-ups. That is quite good fun. It has got lots of quizzes and beauty secrets and things like that in but, generally, I think we get enthusiastic about each one as we are doing it.

Brian Harper-Lewis: But, on a more serious note, the music industry has not so much addressed but almost tried to create by default a layer of copyright evasion. I can recall some press dialogue about people like James Brown getting very upset how many times he has appeared in other people's records; little bits of other people's music is turning up all over the place. When it happens the first time it is a tribute. Then it becomes repetitive. How many seconds do you have to sample before it is straight theft, not just a tribute? The technology that they are working with in sampling in any pre-production studio for audio is philosophically very close to the principles of what we are handling here. And, again, the sound issues apply just as much. So do we begin to address an industry which is going to drive itself downmarket, straight from the word go, in order to meet its own production costs? I do not have the answers. I do not know if anybody does.

Jerry Kuehl: There is a paradox which is that this extraordinarily rich base of imagery may become restricted because you will only use the sources which are in-house. So you will have the *Fox Movietone History of the Twentieth Century* which will not even use images from Pathé and so on.

Sheila Rodgers: I think there is a lot of room for collaboration, though. Recently we have been approached by one of the big book publishers and they want to do a certain title that we know a television company has produced as a drama. And so we are setting up collaboration deals there so that we can use some of the material from the television company, but the book publisher is the one who actually is pushing the thing forward. So there is a lot of room for that as well, I think.

Unidentified questioner: My concern follows Garrett O'Leary's session yesterday about the advertisers and the fact that they are freezing their spend on the advertising which is the main revenue source for the producers, be they independent or be they with the networks. My question is: what do you think about this? What do you think can be done about this and how does it affect you?

Sheila Rodgers: I do not know that I am qualified to speak about this really because, obviously, advertising is not a feature of what we do at all, although it has been suggested there is absolutely no reason why you cannot sell advertising space on multi-media disks.

Chris Griffin: The point that I was trying to make was about the fear of the control of the advertisers and how it is going to affect the sort of programmes that we might be able to see in the future. I mean drama is expensive. It does not always capture the biggest audiences. That is why I am very worried about the BBC if it gets too embroiled in a ratings war.

Unidentified questioner: I think that BBC, ITV and Channel Four are producing all the original programming and all the rest of the multi-channels are basically repackaging. So it is worrying because those who are repackaging are making a few bucks but they are depleting the stocks of new material and new jobs for the production industry. And I wonder if there should be some regulation so that those people who are repackaging ought to have to produce original programming or have so much money set aside so that the production industry is not eroded or fragmented.

Chris Griffin: It depends what they want. And I would hope that sooner or later if they ended up just getting games shows and frothy items, they would not be able to do very much with them. I think you tend to work on what I call the quality programmes, documentaries, dramas, news and what have you. So I think there could be a backlash. But what worries me is whether people are addressing that thought in advance rather than letting it happen and allowing in the power of the advertising men, the Zip Zap merchants.

Philip Reevell (Mersey Television): We make *Brookside*. I am interested in the point you are making about both advertising and new media because I think they are two sides of the same coin, which is growing commercial pressure within main-stream broadcasting. This is exemplified, as far as we are concerned, on Monday evenings, when you find a one hour version of *Coronation Street,* a new episode of *EastEnders* and *Brookside* all shown simultaneously at eight o'clock, which is not exactly increasing choice for people especially since it bumps *World in Action* at eight-thirty out of peak time. So I think the growing commercial pressures which are being introduced by the growth of satellite and cable are unhealthy if they restrict viewer choice. I think the answer, however, is not necessarily to be as de-terministic or as gloomy as some people are. I think if you were to stand your ground it would be possible to get some results. By standing their ground I think there are some implications for what an independent producer actually is. I think they will have to become far more closely involved in the programming as well as the creative side of development of drama in particular, and also factual program-ming in peak time. So that means that the kind of responsibilities an independent previously might have undertaken will end up being wider.

But I am also interested in your point about looking back thirty years because I think if you look back thirty years at the demise of the single play, I wonder if it is a question of form rather than of content. I am very interested in the kind of social realism that was introduced thirty years ago by *Coronation Street* and *Z-Cars* which was in many ways a reflection of what was going on in single plays and film and theatre. If you take that today you could say that social realism has gone from British primetime but you could also say that realism in itself pays very rich divi-dends to broadcasters. The reason that *EastEnders* is going to a third episode is that it is very popular. It is a realistic programme. The more realistic *Brookside* is the more our audience responds. I suspect that the combination of taking a broader view of where an independent producer should be and respecting traditions but doing it in a 90s kind of way might well be a way of addressing some of the pressures. In the end, it is ultimately a regulatory problem, and I think that the regulator will have to act on some matters such as factual programming and current affairs in prime time. I think that is something that only a regulator can stop being pushed out of prime time.

Chris Griffin: I agree with everything that you said, but I think that there still should be room for every type of drama. If we get a constant turnover of soap after soap after soap, that is fine for part of the audience but I think we are starting not to give viewers as wide a choice as we did years ago. We have to ask ourselves why is this happening. It is not happening because we do not want, as independent producers, to offer up (and I hate to use the term) minority interests, because it depends how it is pitched, and how it it received. And there are some programmes that come out of the air, and become popular through word of mouth, like single plays: 'Did you see … ?' I just worry that the audience is not being given a big enough choice, and I think we are being pressured by the controllers and their worry about ratings, and who is watching, and how many people are watching. And your point about Monday night — three things which are very popular all slammed up against each other, I do not think that that is giving a service, and I think that scheduling is more than that.

Philip Reevell: I agree with you. It does not make any sense to anyone to have three programmes of the same kind on at the same time. I agree with you that there is a potential restriction on viewing choice going on at the moment, but I think that if ITV were to follow that route to its logical conclusion, then they will lose audience, because the British audience, traditionally, likes to have a wide variety of programming in peak time. It does not want to have back-to-back soaps throughout the evening. So if that pressure continues, ultimately ITV will lose share of audience and, therefore, will lose money. At that point it will begin to have to address the problem because its shareholders will require it to.

Chris Griffin: The BBC is doing just that sort of thing at the moment with audience research exercises, going out and asking groups of the population what they want, what they like, what they liked about a programme, what they did not like about a programme and I think the danger of that sort of exercise depends largely on the question is that they are asked. And having said that, they will very often say, 'Oh, we would like something more like such and such'. But then when they get it, they complain because they have seen that and they say that it was just like such and such. So these research questions can be manipulative to the convenience of the power base of the broadcasters, or that of the advertisers.

Liz Ashton Hill (College of St Mark and St John, Plymouth): I see the new media as being very much in its experimental stage. It is quite small-scale in a way, and I, like you, am very enthusiastic about it. And if it actually does take off and gets into the homes, and there is great demand for it, will there be any room for small players like yourself or will the big giants just come in and just rule it and take it over?

Sheila Rodgers: That is a very good question. Multi-media productions are expensive, there is no doubt about that, and we are a small company and we employ twenty-five people. We have have recognised that if we are going to exist in this market we cannot remain a small company with twenty-five people. There will be room for a number of different sections of that industry; for example in our future plans we do not propose to employ full-time drama directors or cameramen, and we do not plan to have editing facilities in-house. We intend to use those facilities that are available in the area anyway, or in whatever area is appropriate. So there will be a lot of room for individuals in that market, but in terms of a multi-media publishing company, which is what we partly are, we still do a fair proportion of commissioned work, because that is the bread and butter. And something like *Cluedo* has taken two and a half years for us to get the contract. By the time it is in the market it will have been another eighteen months since the contract was signed, not just because of the production but because of all the testing and all the other bits that go into it. It is very expensive and you have to wait a long time to get your money back. So there is absolutely no doubt that the people with pots of money are the ones who, in theory, should rule the market. But I think that what we would like to do is find a niche in that market that we can provide and support, and that people come to recognise the company name, and see a title and think, 'Ah, that is a good one. We have had their stuff before,' in the same way that there are video games companies who do that sort of thing. There are small independent production companies who produce for television, and you get to recognise the names. So, I think that there is every chance that there will be an attempt to gobble us up. If we can avoid it then we will do, and try to retain our independence, but in order to do that we will have to expand in size.

Birgit Thiel-Weidinger (*Suddeutsche Zeitung*): Coming back to the question of the future and the financial, or the popular aspect of your work. Are there a lot of companies like you in Britain? Certainly not. Are there going to be more because there is a demand, or how are you developing?

Sheila Rodgers: There is a growing number, but they all come at it from different angles. There are quite a few companies who have traditionally been in the interactive video field, for example. Brian mentioned a company called Epic, in Brighton. They have expanded into this field, and I think they are proving very successful and very good at what they do. So there is a small number of them, but it is a growing number, and they are coming into it from different angles. There are quite a few television independent producers who have come into it. Publishers have come into it; everybody is getting at it from a different angle, depending on what their experience and expertise is. But what is happening quite a lot now is that some of the larger companies are seriously considering getting their own multi-media production facility in-house, whereas traditionally they have gone outside and come to people like us and said, 'We have got this great idea but do not know how to do it. Will you do it?' Because they are now recognising the potential for this market, we are trying to dissuade them from doing this, but quite a few of them are considering starting their own multi-media production facilities in-house.

Jerry Kuehl: Is that your experience, Brian?

Brian Harper-Lewis: Yes, except that there are different horses for different courses. It is not the same equation as the old Betamax versus VHS wars, but there is not only a compatibility issue; there are different aims for the market. What Sheila is doing is different to what I am doing. I mean that for all I am moaning constantly about the amount of resources I do not have, I find it a refreshing, delightful, pragmatic insight into the way the company thinks that a few weeks ago we demolished the board room to build me a studio and a new control room simply for the interactive service and some editing suites. I gave a talk to a Royal Television Society workshop recently. There I found several young people who I had seen as clients making pop promos with me in the years gone by. They have now got quite successful as small multi-media companies. There was a young man who had produced a very elaborate video disk, a CD-I disk as an interactive night-club. Now I am not sure who wants to go to an interactive night-club, but somebody paid for it. When he was quizzed from the floor about what the budget was he had for this programme, he said something between nothing and a million pounds, which does not really quantify it. But there are different horses for different courses.

Session produced by Jerome Kuehl

Face the Symposium: Bob Phillis

Bob Phillis
Deputy Director-General, BBC

interviewed by
Gillian Reynolds
Journalist and broadcaster

GILLIAN Reynolds: I want to ask everyone in the room who left school at fifteen to put their hand up. You get my point. You are a select band. There are three of you, Bob. Bob Phillis left school at fifteen and went back to Nottingham University a bit later on in his life, and took quite a distinguished degree, Bob?

Bob Phillis: I had a good time at university, yes.

Gillian Reynolds: And took a first. And then you worked in various sections of the print industry for quite a while. When did you go into television?

Bob Phillis: I suppose initially it was an indirect route. I did an apprenticeship in the printing industry before I went up to university, and after graduation I trained in regional newspapers. And by a sort of odd route, stopping as an academic along the way for a while, I ended up being asked to run the publications side of ITV and Independent Television Publications. So, it was an indirect route, really, but at that time Independent Television Publications was owned by the ITV companies. I suppose everyone needs a bit of luck along the way somewhere or other. And in 1981, when the IBA decided not to renew the ATV franchise in the Midlands, they could not find anyone daft enough to take on the job of the new, as then yet unnamed, company. And I think they trailed it around most of the industry, and those that knew would not, and in desperation they came to me. So they asked me to go into Central in the end of 1981, I suppose it was.

Gillian Reynolds: Now a year ago, on the same day as Producer Choice came to the BBC, 1 April 1993, you came to the BBC. Why did you join?

Bob Phillis: It is a very good question. I think a variety of reasons. Having worked in communications, having worked in broadcasting and media, I think that whilst I was always hugely proud of ITV and Channel 4, and indeed ITN, it seemed to me that the BBC was a very important part of Britain's broadcasting ecology, both radio and television and internationally. I have always admired and respected the BBC for the quality and range of its work, and the talent of the people that it employs. I think that the opportunity to join the BBC in a senior position, to help in some way to shape its future, seemed to me to be both a challenge and an opportunity, and also perhaps also a responsibility that one could not say no to. And I say that having been very proud to have worked as part of ITV. And I was somewhat disturbed, no not just somewhat disturbed, outraged and deeply disturbed by what Mrs Thatcher's government did to ITV through the Broadcasting Act 1990, and the absurd notion of auctioning licences, and the impact that one feared that might have seen disturbing indications of what might happen. I hope very much indeed that my friends and colleagues in ITV and in Channel 4 are going to be able to put Humpty Dumpty back together again. I think that the BBC is under a similar microscope right now, and let us hope that this government might take a rather more balanced view of the future role of the BBC than might otherwise have been the case. It is at a rather critical phase right now.

Gillian Reynolds: Let's not forget had it not been for the almost accidental extension of the last charter to a fifteen year as opposed to a ten year period, negotiated by Ian Trethowan, the BBC's charter would have come up at exactly the same time as the revolution which hit ITV. So you have had a bit of a breathing space.

Bob Phillis: That is right.

Gillian Reynolds: People here have been listening to conversations and convinced opinion about the future for television in this country. How do you see the future of the BBC once you are through charter renewal? Do you see the BBC as holding on to the cornerstone status that even the appalling 1990 Broadcasting Act appeared to give it?

Bob Phillis: Yes, absolutely. I think that while I am not in any way complacent and the BBC certainly cannot afford to be arrogant in terms of its future, it *is* the cornerstone of British broadcasting simply in terms of the scale and the size of its activities and the funding which makes that possible. I guess that most of you know here that in addition to the two television channels, there are five national radio channels, there are thirty-nine local radio channels and a very strong regional structure to support everything we do. And although it is not paid for by the licence fee, the World Service in terms of radio and television is an equally important part of the BBC linked into core domestic activities.

I think that, of course, it is a privileged position as a public service broadcaster to have secure funding, one hopes, into the future which will allow us to provide that range of services, that range of programming for all people, all ages, all tastes, all interests, across the board, and because we are not directly subjected to commercial pressures of advertising revenue, not only will we be committed to making that full range of programming in radio and in television but also to be able to schedule them, irrespective of ratings wars, which very obviously our commercial friends and competitors have to take account of. And I certainly intend putting whatever weight I can to ensure that the BBC maintains that excellence across the range of programming.

Gillian Reynolds: How mild and distinguished a creature you make the BBC sound! No-one would have thought this week when the extra episode of *EastEnders* came in there that there was any competitive bone in its body at all.

Bob Phillis: Of course we are competitive and I think the balance we have to play is an interesting one. I think one of the interesting accidents of broadcasting history in Britain was the separation of funding from the BBC and the commercial sector. They were secure sources of funding and we competed for ratings, but for different purposes. The ITV companies and now Channel Four compete for ratings because it directly influences their revenues. We compete for ratings but not across the board and unchallenged in every way.

Why are we interested in ratings at all? Well, I think unless we can demonstrate that we are serving all of the licence fee payers, all interests, all tastes, all ages, all types of programming and unless we are able to sustain an acceptable level in terms of ratings, then the fundamental question of the legitimacy of the universal licence fee as a source of funding would be challenged. So I think that we cannot say, and I am not saying, ratings do not matter. I am not saying that we must not strive to provide a range of programming across the board and all types of programming but what I am saying is what we are able to do is to keep the news at nine o'clock rather than the suggestion that it gets shunted to six thirty in the evening for a prime time news programme.We are actually able to maintain a documentary tradition of programme making. We are actually able to maintain our educational programmes and our current affairs programming and we will schedule it in peak time even if it means that for that slot and for that time and for that day we are not delivering the maximum audience compared with our competitors.

Gillian Reynolds: You can do this, though, because you are rich. I mean how much money does the BBC get annually in licence fee income?

Bob Phillis: It is approximately £1.5 billion gross. You have to net off the costs of collection and evasion and, I suppose, currently it is running at about £1.3 billion in total in terms of the current income level. But, as I say, for that sum of money I have just listed the services we provide, we are of course, programme makers and programme producers, we are not just simply programme publishers. As I have said we are committed to making across the range. We are committed to innovation and experimentation and risk taking. And I think that if you do not experiment, if you do not innovate, if you do not create a climate where programme makers have the opportunity to experiment, to try things new and to accept failure because if you are going to take risk, if you are going to innovate, you are not going to get everything right. Unless you can create that climate in terms of programme production you will not get new and innovative programming. I do not criticise the important part that cable and satellite and the publisher-contractors are going to play, but I think there is a difference between buying or acquiring other people's programming and scheduling it as opposed to making and originating and creating new programming and new programming ideas across the board. And I think that is something on which I have expressed a worry for my friends in ITV, and I am sure that when you meet next year and the year after it will be interesting to see how strong the documentary programme tradition is, how strong the current affairs programme making tradition is.

Gillian Reynolds: But your friends in ITV worry about you. They say, look there is Bob. They know you as a formidable man of energy. They know you have considerable entrepreneurial skills but, even so, you have got an unprecedented workload. You are Deputy Director-General and that involves you in quite a lot of public appearances and speaking and policy making. You are also Managing Director of World Services, you are Chairman of World Service Television and Chairman of BBC Enterprises. Now even by your own standards, that is a hell of a lot of work. So how do you divide your time up? Who do you belong to? Because there are those in Bush House who wish you would stop by, if only for a cup of tea.

Bob Phillis: I am sure it has happened to all of you in the room, it will happen to you in your own careers. I think that if you choose to take a position of responsibility, I do not believe you take it, and I certainly did not take it at a critical time in the BBC's life, expecting that I would be working between half past nine and half past five. I do not work from half past nine to half past five. I knew that if I was to play my part in trying to help the BBC through a difficult patch I would have to work long and hard. I have been fortunate in being granted one interesting and useful gift and that is I do not need a lot of sleep. So I can work very hard. Actually I spend, I would guess, as much time in Bush House as my predecessor spent in Bush House. Sometimes it is very, very early and sometimes it is very late. But I think that I am just over a year into the job, and there is an awful lot that I have had to do in learning, in understanding, in asking, in thinking, in trying to shape some of the things that we need to do for the future. And whilst the list that you have identified sounds formidable and, yes, I think I am working harder now than probably I have done at any time in the past, it is a necessary input if we are trying to give some sort of shape to the future of the BBC. And if I have a worry about the BBC, if I have a worry about the issues that this Government and this Cabinet are having to consider right now, it is being able to see a BBC ten or fifteen years out from now when the things you have been talking about, the media explosion and the superhighways and the convergence, are thrust upon us, that there is a BBC which is still publicly funded and which is still making the contribution to British programme making and British broadcasting in the way that it does now.

Now I think that it can only do that if one accepts that the BBC has to have a legitimate role in making its programme assets work as hard as possibly as they can for the future. What do I mean by that? Of course we are lucky to be publicly funded with the licence fee but it is the skills and abilities of the people who work in the BBC, and I do not just mean the producers and the writers and the performers, I mean the craftsmen and the technicians and everybody who goes together to produce that programming. It is those skills which create an asset. And the asset is in the intellectual property. It is in programme rights. And I am utterly convinced, and frankly if I lose this argument then I would regard myself as having failed in my job, I believe that the BBC has a responsibility to make those programme assets work as hard as they possibly can in generating additional income flows into the BBC in order to finance our programme making activity and to offset the licence fee.

Let me put that into perspective. Our current licence fee income is about £1.3 billion net. In addition to that there are commercial activities involved in programme sales and publications and videos and interactive CD-ROM and so on across the board. That generates about three hundred million pounds' worth of turnover to the BBC and I guess we put sixty million pounds of that as a contribution back into programme making and into the BBC's activities. Now £60m is a lot of money, but it is less than five per cent of our total income. The sort of things you have been talking about I think are only going to be driven at the end of the day if there is programme material of a range and of a quality that the viewers, the listeners, the consumers at the end of the day actually want to use, and maybe we will get on to superhighways and all that stuff and maybe we will not. But I think that the BBC, in planning its way into the next century ten and fifteen years out, has to set itself fairly aggressive targets, because if there is going to be pressure on total audience size, if there is going to be fragmentation of audiences, if there is going to be the competition and the choice that you have all been talking about, then government, whoever the policymakers of government are at the time, whoever the policymakers in the BBC are at the time, are going to be faced with a very different world.

All of the changes, all of the new technologies, all of the new opportunities give us the opportunity in the BBC to make the programmes that we make for British audiences under our licence fee work harder, by developing themed channels of programming, for example, both internationally and, perhaps, at home; by developing the interactive opportunities and the educational opportunities that the new technology will allow; and by supporting television and radio programmes more effectively with books and tapes and videos and audios and CD material. And I have said publicly elsewhere that I think that if we have a charter period for ten years hopefully that additional income ten years at the end of the next charter, in 2005 or whatever, ought to be about £200 million worth of income into the BBC. It might be fifteen per cent. It might be more, it might be twenty per cent of our total income.

I make those figures because however hard I and my colleagues work in trying to generate those additional income flows (they will be substantial in terms of real money in making programmes for within the BBC or giving the government of the day, I suppose, opportunities to address the question of a universal licence fee) they will never replace the fundamental importance of a public service broadcaster, financed by universal licence fee across the board. But as programme makers and broadcasters, we cannot expect a universal licence fee as of right, we can only expect a universal licence fee if, in fact, we are providing the range of services, radio and television, and the range of programmes across the board, that has something there of interest and appeal and stimulation to every household that is asked to pay the licence fee.

Gillian Reynolds: Now let me see if I have understood this so far. You are saying that the BBC's stock , the programmes that people make, should be put to more than their present use by being used again in themed channels and in programme sales abroad. Is that right?

Bob Phillis: In part. It is not as simple as that and I am not saying that the BBC has not done this well in the past. What I am saying is that the technology and the markets create a situation which is in my view not going to be driven by the computer companies and by the telecommunications companies. It is going to be driven by people who make programmes, because whatever the technology is going to be in getting those pictures or those programmes to our homes, whether it is on the television set, whether it is interactive or whatever, although the technologists I am sure can make this happen, at the end of the day it has got to be financed. How is it going to be financed? It is going to be financed, presumably, because we, viewers, listeners, consumers, are going to want to pay out money in terms of subscription or in terms of the ad revenue, the finances or whatever, to view them. And people are only going to view them if there is something there, or use them if you want that, if there is something there that people think is worthwhile, think is valuable, is something worth paying for in some way.

Gillian Reynolds: So you are extending the opportunity the licence fee payer has to enjoy the programmes to other audiences globally?

Bob Phillis: Not simply globally, there is an expansion and extension within the UK but, globally, yes. Look, if you take the sort of things that we hear, the Rupert Murdochs and the Ted Turners and the Atlantic Bells and the TCIs saying about multi-channel systems. Where are they going to get the programming from? Where are they going to get it from? Who is going to make it for them? The BBC makes eleven and a half thousand hours of original television programming each and every year. We have a library built up over our lifetime of over 250,000 different programmes. I am certainly not being critical of the BBC of the past; the opportunities were not there. But what I am saying is that if there are going to be education channels or documentary channels or sports channels or entertainment channels or specialist theme channels or parts of channels, the programmes have got to come from somewhere. It is a responsibility of the BBC responding to that opportunity, not making programmes for mid-Atlantic, not making programmes for mid-Pacific, but using the programmes that have been made for British audiences and re-presenting them in whatever way the technology allows us to do it in a way that earns money back into the BBC which can be used for additional programme making or to offset the licence fee if the government wants to do that.

Why do I make so much of it? I will tell you why. Because, as you all well know, the note of the 1980s was privatisation, privatise everything. You still see the residual of that in some of the things that are supposed to be privatised right now. So we have gone through water, we have gone through gas, and now are looking at the railways. And, of course, I would not dream of identifying which party or which wing, but there is an element in Westminster that is saying, 'Well, why do we not privatise the BBC? Why don't we chop this bit off or that bit off?' And there are some that would say, 'The BBC should remain chaste. The BBC should remain a pure and simple public service broadcaster who uses the licence fee to make programmes and you should not be playing in these things which are "commercial." Other people can do it better.' What that means is: give the BBC's programmes away to other people who will exploit them for somebody else's profit. I am simply saying that those assets have been created by the licence fee, and providing the BBC can demonstrate that it is using them to generate more income back into the BBC, that is our responsibility. Because, and I hope and believe it will not happen, but if that commercial element was taken out of the BBC, then the BBC would be condemned to wither on the vine over time, because as audiences fragment, as choice widens, as pressure comes as to whether £83 is the right level or not, you would be reducing the income base of the BBC. And if you reduce the income base of the BBC in real terms we would find it more and more difficult to sustain the range of services and the output that we currently produce. And I suppose some might say that was a good thing, but I do not believe that it is so. You could look to the year 2010 or the year 2020 and maybe there is not a BBC any more. Maybe the market will provide what everybody needs and wants to view. I suspect if that is the case, the market will not produce quite the same range, or quite the same depth, or quite the same quality of programming that British broadcasters — not just the BBC — British broadcasters, ITV, Channel Four and the independent sector have strived so hard to produce. But, you know, I have not got a crystal ball, I just happen to believe that the BBC, for all its faults, is worth preserving and worth trying to sustain as a public service broadcaster.

Gillian Reynolds: Even if you have not got a crystal ball, I know you are a fiend for checking the sources for various bits of information. What does the BBC have to offer as a scheduled service that a viewing and a listening public will need in the age of proliferation of sources when you have got loads and loads of other broadcasting services from which you can pick and choose and pay for as you like? What will the BBC still have to offer that is unique?

Bob Phillis: The world of the next century, in television terms, is going to offer more choice. There are going to be more channels. There are going to be more opportunities to listen and to view. It will be interesting to see what proportion of that choice are programmes originated by the cable provider or the satellite provider or whatever, and how much of them are acquired programmes that somebody else has made and are bought for the second or third showing.

What will be distinctive about the BBC? Firstly, if we are successful in getting our charter renewed in the way I hope we will, we will be producing a range of programmes across the board in the way that I have tried to describe. And that is our test; unless we are providing programmes which will be of interest or entertain or value to you all and to the people that pay the licence fee, we will have failed. I think that you will find the BBC making certain types of programme which will not be made elsewhere in the same volume and range.

Gillian Reynolds: Like what?

Bob Phillis: Like documentaries, like current affairs, like detailed analyses, like natural history, like education, like challenging drama, like experimental comedy, like risk-taking entertainment or situation comedy, where programme makers are taking a risk …

Gillian Reynolds: So you will not need to steal them all from Channel Four in the future?

Bob Phillis: Oh, we are always looking for talent, Gillian. And there is a lot of talent in Channel Four. So, the BBC will offer that. It will offer a schedule which I hope and believe tries to maintain standards, and when I say standards there is no sort of aloof or esoteric concept of standards. I mean standards in terms of the quality of what we do, the quality of our writing, our production, our performance, our craft, our technical standards. I mean standards in the expectations that we have of ourselves, of accuracy and independence and objectivity. I believe the BBC will not simply be pandering to what will put the most bums on seats in prime time, because hopefully we will not be advertiser-funded at that time, because that will be the inevitable impact of advertiser funding. I think it will do all those things. I hope we will set standards in a different way. I think a scheduled service still is going to be a core part of the broadcasting ecology. If one draws the comparison with the States, in 1985 the networks had something over seventy to seventy-eight percent of prime-time audiences, and there were an average of twenty odd cable channels available with a coverage of sixty-three per cent of households. We have had the explosion in the States, and what has happened? Well, you have far greater coverage in terms of cable availability, way above sixty per cent. You have households with an average of forty channels available, and the three networks still account for sixty per cent of prime-time viewing. And you add Fox to that and it still accounts for seventy per cent of total viewing in prime-time. Why? I think it is because the American networks, and here I compare BBC, ITV and Channel Four, have skilled and able schedulers, who can take people through that mixture of entertainment, of information, of education, and of course recognising people will zap in and zap out, and play with channel buttons to find things they want, that scheduling skill, and that taking people through into new ideas and new territories, new experiences, whether it is entertainment or comedy, or whether it is natural history, or whatever it might be. I think the BBC will be doing that. Let me just turn to that tiny element of sex, violence, language, all the stuff which exercises Michael Howard, David Alton and so on. I think that things like the watershed — much maligned, much criticised, and the appalling suggestion that it should be moved from nine o'clock to ten o'clock which I fundamentally am opposed to for a variety of reasons — places a responsibility on a broadcaster with a mixed schedule to recognise those expectations. I mean, for whatever is being said by some of the critics of the broadcast channels, it is a fact that over ninety per cent of people recognise the existence of the nine o'clock watershed.

Gillian Reynolds: How much?

Bob Phillis: Ninety-three per cent. Ninety-three per cent of samples, either taken by the ITC or the BBC or independent television.

Gillian Reynolds: What is the source of this information?

Bob Phillis: I can quote you the BBC's internal research, the ITC's own research, I suspect even the Broadcasting Standards Council has done something along the way. I mean, there are a whole range of bodies that measure these figures. But it is important because I think one can make great leaps of the imagination. I suspect that there are a lot of us in the room that have some sympathy in terms of the availability of some of the material on the shelves to kids that are not supervised in any way in terms of what they choose to view. And you can understand where that pressure has come from. But, as a broadcaster, you have a different set of responsibilities. And that is why I refer to the watershed. I mean, to make that leap of imagination from saying that video nasties are corrupting the population to saying that the watershed on broadcast television must be shoved out to ten o'clock is an absurdity, because the concept of the watershed is understood by all the broadcast channels in the UK. I think quite properly we recognise the need to identify when the nature of viewing and listening opportunities change. We cannot ever replace, and I am not suggesting that we do replace, parental responsibility for the exercise of choice, but we can damn well signpost when there is a change in programming content so that if there is that parental supervision then they know very well that there may be language or violence or sex which some people might find offensive. But it does get a bit out of context, you know. There is a bit of research that I did not believe until I questioned and pushed and asked whether it was really true. It said that more than seventy per cent of households in Britain do not have kids living at home. It is surprising, isn't it? I mean, you think that cannot be true. I am talking about standards and quality and watersheds and those sort of things. You ask me what the BBC is going to be offering in ten or fifteen years time. Some of those things. If we are successful in getting our charter renewed.

Gillian Reynolds: I want to broaden the conversation and bring in as many people as want to speak in the time we have left.

Hilary Bentley (Videotron): I would like you to comment on the BBC's relationship with its viewers and its listeners and how that might change given that in the future the BBC will perhaps be one of a myriad of programme providers. And, today also, I am thinking also of the fact that that close relationship with the listener might have been lost or fudged, I think particularly of Radio Four and lots of criticism about things that have been done to Radio Four.

Bob Phillis: Yes. That is a very interesting question, and I, as Gillian explained, have only been with the BBC for a little over a year. People have said that in the past the BBC has been arrogant in believing that it knows what is best for its viewers and listeners. I do not know whether that is true because I was not part of it. I just make the observation that if it was arrogant, then it did not actually do badly in the sort of programmes that it was able to stimulate and generate over many years. And that is a tradition that has got to be preserved. So, people tell me that the BBC might have been arrogant in the past, I cannot comment. I am not a research freak, I am not a systems freak. But I do believe that any broadcaster, anyone providing a service, has to get a lot closer to its audiences, whether they are radio audiences, or television audiences, in understanding the types of programming people would like to listen to or would like to see; what is appreciated and what is not appreciated. And I think that the BBC is, consciously, devoting more and more to research and understanding and feedback in terms of what its listeners and viewers feel about our programme services. Now, of course we do not get it right all of the time. So there is a commitment in the BBC, I think, to recognise that it is not 'We know what is best for you. This is what you are going to get,' but an attempt to try to understand changing tastes and interests, and how well we are serving those audiences. There will always be traditionalists in many fields, so that if you change someone's favourite programme, or if you experiment and take a risk, or if you change the established order, there will always be people who will react to that and oppose it. I am not categorising all of the BBC's critics in that category, of course I am not. It would be absurd to do so. I do not know whether you are thinking of radio or television, but if you take some of the radio questions, it was extraordinary how the concept of Radio Five was criticised in advance by so many people without any idea of what was going to be produced. And I am not saying that Radio Five has necessarily got every aspect of its service right, you know, three or four weeks in, because it is an evolving process that one has to learn about and one has to respond to.

There is a story that I love about the BBC's Radio Four listeners, who protested outside Broadcasting House last year, and they were very much Radio Four listeners, they were very smartly dressed men and women, and some young folks as well. They were parading outside Broadcasting House with placards, and someone set up a chant, and it went something like this: 'What do we want? Radio Four. Where do we want it? Long wave. What do we say? Please.'

Rod Allen (HarperCollins): Well, I have a worry, and I would like you to reassure me about it. It is to do with the intellectual property rights that you were talking about earlier. You do not own most of the rights that you need for the cross-media exploitation and the re-purposing of a lot of the properties that are in the BBC video vaults. For example, we have just licensed a literary property to you, and we have reserved the multi-media rights; you have only the right to transmit it. The worry that that gives me is as follows: the prospect of re-purposing and re-exploiting the properties that you have created is a very attractive one, and you will say to us next time you want another piece from us, 'License us those rights.' And we will say to you, 'Certainly. Give us some more money.' And you will. And the outcome of that is that you find yourself devoting more and more of your front-end investment in preparing for the back-end exploitation, and usually that means that the profit is lower on such a thing. And the thick end of that wedge is right up at the very end where you find yourself purposing the *original* programme for cross-media, multi-media, international exploitation. And the danger is that you defeat your own purposes. The purpose of creating additional income streams in order to re-invest in programming seems to me to be admirable and absolutely right. The commercial seductiveness of doing it successfully has its dangers.

Bob Phillis: You have raised a lot of points, Rod. There are two that I would like to pick up on. First of all, I make no apologies for the fact that people of skill and ability, and organisations which create an intellectual property, have a right to it. But it seems to me that there is a fundamental relationship between who owns those rights, and how things are funded. And I would defend the BBC's rights, say, in something that we would wholly fund, and where the idea is our generation and something that our people have created, that we would be foolish not to try to exploit those rights, to develop those rights in whatever way we can. Equally, Rod, where the ideas and the concepts and the element is brought to us by folks outside, or independents, or publishers, or whatever it is, then there is a proper negotiation, it seems to me, as to how those rights are split, what they are worth and who has the right to exploit them.

I think there have been problems in terms of clout where ITV, Channel Four and the much disadvantaged independents have gone into co-production or co-funding arrangements. The big American boys would say, 'Fine. We want all rights in perpetuity, in these defined territories.' What a rip off! If you give, in the context of what you have been talking about for two days, all rights in perpetuity, and you do not quite know how interactive is going to develop, or what other technologies are around the corner, I think that is irresponsible. And I have no difficulty in saying to an American that comes to the door with the big fat wallet saying, 'Right, I will put the money in, but by the way, I want all rights, unrestricted, in perpetuity, forever, in whatever that market place is.' To that, I say, 'Go away.' Because if we create the programmes, we do not know what these opportunities of interactivity or CD-ROM or the database exploitation is going to be, then that is something which not only the BBC, I would argue as strongly for the ITV companies and Channel Four, and the independents if they had the financial muscle to be able to deliver that issue. So, there is a relationship between rights on one hand and finances on the other. And that seems to me to be a commercial relationship one gets in to.

Gillian Reynolds: Good idea for a participative exercise next year. 'Watch Your Rights'.

Bob Phillis: But I do not want to be misunderstood, meaning I do not want to leave you with the wrong impression. The BBC, for as long as it remains publicly funded, has a prime and sole purpose, and that is to serve its licence fee and its British audiences by radio or by television. And we must make programming that the British audience, who fund us through licence fee, want to see or want to listen to. We must never, Rod, make that fatal mistake that you have seen in so many appalling so-called international co-productions which try to cast its German, its Dutchmen, its Italian, its Australian, or its American.

Gillian Reynolds: Nobody mentioned *Eldorado*.

Bob Phillis: No, no, no, no. Well, we did not cast so many of those. And, of course, we stopped doing it. I think what I am trying to say is, I am not in anything that I have said suggesting that the BBC has to make for the mid-Atlantic or mid-Pacific or whatever. It must make its radio and its television programmes to serve the people that fund it, and that is the licence fee payer. If we can then exploit that and develop that outside, that is fine. But we must not fall down the route that you have correctly identified as a possible route.

Granville Williams (Campaign for Press and Broadcasting Freedom): In the *Evening Standard* there was a speculative story about the two BBC satellite channels. First of all, do you confirm that that is part of the planning? Also, could you expand a bit on the thinking behind that? That is a very quick question. Secondly, just on the point you were making about your priority being serving the British public, and the other commercial criteria about the World Services and so on, I am reminded of the Saddler enquiry into cross-media promotion, and the way that what was actually meant to be a look at the use by Sky and News International to promote their services turned into an enquiry into the BBC's magazines. On an international scale, I wondered if you could say anything about what happened with Star TV, the Murdoch Asian TV satellite, and the way that your service was taken off? It seemed to go very quietly.

Bob Phillis: There are three points. First of all, the *Evening Standard*, as you say, ran a headline which said the BBC had asked for two new channels. This is a first class example in which a newspaper was able to run a story about a technology which does not yet exist and about a decision which has not yet been taken and gave us a press headline which is a total distortion of anything that the BBC is trying to do. The simple and short answer to how that story found banner headlines on the *Evening Standard* is simply this. As you know one of the technological opportunities that exists for broadcasters everywhere is the move from analogue technology to digital technology. There is a question which this government and the DTI are properly asking: 'What is the time horizon for digital television technology?' Because it creates the opportunity for more channels. Should it be terrestrial or should it be satellite or should it be both? The issue is one that relates to the concept of the new Channel Five because if the DTI decides to introduce digital terrestrial technology in the UK rather than simply wait for satellite, they have one opportunity to do it and that means using the spectrum frequencies, bands thirty-five and thirty-seven, which are provisionally allocated for the introduction of Channel Five. The genesis of the story was one of our technical people giving a technological and engineering appraisal of if Channel Five were not to occupy those spectrums then there is an opportunity for a terrestrial digital television and if that were to happen in place of Channel Five there could be up to sixteen new channels made available — not for the BBC — for allocation in whatever way was possible and, obviously, if there were ever to be sixteen new channels made available the BBC would hope that it would have sufficiently good ideas that it might be able to use a number of them. But that is the genesis of the story. It is an engineer's assessment of what might happen; it will be for the DTI to decide whether they go with Channel Five on those frequencies or whether they want to reserve them for terrestrial. That is the first point.

The second point is about the question of the Saddler enquiry and fairness and so on. Well, our critics and there are many of them and particularly those in the commercial field who would like to get their hands on BBC's property, programme rights, who will say, 'This is outrageous. You cannot have a publicly funded organisation abusing its position to give it an advantage which other people do not have, with cross promotion on the airways, on television, and on radio. We published this week a document called *The BBC's Fair Trading Guidelines* and it is saying, 'Look, because we are publicly funded we are going to set a number of very strict standards of behaviour within the BBC which any commercial activity that is trading has to abide by and we will be fair, we will be above board, we will be transparent, we will be accountable. There will be no misuse of licence fee funding. There will be no misuse of grant-in-aid funding in terms of the World Service.' And, in fact, we are setting higher standards than some of our commercial colleagues.

I must admit I do, personally, bridle a little bit when I get preached at about level playing fields and the need for everybody to act in a fair and proper and gentlemanly way. Do you really think that all those commercial organisations, I am not only talking about the ITV companies, I am talking about all those commercial organisations which would actually like to take advantage of the BBC's intellectual property are going to play on a level playing field and fair and above board and do things in a proper way? Of course they are not. They are going to try and make profit out of that and they are going to try to serve their shareholders out of that. But the BBC will play fair. We have published our guidelines and they will be strictly imposed. So those who try to criticise us, pre-Saddler, post-Saddler and currently I think will find it very difficult to pick up the BBC on that score.

Your final point was about World Service Television, to which Mrs Thatcher's government chose not to allocate any public funding of any sort but said that if we wanted to do it we had better go and find some partners to work with. And in 1991 when that task was set the BBC entered into an agreement with Star Television, which was then owned by Hutchvision in Hong Kong, and because neither they nor we knew whether the thing was going to have any chance of success, we signed a ten year agreement but with a chance for either party to get out after three years. And that was part of the contract. Either party could get out after three years. What we did not foresee was the ownership of that company was going to change and an Australian, or do I mean an American?, but an international media player bought Star TV. One had hopes last September when Rupert Murdoch proclaimed that one of the things the new technologies would do would bring free and unfettered information worldwide and, of course, no totalitarian regime would be free from access to this news. It was a high ideal and I applaud him for that high ideal. Unfortunately the commercial realities of Star TV in Asia meant that he had other considerations that he wished to recognise. I am not suggesting that he acted improperly in any way, but he had the right to give us notice for the totality of World Service Television in China and Korea and Taiwan and the Indian sub-continent and right the way across the Gulf. Against that background, I regret very much World Service television not being available in China, I regret it very much indeed. Fortunately our radio services are still broadcasting to China. We entered into a negotiation within which the BBC had no option but to negotiate faced with the opportunity of no World Service Television anywhere in Asia at the end of the year. What we actually did, with great reluctance, was agree to come off the northern beam to China early but to protect our broadcasting across the southern beam which goes across as I say from Hong Kong all across the Indian sub-continent and right the way to the Gulf, until 1996. There is a lesson to be learned there. One of the things that I am suggesting in our discussions with government is that whilst no British broadcaster will own the satellites in the way that the powerful organisations like News Corporation and others might, it is essential that if the BBC is going to retain editorial and managerial control over its programme content, as it always will, it ought to also be allowed and permitted to be in a situation where together with other partners, it can actually have some access to the means of delivery and not available to being ejected in the way that we were off the northern beam.

Liz Ashton-Hill (College of St Mark and St John, Plymouth): It is a bit of a cheeky question to you, Bob, because I used to work for the BBC in this particular area. You mentioned earlier that that BBC wants to get involved in risk taking activities to a certain extent, and the BBC got involved with terrestrial subscription analogue broadcasting with BBC Select. Can you give me an assessment of that experiment and whether it has, in fact, a future life or whether it can be seen as rather an expensive experiment?

Bob Phillis: Thanks for the question, Liz, and I think it provides an opportunity to clarify one important thing. When I said the BBC should be involved in risk-taking, I meant risk-taking in programme making. I meant the ability to innovate and to experiment and the risk of failing in a new programming idea that does not work. That is the risk-taking I was talking about. I believe that the BBC should not take risks with licence payers' money in getting involved in commercial risks it should not be involved in. And we have in that context a strategy before government which would permit the BBC to be involved in commercial risk-taking activities but where the BBC's leverage, where the BBC's contributions are its programming, its programme assets, its programme archives and the skills it has as programme makers and broadcasters. That is a massive asset to bring to the table, but if people want to partner with us they have got to put money up front on the table so that we do not take financial risks with licence payers' money.

You asked a specific question about BBC Select which is the night-time subscription service. And I would say two things. The BBC has many skills historically; they are programme making skills, they are broadcasting skills, they are production skills, they are craft skills. The one thing that the BBC has not had historically, and has not needed to have historically, was any particularly well developed commercial skills or expertise. Very often one can point to examples where the BBC has gone into an activity for the wrong reason. If I am candid, and it is a personal view, I suspect that the driving force behind the BBC getting into BBC Select and the subscription services was as much motivated by a desire to block off the night time down time hours from being passed to other broadcasters. It seems extraordinary now, but there was a suggestion back in the Thatcher years that the down time on BBC 1 and BBC 2 should be auctioned off or given to some other broadcaster to exploit. And I am not saying it was wrong, but I think that what might have motivated my predecessors in the BBC was saying, 'For Christ's sake, if Thatcher or someone has got the bright idea of auctioning it off we had better put something there in order to maintain it as the BBC.' And that is the wrong motive. It might have been the right short term political motive in terms of a perceived threat but, fundamentally, the proposition was unsound. And I know you worked in that area, Liz, and I know it has been a very dedicated bunch of people, with great skill and enthusiasm working in there. But, fundamentally, it was only ever, in my view, going to lose money. And it did.

Roger Wilson (Learning Television): Bob, one thing you have not talked about at the moment is Producer Choice and the success that you see of it. I worked for the BBC for sixteen years; I have a lot of friends in the BBC and I pick up a strong sense of very low morale from people. That may be temporary, that may not. But would you like to reflect on that?

Brian Kelly (Open Campus Television): My question is really about the licence fee. Why should £1.3 billion of a licence fee be used just by the BBC? Is it not possible that a fund could be set up from the licence fee so that other people outside the BBC who provide public service broadcasting get some of it?

Mike Davis (University of Manchester): You did mention earlier on in your talk that that BBC was willing to accept failure, and I am just wondering at what point it will accept failure in relation to the audio nasties of *Anderson Country*.

Bob Phillis: Let us take the morale first. I do not know of any organisation anywhere in Britain that could have gone through the agony of losing twenty per cent of its staff, five thousand people, and not have low morale. And in a circumstance where people are still worried about losing their jobs, it is the most insidious and undermining situation that I am aware of. I am not excusing any of the things where, clearly, we might not have got it right. But people say there is low morale in the BBC, and I agree there is low morale in the BBC and that is not going to go away until the surplus capacity which exists within the BBC has been taken out.

Gillian Reynolds: What does that mean, more job losses?

Bob Phillis: No. That surplus capacity is not a criticism of any of my predecessors. It was a government that said that twenty-five per cent of all our output would have to be made by the independent sector. They said that to ITV and they have said it to us. And, actually, I think there has been huge benefits in stimulating the independent production sector. But just like the ITV companies, we had to adjust. Gillian says, 'Will there be more job losses?' Yes, there will be more job losses this year. I hope very much that by the end of this year the major structural reorganisation in terms of the numbers employed will have come to an end. But let me not kid this audience. I defy anyone in broadcasting, whether they work for the BBC or ITV or Channel Four or cable and satellite or the independent production sector, that is going to be working in the world you have been talking about of change in technology, in markets and whatever, is not constantly going to say, 'Can we continue to work in this way?' And I think every broadcaster, every programme maker in Britain and worldwide has got to say, 'What are the opportunities of this technology? What are the requirements in terms of audiences?' And there will be a constant change in terms of the way we work. The notion of going into a job in broadcasting and believing that the job that you take up when you are eighteen years old or twenty-two years old is going to be the same job in the same way when you retire is, you know better than I do, absolute and complete nonsense.

So the morale question, I think, will begin to change when we reach this equilibrium. At the moment people have suffered a lot of pain and a lot of agony in the BBC and I do not deny that. If, at the end of the day, and that will be the acid test, we get the charter renewed and the BBC remains intact and the BBC is properly funded, then I believe it would have been worth it, despite the pain. If we fail in that, and if they want to break the BBC up or if they want to put advertising on the BBC, then it would have been a pointless sacrifice.

Now to Producer Choice. I do not know why the BBC gives names and labels to all of these things. I am not an accountant. I do understand numbers. I do not know how to manage anything at all unless I have the information. And what the BBC has not traditionally been good at is financial information and knowing how it spends its money. Forget the label Producer Choice and ask whether any organisation which is publicly funded should know where it is spending its money and how much programmes cost. I am not an accountant but I do not apologise for that. I tell you one thing that as a result of Producer Choice in this last year, for all its faults, and it has had many faults in presentation, faults in detail, faults in application, for all its faults it is going to release massive investment back into programmes this coming year and the year after that. And I do not mean five or six million, I do not mean ten or twenty million, I mean many, many millions of pounds which by addressing the painful questions of Producer Choice has released money that we will spend on new programme making.

The notion of a public service broadcasting fund was one of Melvyn Bragg's brighter ideas. I think that if you look at the totality of a broadcasting organisation, the corollary of what you would be saying is if the licence fee went into a general pot, and it was allocated to worthy public service programming, who is going to find the rest of what the BBC does? Now some would say, 'Well, that is easy, you put advertising on the BBC.' Put advertising on the BBC and I think the schedules and the range of programmes that we make and the way it would affect the schedule, because of the need to generate advertising revenue, would actually fundamentally break the concept of public service broadcasting.

Gillian Reynolds: Aren't you, in effect, doing what he is asking by investing in independent production in the public service segment? No?

Naomi Sargent (VLV): What it would mean is that Melvyn Bragg would get money from that fund for *The South Bank Show* and ITV would not have to pay for that type of programme. That is what..

Bob Phillis: Or put it another way, Naomi, which maybe the new ITV might not *want* to pay for. The concept of a publicly funded broadcaster like ourselves is we have to use that money to make programmes across the board. We can only make programmes like *Middlemarch*, on the one hand, or some of our comedy or some of our education on the other, because we have to spread that money across a range of programming. If you carve out a category of programming in the way that you have suggested, money that we were, if you like, to take out of our funding, into cable into satellite or to Melvyn or to fund those sort of programmes that the commercial sector does not want to make, it will only reduce the funding available to the BBC to produce the range that we currently wish to do. Now, of course, it could be argued, and it was argued by some, that the BBC should not worry about situation comedy or light entertainment or popular drama; it should just concentrate on a narrower range of programming. But if you accept that concept, then I think you end up looking something like American television looks like where you have mass entertainment on the three network channels and you have a public service broadcasting organisation that survives by broadcasting on air and saying, 'Will you put a penny in the bowl, please?' I missed a question..

Gillian Reynolds: At what point do you admit failure and take a programme which has failed in audience terms, or appears to be failing in listener reaction, off the air?

Bob Phillis: I believe, whether I was running Central or ITN or Zenith Productions or the BBC, that anyone within an organisation has a responsibility to support its programme makers in everything that they are trying to do. And the one thing that I would not do — I am not avoiding the question, whatever programme you identify— is publicly criticise my programme makers in things that might not be working out in the way that we would want. That is not to say that I do not recognise — not the programme that you talk about, but anything that we happen to be doing that we are not aware of that. And the issue must always be if a programme is not working, why not? If a programme is not working, can we make it better, how do we change it? And if we cannot change it and make it better, whatever that programme might be, well then you have to say, 'We have failed. We had better replace it and do something better.' That is the sort of debate that went on over *Eldorado*, if you take something that is dead rather than something that is living in the way that you are talking about. We do not get everything that we do right in programme making terms, we do not do everything that we do right in scheduling terms but I would be letting down my colleagues and my staff who are working bloody hard actually to innovate and create something new, if I were to stand here and say 'I think *Middlemarch* is a lot of rubbish or I think *Life in the Freezer* was a big con.' I happen to be taking two programmes which I do not think one can criticise for obvious reasons. I do not think any broadcaster should do that.

Gillian Reynolds: Well, once again, the Manchester Broadcasting Symposium got it right by inviting a terrific spokesman for your final plenary session. Thank you very much indeed.

Session produced by Colin Shaw

The future of regulation

Colin Shaw CBE
Director, Broadcasting Standards Council

I N William Cowper's poem, John Gilpin, it may be remembered, was a London citizen of credit and renown. To mark his wedding anniversary, he hired a coach to take his wife and family to dinner, while he himself borrowed a horse. Alas for him, the horse bolted back to its stable and Gilpin was obliged to explain his unexpected arrival miles from where he was meant to be. 'I came', he said, clearly a stickler for the truth, 'because the horse would come'.

Technology, playing horse, has landed society in Gilpin's place. Before us unroll the superhighways with their apparently limitless promise. What are we to do about them and can we hope, in some way, to ensure that the promise is not allowed to be dissipated, turning to gold for a handful of people and dross for the rest? The evidence of the past twenty years, if no longer, shows that, left to itself, the market will not protect us. A combination of the market and regulation may offer more promise. After all, during the debate on the Broadcasting Bill in 1990, David Mellor said, for the Government, that a light touch approach could be accompanied, where appropriate, by a touch rather heavier.

Speaking in Buenos Aires to the ITU Conference in March 1993, the Vice-President of the United States, Al Gore, outlined his thoughts about the evolution of the global information infrastructure upon which could rest the information superhighways of which much has been said.

The Vice-President set out the five principles upon which he believed the infrastructure would be based. These principles were:

(i) the encouragement of private investment;
(ii) the promotion of competition;
(iii) the creation of a flexible regulatory framework;
(iv) the provision of open access to the network for all information; and
(v) a guarantee of universal service.

Well, it depends what you mean … but at least there's nothing there to make an old-fashioned liberal recoil from further exploration.

The modern world contains many states which have been in the course of evolution for many centuries. They have enjoyed an organic form of growth: they have histories, customs, and traditions to provide them with a confidence to encourage their own further development. They have systems of belief and of law which are an added source of strength. They have roots which reach down far enough to help them withstand the tempest when the tempest comes.

But the modern world also contains many nations which, born in circumstances of unreasoning hope, have grown up in conditions of conflict and turbulence, lacking the security which deeper roots can offer. They are often poor and lack almost everything that might help them to help themselves.

It is for them that the future sketched by Vice- President Gore is the most peril-ous, just as, within nations more securely founded, it is the poorest of their citi-zens, ill-resourced and ill-educated very often, who stand to suffer most in the brave new world which, we are told, the global information infrastructure can bring us.

Not long ago, Mr Rupert Murdoch was reported in a British newspaper as say-ing: 'technology had carried us beyond the politicians and the regulators'. There is little evidence that those who increasingly control the media are characterised by an ability to put broader concerns before the expansion of their own businesses. Dr Johnson's dictum that a man is never so innocently employed as when he is making money does not apply to them. Indeed, it is aggrandisement focused on themselves which drives many of them and, if they showed a serious inclination to be diverted from their dominant task, then they would be very rapidly replaced by people whose determination was less questionable.

But how can the legitimate energies of the businessmen be reflected in the serv-ices given to the public, services which, in many countries, have by tradition em-braced both the needs and the wants of the audience, often through the creation of public institutions?

The responsibilities of authorities, global & national: technical
There is a clear role for national authorities in making sure that the technical promise of the new developments is fulfilled as far as it is practical. There ought to be the means for every citizen everywhere to have reasonable access for their informa-tion needs: the right to communicate and, its accompanying right, the right to be communicated with.

We should, therefore, welcome the Vice-President's insistence on the provision of universal service. If it is to be a reality, then a degree of national and interna-tional regulation is inescapable. Mr Gore says that the goal is a kind of global conversation in which everyone who wants can have his or her say. Access, he says, means making the service available at affordable prices to everyone. It also means making the service available everywhere, despite the geographical prob-lems which may have to be solved.

At the end of his speech, the Vice-President talks of the creation of a Global Digital Library, to which there would be access for anyone anywhere in the world. It is of the greatest importance that access should be freely available — nobody should be allowed to achieve a monopoly of information available only to the rich or, more sinisterly, to those of whom the monopolist approves, with those of whom he does not approve denied access.

The Americans are talking of reserving a significant proportion of the superhighways for public access, following the reservation of a right to public access on cable services within the United States. However, while this is to be applauded as a first step, there will be no second step unless funds from public or private sources are provided to enable full use to be made of the facility.

We should not be encouraging the growth of further divisions within the world community by establishing alongside the 'information haves' a multitude of 'information have-nots' who, though facilities exist, are denied access to them by a lack of resources sufficient to make them of any interest to the operators of a commercially-dominated system.

The denial of universal service and of access are clear dangers which exist if commercial judgements are allowed to exercise undue influence and the means to challenge them are not available to every nation. If, as Mr Murdoch is reported to believe, technology liberates us from politicians and regulators, he is offering a confrontation which no nation can afford to overlook.

The responsibilities of national authorities: programmes

But beside the right to communicate and the right to be communicated with, there is a further right: not to be communicated with. Between them they give rise to two significant dilemmas:

- the exclusion of unwanted material; and
- the maintenance of programmes which it is considered are of particular value to individual states.

The first of them is the more controversial for it involves restrictions on free expression and the individual's right to decide for himself or herself what he or she will watch. It also raises practical problems since the ability of governments to prevent the installation of receiving equipment is in question, as it is suggested the Chinese government is finding in its attempt to deny Mr Murdoch's satellite operation to the Chinese audience. But it should not be forgotten that the providers of the new services will have an interest in recouping their costs from the audiences they will be serving or the manufacturers whose goods they will be advertising.

I can offer no expert advice on how that movement of money might provide opportunities for striking compromises on programme contents. It is a small example, but it is worth recalling that, when Britain was surrounded by ships broadcasting illegally to British audiences, the British Government took powers to prevent trading with the operators of those ships: no sale of advertisements, no provision of supplies to the crews, for example. The restrictions proved rapidly effective.

The rights of nations to take action of that kind should be affirmed and, beyond that, it should be possible to secure broader agreement over the general unacceptability of certain kinds of material, including excessive displays of violence. Although violence can be shown not to be the most popular programming throughout the world, it is nevertheless attractive to large numbers of people and, with its emphasis on action rather than on speech, it travels readily and is often available more cheaply than other kinds of material.

Less controversial than the question of restricting or hindering the transmission of certain classes of material is the question of how domestic television services may be organised so that they provide a balanced reflection of many aspects of the national life: from major occasions of State to the work of the country's dramatists and actors, the education of its children, the variety of its minorities and its prime sporting events — the things which unite the nation as the occasions for national pride as well as those which highlight the diversity of lives within its borders.

There must be a very real apprehension that individuality of all kinds will be under threat when the global market truly arrives. Not only the individuality of the single man, woman or, perhaps especially, the child, but the individuality of separate nations, new or old.

Those needs include many forms of education, forms of specialised information for minority interests, provision for believers of different faiths and for linguistic minorities, and an adequate service of news and current affairs capable of sustaining an informed public. The list is capable of being extended, but it may be valuable to describe in more detail some of the elements already set down. In considering them more fully, it may be useful to have in mind that, while some of these areas of output may be covered by the workings of the market, it is almost certain that the market's provision is geographically selective and does not reflect the principle of universal coverage which, as has already been suggested, is an additional, and crucial part of the interventionist case.

The protected species: education

Broadcasting can supplement the work of the schools at primary and secondary levels, offering illustrative material which is often beyond the means of the individual teaching institutions, especially as public funds run low. The greatest value will be derived from programmes directed to schools if they can be fully integrated with the work of the schools themselves.

At the level of university teaching, the contribution has been less in Britain, reflecting the different nature of education at the tertiary stage. Reference should be made to the development of distance-learning in many countries by the public-service broadcasters.

There is formal education which can be supported in broadcast programmes, but there is also the possibility of supplying programming which can be called educative rather than formally didactic. Programmes, for example, dealing with citizens' rights or explaining how to deal with officialdom render a valuable social service, often capable of reaching audiences in their own homes who remain impervious to other, more public, forms of approach. Successful campaigns to encourage literacy have been organised to take advantage of the special aspect of privacy afforded by broadcasting.

Minorities

All of us, in viewing television, form part of both majority and minority audiences. As followers of a particular sport or fans of a particular comedian, we are likely to be viewing in common with many of our fellow citizens. As amateur photographers or sporting fishermen, we are likely to be in a more exclusive, though not necessarily less fanatical, group. If our minority interests do not command a place in the market, then we are likely to be by-passed under a system where the market is dominant. Protection within a more regulated service will serve our needs better.

125

Children's programmes

Children need instruction and broadcasting can help in that, but they also need all kinds of entertainment designed not simply to amuse, but also to stretch their imaginations and tax their developing mind. With honourable exceptions, it is apparent that a television service operated solely for commercial ends can offer only a more limited range of programmes. already defined is likely to concentrate on those programmes for children capable of making a profitable return directly or in the form of merchandise. The range of programmes likely to be offered to children as a result may not be as wide or as committed to the children's stimulation as many parents would wish them to be.

News and current affairs

Although there is evidence to show the popularity of programmes reporting the News, competitive pressures carry with them the risk of the trivialising of the content of the bulletins themselves, whether by the shortening of individual items to a series of sound-bites, by the import of stories with a tabloid quality to them, or by a concentration on domestic stories to the exclusion of stories from other parts of the world. The ability to give more measured treatment to the news, setting the stories more completely in their contexts, is an important contribution to the working of a democratic society.

Promotion of the culture: protection of the heritage

The pressures of commercial broadcasting may not be well-disposed to protect those aspects of the national life which would be widely recognised as an expression of the national spirit. In some countries, there are musical forms and even musical instruments which come out of the national history, just as forms of dance do. Dialects have a strong place in many cultures, as do costume and national dishes. At best, intervention would be justified by the maintenance of the traditions represented by these things or, at worst, by the possibility of delaying their inevitable erosion and eventual elimination by the incursion of other values deriving from different, more potent cultures.

Protected species: paying the price

There is no point in pretending that many of the programmes described above, as well as certain other classes of output, will pay their way. Their continuation is, therefore, a matter of political will if they are valued sufficiently. It would seem appropriate if some at least of the financing came from the new services. Businessmen have often said that the revolution they are promoting will be 'entertainment-led'. If they are going to base their prosperity upon the skills of programme-makers of many different kinds, then it would seem equitable to insist that they provide financial support for that wider range of services which broadcasting has traditionally delivered to many different societies. An alternative approach would be the provision of Government funds, but it would then be necessary to secure the independence of the broadcasters.

If there is no political will to make equitable sense of the future offered by superhighways, assuming that, in some form at least they come into existence, then a huge opportunity will have been lost, with incalculable consequences. To return to John Gilpin and reverse the words of a second poet, Roy Campbell, we've got the horse, but where are the bloody snaffle and the bridle?

This paper also formed the basis of a speech given in June, 1994, to a conference on digital television in Fez, Morocco.

Spoilt for choice: the particular in pursuit of the palatable

The 1994 Symposium's participatory exercise reviewed by
Mike Davis
Centre for Adult and Higher Education
University of Manchester

UNTIL 1987, audience participation in the Manchester Broadcasting Symposium was characterised by the gentle interrogation of presenters and by group discussions held in rooms around the hall of residence used for the symposium. This procedure up until this time was neatly summed up as: "... polite questions in plenary sessions and ... strangely titled syndicate groups named after Scandinavian countries." (*The Beast*, 6.1.1) Since then, to avoid this mundane activity, the University of Manchester Broadcasting Symposium Steering Committee has worked to produce novel ways of exploring the Symposium themes through active participation. The intention has been to create activities that have the capacity to involve all conference participants in an exploration of the theoretical issues presented in the main sessions, through practical application, within a simulated environment. This use of simulation has a widespread acceptance within a number of fields, including education and training and while not being seen as a mechanism for replicating the real world (whatever that is) it is, rather, regarded as an opportunity to explore some elements of organisations and processes, in conditions of safety. In other words, while the consequences of actions are real within the context of the simulation, they do not pass beyond its boundaries. A well-designed simulation will, therefore, encourage experimentation while retaining authenticity, and without the (often imagined) constraints of the environment being simulated. The procedure used to achieve this include accelerated time scales and an assortment of tokens representing a range of phenomena: outline characterisations, money, power and influence, achievement. The process is widely regarded as making possible meaningful learning: "... since participants become involved at an emotional as well as an intellectual level." (Miller, 1990: 3)

On this occasion, the theme to be explored throughout the three days was that of *The Nintendo Millennium: communications, democracy and culture in the post-broadcasting age*. In his opening key-note address, Professor Roger Silverstone of the University of Sussex supplemented this theme with three sub-themes: control, access and choice, making possible a range of alternatives that he then made further problematic by pointing out uncertainties and instabilities, even into the near future. Thus, as with weather forecasting, where the next minute is (almost) predictable, and the next one and the one after that become more elusive and subject to unknown and unaccountable influences (Gleick, 1987: 21), so too with social and cultural change in the light of equally uncertain technological advance. And while the participatory exercise is set in the future, its purpose is not to predict the detail: rather to explore some of the human constraints that will continue to exist regardless of the nature of the technological changes that take place. It is against this background of uncertainty that participants in the Symposium lived up to the challenge of the exercise entitled *Spoilt for Choice.*

The broad aim of the exercise was to explore such questions as:

- How will households choose the channels to which they subscribe in a world where they are spoilt for choice?
- How will broadcasters and cable operators promote their channels or combinations of channels?
- How will market forces operate?
- How will channels be regulated?
- How will channel space be filled?

The briefing document set the scene as follows:

> It is the year 2001. At last, the whole of the UK has been cabled up with a broadband fibre cable direct to their home by Myriad Cable plc, and video compression is a reality. This means that every home is capable of receiving five hundred television channels. Not everyone will be able to afford to subscribe to all five hundred channels. So rival companies will create channel packages, and they will try to persuade people in cable homes to subscribe to their packages.

The opening activity, following the introduction given by Symposium Director Nod Miller, one of the exercise designers, was to self-select groups who then were to establish company names. The briefing document continued:

> Each team member will contribute £1, and this money will be used to buy five packages of channels from The Channel Shop ... These packages are made up from a list of five hundred channels ... and each contains a wide range of services. Extra packages can be bought from The Channel Shop for £1 each.

The channel names ranged from Academic Conferences, Gay TV, Hello!, Live White Females, to Vaseline and Your Ailments. Interpretation of the content of each channel was left largely up to the group and while in some cases that was quite severely constrained by what is shared knowledge (e.g. Coronation Street) in others, there was a range of ambiguity in the channel name (e.g. Log Fire, PCTV).

The briefing document went on the describe the next stage:

> Groups will be able to trade channels with each other and may wish to create alliances. Their main task is to create an attractive package which will:
> - attract subscriptions;
> - appeal to investors;
> - satisfy the regulatory authorities; and
> - attract advertising and / or sponsorship revenue.

Each of these components will affect the earning power of each group. The winning team is the one which ends up with most cash, by raising advertising and sponsorship revenue, by securing subscriptions from family groups and by avoiding the wrath of the regulators. They will also apply for investment income from bankers. Groups will create posters, which will be the main way of promoting their channel packages. They will also complete forms showing details of their packages which will be checked by the regulatory authorities and by the advertisers and sponsors.

The foregoing was designed to occupy the first element in the simulation and followed the pattern of enabling participants to interpret functional roles (e.g. Finance Director), rather than biographical roles (e.g. Michael Grade). In the second stage, however, there was to be a role switch and participants had to regroup according to their Happy Families household names which were printed on the reverse of their Symposium name-tags. The briefing document described the process thus:

> ... each household will decide how to spend its limited viewing budget on the basis of the posters created by each group. Some households will, of course, have less disposable income than others, so they will only be able to subscribe to a limited number of services. The number of households choosing a particular package will determine the amount of subscription income its promoters receive. The population contains a wide variety of households whose viewing budgets range from 50p to £3; companies will need to decide whether to target richer (and possibly fewer) households to try to appeal across income groups.

There were, in fact, 22 families, which were intended by the game's designers to represent the variety of the populations. As The Beast reported:

> Plans for the microcosmic social system ... spared no scholarship in delving into Social Trends and formulating a set of families demographically sound in almost every respect, from the one-parent Buns to the aspirant Birts, the elderly residents of the Twilight Home and the penurious Students and Subculturalists to the dual income Hypes and Boffins.

For each member of the household, there was a very brief biography (e.g. Fraulein Hilde Himmelweit, aged 19, au pair) and the combination of the different biographies within each household was the intended source of tension for the phase of the simulation when selections of channels were to be made.

The remaining dimension in the simulation was represented by the 'Public Goodness Authority', described in the briefing document as having responsibility to protect against offence and against failure to provide a degree of public service content. Despite both criteria being open to interpretation, the PGA had the authority to inflict financial penalties if complaints were made and upheld.

The following section will draw primarily on my own experience as a participant/observer. Their was no systematic attempt to gather evidence from other participants during or after the event, in contrast, for example, to the approach adopted by Jim Brown in Miller & Norris (1989: 150) and the significance of this will be explored later.

After self-selecting the group and establishing our company name — The Best Channel — (a process I discussed briefly in Miller and Allen (1994) in the context of the 24th Symposium exercise) we identified key personnel: Managing Director, Programme, Finance, Marketing Directors. Capitalising the company came next and then the purchase of the cable packages. The next stage was to decide the way in which the channels we had bought could be grouped for marketing purposes. Among the channels we obtained in the blind auction were UK Gold and UK Bronze. After successfully negotiating with another company, we obtained UK Silver and this encouraged us to feel confident enough to offer a cable package called The Best Channel, built primarily on these three collections of classic programmes from the past.

It was evident that in other groups the process of creating company characteristics was under way. Through discarding unwanted packages and trading others, and on rare occasions after obtaining further capitalisation, buying additional packages from The Channel Shop, companies reached the point at which they could begin to attract their potential audiences by the publication of advertising material. The rules of the exercise allowed for one sheet of A0 paper to advertise the packages, an injunction broken by at least one company, as revealed by The Beast:

> Delegates were stunned by the rumour that arch regulator Colin Shaw was going to be hammered for violating conditions of tender in yesterday's Spoilt for Choice proceedings. Insiders claimed that three garish posters advertising the consortium in which he was managing director exceeded by two the number permitted.

Needless to say, despite the much-vaunted vigilance of the Public Goodness Authority in other matters, no action was taken by any regulators considering this clear breach of the tender conditions.

While preparation of advertising material was under way, other activity was also in progress. As explored above, companies had three sources of income once their channels were ready to go on sale to the public: the subscriptions themselves; potential investment capital from two banks; and advertising or sponsorship revenue. Representatives of the latter two agencies were available for consultation during the second session of the exercise and it was the responsibility of company members to look for ways in which income, either in the form of loan capital or as sponsorship or advertising revenue, could be raised. Given that criteria for success in the early stages of each company's existence (i.e. during the life of the Symposium) was the level of capitalisation, there were good reasons for making a strong case to either of the two banks which were operating in this field of media-related venture capitalism. In the outside world, banks' decisions strike me as being somewhat opaque, and this was also the case during the exercise. Bank officers were allowed to offer loan capital on the basis of presentations made by managing and finance directors but the criteria were never explicit. A plausible, well-presented case seemed to be important, thus:

Banker: … and your board has a background in business?
Finance Director: No, we are all from the higher education sector …
Banker: No, you are not.
Finance Director: … students, lecturers …
Banker: Banks look for a substantial track record of experience in an industry.

Finance Director: ... but with a background and substantial experience in the industry at a variety of levels. The outcome of this consultation was the allocation of capital of 50p and this was a source of much satisfaction at the time, as it provided outside financial support without tying us too tightly to the financial sector.

Negotiations were also conducted with advertisers who seemed much more hard-headed and systematic than the banks, looking for clarity and explicitness rather than general goodwill. Brook Sinclair, one of the activity's designers, wrote of his reaction to the bidding made by the company I belonged to:

> Best, which made three excellent suggestions about sponsorship, would not discuss the rest of their schedules. They got 50p, they might have got more.

Sinclair wrote more generally about the event from the perspective of the advertisers:

> The two 'advertisers' attempted to introduce the 'real world' into Spoilt for Choice in two ways:
>
> 1. Making use of a 22-category breakdown of real life advertising expenditure. This told us motor manufacturers, drink, retail, household and finance industries would have more to spend ... than education, charities, horticulture and entertainment:
>
> 2. Creating a list of the top 100 UK advertisers' individual expenditure, in case groups mentioned clients by name.

We found, early on, that the 500 channels and real-life spending were markedly out of step. Few channels were obvious choices for advertisers and, during the game, companies named only four major manufacturers. Determined to spend our £10 anyway, we devised a scheme to reward companies who attempted an appropriate mix of channels or who had geared channels to audiences some advertiser might like. Companies who laid out a full scenario and asked for our help, did better than companies who tried to hide things. Within the full scenario we could find items worthy of advertising support which a company had not detected.

Concluding that in general, most participants showed themselves to be out of touch with commercial life, Sinclair believed that suspicion characterised the relationship between intending broadcasters and advertisers and sponsors.

To return to The Best Channel, we regarded ourselves as a successful and competent company with an attractive range of packages representing a wide range of viewing interests: films, TV greats, music and sports. We had worked well together to produce the subscription campaign and despite having had limited success with the bankers and advertisers, we were fairly confident that we would go into the final stage with a package that would be as attractive to the well-off Birts as to the financially embarrassed Underclasses.

The transition to the Happy Families was, I believe, the least successful part of the activity. Tucked away on the final part of the second afternoon, participants had little opportunity to try to fill the biographical roles and for a variety of reasons, not all participants were still attending the Symposium or they were unavailable for unspecified reasons to take part in this stage. I will return to this issue later. In consequence, however, purchasing decisions were made on the basis of hurried discussions which, in turn, depended on stereotypical expectations of the choices that may have been made. For example, my interpretation of the role of Dr Tabitha Tinker, family therapist, was only marginally less inauthentic then that made by my 'husband', a sociologist, or those of our two children. This, perhaps, could have been anticipated. Role-playing demands a different set of responses than the role-taking as required in the earlier stages of the simulation. While the latter demands "... a repertoire of behaviours which are expected of that role" (van Ments, 1983: 18), role playing demands a more constrained set of responses. As Morry van Ments continues:

> ... the role-player is ... concerned only with himself (*sic*) and his fellow role-players. His aim is to feel, react and behave as closely as possible to the way someone placed in that situation would do. (*op cit:* 20)

The difference is, perhaps, a fine one but significant nonetheless. When participating in the early stages of the simulation, I was filling a procedural role: I was Mike Davis and I had certain tasks to undertake and I was to bring to those tasks whatever abilities I can from other relevant contexts. The only thing to constrain me is my lack of knowledge about some aspects of the simulated environment: for example in the case of Spoilt for Choice, the range of acceptable criteria that would appeal to the bankers and advertisers. These and other areas of specialist knowledge can be furnished by sharing information in the group (who are likely to be, at the very least, interested bystanders) and by appeals to 'common sense' understanding to fill any remaining gaps. My role of Dr Tabitha Tinker, however, had no such room for interpretation: each element of the individual biography and family profile serve to limit freedom to respond. In this sense, the strength of role-play is also its weakness: in providing opportunities to stand in another's shoes, it can pinch the feet.

Needless to say, we made our selection based on an assortment of implicit and explicit criteria: my recollections are hazy but, working towards/against the stereotype, I remember that my sociologist husband was keen to buy some sport. My role performance, on the other hand, was suffering from 'leakage' and I argued for the merits of The Best Channel. In any event, it wasn't enough. Our combined income from the three sources put us in fourth place behind a company heavily in debt to the bank and up to their toe-nails in public service broadcasting difficulties in their over-reliance on dubious advertising link-ups. Interestingly, our company board's guess that we would have a broad appeal across the social spectrum was generally confirmed: we attracted subscriptions from the Birts, the Fortnums, the Tinker-Taylors, (available income £3); the Fixit-Foggs and the Dimbleby-Delors (£2); and the Twilight Homes who dedicated 50% of their available resources to one of our packages.

The exercise concluded with the ritual prize-giving during the final session and the extent to which people were still engaged in the outcomes of the competition was, perhaps, an indication of how successful it had been. It had seemed to me to be more engaging than the 1993 Thursday Night Schedule exercise I had taken part in and reported on last year (in Miller & Allen, 1994: 149ff) but that may have been the product of a number of different criteria, including the Symposium theme, the participants, other sessions and the different ways that these combine. Perhaps what needs to be examined in more detail is the extent to which the participative exercise contributes towards participants' understanding and enjoyment of the Symposium as a whole: whether it achieves its intention to make the theme more available and the learning in the other sessions more powerful, and it is this that I turn to now.

I share with Jim Brown (Miller & Norris, 1989: 153) two reservations. In respect of one, he wrote:

> From my own point of view, I was unsettled by the confirmation that participative exercises rely more on the skills of participation and team management that they do on any particular knowledge or understanding of the issues being examined.

Either that is the way broadcasting (or any other) decisions are made, or it could be a weakness in the exercise design. In any event, it might account for Sinclair's comment that "... most groups seemed out of touch with commercial life." Or it may be a product of Brown's second concern: his thesis that "... the more well-known you were the less likely you were to take part in the participative exercise." I didn't keep a track of Symposium VIPs but *The Manchester Daily Beast* is an invariably reliable (although scurrilous) source of information, and by Issue 3, gossip columnist Mr Manchester was reporting on the significance of the Happy Families roles for at least four of the Symposium's 'stars', including a Member of the House of Lords, a C.B.E. and a Professor (in no particular order). The extent to which participants in general are drawn from the broadcast professionals is less certain and it may be that while the exercise is attractive to the academic community in attendance, it is less so to the the broadcasters. Brown depicted this as "unconscious elitism ... indicative of how the broadcasting industry operates on a norm of power, hierarchy and social distance" (Miller & Norris, 1989: 154) and that may be so. It may also be, however, the product of misperceptions of the purpose of the exercise. The literature related to experiential education is littered with concerns about signifiance, intention, objectives and the relationship of 'experience' to 'learning' and it may be these factors which inhibit participation by some people. To appreciate the weight of this requires a return to the generalities about simulation exercises that were discussed briefly at the beginning of this chapter.

In the opening paragraph, the simulation was depicted as "an opportunity to explore some elements of organisations and processes, in conditions of safety ...While the consequences of actions are real within the context of the simulation, they do not pass beyond its boundaries. A well-designed simulation will, therefore, encourage experimentation while retaining authenticity, and without the (often imagined) constraints of the environment being simulated. The problem is not with this definition, but with other components of simulations, and, for that matter, experiential learning in general, for example, as identified by Jones (Jones, 1987:11):

> Nor is it essential that the action part of a good simulation should include effective learning. Experiential learning frequently occurs after rather than during an

event. The action part of a simulation can include muddle and mistakes, and participants can become completely convinced that their own arguments and solutions are the best, and that other people are being unreasonable. ... This does not make the event a non-simulation or a bad simulation. In a simulation it is not a crime to make mistakes, the crime is not to learn from the experience.

The ability to learn from experience and to facilitate that process in others cannot be assumed. It is increasingly seen as problematic in the intellectual community where it had some of its origins (see, for example Boud & Walker, 1993: 73ff) but it is beyond the scope of this chapter to explore it in detail here other than to explore a possible future of the participative exercise at the Manchester Broadcasting Symposium.

It would, perhaps, be hard to imagine a Symposium without some form of interaction between participants from the different sectors which make up its membership. Given that there are difficulties, however, in gaining access to its nature and significance, particularly at the time, it might be worth considering ways in which follow-up studies can be built in to the planning of future exercises. Questions that occur to me include:

- who takes part? why? who doesn't? why not?
- how do participants characterise their experience a) at the time; and b) later?
- how would they describe it to fellow professionals (whatever their sector)?
- how successful is it in relating to the Symposium themes?
- what is learnt, about (a) content; (b) process; and (c) self?

By attempting to answer these questions, and others, there could be a significant contribution to understanding that goes far beyond the boundaries of the Symposium.

References

Boud, D., Cohen, R. and Walker, D. (eds) (1993): *Using experience for learning.* Milton Keynes: Open University Press/SRHE
Boud, D. and Walker, D. (1993): 'Barriers to reflection on experience' in Boud et al (1993)
Brown, J. (1989): 'The participation exercise: an outsider's view' in Miller & Norris (1989)
Davis, M. (1994): 'The Thursday night schedule: in pursuit of public service principles' in Miller & Allen (1994)
Gleick, J. (1987): *Chaos: making a new science.* Harmondsworth: Penguin
Jones, K. (1987): *Simulations: a handbook for teachers and trainers.* (2nd edition) London: Kogan Page
Miller, N. and Norris, C. (eds) (1989): *Life after the broadcasting bill.* Manchester: Manchester Monographs.
Miller, N., Norris, C. & Hughes, J. (eds) (1990): *Broadcasting standards: quality or control.* Manchester: Manchester Monographs.
Miller, N. (1990): 'Introduction' in Miller et al (1990)
Miller, N. and Allen, R. (eds) (1994): *Broadcasting enters the marketplace.* London: John Libbey
van Ments, M. (1983): *The effective use of role-play.* London: Kogan Page

Five hundred channels

The group which devised the participatory exercise 'Spoilt for Choice' identified 500 more or less serious suggestions for digital channels. The list is reproduced below.

Academic Confer-
  ences
Accounting
Adult Channel
Adult Education
Aerobics
Africa
Africa TV
After Dark
Agatha Christie
Algebra
All about soaps
All Our Yesterdays
Amateur dramatics
Ancient history
Angling
Anoraks
Antiques Price
  Guide
Antiques
  Roadshow
Apple Channel
Arabic
Archaeology
Architecture
Arguments
Arithmetic
Army & Navy
Aromatherapy
Arson
Art Deco
Art films
Art Nouveau
Astrology
Astronomy
Asylum
Autobiography
Awards
B&B
Back packing
Ballet
Ballroom

Banking for All
Bankrupts
Baptist Channel
Barbara Cartland
Beastvision
Beautiful Music
Bedding plants
Bengali
Bereavement
Best Aussie Soaps
Best of chat shows
BFI
Big Dogs
Bikers
Biology
Bird Watching
Birmingham
Black & White TV
Blackmail
Boating
Bodice-rippers
Body building
  (female)
Body building
  (male)
Body language
Books
Boxing
Boys' own
Brain Surgery
Bravo
Brazilian soaps
Bridge
Brighton
Brookside
Brownies
Buddhism
Bungy-jumping
Bureaucracy
Burglary
Burmese Cats
Bus spotters

Butchery
Calculations
Canoeing
Car boot
Caravanning
Carnival Channel
Carnivores
Cars
Cartoon Network
Cartoons
Casualty
Cathedrals
Cats
CDs
Celtic
Channel guide
Channel of Colour
Charity
Chemistry
Chess
Childcare
Children
China Channel
Choose your Victim
Christian
Christie's Auc-
  tions Live
Church music
Citizens advice
Clairvoyance
Classic cars
Clothes
CNN
Cocktails
Coins
Collecting
Comedy Channel
Competitions
Complaints
  Channel
Computer Channel
Consuming

Passions
Cookery
Coronation Street
Cortinas
Counselling
Country living
Court TV
Covent Garden
Cricket
Crime
Croquet
Cross Dressing
Culture Vultures
Cycling
Daily Mail TV
Daily Telegraph
  Channel
Dance
Darts
Dating
David
  Attenborough
David Frost
David Mellor
Dead comics
Dead white males
Debating
Derby
Desk-top publish-
  ing
Destination Asia
Diabetes
Digging
Dinosaurs
Disability
Disasters
Discovery Channel
Disney Channel
Dissection
Divorce
DIY
Drama Queens

Drama School
Dressage
Dressmaking
Drink
Dublin
Dutch
East Anglia
Easy watching
Economics
Ecstacy
Edinburgh
Edwardian Channel
Eighties Channel
Embalming
Ends of films
Enjoy Your Retire-
  ment
Estate agents
Euro-royals
European art
Eurosport
Exhibitionists
Exotic pets
Family Channel
Family planning
Farming
Fashion news
Feminism
Fifties Channel
Finnish
Fire brigade
Fish
Fishing
Flower arranging
Fly fishing
Folk dance
Folk music
Food
Food shopping
Football
Footwear
Forties Channel
French
French theorists
Fretwork network
Fruitarians
Funerals

Game Show
  Channel
Gay TV
Geography
German
Ghosts
Glasgow
Go For It!
Going for a Song
Golden age of
  murder
Goldfish
Golf
Good News
Gospel music
Gossip
Granada TV reruns
Great dead actors
Greek
Greenpeace
Greyhounds
Guardian TV
Guides
Gymnastics
Hacienda
Hairdressing
Hang gliding
Happy endings
Healing
Health
Heart channel
Heavy metal
Hebrew
Hello!
Heritage
Hindi
Hip replacements
History
Hockey
Holidays
Home design
Home doctor
Hooray
Horses
Hospital Watch
House and garden
House of Commons

House of Lords
Household hints
How to paint
Huddersfield
Hymns and carols
Hypochondria
I Love Lucy
Ibsen
Ice skating
Improvisation
Indian movies
Italian
Japanese TV
Jazz
Jewellery
Jewish
Jive
Jokes
Karaoke
Karate
Knitting
Landscape
Learn to dance
Leeds
Left Bank
Lesbian interest
Libraries
Lingerie Channel
Literature
Live white fe-
  males
Liverpool
Local government
Log fire
London
Lost and found
Low technology
M&S
M25
Mafia
Marriage bureau
Marriage TV
Massage
Mathematics
Memorabilia
Men's issues
Mensa

Methodists
Mexican
MI5
Middle ages
Midnight Fun
Militaria
Mills & Boon
Missing persons
Moral maze
More Music
Morris dancing
Motor racing
Movie Channel
MTV
Mud wrestling
Museums
Music hall
Muslim
Naturist
NBC Superchannel
Neckwear
Needle Channel
New Age
New News
News of the
  World TV
Nigel Dempster
Nineties Channel
Nintendo
Norwegian
Nostalgia
Nursery
Nuts
Office systems
Old advertisements
Old movies
Old sexist comedy
Opera
Operating Theatre
  Live
Operations
Oz Channel
Pagan
Painting
Panda Channel
Pathe News
Patience

PC TV
Pensions
Peru
Pets
Photography
Physics
Piranhavision
Police
Police station
Polish
Portuguese
Post office
Post-modern TV
Post-structuralist
Pottery
Primary health
care
Prisoner Cell
Block H
Private Eye
Problems
Psychology
Public service
broadcasting
Quantum Shopping
Quizzes
QVC Shopping
Radio choice
RAI-1
Readers' Digest
Reconstructions
Records
Red TV
Reggae
Religion
Restaurants
Rich and famous
R. Attenborough
Road accidents
Rock and roll
Rodents
Roller blading
Roman Catholic
Channel

Roulette
Royalty
Rubber
Ruling Class channel
Rural development
Russian
S&M
Salford
Satire
Save the whale
Science fiction
Scouts
Sculpture
Secret societies
Sega Channel
Semaphore
Semiotics
Serbo-Croat
Serial killers
Seventh Day
adventist
Seventies Channel
Sewing
Sex
Shakespeare
Shoes
Silent movies
Silent pics
Sixties Channel
Skating
Sky Movies
Sky News
Sky One
Sky Sport
Small Dogs
Small railway
journeys
Smokers
Snooker Channel
Soaps
Sociology
Soul Channel
South America
Space

Spanish
Spelling
Stamps
Star Trek
States of America
Steeplechasing
Stock market
Street scenes
Stress management
Student life
Sumo
Supernatural
Surrey
Swedish
Swimming
Tabloid
Tai Chi
Tarot
Tate Gallery
Teach Yourself
Hairdressing
Teddy bears
Teletext
Tennis
Thai TV
The Simpsons
Thirties Channel
Thought for the day
Time Channel
Times TV
Timeshare
TNT
Traffic news
Travel
Trees
True Confessions
True Crime
True Romance
Tudor times
Turkish TV
TV Asia
TV TV
Twenties Channel
UK Bronze

UK Gold
UK Silver
Undertakers
University Chal-
lenge
US TV reruns
V&A
Vaseline
Vaticanvision
Vegans
Vegetarian
Very Old Movies
Video diaries
Video games
Volleyball
War games
Wars
Weapons
Weather
Weaving
Wednesday Play
Today
Weight watchers
Welsh
What the papers say
Whist
Wicked women
Wild Life
Wine buffs
Witchcraft
Woodwork
Word games
Worst of chat shows
Wrestling
Xmas
Yachting Channel
Yoga
Your ailments

'Spoilt for Choice' was devised by Rod Allen, Genevieve Clarke, Nod Miller, Pam Mills, Brook Sinclair and Veronica Taylor.

Part 2

Diversity, regions and communities

Diversity, regions and communities

Chair: **Colin Shaw**
Broadcasting Standards Council
Chair, University of Manchester Broadcasting Symposium steering committee

Gillian Reynolds
Journalist and broadcaster

Opening remarks: **Professor Roger Iredale**
School of Education, University of Manchester

PROFESSOR Iredale: Welcome to the Symposium. I am Roger Iredale, Head of the School of Education at the University of Manchester, and it has fallen to me to open the Sympo-sium. I extend a very warm welcome to you all and hope you will enjoy what I am sure promises to be an extremely interesting session.

The School of Education is very glad to be hosting this Symposium, as it has done for many years. We have an extremely wide and varied range of offerings within the School from teacher training to areas such as social ethics and policies connected with the ethics of biology and medicine in their legal senses. So we are a Faculty with a tremendous range of interests, and among those interests is an extremely effective and successful series of media courses which we mount at various levels, but particularly at Master's level annually. They are extremely well supported with important international dimensions.

The School of Education itself has a long history of experience in developing countries internationally, extending over many decades and we are interested, in a different sense perhaps from today's theme, in the issues of pluralism as we enter an increasingly complex world, as all universities are having to do, of competition — competition across a whole range of activities and, particularly, in the international field.

We also have a very strong sense still of regionalism and I am conscious that at the conference you are going to be discussing definitions of regionalism in relation to broadcasting, a particularly topical thing to do when television viewers in Newcastle aren't able to see what the rest of the country sees, let alone those in Scotland. We have a very strong sense of the regional, being one of a number of universities of the north-west and, in the case of my faculty, with very close contacts with the north-west across the whole range of our activities, whether it be broadcasting, whether it be in-service and pre-service teacher training.

I am extremely pleased that we are offering this theme for this year. I am not going to say any more. I think all I have to do now is invite Colin Shaw, Director of the Broadcasting Standards Council, to introduce Gillian Reynolds to give the keynote speech.

Colin Shaw: Thank you very much for that introduction. I am particularly glad to welcome Gillian Reynolds to give us the keynote address to this Symposium. Gillian and I were debating earlier whether we would ever call ourselves Merseysiders. We decided that Merseyside was a late invention and although our youths are, I hasten to say in all gallantry, considerably separated by a number of years, nevertheless we do both come from Liverpool and I think we take a certain pride in coming from that militant, with a small 'm', city.

Gillian has been around in the industry in a variety of guises. She is now a most distinguished critic, but what comes out from her experience is a profound affection for the business of broadcasting and for the people who play a part in broadcasting. Most clearly her first love lies with radio but, as you will hear, her experience goes far wider than that and she now brings to the things that she writes each week a wisdom, an insight and a clarity of thought which I think greatly enrich the broadcasting debate in this country. I hope that she is now going to add to our indebtedness to her by the things that she is going to say when she talks about diversity, regions and communities in broadcasting.

Gillian Reynolds: If people ask me where I am from I say 'Liverpool'. It does not matter that this autumn I will have lived in London for twenty years, and long before that the length of my native 'a' sounds, which of course are 'bath' and 'glass', changed to something closer to those of the BBC Radio announcers I grew up listening to, as in 'bath' and 'glass'. If I speak to people and hear their reply come in that particular combination of flat vowels, tongued consonants, salty expression and an intonation that starts high and swoops low, as in, 'I never said anything like that,' or "e turned round and give me down the banks,' I always say 'Which part of Liverpool do you come from?', followed by 'What school did you go to?', the answer to which will at once reveal religion, class, age and aspiration. I think you could call this a form of tribal recognition. Once this first tribal greeting is over, however, there remains the recognition of the branch of the tribe, as in 'Oh, Crosby, well, that's not really Liverpool , is it?'

What I don't easily recognise is the notion of Liverpool belonging to a region. I also come from a time when the word community was not used much, except in law and definitions of property. Liverpool is where I'm from, Norris Green or Club Moor was where I lived, Blackburn House was my school, and Kelly was my mother's maiden name. Mine is a matriarchal family. Region meant North region, as in the Home Service of the BBC. That, as far as I was concerned, was the BBC's way of splitting things up. It was nothing much to do with me.

Then, when I went to Blackburn House, which I might tell you is the oldest girl's day school in England, or was until Derek Hatton closed it down ... anyway, when I went to Blackburn House and did Latin, I began to understand the notion that people do tend to split things up for access and convenience, as in *omnia Gallia divisa in tres partibus est*. The opening of Caesar's account of his conquest of Gaul, translated by Handford in the Penguin Classic of 1951, comes out as 'Gaul comprises three areas,' which to my ear does not quite have the impact of Gaius Julius himself. Caesar and the Romans are actually not a bad introduction to any study of the BBC. A huge empire, ruled from the centre, with vast power vested in the ruler, battles fought to conquer new territory, rebellions subdued after the conquests.

Any account of broadcasting's effects on and connections with regions and communities must begin with the BBC. And the BBC began with radio locally, regionally, because that was all the first transmitters could do. It is one of those accidents of history that the BBC, sometimes uneasily, and at other times very uneasily indeed, has lived with ever since. Since those first beginnings the story of BBC policy towards local and regional broadcasting has been one of promises made and promises broken, of powers developed then checked, usually for good reasons. Of this I will speak more.

Bear in mind, meanwhile, that regional broadcasting became a Directorate of its own in 1987, and that last year the BBC announced another £75 million would be going into it. So, why are the Bishop of Oxford and the Mayor of Coventry both now laying siege to the regional managing director, Ron Neal?

For almost thirty years the BBC had a monopoly of the airwaves, TV as well as radio. This September it will be fifty years since a great Whitehall banquet marked the start of ITV. Next year it's Granada's half-century. Commercial radio arrived in London in 1973, has grown, and will go on growing all around the UK, either until the Home Office runs out of frequencies or the Association of Independent Radio Contractors screams 'market saturation!' Both were based on the regional and local premise. Both have been radically affected by the 1990 Broadcasting Act. Of this too, and why independent local radio is growing less local, and ITV less regional by the moment, more in a few moments.

Broadcasting is a mirror of the way we live. By that I mean that forces at work in politics and society are bound to be reflected not just in the output — the programmes — but in the structure and the aspirations of broadcasting organisations. In the years since the first Thatcher government in 1979 this country has passed through a major upheaval — a radical reappraisal of all its institutions, some of them post-1945, some of them pre-war, including health and education services, including universities, museums, orchestras, all those premises of the Welfare State which upheld the principle of universal access to good education, sound health and high art. The Thatcherite reappraisal included all of broadcasting. The forces which drove the reconsideration have made fluctuations in the fortunes of regional and local broadcasting inevitable.

What changes lie ahead? The BBC is facing up to the results of Producer Choice, and a promise to pay off its £200 million overdraft by the end of next year. ITV has the prospect of Channel Five to ponder. The regions always feel the chill first whenever troubled breezes blow. But I think I see something which may prove an unexpected future force for putting the regions on a new footing. If regionalism in British broadcasting was, as we know it was, fashioned by technical happenstance, it has in a very British way become sustained by custom, and by political intent, and I must define now that what I mean by 'political' is both political as in Westminster and political as in the boardrooms of broadcasting organisations.

The BBC's regional scheme of 1928 was devised by engineers and based on high powered medium wave transmitters. The boundaries of what became the BBC regions were fixed by radio's engineering possibilities. They did not make sense geographically or tribally — the North region, for instance, stretched right across the Pennines and as far down as Lincolnshire. But once the English regions were there they took on an existence and a purpose of their own. That, though, has led to a continuous debate within the BBC which has ebbed and flowed but continues to this day.

The lines of the debate are roughly this: What are the regions for? How can we afford them? How autonomous could or should they be? How can they fulfil a real function without becoming a threat to the central power base in London? If radio was the marvel of the age in the 1930s, with people clustering round their sets to hear bands from London and voices from the other side of the Pennines, it became the nation's lifeline between 1939 and 1945. Despite Colin's very kind remarks about my age I do remember all of this quite vividly. Television, in its first experimental stages and broadcasting only around London, was suspended for the duration of the war. Radio became two streamed networks — the Forces Service for music and light entertainment and general cheeriness; the Home Service, based on the regions, for news, discussion, debate, drama. It came into its own, did radio. The place where you heard what happened in last night's air raids, where the Prime Minister spoke to the nation, where *ITMA* only had to rattle a doorknob for the nation to fall about laughing. For a decade after the war the BBC's regions had a large degree of autonomy. In 1955, though, minds were no longer on the wireless. Television was growing. ITV was round the corner, and BBC television was not based in the regions. So, here was this structure which had started back in the 1920s, had put radio on the map in the 1930s, served the nation well all through the war. What was to be done with it?

In 1955 the BBC ordered an internal review. It was conducted by Frank Gillard, and in his report he said, and I quote, 'A healthy national culture is based on a healthy regional culture.' He saw broadcasting as nourishing that culture, and I quote, 'from the roots up. Regional broadcasting had two responsibilities,' he said. 'To serve the regions themselves; to reflect the regions in a national context.' News was the first priority, entertainment second. But he wondered about going further, providing a real community service, concentrating on areas smaller than the regions, putting a transmitter in every community. This, and remember it's 1955 here, he said, and I quote, 'would no doubt flatter local pride enormously.' What an interesting verb that is, 'to flatter'! Gillard was then Head of Programmes, West Region, based in Bristol. He had been a distinguished war correspondent . To this day, and he is well into his nineties, he remains a BBC man to his fingertips. As such, he has that fine — you might almost say Roman — knack of combining the bold with the practical, the pragmatic with the progressive, which marks the effective public servant. There are some who will never forgive him for being the man who took off *Children's Hour.* There are others who say that without his bold vision of what BBC Radio could and might do, there would be no BBC Radio at all today.

This prefiguration of BBC local radio was examined by — yes, you've guessed it — another BBC committee in 1959, the secretary of which was Colin Shaw. It was a time when competition from regionally based ITV was beginning both to be felt and taken very seriously by the BBC. They declared in favour of local as opposed to area broadcasting. In 1961, though, the BBC was still talking about not being able to serve the 'whole man' (language that would not be permitted today) unless there was a local dimension. BBC local radio, on VHF only, was prescribed. It ought to be mentioned here, that out in the wider world beyond Broadcasting House, and indeed beyond the BBC in Manchester, there was a very vigorous lobby working for commercial radio. The Conservative Party had pledged official support for it; the manufacturers Pye had plans for stations based on towns of a population above fifty thousand people. There was vivid interest from newspapers.

The BBC, with Hugh Carlton Greene as Director General, was talking about a local radio service emphasising education. Gillard was saying that stations should not be juke boxes but responsive to local needs — to be flexible. In 1963 a BBC policy statement emphasised democracy over education, warned against parochialism, and said nothing would be standardised. There was, apparently, no vast known public interest in local radio of whatever stripe. But a BBC brochure in 1966 said listeners should come to regard their local station as 'their own,' and not, and this is quite significant, as 'the BBC station in our town.' Station managers were to have a charter and would be free to provide what they thought best for their communities, enjoying an extremely high degree of independence. And where would the money come from? Partly from the BBC, partly from local authorities. Would that explain the 'democracy' in the definition? Leicester Corporation put £104,000 into their BBC local radio station, the first to be opened, in 1967. All of the nine radio stations in that first wave had promises of finance from their local authorities. But the birth of BBC local radio was, as you would have guessed, the death of the regions. After that decade of 1945 to 1955 of autonomy, power and acclaim, of Geoffrey Brideson, Olive Chapley and Joan Littlewood in North Region, of the actuality pioneer Charles Parker in Midland Region, of *Any Questions?* in Bristol and *Have a Go!* in Manchester, the shift in the BBC's internal emphasis towards television meant the regions with their basis in radio history were increasingly pushed towards the margins.

New money came, but for the provision of news. In 1959 Midland Region gave birth to its own news magazine. *Points North* followed here in the North Region a year later. London was calling the tune. But we should bear in mind that the new band in town, ITV, was surging rapidly up the popularity charts. BBC managers, some very reluctantly, agreed to back a plan for local radio plus a bid for the second television channel, BBC2. But the Regional Advisory Councils were another matter. In this part of the country they were incensed. They declared that North Region had a right to its own domestic programmes which express the particular character, interests and problems of its people. Hugh Carlton Greene saw them, he talked to them, he persuaded them to emphasise achievements not problems, and he won them over for the time being.

When the Pilkington enquiry into the future of broadcasting came out and was lukewarm to the claims of the English regions — as opposed to the national regions of Scotland, Wales and Northern Ireland — the North Region's Advisory Council went into the attack. They said the north was suffering from a drift to the south and they despatched their own deputation, dubbed at the time 'The Pilgrimage of Grace,' to London. On paper the BBC said it welcomed 'a forceful and articulate council.' Actually, because they had gone straight to the Government to be 'forceful and articulate' and had gone over the heads of Output Directors, they were not just doomed but double-doomed. Always remember that if you play with the BBC, even when you think a part of the field is yours by right and agreement, it isn't. It is theirs, and the rules will always vary accordingly.

There was something else, too. The North's Regional Advisory Council may have been speaking up for their BBC programme makers. In London there was not that degree of professional regard. Then, as now, there was a degree of haughtiness, a certain scorn for people outside London making programmes. 'Amateurs playing in a professional league' is how Lord Briggs in his masterly final volume of BBC history (and all of us must regret deeply that it will be the final one) reports this kind of thinking. It was not, as we know, his own. BBC2, it had been hoped, would be a place for regional output. It was not to be. So the BBC started talking again. Should they shift big departments to the regions, education for instance to Manchester? 'No,' they said, and hushed up the very suggestion. Everyone could think of good things the regions had done. As Gillard himself said, 'Forty years of enquiries had commended the English regions.' But what were they for? And how, when competing for mass audiences, could the money be justified to keep them providing minority audience programmes outside news?

News, of course, there had to be. People want news about their regions. MPs expect to be on it. But is that all there can be, and should be? Evidently not. According to *People in Programmes,* published just this February, the latest in a long line of BBC declarations on the subject, research fwas undertaken throughout 1993, and here is a quote: 'Those who lived outside London, and especially Scotland, Wales and Northern Ireland, bitterly resented what they saw as the south-east bias of much of the BBC's drama and entertainment output, the ignoring of regional talent and culture.'

Now the events of this week have added a slightly different skew to those words but let's stick with the drama and entertainment for a moment because I wonder about this. I have learned as much about Northern Ireland through BBC drama on radio and television as through the news. I adored Scotland's *Naked Radio* which became *Naked Video*, and, in the course of time produced one of the great comic creations of the age, the peerless Rab C. Nesbitt, written by Ian Patterson and performed by Gregor Fisher. I enjoyed the *Animated Shakespeare* co-produced with S4C in Wales. So is this some regional revisionism going on here? Are memories so short now at the BBC?

There is something very odd about this report. Take the licence fee payer quoted in the margin of page 30. This licence fee payer says, 'I always think of the BBC as down south whereas Tyne Tees is up here.' I would love a word with that licence fee payer. I bet he or she knows who Mike Neville is better than Paul Frost or whoever is fronting the Tyne Tees news magazine these days. But there was a time, and not too long ago at that, when Mike Neville's future as a regional anchorman, the friendly face of the north-east region, was in doubt. He, like all the other friendly regional BBC faces, was shunted off and replaced by identikit teams of younger men in grey suits and young women with bright jackets and lipstick. Those of you who were at the Edinburgh Festival and saw the Frank Magid [a news broadcasting consultant from the US — *Eds*] presentation about selling news formats across television will well remember the Frank Magid format newsteams who, research claims, do better than squashy regional types with regional voices and personalities of their own. Except that they don't, which is why, praise be, Mike Neville is back on the BBC is the north-east but also why many another BBC regional news magazine has gone through rather a bumpy grey suit and red lipstick ratings ride over the past few years.

You can't have it both ways. Either you are regional or you're not. You can stuff money into unenhanced regional TV news service to provide vast response capability. You can bring in new weekly sport and leisure magazines in the English regions, both of which spring directly from the programme strategy review described in *People in Programmes* and which put another £6.3 million into the coming year's regional budget. But if you don't trust the programmes to regional talent, people who know the history of the area, the character of the people and how to say its place names, you might as well spend a lot on more glossy brochures. If it is not real, it won't work.

The trouble with BBC regional news and sport, as far as my own viewing goes, is that it seems often unreal — to speak too much with a voice that has been bought in, not bred up. But now that I have mentioned money let's not pass lightly by the additional £75 million that went into regional broadcasting this time last year. I quote from the press release at the time:

> In line with its commitment to reflect the regional and cultural diversity of the UK, the BBC is increasing the amount of network TV and programmes produced outside London from one-fifth to broadly one-third by 1997.

The press release also mentioned Director-General John Birt's intent that it must be the *British* Broadcasting Corporation, not the London Broadcasting Corporation. £65 million to TV, £10 million to radio, an increase in network spending in Scotland, Wales and Northern Ireland by an average of sixty-seven per cent. Manchester is to get a regional arts base. Light entertainment output from the regions is going to be doubled from eight to sixteen per cent over four years. Continuing education and schools output is going to be tripled. No wonder Regional Broadcasting Managing Director Ron Neal commented, 'This is the most dramatic move of radio and television production to the nations and regions in the BBC's history.' Is it appropriate, then, to wonder whether one-tenth of radio's new money, one million of that ten million pounds, is being spent on a permanent off-air help-line based in Glasgow? Is it appropriate to wonder whether it's a better investment than putting it into programmes? Is it the moment to ask whether making Radio 2's four nights a week show with Derek Jameson into an independent production, giving that show to a London-based company, Unique, who have since, of course, opened a Scottish office, but still shipping a team up there to do the show four nights a week — is that really the best instance of broadening the regional base, tone and style of BBC Network Radio? Perhaps not. But, as David Hatch, the DG's advisor who did the review, said, 'The policy is editorially driven. In the long term those with the best ideas will benefit most.' Are these, then, the best ideas?

Those of us who have learned a little about the language, new and old, of BBC management (although only native citizens of that native state, Bibiciana, can ever fully comprehend all the nuances of its language) may feel inclined to paraphrase here. My paraphrase would read, 'We have got to do something to look as if we care about the regions especially with the White Paper and the Charter coming up. So we have shuffled the money around the board a bit.'

Such irreverent thoughts are sustained by Steve Clarke and Chris Horrie's entertaining unofficial history of recent events, called *Fuzzy Monsters: Fear and Loathing at the BBC*, in which the authors recall John Birt criticising Michael Checkland for placing too much importance on the regions. They also recall a particularly memorable episode in which John Birt visits Manchester with a taskforce team and, almost before a word is uttered, says the whole new Oxford Road Centre ought to be closed down. But hark! Here come the governors with an insistence that the BBC should maintain a strong regional presence for political reasons. Shortly afterwards, you will recall, the regions were designated centres of excellence. Personally I find there is something vastly irritating about that term 'centres of excellence.' Does it imply they were centres of mediocrity before the diktat? What an insult! By the way Clarke and Horrie also say that the Birt Report of 1991 on Network Resources cost £2 million in consultants' fees and resulted in a forty per cent cut in core regional production units. No wonder that £75 million was so welcome last year! No wonder the new £6.3 million this year is such a tonic.

So why are the Bishop of Oxford and the Mayor of Coventry fizzing with fury? Because the Regional Directorate has plans to shut down their local radio stations. Meanwhile, fourteen Members of Parliament have tabled a House of Commons motion opposing proposed engineering service cuts to BBC Radio Merseyside. Meanwhile, at Radio York, budget cuts mean that they can't manage on their income without hiring out their studios, except they need their studios to do the programmes. Station managers' autonomy went long ago. There is now, I read in *Broadcast*, a hit-list for local radio stations.

Here's another quote. 'The £6.3 million package of new developments in regional television are not being funded by radio but by efficiency savings across all areas of regional broadcasting.' And a bit further on, this letter says, 'We are focusing on how we will be able to provide high quality local and regional services relevant to people's daily lives which take account of technological change and developments in the broadcasting marketplace.' I bet if Mark Byford, who wrote that, were to say something like it to John Humphries on the *Today* programme, he'd have to brace himself for at least thirty-two interruptions.

But why is it that whenever even mere mortals like us see a word like 'focused' used by a BBC mogul, we reach for the BBC dictionary and attempt a translation? Now, I happen to like the regional moguls of the BBC and Mark Byford is a good lad. He doesn't even live in London, he's that good. So, I'll be generous in my paraphrase. I think what he is really saying is, 'Sorry about this, but we haven't got enough money to keep all the radio stations open. We can't say this straight out, because every councillor and MP in the country will go bananas.' Out loud, meanwhile, he has said that the closure and merger proposals for four local radio stations are not open to negotiation. We are back to the question of how the BBC is strapped for cash, because the government has kept it that way, and it has also spent perhaps more than it can afford on management consultants and new systems of internal accounting.

There are seventy years of tussles on this same question. They run through the history of the BBC like the words in a bar of rock, and like rock they are always either eaten or left to turn sticky. Of all the messes the BBC has got itself into over regionalism, I can think of few stickier than the one which resulted in this week's fracas over the broadcasting of *Panorama*, which you will remember features a forty-minute interview with the Prime Minister in Scotland three days before the Scottish local elections. Did London really think it could ignore the Scottish political calendar? Did the BBC think no-one would remember the cancellation this time last year of a *Panorama* about corruption in Westminster City Council ten days before local elections in London? It has been for those who care to compare and contrast the regional rhetoric in *People and Programmes* with the more brutal reality — an instructive but sorry episode.

I recommend people who work in regional broadcasting for the BBC to flick to the end of Caesar's conquest of Gaul, where they will find this note on how that great man kept his tribes loyal:

> He made their condition of subjection more tolerable by addressing tribal governments in complimentary terms, refraining from the imposition of any fresh burdens and bestowing rich presents upon the principal citizens. By these means it was easy to induce a people exhausted by so many defeats to live at peace.

I am thinking of putting that on T-shirts and sending a couple off to Ron Neal and Mark Byford straight away.

But although it was there at the very beginning, the BBC is not the whole story of regional, local and community broadcasting. Since 1955 we have had a competing television service — ITV — regionally based. Since 1973 there has been independent local radio, locally based. Since 1982 there has been Channel Four, which can take regionally produced programmes and put them on for a national audience. Since 1992 there has been independent national radio, first Classic FM then Virgin 1215, and since February Talk Radio UK, all of which try to show they are not just London radio stations. Is it real, though, or is it just flavouring from the regional bottle?

It is worth going back to the beginning here. ITV as we know it, with contracting companies based in Manchester, Leeds, Newcastle and so on, was not born directly out of an Act of Parliament. It was the Independent Television Authority, under its first chairman Sir Kenneth Clarke, who decided on the federal structure — the division into franchise areas to encourage competition and promote regional identity. And, of course, to be very different from the BBC.

I grew up with Granada Television, and I have to say I felt an unreasonable surge of tribal pride when it took over London Weekend TV last year. It's now, of course, the longest-serving ITV contractor. So how did a London-based cinema chain come to provide television for the north? In Caroline Moorehead's biography of Sidney Bernstein there is a report of him talking to the Manchester Publicity Association in 1953. This is what he said:

> People have asked me why I applied for the North region. I have answered that London is full of displaced persons. The North is a place — close-knit, indigenous, industrial society, a homogenous cultured group with a record for music, theatre, literature and newspapers not found elsewhere. These reasons are true. But I am now going to tell you how I really came to my decision. It was brought about by two maps — a population map of Great Britain and a rainfall map. Any sensible person after studying these maps for a few minutes would realise that if commercial television is going to be a success anywhere in the world, it would be in the north of England.'

A week later he was awarded the contract, not for seven days a week but for five, with an area stretching right across the whole north from Liverpool to Newcastle. Granada went on the air in May 1956. In news, he was determined to get away from the stuffiness of the BBC. He did, and the BBC soon knew about it.

The man who headed the ITV weekend company for an area combining the north-west and the Midlands, a huge area, ABC Television, was Howard Thomas, the inventor for the BBC, on radio of course, during the war years of *The Brains Trust* and *Sincerely Yours, Vera Lynn*, the programme of which the BBC governors wrote '*Sincerely Yours* deplored. But popularity noted.' Thomas knew the value to any broadcaster of being seen around the territory. He bought three outside broadcast units capable of broadcasting from football matches, churches and all kinds of halls right across the region, 'from the Mersey to the Humber,' in his words.

In the mid-60s I used to do a show for ABC. It was live, studio-based, at that former cinema in Didsbury just up the road where Hughie Green used to do *Opportunity Knocks* and the great days of *Armchair Theatre* — live drama with all its attendant hazards — were lived out. In his memoirs, *With an Independent Air*, Thomas recalls watching at home one Sunday night and getting an urgent message from the general manager at ABC. 'One of the actors has just died and is lying on the studio floor. What shall I do?' Thomas says he could only answer 'Get him out of the picture and get on with the play!' And they did. Thomas bought the best for *Armchair Theatre*. The region served by ABC — the North and the Midlands — loved it. The network wouldn't let *Armchair Theatre* on at first . But, when they did, in the 1959 to 1960 season, *Armchair Theatre* plays by, amongst others, Harold Pinter, Angus Wilson, Alun Owen, were in the Top Ten programmes for thirty-two weeks out of thirty-seven.

On our much humbler programme, called *ABC Weekend*, the forerunner of all the ninety-minute regional debate shows that have come down the line ever since, and God knows I've done most of them, there was always an outside broadcast link. Where it was depended on where the OB unit was — usually half way between Saturday's football match and Sunday's Church service. At that place, whether it was in someone's home or in some beery club, I'd be the person on the end of the line. I once said to my distinguished friend, a producer here for BBC North region radio, I said, 'Why is it that I am always our man up the slag heap?' And, she said, 'Well, dear, horses for courses.'

Anyway, at that place I'd be the focus, and the lines would go down, and you'd have to continue in sound only. It kept ABC totally visible. Even in the sophisticated days of the swinging 60s Howard Thomas knew his audience. Those Saturday night OBs made me famous from Morecambe to Wolverhampton. The glamour of it all!

A year or so before, in 1964, the BBC was still struggling to reconcile its regional output with social reality, for devolution was all the go just then, and for a while it even looked as though Harold Wilson's Labour government might lay some serious power on the regions. He didn't, of course, but you did not know that at the time. There was a conference organised with the University of York. All sorts of grand people were there, including the Assistant Head of North Regional Programmes, Colin Shaw, to discuss drama, news, writers and the arts in BBC North region. The word 'provincialism' was daringly used in the title. (Now there's another word you would think about using twice today). Anyway, the report is fascinating. Sid Chaplin, the writer, says that it's inevitable that there would be a flow to and from a capital city. Stan Barstow, another writer, said rejection by London didn't mean total rejection. William Hardcastle said that community news made sense, and of course there wasn't too much news on radio. Richard Hoggart talked of links across cultures rather than between regions, accused the BBC of going in for mere 'parish pumpery', said Granada was the adman's north, but also said that Granada had caught the spirit of the north better in *Coronation Street* than anything the BBC were doing. The BBC, he said, went in more for 'clog dancers'. By the way, out there in Viewerland *Crossroads* had started just a month before. How long ago it seems; how long ago it was!

We've had a few reallocations of TV franchises since then, many a BBC D-G and several Acts of Parliament. The last one, in 1990, the one which made ITV applicants bid for their licences in money and not just fair words and lifted away entirely the public service requirement from independent local radio, left the shape of ITV once more to the IBA to decide. It astonished a lot of people that they stuck with the same map — the fourteen regions and GMTV — and the same time clock which splits London into two licences. I've heard Sir George Russell, then of the IBA and now the ITC chairman, say they did so because ITV is a very powerful brand name. Sir George, of course, is a Geordie who courted his wife on Otterspool Prom in Liverpool. He is the same age as me, and I bet his regional imprinting is every bit as strong as mine. But it can't just have been sentiment; regionality may be an administrative convenience more than a notion of real tribal affinity. It does seem to matter, though, in how devoted you become to what you see and what you hear. I worked for ten action-packed years doing local and network programmes at Tyne-Tees. I know that both the affection and the annoyance people felt towards me was real. A cynic, a distinguished BBC producer, who does not come from Geordieland but lives there and loves it enough to have become totally enmeshed within its masochistic tendrils, once said to me, 'The problem with this place is that they will support anything — any football team, any television company, any crooked politician, as long as it is *ours.*'

In the last round of ITV contracts we saw weaker companies bidding blind against the strong ones. The result, as we all know, was that Tyne-Tees and Yorkshire paid far too much for their contracts to stay in business on their own. Sir George Russell helped them to find a way to combine and stay in business. It can help to have a Geordie on your side sometimes. But what if the Government decides the ownership rule should now be radically changed? Granada said last year that it would be interested in the action in a Yorkshire/Tyne-Tees area. Will we see the big amalgamations? Those four big companies of the first ITV years reforming themselves in the light of business sense and hard experience? How strange that would be! But preferable, perhaps, to some French water company or some German publisher or some Australian newspaper magnate coming in. I think so. I fear the effect of foreign ownership in a lightly regulated market.

Some of you may have seen Channel 4's documentary on Sunday night on the impact of satellite TV in India. Did you feel, as I did, tremors of premonition down your back as Rupert Murdoch said that everywhere he goes people are turning to local programming? I don't think he means *Calendar* in Yorkshire or *Look North* on Granada; I am sure that he does not mean drama done co-operatively between Granada, Yorkshire and Tyne-Tees. He means a gorgeous local babe talking over a confrontation done in action camera style. Bring back the BBC's clog dances, I say!

Back in the present, things have already changed a lot. In the last five years, through the impact of the Government's policy on commercial television, we have seen a major shift in the labour market. ITV has shed jobs, local jobs, by the thousand. Two years ago on this very spot, at this very Symposium, Mike Watts, then Director of Programmes at Central, spoke of a third of the ITV working force having gone, and one-third of that third going entirely out of the trade, one-third going independent or freelance and moving to London, the final third trying to make a living in television on their own patch. Since then, following the Carlton/Central merger, Mike Watts has become one of his own redundancy statistics. Data from SkillSet, the industry training organisation for broadcasting, film and video, shows that of the television workforce throughout the UK, fifty-four per cent is now freelance. Two-thirds are based in London. They are mostly male and middle-aged, and only half had worked in the previous year.

The craft base of all regional television has changed. Tyne-Tees no longer employs three people in make-up. It has one and some freelancers. ITV contracts, however, still stipulate regional programming as one of four mandated categories. Is this just sentiment, or is it good business? If the experience of independent local radio is anything to go by, and I think it is, those broadcasters whose voice is rooted in the local community and whose programmes reflect the reality of regional experience always do better. Look at Radio Clyde in Glasgow. For the last year its RAJAR — that is the Joint Industry Radio Audience Research — has been, as we would say in Liverpool, 'the talk of the wash-house.' It has two services, AM and FM, and together they beat the BBC's five networks and Virgin and Classic FM and BBC Radio Scotland all combined. For Radio Clyde talks in its own voice and has done for all its twenty-one years. It is not put on. It is not mandated by some distant person who sets out a pattern. It is real.

In commercial radio, stations come and go, change hands, move on. Liverpool's Radio City, where once I was the first Programme Controller, used to be a local consortium. Now it belongs to EMAP, regional newspaper publishers from outside who also own Kiss FM in London and who devised an ingenious way to accommodate the Radio Authority's ownership rules when they took over the Transworld group of radio stations, Piccadilly in Manchester, Red Rose in Preston, Radio Aire across the Pennines in Leeds. All of those stations began as locals, locally owned. Piccadilly's first chairman, Neil Pearson, was once chairman of that bolshie BBC North Region Advisory Council. Those days are gone. Radio is a business like any others — buy shares, sell them. Fine. But take away the regional reality, the local tan, the people who know how to say the place names and your investment won't be worth as much.

Interestingly, the buying of Transworld by EMAP is a deal which isn't yet complete. Their way of going round the ownership rules hasn't actually yet been accepted by the Radio Authority. They referred it to the Department of Heritage when it happened. And a year or more on we are still waiting for Heritage to say whether the deal can go through. If it does it will show the way for TV companies to eat each other up. But so far, mysteriously, Heritage hasn't spoken. Although other groups have asked for the same freedom, the Radio Authority has granted it to none. Watch this space! Radio, so often the seed-bed for new talent — Chris Evans, Mark Radcliffe and the rest — is also the forcing house for new ownership patterns, new working practices and different approaches to audiences. It is much more crowded out there in Radioland. A pound has to go further, but ideas can travel much faster.

How long is it going to take, though, before people realise that what brings Radio Clyde such huge audiences and keeps Capital top of the heap in London is that they make you feel good about the place you live? By feeling good I don't mean just sunny jingles and big cash give-aways. I mean they tell you stuff about the city you didn't know before which you find useful and which is done in a way that doesn't come clonking through the airwaves in the aural equivalent of flares and platform soles.

I hear the Labour Party is eager to put a regional obligation on local cable operators. I wonder why? It makes sense in audience terms and in business terms and without any legal requirement whatsoever to show regional commitment and awareness, to grow local talent, to bring it to local news, to try new local programmes. Look at the ratings if you doubt me, but it needs to be real to be right.

The first year of ITV contractors' annual reports in the ITC show that on the surface they are keeping their promises on regional programming. Every company, bar one — Westcountry — and that for a pretty good reason, has kept, and more than kept, to their stated regional quota of programmes. Most exceeded them. Yes, there were shortfalls in some areas — Meridian for arts, HTV for using inexperienced presenters, Scottish for 'limited range and quality in religious programmes.' I understand this year the picture on meeting regional commitment remains broadly satisfactory. There is growing concern, though, over marginalisation in the scheduling of regional programmes, and a general tendency to bulk things up with news — when in doubt, stick in a sub-regional bulletin. Against attempts at the regional quiz format where the regional content clearly falls way behind the money saving and fill-up-the-time motive, it could be worse.

It could also be much better. The ITV companies are still making huge profits, even though they have to hand over so many heavy bags of gold to the Treasury. Carlton, the London weekday contractor, has taken a pasting from the ITC and the newspaper critics for being particularly feeble in programme output. Well, *Hollywood Women* was a bit of a freak show. But I have to say that Carlton's local shows are a pleasant surprise. Their nightly news magazine is my preferred slant on life in London. They have done their bit for art and artists. They make living in the city feel a bit more like fun than those grim-faced duos, the ones with the grey jackets and the bright red lipstick, though not both together, over on the BBC, broadcasting by numbers.

As long as there is business in local and regional identity, then commercial broadcasters will do it. But, with no disrespect to the ITC's power to keep people to their licences, it will always need hard competition from the BBC in range and quality to keep the standard high. That's for old-fashioned TV, of course, the kind that comes through the air or down a cable on to a set. The next big thing on the horizon is the Little Screen — the computer — taking over from TV, being your personal guide to what it is you want to know. Already, I am told, it is possible to put in 'cheap', 'Italian' and 'Manchester 'into your *Daily Telegraph* CD-ROM and up will come at least six suggestions for restaurants. But that's information, not entertainment. The BBC, I know, is much exercised lest the computer screen take over from the TV screen within the next decade. Personally, I think the computer-screen based stuff like the Internet and interactive is much more of a threat to radio than to TV. If it takes off, it is radio that faces the loss of a young audience, and that, any way you look at it, would be the beginning of the end.

ITV has other things on its mind. What about Channel Five? There's no obligation to carry regional or local programmes on Channel Five. Interestingly, the first time it was advertised, the only proposal received was for a network based on cities. The ITC, in circumstances which to this day make David Elstein, who headed the bid, grind his teeth, turn them down. None of the groups bidding now — Pearsons, Mirror Group, BSkyB with Granada, Yorkshire and Tyne Tees, is openly planning a regional element. Maybe it will be someone's secret weapon.

Out in the wider political world things are changing too. Like it or not, we are members of the European Union. And the basis of much of EU thinking is regional. The north-west, for instance, is a region of the European Union. Lancashire got grants worth over 1.7 million ECU in 1990 to 1992 to help with the reconversion of run-down coal mining areas. Liverpool is now getting £375 million from the European Development Fund. They say over there, but only behind their hand, that it would have been a billion, except that Mr Major nicked some of the millions to buy off the Ulster Unionists on Maastricht, but that's only gossip.

Anyway, my old school, Blackburn House, is now a centre for women's' technical training, and a large slice of the money to make it possible came from Europe. Roads, rail links, education, communications — they have all had funds from the EU, and this is a pattern which will grow. The political pressure for devolution is therefore back. Labour, pressing for regional power to the people, committing to regional assemblies, is only keeping step with the EU. We are, after all, the only European country without a regional tier of government. Did you know, though, that already there is a new committee of the regions established by the Maastricht Treaty, and this region, and every other, sends three representatives to it? Where there are politics, broadcasting will follow.

If there really is a growth in regional political power over the next five years, it will need to be reflected on radio and television. Imagine in 1999 trying to broadcast a *Panorama* interview with Tony Blair the week of elections to a Labour majority Scottish Assembly with an unpopular record on public spending. My observation of both BBC and commercial broadcasting seems to indicate that regional output often becomes richer and more varied the closer we are to renewals of charters and franchises and the nearer we come to elections. I sniff change in the air. May the wind blow northerly.

Bibliography

BBC (1995), *People in Programmes*. London: BBC.
Briggs, A. (1979), *History of Broadcasting in the United Kingdom, Vol IV: Sound and Vision*. Oxford: Oxford University Press
Handford, V. (tr.) (1951) *Caesar's Gaul*. Harmondsworth: Penguin Books.
Clarke, S. and Horrie, C. (1994), *Fuzzy Monsters: Fear and Loathing at the BBC*. London: Heinemann
Moorehead, C. (1984), *Sidney Bernstein: A Biography*. London: Cape.
Thomas, H. (1977), *With an Independent Air: Encounters during a lifetime of broadcasting*. London: Weidenfeld and Nicolson.

Session produced by Colin Shaw

Does regional culture matter?

Chair: **Rod Allen**
HarperCollins Interactive

Steve Avery
Kirklees Economic Development Unit

Professor Colin Fletcher
University of Wolverhampton

Phil Wood
Kirklees Economic Development Unit

ROD Allen: My name is Rod Allen; I am editorial director of HarperCollins*Interactive*. I was interested to hear from Gillian Reynolds this morning that I am a big threat to regional news. I hadn't though of it like that, but she is probably right, actually, particularly in terms of our on-line publishing activities, which are swift, interactive and topical. So I don't work in television any more, which gives me a chance to sit back somewhat more objectively and think about the debates that we are participating in in these two days.

In this session we wanted to look at some of the assumptions underlying the debate and discussion about regional and community access — regional and community broadcasting, and we have got two very different presentations which we hope will then stimulate some discussion from the floor.

Colin Fletcher, who is Professor of Educational Research at the University of Wolverhampton, has been studying the issue of regionalism and what it is we mean by regional for some time now, and he is going to share with us some of the insights that he has arrived at during this work and look at some of the underlying assumptions.

We are then going to look, with Steve Avery and Phil Wood, at a community cultural communications initiative actually in action. Just before we do that, though, because Steve and Phil come from the Kirklees Economic Development Unit, would you put up your hand if you know where Kirklees is?

Many hands go up

Good. About half of you. I only learned last week that it is another word for Huddersfield. Kirklees is where this deliberate local cultural policy is being pursued and we are going to find out here about how that is being done.

Colin Fletcher: I am concerned with the public use and place of media in empowerment as distinct from entertainment. I am concerned with the way in which media feature as part of the process whereby people realise and whereby people resist.

So, in order to do this, of course, I now need to establish an academic offering. I will need to advance to you the different definitions of community and region since Chaucer. I need to give a lot of references with suggested names. I need to give a heap of inconclusive data about how forty-nine per cent do, fifty-one per cent don't and the rest didn't know. And I need to conclude with the plea for further research, preferably located at my own institution. I have done that. OK. Can we take that as done?

The interesting thing for me with regard to what Gillian Reynolds had to say was that she used her sense of community to discuss region. She used what she called her 'tribalism,' her location in terms of school, in terms of place, in terms of language, in terms of her very self. Twenty years on and the fibres are still strong.

For those of us in education there are two quite distinct sets of communities. There are communities of residence, which have a fairly obvious corollary with neighbourhood, town and village, and there are communities of interest; these are groups of people who are banded together because they like fishing or because they are bringing up children, or whatever. The interesting thing, as far as I am concerned, is the way in which communities of interest tend to be under-represented in discussion, whereas we tend to assume that community always means residence. And, of course, we always assume that community is a warm, wholesome, homely sort of thing. As Raymond Williams said, 'There is no known antidote, let alone opposite to community.' Each one of you could affirmatively answer the question 'Where are you from?' You would all say a place. You would all say, quite clearly, that you have roots and possibly also the realisation of the ways in which those roots have been pulled, or the ways in which you, yourselves, have been removed.

One of the most interesting features of the English demography is that seventy per cent of the population of England and Wales have not moved more than twenty-five miles in their lives. And that applies with remarkable consistency from 1801 onwards. Cosmopolitans are in the minority, the locals are in the majority. Most significantly of all, those who are the most intensively loyal are young people. They are the ones with the very profound sense of territory, the very profound sense of language, local significances and circumstances.

I suspect that my quarrel, if you like, with the terms and title of this conference is the over-statement of the notion of region. I am fascinated with the struggle that will take place over the next two days to give a reality to what is palpably a myth. It is a *political* reality. It always has been. I firmly believe that regions are probably pre-Norman. They are almost certainly made and maintained by a combination of land-owning interests and the masonic order. I see very little evidence of regions having a clear edge, a clear boundary or a clear meaning. What I do see, of course, is every institution in the country having a profound sense of struggle over what region means to it — whether it is a health authority, whether it is education, you name it. And now, of course, broadcasting. And I will put it to you very plainly that the joy of the struggle is not to succeed but to engage. The purpose of this is to fulfil that well-known maxim from T.S. Eliot, 'The centre will not hold.'

What we really see in the concept of regionalism and the concept of region are different ways in which the centre can be resisted, different ways in which we can represent the centre. Gillian Reynolds was quite right in saying that without the European Union, as it now is, most regions would be feeling a lot colder than they do now. I currently work in the Black Country, which has little, if any, relationship with the national government. But, by jove, we have got little flags with blue backgrounds and stars all round them on every road, street and, on some occasions, major houses. It is fascinating, therefore, that the European Union is, I would argue, in the process of encouraging regions as a countervailing force to the nation state. You can't get through to the Government. but at least you might be able to get through to the localities.

So here, then, are my three propositions and they don't exactly, as yet, connect. My three propositions are:

- There are communities of residence, localities, neighbourhoods;
- There are communities of interest which spread from localities right across the country; and
- There is a struggle over the nature and realisation of region, and that the signifance of this struggle is about tackling the centre as best one can.

I don't wish to convey by this means the idea that community is somehow or other simply this warm, wholesome, wholemeal thing. William Hazlitt, on his celebrated rides around the country, wrote an essay on the English village the first sentence of which was 'All village people hate each other.' And William Hazlitt's argument was that it was conflict which actually cohered. It was the right to engage with others, it was the right to argue with them, it was the right to be a character and to be challenged as a character which gave so much of the colour to the countryside.

So if we can accept, then, that the *locus* of most people's identity is probably to do with the conflicts and loyalties, the languages, the families, and the follies, the staggering follies of local communities then, in my view, what we have in broadcasting is the representation of communities as more or less standing models in the national theme park; that we have these interesting characters (and the older the better); we have communities of interest largely under-represented, except when it comes to sport and recreation and, in that sense, mis-represented; and we have regions as nodes, or what we would call sites of conflict. Regions are, therefore, always in dispute.

The work in regard to community education and community development basically says that the two real challenges for the representation of social life are tokenism and parochialism. Tokenism means that you talk about a few people endlessly — good old England, as it were. And parochialism means that you talk about us lot as distinct from them lot. And us lot being different are, therefore, better.

I would argue that every account of communities of residence and every account of region has a way of tending towards these two key problems of taking a very small part of something that is very obvious, tokenistically, and advancing it in such a way that there is actually no real social gain; there is simply the warmth of some sense of being better than others. And it was interesting that Gillian Reynolds, as it were, pitched us into a state of perpetual motion between the football match and Sunday's church service to that effect. My basic feeling about the problems which may occur over the next two days with regard to the debate is that we may never actually leave the outside broadcast dilemma; that there are certain realities that we hold true and dear, that we live in particular neighbourhoods — we like our neighbours and why shouldn't we? — that there are certain enthusiasms that we have for particular activities and, to be quite honest, the more bizarre, the better and there are certain ways in which we think. We may well live in a region; we are not quite sure precisely where its edges are; we are fairly convinced that it has a major urban centre and that somehow or other this major urban centre is our way of tackling the major national urban centre. So our gang is better than their gang.

In this way I believe it is important not only to expose the assumptions but also to expose the inadequacy with which they are actually pursued, the under-representation of communities of interest. Whoever does it — whether or not it is handled by regional broadcasting or national broadcasting — for me is neither here or there; it is the degree to which there are interests. I happen to be very keen on environmental issues; I am sure some of you are, but you may also have concerns specific and special to yourself. I am fascinated by the way in which these specific concerns about where we are going as distinct from where we have come from can be overlooked if we concentrate solely on the charms of our communities historically achieved and upon the realisations of our regions as a way of resisting national government.

I don't deny that there is something significant about the forms of speech and humour. I don't deny that there are cherished phrases and holy places. You have probably gathered that I am the third Merseysider in succession. Neither do I deny that there is a kind of folksiness to us which will always come out. There is a kind of sentiment, a kind of sentimentality which I would never rubbish. What I am concerned about is that we adopt a genuinely sceptical attitude to the ways in which we will represent the future of things as distinct from the past of them, to the ways in which, especially, communities of interest are actually best served.

These are the emergent forms, as distinct from the communities of residence in which most people live and will stay living and regions. Where I want to come to rest with regard to the examination of the assumptions is: if you can accept that for me mass media are the most powerful significant phenomena in social change then without them there is very little, if any, genuine communication between people, particularly between countries and now, I would say, especially within countries. I am proposing these as forms of debate rather than things which I have simply said and see as closed.

Then whilst I can obviously acknowledge the emphasis and concern you have for media as entertainment, it is media's empowerment which draws me back. It is this which I think has taken me much more now to interactive media and to hyper-media, working with community groups than to the kinds of ways in which we used to videotape programmes ten or fifteen years ago and show them endlessly. We are now turning much more to the development of interactive media with local groups.

So my drift is this: I accept that many of you, if not most of you, are concerned with media as entertainment and I don't deny the validity of that. I enjoy it, why not? For me there is also the question of empowerment. There is the question of human engagement. And what I see at the moment in this debate is the under-representation of communities of interest, the staid and stereotypical representation of communities of residence and something about the region which I regard as essentially and ultimately unresolvable. It is challenging, for sure, and something in which to engage, clearly aided and abetted and encouraged by the European Union and clearly for many of us in the more deprived parts of the country, particularly where I am now working in the Black Country, perhaps the most important single straw we have to clutch. Perhaps for us in the Black Country there is this feeling that without the European Union nothing would be happening. We wouldn't have training for women, we wouldn't have work in local communities, we wouldn't have stations that function. There is no doubt about this is any of our minds. But how we see it is that we are being set up, in the nicest possible way, as a form of one and a half fingers to the national government, and there is no way we can be convinced that anybody believes that our region is meaningful, either to ourselves or to yourselves, without this focusing of a national struggle.

So there are my propositions. OK with regard to communities of residence. Lots and lots of air-time for those. Under-statement with regard to communities of interest. And the question of region partially, but not wholly, a red herring.

Rod Allen: We will hold some of those propositions in our minds for the debate afterwards and we will come back to them. Now we are going to focus a little more on the community issues and Steve and Phil are going to tell us about Kirklees and its community cultural policy.

Phil Wood: Who needs a cultural policy anyway? Did Salzburg need a cultural policy to produce Mozart? No. Did Kansas City need a cultural policy to produce Charlie Parker? We don't think so. Did Liverpool need a cultural policy to produce the Beatles? Hardly.

But if Liverpool *had* had a cultural policy in the early 1960s, might it have made rather more of the remarkable cultural explosion of Merseybeat? Liverpool today is one of the most sussed cities in Britain in terms of maximising the potential of its cultural assets, but for twenty years up to the mid 1980s, it squandered its wealth with a profligacy which is quite breathtaking.

This brings us to the key theme of our paper — that civic authorities cannot create creativity, but they can do a great deal to frustrate or even destroy it. The adoption of local cultural policies is designed to produce a condition of which creativity — when it is does emerge — is best able to flourish to the mutual benefit of the creator and a wider society.

Before we talk about Kirklees' adoption of cultural policy, a brief preamble setting out the socio-economic and cultural developments of the last few decades which influenced the thinking of Kirklees and other local government policy makers. (Acknowledgment is due for this section in particular to our consultants Franco Bianchini and Charles Landry of Comedia).

Cultural policy in Britain up to the 1970s had barely changed for decades. The arts were a pantheon of good taste and breeding into which only the chosen might enter. The creation of art was an end in itself — arts for arts' sake. Liberal elements in the 1960s called for a 'democratisation of culture' — could not the doors of the pantheon (or the Municipal Art Gallery) be opened a little wider to let a few more people in? During the 70s, some leftward leaning authorities began talk of there being a 'role' for the arts in achieving a better and more just society. The community arts or cultural democracy movement gave local government the notion that there might be more to the arts than simply art itself.

However, it was during the 1980s that two key forces emanating from opposite poles converged to achieve a most significant impact. Firstly, Thatcherite monetarism penetrated the bastions of the Arts Council to the extent that it began, in the mid-1980s, to start parroting the language of its arm's-length master. The Arts Council's invite to the public and private sectors to 'invest' in British Culture bestowed upon culture the sense of it being a commodity or a national economic asset. The link between culture and the (market) economy had been made.

Just across the Thames meanwhile, Ken Livingstone and Tony Banks's Greater London Council was arriving at a similar conclusion by way of a radically different route. The GLC employed its grants for the arts function as a strategy to empower hitherto under-represented social and cultural groups, such as feminists, black groups, gays and the disabled. The arts became a battle ground on which the *causes celèbres* of equal opportunities were fought out, as the pages of contemporary tabloids would testify. Perhaps more significant, however, was the GLC's role in discovering London's 'cultural industries' and defining a new role for local government in this sector. Through the Greater London Enterprise Board, a cultural industries strategy was devised and implemented, recognising for the first time that this was one of London's most significant economic sectors in terms of employment, turnover and export potential. The once radical notion that culture could employ lots of people in real, wealth-creating jobs was first pioneered by the GLC and finally received universal acknowledgment with the publication of John Myerscough's major study *The Economic Importance of the Arts* in 1988.

During the 1980s, local authorities were also starting to look further afield than London for policy inspiration. It became clear that in continental Europe and the USA cities and municipalities were re-inventing themselves through processes of urban regeneration which were either led or heavily influenced by culture. Old American rustbelt cities like Pittsburgh were combining cultural projects with high-tech inward investment to shake off their dowdy images, whilst prosperous but boring Frankfurt was trying to project a more frivolous image through the arts.

Therefore, by the time that Kirklees Council began to address itself to cultural policy-making, there was a rich store of past experience from which to draw. As with most experience, it was often contradictory and apparently illogical, but it is possible to identify common themes, or at least positions on common continua, from one city to another. These have been called the dilemmas of cultural policy development:

1. *Elite/Prestige/Flagship v Community-orientated/small scale*
   From the American experience in particular, we see examples of whole down-town development schemes being driven by an opera house or theatre devel-opment, whereas the European experience has often been a small groups of artists or community activists building from the grass roots.

2. *Artistic Content v Spin-offs*
   Should cultural policy's first priority be to benefit the arts or is the arts' impact on the economy, environment, education, etc. the most significant?

3. *Challenging v Reassuring*
   Surely good art should ask questions of the status quo, but is there a tempta-tion for the artist involved in urban regeneration to compromise and play it safe to please the paymaster?

4. *Ephemeral/Events v Permanent/Buildings*
   High profile events can often radically alter the way in which a city is viewed by the outside world, for example Glasgow's Year of Culture in 1990, but the lasting benefit of these can be limited, whilst the natural instinct of a local elected member is often to invest in something that will last like a building .

5. *Local v International*
   Should the policy celebrate everything that is local and home-grown or is there a case for bringing in new ideas and influences from abroad?

6. *Past/Heritage v Future/Experimental*
   Some policies have been used to repackage a worn-out industrial past as cul-tural heritage, whilst other cities have sought to re-invent themselves by in-vesting in new high tech media and experimental art forms.

7. *Arts v Media*
   A false dichotomy, it seems to us, but all too real to some, is whether cultural development should be lead by the traditional subsidised arts or by the mod-ern semi-commercial media industries.

8. *Consumption v Production*
   A city like Bradford has chosen to promote itself as a place where you can go and have a good time at its festivals, in its concert halls or in its curry houses, whilst, in contrast, Sheffield is developing, through its Cultural Industries Quar-ter, as a place where cultural commodities are produced, often for export.

9. *City Centre v Periphery*
   For years Liverpool Council deliberately neglected its city centre in order to invest in suburban re-housing projects — and it shows, whilst Glasgow has faced stiff criticism from its own electorate for concentrating disproportion-ately on the centre during its Year of Culture.

10. *Authenticity v Gentrification*
    The case of Soho in New York is interesting here — an area of cheap housing was populated by artists who developed an authentic loft community, only to find that this artistic cachet raised property prices to a level which meant they had to leave, to be replaced by the gentrifiers and pastiche merchants.

These are ten dilemmas to which there is no definitive right or wrong, but which cannot be overlooked by the cultural policy maker. Our instinct in Kirklees, and one which was reinforced by our consultants, was that the best policy is 'be yourself'. In order to assist a puzzled local authority to discover what being oneself really is, Bianchini and Landry offer a policy making model — the Cultural Resources approach.

They point out that each locality has its own cultural resources, be it an ivy-clad university town or a pit village, through the commonly held values, experiences, rituals and aspirations of its people; and that the role which culture can play in the well-being of that locality can be manifold:

ECONOMIC
Media Industries
Technology
Cultural Tourism

SYMBOLIC
Civic Pride
Image
City Marketing

SOCIAL
Cohesion
Harmony
Community Safety

ENVIRONMENTAL
Urban beautification
Public Art
Raising property values

POLITICAL
Active citizenship

EDUCATIONAL
Delivering School Curriculum through culture

In trying to understand this approach it might be useful to draw a comparison with our understanding of the natural environment. Twenty years ago, a local authority's perspective on the environment did not extend much beyond ensuring the drains were kept clear. Nowadays, they are all avidly identifying and conserving important habitats for all sorts of economic, social and moral reasons. Through this 'greening process' we all now understand that if a species or habitat is lost, it can never be replaced. In the same way our local cultural resources are being swallowed up by the slash and burn of global homogenisation. Many local authorities never recognise their own cultural resources until they are gone — and some then go to ridiculous and expensive lengths to re-create artificially what they have lost — but it is locking the stable door after the horse has bolted. The Cultural Resources approach is a technique for recognising what you have got whilst you still have it. One should not, however, think this is an attempt to freeze in time some romantic idyll. This is a dynamic model which needs constant replenishment from new and challenging cultural hybrids.

This is the context out of which Kirklees' cultural policy was born. There would have been no point in borrowing Glasgow or Manchester's policy because Kirklees is a singularly different entity — a hodgepodge of town and country displaying great contrast and diversity. Maybe it is significant as the beginning of an alternative to the big city models quoted earlier. Maybe Kirklees can provide a clarion call for all the Seftons and Haltons, the Tamesides and Calderdales, the anonymous creations of the 1974 local government reorganisation.

The Council's policy, adopted in 1994, is entitled 'Made in Kirklees', a means of linking past with present. Kirklees draws its identify from people making things, be it worsted cloth and gear boxes or choral and brass band music. It has three guiding principles:

> 1. *Celebrating Diversity* — for years the geographic, political, economic and ethnic diversity of Kirklees was seen as its disability, but now the district has found a way of working collaboratively and synergistically and diversity is now seen as a positive asset.
> 2. *Maintaining Distinctiveness* — recognising what makes us different and special and keeping it that way. This doesn't mean you can turn back Macdonalds and CNN at the borders, but it does mean intervening to ensure local tendencies hold their own.
> 3. *Harnessing Creativity* — as we said early, you cannot will a Mozart, a Parker or the Beatles, but you can ensure the local state has the flexibility to recognise and accommodate them. Creativity whether in the arts, business or public administration, is the lifeblood of any viable town or city.

Physical manifestations of the policy are often difficult to pin down. Nevertheless, the spirit which the policy encapsulates has been very much in evidence during the 1990s; it would not be hyperbolic to speak of a 'Kirklees Cultural Renaissance' in recent years. 1994 alone saw:

> (a) the opening of the unique Alfred McAlpine Stadium, a £15 million for football, rugby and music spectaculars displaying all the typical Kirklees characteristics of financial risk taking, public/private/community collaboration and quality execution;
> (b) the national media proclaiming of Huddersfield as "The Poetry Capital of Britain" acknowledging a remarkable upsurge in new writing activity in the town;
> (c) the opening of the £5 million Lawrence Batley Theatre which achieved national acclaim on becoming the new home for the Huddersfield Contemporary Music Festival; and
> (d) the advice of none other than the then Secretary of State for National Herit-

age, Steven Dorrell, that the travelling culture vulture should forget Paris and look instead to Huddersfield for inspiration.

As this is a Broadcasting Symposium, however, you are likely to be interested less in poetry, theatre and tourism and more on how we have adopted our policy to the challenges of the contemporary media industries and for this I turn to my colleague Steve Avery.

Steve Avery: For those of you who still do not know where Kirklees is I will briefly point it out. It is in the middle of the country, almost in the middle of Great Britain. It is an area of great scenic beauty.

I am not from a cultural background. I come from an economics background and you are probably wondering why I am speaking here on behalf of a cultural policy. From a point of little if any media production activity within the area maybe four or five years ago, we now have a Media Centre. We had the thank-you drinks party for the Media Centre last Friday. We have a film commissioning distribution company who are going to be locating within that centre. We have the Campaign for Press and Broadcasting Freedom who are going to be in there as well. We have within the Media Centre a fibre optic network which has actually been provided for us by Cabletel, the local cable franchisee. That gives you an idea of the beginning of the economic justification that I can claim for the diversification of the local economy into the media.

Last week we also had a group of senior councillors round, and in Kirklees they do tend to be a bit conservative with a small 'c' if not a large 'C.' They agreed to take forward a report on developing joint initiatives with Cabletel and that included a local television channel. And that shows just how far we have taken the political understanding of how important media are over that five year period during which we have been developing the cultural policy. We would not have got that sort of decision five years ago.

Recently our Chief Executive hosted a meal for the top businessmen in the area to introduce them to a group of community activists who have been lobbying for the local community radio licence to be released. That shows how far we have brought the senior management within the authority into this.

The cultural policy helps us weave this support into the fabric of work. Clearly there are some of us within Kirklees who require no convincing that the media sector will provide employment and ought to be invested in. We believe let's say by the year 2010 that within our travel-to-work area, media will employ more people than are employed within the textiles industry, which is the traditional industry of the area and that is despite our knowledge of the fact that independent television is cutting jobs at a rapid rate.

The question is: how can we develop the ability of the local communities to take advantage of the regional job opportunities? And the cultural policy provides us with a platform for that debate. It allows us to go in and talk to the people who do not believe in the media as being a means of employment that we can actually get there.

It has some practical benefits as well. Most of you, if you come from a big city, will at the moment be facing the problem of how to deal with the cable operators as they go through. If you are in television you will be wondering what effect cable is going to have upon your market share. Most local authorities have a fairly negative relationship with the cable providers. They see them with respect to the first two points on the list — how can they reduce the inconvenience caused during the build-out programme and how can they maximise the improvement in the quality of the pavements?

I will start giving some examples now of where we have actually moved forward. I suppose we have come to it very much from a community base and that, in itself, is important if you are looking at a regional policy. We have to work with the existing community and the existing culture. There are a number of organisations that existed when I moved across to Kirklees in '89. Arty Van was one of those. A basic community arts body went out. He had his printing room and his darkroom in a van and he went from pit villages to wherever helping people make books, get photographic exhibitions on. Arty Van has now moved to become Arty Media. They deal with multi-media production. They are doing CD-ROMs. They are making material to publicise local companies as well. They have helped us win our bid, as a region, to become involved in the year for photography and the moving image in 1998.

We have EAV, which is a video production training facility. It is very small-scale, local community, very common up and down the country. But it still exists. The fact that it still exists in this day and age I think is a consequence of that cultural policy. We have Beaumont Street Recording Studio, a local community studio — again most of those, nationally, have a very bad track record. Beaumont Street have expanded; they are now multimedia. They do single media production and training, they put people through journalism. They have facilities both in the north and south of the area. They are picking up money from all the government programmes.

And we have got the Media Centre, the physical base in which a lot of these organisations will be having a presence. It provides work space for those businesses, conference facilities, gallery and a cafe/bar facility.

We can also say, and more importantly for me and also I think for yourselves, is that we have been able to get the Council involved in looking at the establishment of a local television channel. We are not able to take more than a five per cent share in local television. We are forbidden from doing to stop us from politically influencing programmes. I don't know why they restrict us as local authorities but it is maybe so there can't be competition for national governments in that line but consequently we are restricted in our role to playing that of an honest broker, and that's what we have been doing. We have got the officers and we have got the councillors to agree that we can go out. And we are out there talking with the local further education colleges, we are talking with the local newspapers, we are talking to everybody about how we can get that local channel going.

And we are being successful. We have got Cabletel to take us very seriously. They have recently poached someone from Yorkshire Television to come in and advise them on how they can deal with the local programming issues. So we are having an effect there.

We are moving into an educational market. We have got our education services. Again a normally traditional, conservative sort of service in the local authority, they are pursuing the development of educational material, and asking how they can become a producer. They are not just interested in just being a consumer. They know they are going to become a consumer. Microsoft is releasing huge quantities of information and educational material on to the market. I am sure Rod Allen at HarperCollins is also producing huge quantities of material for the market, seeing our educational services as being a consumer of that. Well, the Microsoft stuff has an American culture underlying it, not a British one. Rod's stuff may have a British one. I'll have to check what he has got. But we would like some local culture within there. If you going to maintain a local identity, you have to be teaching about your local culture within, I think, that educational system.

That is a cultural reason why we are investing, but it is also a negative reason. Looking at why we might have a positive reason for investing it in that production, if we do produce local material, we want to do this locally whether it is for CD-ROM, remote database accessing or transmission by broad or narrow band, that requires local facilities. If you operate local facilities, you need local skills and, therefore, you are beginning to create a local economy. This encourages our local colleges and universities to increase their training programmes to take up those opportunities and, therefore, provides more opportunities for training people into the regional market.

That is simplistic. It is small-scale. But when you start, as we did, in Kirklees from a base where less than forty per cent of the national average of people were working in the high tech and media sectors, you have got to take some positive steps to increase that figure.

Now there are other issues that lead us to looking at why we should be supporting the media, why we are looking at a cultural policy. As has been mentioned before, there is empowerment. And that is an important issue for me, despite coming from an economic background. I deal with employment initiatives supporting people. We deal with co-ops and community enterprise and that is about empowerment. That is about providing resources for people. There is an increasing interest within our local authority in democratic involvement and how the media can bring people back into the democratic process. The initiatives they are talking about, such as a young persons' parliament, are not, perhaps, going to cause a significant increase in the numbers of those taking part in the political process but I think it will slow the rate of decline that we seem to be experiencing at the very least.

I think there was a programme on Monday night about the return to the Middle Ages that we are witnessing at the moment, not much of which I would agree with — but I do see that we are moving more into a situation of rich 'haves' who get involved within the decision making in society and those who 'have not' who do not get involved in the decision making.

I am very clear that the role of culture and media in dealing with those issues is quite central. We talked before about the use of cultural activity in terms of bringing people back into questions of community. We need to be looking at how we can get culture and media in getting people back involved within those democratic processes, involved in the central questions that influence their lives.

We are, though, in this modern age, looking also at the person who is involved as a consumer of the media. We are looking at trying to make the consumers also active, involved players within the media in putting their point of view forward. Interactivity has to be developed. We recently carried out a survey which showed that the great majority of people within Kirklees wanted information about the local authority in their home. They didn't want to go to libraries and get it, they didn't want to go to civic meetings and get it. What they really want is information on us through their televisions. Ninety-eight per cent of homes in this country have a television; only eighty-nine per cent have a phone. We have to use new techniques; we have to look for techniques whereby we can use the television set, whether it is moving towards the television as an adjunct to the computer, or the black box the cable companies would love to have but don't appear to at the moment. We have got to look at how we will utilise that technology. Having a cultural policy means that we in Kirklees are beginning to look at those questions. We are having those debates now, both at an officer level and at a councillor level. That's important.

Overall, then, there are a number of reasons why we need a cultural policy but I can sum it up by saying that the cultural policy is important to what we would describe as a sustainable regeneration of Kirklees both economically, politically and culturally.

And to return to an earlier theme of Phil's which was about why a cultural policy helps you benefit. At the turn of the century Yorkshire was at the forefront of the film industry in Britain. It was competing, a major rival for Hollywood. Not surprisingly, I suppose, given the climate and also the cultural differences between Yorkshire and California, Yorkshire lost out. We are looking for our cultural policy to move us back to being a producer of media products in the long term. We know, though, that that's not going to get us to a position where we can rival Microsoft. Microsoft are probably going to be the major media producer in the long term, if not the BBC. But there is no reason why we should sit back and allow you and the rest of the country to imagine that what we are really is nothing better than a backdrop to *The Last of the Summer Wine*. Our cultural policy allows us to escape from that ghetto.

I would like to finish with a question for people here. And it is more one for a wider audience again but as we are, without doubt, within the information age, can any authority afford to be without a cultural policy?

Rod Allen: Colin spoke about the issues of media as a means of empowerment rather than as a means of entertainment. I don't want to have the argument about the extent to which entertainment and empowerment cross over. He talked about the under-representation in the debate of communities of interest, about stereotypes of communities of residence and the challenge of understanding what we really mean by regions.

Gillian Reynolds (journalist and broadcaster): Could you please give an example of the communities of interest you see as under-represented? Because if you listen

167

to the radio and watch the television noticeably in the last three years there's been a growth in pressure group politics. Is there a dividing line between pressure groups and communities of interest?

Colin Fletcher: It may be that the radio is better placed, I suspect, and I would not challenge your primary impression. The kind of concern I have with regard to communities of interest is where, in a sense, we represent each of our demographic sections as having essentially one particular quality. So we talk about young people needing to bounce balls about, but they have no spiritual interest whatsoever. We talk about old people needing day centres in which we can park them, but it is not recreation. What fascinates me is that segmenting. You can then start to talk about emergent social issues when we are discussing interests. One particular area that I am concerned with at the moment are parents with physical handicaps bringing up able-bodied children and where, very often, it is the child who is represented as being, you know, spiffing and splendid and heroic, as distinct from the parents' capacity immediately to share parenthood. But the message coming back from society that if you don't cope on your own, as the little woman and the little man, then you are less than adequate. Parents with physical handicaps learn to share parenting from the word go.

These are very simple examples but they show the nature of specific minorities who are largely invisible. The nature of the segmentation of our demography into having a particular capacity and that's it. And to that I would then add the ways in which we are now struggling with what our colleagues from Kirklees were discussing as how to overcome the alienation of the democratic process — just what to do about the extent of sheer turn-off. And people are trying. People are trying largely in reaction to things like roads or chopping down trees or whatever. But they then move into other areas.

The part that I am concerned with is how people learn how to work together. That is the bit that I am most interested in. I don't just want to see programmes which show people doing splendid things with wheelchairs. The real art, I think, is that of mutual cooperation .

Rod Allen: Does that really address Gillian's point about pressure groups, though? You mentioned people trying to stop roads being built across their backyards who have a legitimate, or so they say, a legitimate political point to make and they use all the mechanisms of media access to do it. They are not, as I understand it, an under-represented community of interest.

Colin Fletcher: I don't know. We then get into an argument about what constitutes a media share as distinct from a market share and I'm not in a position to say. What I tried to do this afternoon was make a very simple pitch and say if we are stuck in that stereotyping, then I personally am going to take routes other than by broadcasting. I have got one life to lead and doing battle with the major mogul interests isn't one of them. So my own feeling is that where I am at the moment, our concern is very comparable to that which is Kirklees'. How we normally cut it is that we got the name the 'Black Country' from Queen Victoria drawing the curtains as she passed through. Very little has changed since. We are, if you like, the oldest industrial area in the world and one that is now assumed to be dead. And if the one and a half or so million of us wouldn't mind just lying down evenly, then it would be obvious to all concerned. And it is this refusal to lie down that fascinates me. Here is a group of people who, for a hundred years, have seen deterioration and, to a large extent, dismissal. Our problem at the moment is to convince people that they can in fact make a difference.

Martin Spence (BECTU): I am here representing the broadcasting workers' union. I have a couple of points in response to Colin's contribution, the first of which sounds nakedly self-interested but I hope isn't. It is just an example of what has always struck me as being a community of interest that is desperately under-represented in the broadcast media. And it is a community of interest that encompasses what must be the majority of the population of the country which is people at work, in their capacity as people at work. I mean most of us are employees, and there is programme after programme, radio and television, addressing us in our capacity as consumers, or with consumers' rights, consumers' problems; but we do actually have problems as employees. And it is not a self-interested appeal for a re-run of *Union World*. It is not about a trade union programme. It is about a programme that addresses our problems as employees, as people that work. And very insecure most of us are now as people at work. I can never understand why that is not addressed. And, if I have understood you correctly, that is precisely the sort of under-represented community of interest which we might address.

And, secondly, as a sort of case study, I wonder whether this touches your issue about regions and the constant struggle for regional identity. I live and work in the north-east of England and it seems to me that we are going through a battle now which is precisely a case study of that sort of issue because institution after institution is fleeing from the north-east down to what is increasingly talked about as the combined region of the north-east and Yorkshire. I think from the north-east we perceive ourselves as having lost all real autonomy as regards the BBC. With the Yorkshire-Tyne-Tees merger, we have lost our autonomy in the independent television broadcasting system. Regional government offices are increasingly now based in Leeds. I mean we have even lost the bloody Labour Party. You know the Labour Party — what greater institution could there be representing the political identity of the north-east? Now it is the combined North-East and Yorkshire region of the Labour Party. And yet there is no question that the north-east region exists and people who live there experience its reality very powerfully and passionately. So it is just a case study. There is a battle going on there which I think illustrates very well what Colin was referring to earlier on.

Colin Fletcher: Thank you. There is not a question. It is a wonderful statement. Where the particular focus comes, I think, is in the emergence of contract work. Now less than forty per cent of people have secure employment, and what we are really saying to most people now under the age of thirty, and most people over the age of forty-five, is to expect contracts. And with that goes financial insecurity. With that goes problems of borrowing. With that goes God knows what. And somehow this is not a national issue, it is of no particular concern and, you know, the fact that some people may be trying to set up a home and so on ... It is fascinating. There is almost a conspiracy of silence against the denudation that is occuring through contract employment.

Rod Allen: Before I come to the next question, can I ask the people who are concerned with programme commissioning, or have been, is there any particular reason why there aren't programmes addressed to people at work? Paul Bonner, have you got any ideas about that?

Paul Bonner (former director, ITV Network Centre): I was the person who commissioned *Union World* at Channel 4 and the last speaker was absolutely right, it would now be an anachronism; that does not devalue the fact that there are a whole lot of problems for people at work. Whether there is a coherent slot that could be devoted to that depends on the skill and the imagination of the producers.

John Gray (independent consultant): You are picking up some of the things that Gillian said this morning. We are talking about regions and we were saying how local radio ceased to be local and became regional and how television is ceasing to be regional and is becoming multi-regional. And I am going to bring us back to the fact that broadcasting can be a cottage industry as well. When you come to rural radio, the community of interest and the residential become almost identical. In the rural community there is a great deal of homogeneity. I admit there are exceptions. I have one would-be radio station in Scotland which wants to cope with the anglophone minority in the Isle of Lewis, which is taking a sub-group about as far as you can go. But I do think that we should remember that it can be small-scale — radio more easily than television, but not necessarily exclusively. And a community can not only talk to itself but really positively develop a great range of community activities both economic and cultural. So although we are talking about regions, there are sub-regions and sub-sub-regions with which broadcasting can effectively cope.

Andy Griffee (BBC South): I am editor of news and current affairs for the BBC in Southampton. My nightly news programme broadcasts to five and a half million people across eight counties, that is Weymouth, in Dorset, down to Romney Marsh on the Kent and East Sussex border, and then up as far as Berkshire. It is one hell of a region. And I would like to pick up what Colin was saying about regionalism or regions essentially being unresolveable. I feel that with quite a passion.

I mean the government's regions are different, public sector regions are different, broadcasters' regions are different to anybody else who happens to organise themselves on a regional basis. I don't know whether you know but the Local Government Commission is part of its on-going farcical attempt to carve up the country, or re-carve up the country. It carried out nine thousand interviews around the country which asked people where their sense of belonging was and they spent an awful lot of money speaking to these nine thousand people to find out — surprise, surprise — that people had an incredibly strong sense of belonging to very small communities. They had a very strong sense of belonging to neighbourhoods and villages and, as the area got larger, that sense of belonging diminished pretty drastically. So it was far less of a sense of belonging to people's towns, even less to their counties.

I think you have to resolve that tremendous sense of localness that still exists. You know, people don't move house as much as we might think. I think there is an extraordinary figure like something like thirty-three per cent of the population are still living within twenty miles of their Mums. They are not travelling to work. The average distance of journey to work hasn't increased very substantially at all in the last twenty to thirty years.

And yet we all have this idea that we are all becoming much more cosmopolitan and moving round the country much more and eating Macdonalds and watching Hollywood movies and we don't really care about our neighbourhoods. That is not really true. But you have to resolve that with the tremendous popularity of regional news programmes. There has been some research within the BBC which I think probably disappointed the centralists in London but it discovered that regional nightly news programmes are the second most popular thing on the BBC after *One Foot in the Grave*.

You also have to resolve it with the fact that a combination of transmitter technology, economics and, if you like, some centralism is preventing broadcasters from taking their definition of regions any smaller. So I don't see ITV regions being carved up any smaller than they are for the next three or four years. And I don't see the BBC investing in the huge sums of money necessary to set up new sub-regions. Therefore the only way to square that particular circle is to look at what you defined as the communities of residence and the communities of interest. This really struck a chord with me as somebody who is struggling to produce a nightly programme of interest to such a large region. The bottom line, I think, is in the intelligence of the journalism that is being applied.

If I have my fifteen reporters starting their day, ending their day, editing and working the local cameramen across that region, then our programme will achieve a normal geographical spread. There is a community of residence for those particular stories but, at the end of the day, that's meaningless because effectively part of my audience will engage for two minutes with one report and to be turned off with the other twenty-four minutes. And the fundamental thing that broadcasters and journalists have to resolve is to mesh that community of residence that you are talking about with the community of interest. The only way to do that is go beyond the knee-jerk, old-fashioned, dare I say it?, local newspaper journalism of the past and say not only what is happening but why is it happening. Draw out the underlying context and then you make the story travel.

Can I just give one basic example? A bakery closed in Bournemouth two weeks ago. Two hundred people lost their jobs. Now those two hundred people would have been very interested in a report on *South Today* that night. I imagine people in Bournemouth would have been very interested, people in neighbouring Poole less interested and people in Hastings quite frankly probably wouldn't give a damn. But as soon as the journalist starts to ask himself why these jobs are going he discovers that it is actually about a price war over the loaf of bread in supermarkets. Supermarkets are using bread as a loss-leader. As soon as you tease out that story and as soon as you explain the background to why a small bakery is closing, then everyone who buys bread in my region is going to engage with that story. It touches on an aspect of their lives. And that is why fundamentally the BBC has been right in investing in specialist correspondents in the regions. I have six special correspondents in environment, health, defence, business and education.

Equally, picking up this point here, we could have not gone down the consumer route. We could have gone down the route of looking at workplace practices. And that, equally, would have made that story of relevance to people across the region. And it is only by engaging the brain and doing a different type of journalism that you can square the circle.

Rod Allen: But the relevance, though, does not stop at the regional boundaries, does it? You are still describing strategies for dealing with the problem of serving a region. You are not expressing regional identity, which may be a chimera anyway.

Colin Fletcher: It may or may not be a regional matter. But you have put your finger beautifully on the two key characteristics which you identify as making your regional news work. The first one is you are using a local accent but it is intelligent. You know it is not, 'E, by gum, 'ey up me duck.' Yes? And the second is it's wonderful to hear your own accent used intelligently. It speaks to you about ways in which your own brain rhythms are getting sloppy and slack. And the second thing is that you are asking the question not just why, but why now? Why is this happening to us now? And it is the 'why now' which gives the news capacity. So it is not just a matter of some eternally spinning wheel.

Rod Allen: I have a question for Steve Avery and Phil Woods which is worrying me and I should like them to address it. Your whole presentation suggests to me that what is underneath what you are doing is the idea that culture is good for the economy. Is that all it is?

Phil Woods: I hope that is not the message that came across. I think in the cultural resources approach I was trying to expound upon, the economic spin-offs are merely one thing. We talked about symbolic spin-offs, political, economic, environmental, educational as well as art for art's sake — wow, let's enjoy ourselves! Those are all lots of equally important reasons. But, as we said, Thatcherism plus the influences from the GLC made culture a commodity and, at the moment, if you are in local government with tight budgets and you want to do something, it is the economic arguments that carry the most weights.

Russell Clark (Falmouth College of Art): I moved to Falmouth from the West Midlands, from Walsall, where a very similar kind of project was aimed — you'll be familiar with this — a Media Centre. A proliferation of media activity, encouraging and nurturing production was intended to take place and never got off the ground because it became, to use a much hated cliché, a political football. There was a minority Labour authority which did not have the numbers to carry it as a policy. I would be interested to know what the political mix is and what the numbers are, whether or not you need that to sustain a policy of this sort in order to sell it to an electorate, because in Walsall the whole thing faltered, whereas in neighbouring Wolverhampton a similar initiative got off the ground and proved to be very successful.

Steve Avery: I have to say in answering that point I think the media centre is still a political football. Whilst we had the celebration drink last Friday I was busily editing the report to try to get some more financing to another section of the media centre, so we have not escaped that particular problem. That word 'media' itself I think makes it a political football. We didn't get it through because we have a Labour majority, though, because at the moment we haven't. So we have had to work very hard to withdraw it, if you like, from being a football. We know it is contentious and that is why in some ways, as Phil said, what we've had to do is utilise those arguments which are based on the economics, the arguments which are based around the financing of the project. We have had to convince some very sceptical people of the immediate value our building will bring to the town.

Session produced by Rod Allen

New regions for old

Chair: **Sue Caro**
Channel 4 Television

Paul Bonner
Former director, ITV Network Centre

John Whiston
BBC Manchester

Duncan Dallas
XYTV, Leeds

S
UE Caro: We are going to explore the idea of new regions for old and we have a very distinguished panel to help us do that. On my right is Paul Bonner. For those of you who don't know him, he was recently Director of the ITV Network Centre with a very long distinguished career in broadcasting, starting in the BBC in radio in 1955. Then he was introduced to the delights of television under what was then called the ambidexterity policy (which sounds very familiar somehow) which enabled him to move over to TV, where he was a studio and OB director for five years. And then he had a fortuitous meeting with Grace Wyndham Goldie and as a result moved on to producing and directing the first ever BBC consumer programme, *Choice*. He had a distinguished career as a documentary maker including *Who Sank the Lusitania?* and *Jack the Ripper*, then he was responsible for starting, or opening up, the *Open Door* of the BBC2 community programmes unit and for the advent of *Write On* on BBC1. He became head of BBC Science and Features and then in 1979 he was enticed to join Jeremy Isaacs to become his Channel Controller at Channel 4. And we have to thank him for persuading Martin Lambie-Nairn to design our logo, which is still going strong to this day which we all love. He was also responsible for *Right to Reply* along with Gus Macdonald. 1987 saw him take over as Chair of the ITV Controllers and he was responsible for that change in ITV's fortunes which pushed their ratings up past the BBC where they have remained more or less ever since. Since '92 he has helped to set up the ITV Network Centre.

On my left is John Whiston who is now the head of BBC Youth and Entertainment Programmes and he is based in Manchester. They have a total of 300 hours of output on BBC1 and 2. He has regional qualifications. Born and educated in Scotland, he came up through Music and Arts and helped to launch *The Late Show* under Michael Jackson's editorship and has done much, much more, including a lot of archive productions — *A Night in with Alan Bennett* (this is stressing his regional connections here), *Granadaland, ATV Night, TV Hell, Thirty-six years in the Tardis,* and *Later with Jools Holland* are amongst his many credits.

And we have Duncan Dallas, who now runs his own production company XYTV. I don't think I need to explain the pun. He started off with the BBC and moved to Leeds in 1968 where he has been ever since, but he was working with YTV where he became Head of Science and Features. He claims the possibly dubious distinction of having popularised Magnus Pyke, David Bellamy and Miriam Stoppard. He has been running his own company since 1992.

Paul Bonner: One of the penalties of coming on so late down in the order, with a keynote speaker as able and perceptive as Gillian Reynolds, is that if you have anything worthwhile to say at all it's liable to be a faint echo of what she said. So forgive me for the occasional repetition.

Regional cutting, regional expansion, regional rationalisation, ambidexterity, as was said, regional independent production, were always on the agenda at Whitehall, Westminster, Shepherd's Bush and Fitzrovia — so much more cultural than Knightsbridge — (that's a London joke). Sometimes when we look at peak time in television in Manchester, you might not believe that the region was in everybody's minds all the time. For David Hatch, being the longest serving BBC Board of Management member means he has been a participant both in regional cuts and in regional expansion. He was part of the famous, or infamous, 'Black Spot' team way back in the early 80s and then again distributed the largesse, this time last year.

So it really is the most ludicrously cyclical business and, in some ways, I am comforted by Colin Fletcher whose view that the association geographically between people was not actually terribly important when compared to associations of interest.

Where did we go wrong, then, as broadcasters? I think the road to regional hell ws probably paved with happy accidents. Radio, the wireless as it was, could only radiate locally when the British Broadcasting Company was set up in 1923. Freak meteorological conditions occasionally allowed 2LO, the London station, to be heard in the north and 3PY from Plymouth sometimes confused cat's whiskers set listeners in Crewe.

But it was just after the BBC became a corporation that in 1928 the Daventry 5XX transmitter (sounds like a beer, a powerful beer at that) came on the air. Then the national service truly was formed. And so, in a sense, that was the end of the English regions and in the main technical progress became a matter of better sound quality reaching further.

In terms of independent television, or commercial television (a title that it proudly fought to avoid) it was on 14 October 1954 that the die was cast for ITV by the Independent Television Authority, when the Authority members agreed with the recommendation of both their Chairman and their Director General that the channel should be regionally based. This, in a way, was also to do with technical limitations at the time. But it was a politically astute decision to avoid a *de facto* visible monopoly with absolutely no competition as a reult of there being, at that time, only one VHF transmission band available for the new channel.

Sir Robert Fraser, the then Director General, decided that the answer to this *de facto* monopoly, which certainly would not have been politically acceptable, was to create internal competition between regionally based contractors. London would do battle with Birmingham and Manchester for a share of the glittering pile of gold that advertising would surely bring. In the first two years, actually, they were doing battle over a hole in the ground down which gold was being poured and disappearing fast. It was as a result of this that the ITA had to reduce the internal competition and allow the less wasteful form of networking programmes with national appeal — the so-called carve-up. Even so the companies were still getting their revenue in competition with one another, selling advertising against one another. So it was a balanced carve-up, so much so that by the time the Office of Fair Trading came on the scene they accepted in 1978 this form of competition as registrable, that is to say legal under the Act. Note that in neither the BBC nor the ITV case was the prior objective to recognise regional identity and aspirations. At least in the BBC's case the coverage was originally of the region, by the region and for the region concerned.

Then by a sequence of people and events on which Gillian, again, touched which included John Reith, the Second World War and the Bernstein brothers, the roles became reversed between the BBC and ITV. The BBC became the voice of the nation as seen from London. Broadcasting is a powerful uniter if it is used in that mode and most ITV companies decided that it was politically, and therefore ultimately also commercially, wise to embrace fully the regional terms of their contracts. So firmly did they embrace them that in one region the company sought in its advertisements to superimpose the company identity on the rather artificial region that it had and that was the 'Granadaland' that was celebrated in their ads.

Is the richness — and there is a richness despite all the contradiction that Colin wisely pointed out —of Britain's tightly packed but distinct regional culture reflected by the broadcasting structure? Surprisingly, perhaps, given what I implied at the start, the answer is 'yes,' a qualified 'yes' but a definite positive. If you doubt that there is a simple test that I have tried myself. I did it in North Devon but you can do it in any region of the land and I suspect the result is, to a great extent, the same. Watch twelve hours — midday to midnight — of BBC1 or ITV and then, the following day, watch twelve hours of Sky One or Super Channel. And there you have a clear picture however edited, however unsatisfactory, of the fact that the regional culture view is reflected in terrestrial broadcasting still.

Now that is in England. The position in the national regions — Scotland and Northern Ireland — is radically different. In Scotland, and I speak having talked to Scots recently, BBC1 appears positively offensive. Why? Because it is so English. Not in its accent so much as in the judgements, the agenda, all the inherent approaches that it takes. They are clearly London-based.

I remember when I started in radio, I started in the West of England Home Service and I sometimes thought that London BBC saw us down the wrong end of the telescope. Everything we did, every value we had, was in some way diminished. And I think this feels particularly so in the national regions because they are just not cultural entities but political entities with stronger political aspirations than I think any English region would ever have.

ITV seems somehow less alien because the companies providing the programmes are now truly regionally based. STV has not been a Canadian-owned licence to print money for nearly thirty years, though the phrase lingers on. And the Broadcasting Act requires STV and Grampian to carry some programmes in the Gaelic language. I will return to language and regional culture later. But, in fact, there is regional culture reflected in not only STV and Grampian but BBC Scotland as well.

However it is not enough. And as Gus Macdonald, STV's Chief Executive, if he were here, would point out in no uncertain terms, those companies are still subject to London-based regulations, something about which certainly the more political active members of their viewership feel strongly, and their ownership is not subject to any formal regional qualification.

And I have to say that evidence I received at a BBC seminar only last week before the *Panorama* fracas indicates that there is likely to be a recrudescence of the campaign in Scotland for licence fees from Scottish viewers to be made available to a new Scottish Broadcasting Corporation. This would commission and schedule Scottish programmes for the Scots as it liked, and it would only fill in its schedule with BBC network programmes or even programmes from other sources when it wanted to. Whether such a service would or could be financially viable or self-sustaining without a considerable discount on the programmes from south of the border must be questionable. But, clearly, the aggravation level is such that this is likely to be on the political agenda by the next general election. And, as we have already heard, the BBC's behaviour on Monday in scheduling an interview with the British Prime Minister (who is, of course, seen in Scotland as the leader of a minority party in that country) just prior to local elections in that national region, demonstrates precisely the type of London-based insensitivity that so offends the other parts of Britain. Perhaps the Director-General of the BBC should have attended his own Managing Director's seminar at which this issue was raised with me. Where the Controller of Scotland, John McCormick, and the Managing Director of Regional Services, Ron Neal, stand in all this has yet to be revealed. But it could not have come at a worse time for regional efforts within the BBC, and we have not heard the last of it.

Nevertheless, the fact is that in Scotland and more particularly in Northern Ireland regional programmes feature in the Top Ten ratings week in and week out. So national regional services are provided in those provinces and they are popular but they do not, as I have said, go far enough to satisfy nationalist sentiment in Scotland, at least. Nationalist sentiment in Northern Ireland is a contentious and difficult issue that I would not address.

In Wales we do find a true national regional cultural reflection in S4C. A Welsh Nationalist MP promised to starve and a kindly, nice Home Secretary took him seriously and at a very late date indeed in the legislation concerned a Welsh fourth channel authority was set up as a separate entity, quite separate from the IBA, and put in charge of setting up a channel which is now Sianel Pedwar Cymru, the

Welsh fourth channel. But is it a true national cultural reflection? After all, the language in which it broadcasts is the language of the minority in Wales. Is the preservation of minority languages, though a desirable aim perhaps, truly a function for regional broadcasting? And is it so at a cost of £40 million a year?

If it is, where do the new minority languages of Urdu and Hindi stand in all this? Because regions don't stand still. They change their demography, their industry changes. Some ITV regional companies, Central and Yorkshire for instance, do broadcast series in Urdu. I believe the BBC Midlands does as well and there may be others. Certainly there are many local radio stations set up to do so and other stations catering for communities with a large population of Asian or Asian-derived people. They broadcast because they see it as part of their function of regional reflection. But does that make, for instance, Central Television more or less regional than Westcountry which though it reflects Cornish culture in many of its programmes does not broadcast complete programmes in Cornish even though that language, once nearly dead, has received the kiss of life?

You must judge, I think, to what extent regional broadcasting may actually be a unicorn. Rod Allen called it a chimera. In any event it is a mythical beast whose function is solely to fulfil romantic illusions. Or is it?

Most objective observers acknowledge that regional broadcasting currently fulfils a function on terrestrial television and, however imperfect that function may be, it is valued by the audience. And if it is valued by the audience, it deserves encouragement, preservation and expansion within financial reason.

Maybe a unicorn is in reality a handy workhorse upon which some dreamers wish to place a horn and ribbons but which actually does do a good job of hauling an important load. Down the road, though, there lurk half-realities that could hobble that horse. For the BBC there lurks the finite nature of the licence fee and for ITV the twin demons of greater competition from ever greater numbers of broadcasters and from the combined and further combining ownership of ITV companies which will lie in fewer and fewer hands and mostly, almost certainly, in London.

Ironically if political regional devolution, toyed with so recently by the Labour Party, were to come about, some money might be added to the licence fee to enable the BBC, as the national instrument of broadcasting, to respond to the regional and national assemblies' inevitable demands for more and better regional coverage of their work. Perhaps part of the money might have to be raised locally but it would raise the revenue input specifically targeted to regional broadcasts. However, I fear that the more likely scenario is that whatever the complexion of the party in power, the inevitably increasing competitive pressures on revenue for broadcasting will drag most of whatever money is available to broadcasters down to London to make glitzy cost-effective programming that will continue to justify the BBC licence in terms of audience share and continue to fund the ITV network, some of whose programmes will continue to be made in the regional centres for the remainder of this licence period, at least, and Channel 4 with sufficient advertising revenue to survive against increasing competition.

The ITC will fight a brave rearguard action. Regional advisory bodies will dig in until overwhelmed by the enemy. And there will be questions in Parliament, particularly in the Lords. But all that will avail nought. Channel 5 will have to be primarily national, as we have heard, in order to recoup its capital outlay, swollen to horrific bloated proportions by the cost of retuning of domestic VCRs and for meeting the other technical peculiarities which seem to emerge year by year.

Digital technology could, in theory, be applied regionally, but it will multiply twelve-fold the demands on advertising and licence revenue to sustain broadcasting and it won't increase either of those sources of finance by more than a single figure percentage. And that new manner of broadcasting, subscription television, needs a national base, not a regional one, to be viable.

So, in conclusion, I fear that the title of this session may, in reality, be 'No Regions for Old.'

John Whiston: Saturday morning, eight o'clock in the morning, April Fool's Day. My girlfriend came into the room and said 'So have you heard the news?' And I said, 'No,' and she said, 'John Birt has gone to CBS.' And she then went out of the room leaving me lying in bed for half an hour contemplating a new future. Of course, the first thing that one does is one spends about ten minutes of shuffling the pack and working out who is going to come to the top of that pack. The next ten minutes one spends thinking about all the reports that one won't have to write and then in the final ten minutes, though, one starts to think, 'Well, what if what that one man has done will actually survive him going?' And that was a very interesting ten minutes before my girlfriend cracked and came back in. I think the fact that I was reaching for the 'phone and about to talk to a few people and make a huge fool of myself softened her a bit.

But one of the things that I was rather scared about was that in about a week's time we had Perfomance Review at which John Birt comes up himself and ticks off on a list the extent to which we had managed to achieve some of the policies, particularly the regional policies. It is the sort of annual self-denouncement beloved of Maoists and Catholics. I am probably both and he is certainly one of them.

What I was concerned about was that we have created some achievements in the year that we were designated to be a centre of excellence in music and arts and entertainment. In terms of spend, we've brought in about eight to nine million pounds worth of new business — things like *Weird Night,* which was a sort of music and arts documentary, *Mrs Merton,* which is a co-production with Granada, *University Challenge,* another co-production with Granada, and *Memory Master,* which is a new quiz that is about to be launched on BBC1 from Action Time here in Manchester.

I will come on to later to talk about whether those programmes have any regional resonance at all. It is an amount of spend that was promised and is starting to be delivered. But it is hard. And what is hard about building up regional production is that it is hard to convince controllers to take a risk because that is, frankly, what they think it is. That is despite the fact that one controller was brought up in Macclesfield and the other went to university here in Manchester.

It is even harder to wean some fiefdom away from the London heads who are quite protective of their output. But the great thing about John Birt is that he puts you between a rock and a hard place so there is, in effect, no escape. We have to deliver this expansion and I personally believe that expansion is so locked down now for various reasons that there won't be the black spots of the past; the BBC is committed to spending more in the regions and getting more programming from the regions.

You can say well, that is very cynical; the BBC is doing it for cynical reasons. It depends on where you stand on that. I believe there is a mood abroad in the BBC, especially in these caring, sharing '90s, that we have to do our bit to be part of re-building the community. Now that it is not because the BBC is full of jolly nice chaps who have all got their hearts in the right place. It is because the BBC is hard-nosed enough to know that that sort of commitment is part of its USP, to use the jargon — its unique selling point. Quite basically, it's what will get us a licence fee next time around.

So then you have to ask the question 'So what? Why does it matter if it is a cynical exercise?' I mean putting more women on *Question Time* was a cynical exercise, a deliberate one, and perhaps has made it marginally more watchable. But the question about positive discrimination is only really a question if it's posi-tive discrimination versus excellence. It is only a question if you think that the talent pool is very narrow, and I don't happen to think that. I think that positive discrimination is bad if you are replacing good people with bad, good programmes with mediocre. But it is not a bad thing if you are replacing the old with the new or the entrenched with the fresh, particularly in the area that I am working in which is youth and a crossover into entertainment. I think that that is what one is trying to do, especially here in the regions.

I think the BBC's initial commitment to the independents could be seen as a cynical exercise, to jump before it was pushed, but now twenty-five per cent of all programmes and in my department forty-nine per cent of programmes are made by independents. So cynical exercises can grow into something more.

You shouldn't knock cynicism, actually, because it is a more powerful motiva-tor, I think, than the old-fashioned dewy-eyed paternalistic sentimentality that the BBC used to have in terms of its regions. You can either say it is recognising a mood in the country and doing something to help bring about that mood or you can say it is recognising the mood in the country and ingratiating itself with that mood. Whichever way round it is, I don't think it matters so long as it gets the results. But there is something behind the accusation of cynicism towards BBC. The question is: If it is cynical then when the new wave comes in, will it stick? Well, I think it will stick because of a number of factors.

Firstly it is in the Charter and things that are in the Charter generally stick. I think it is one of those things like, you know, 'Don't mention pink elephants.' As soon as you have brought this issue to the fore, it is not going to go away and it is not going to go away in the next ten years as the BBC lumbers up towards another Charter renewal.

And the other thing is, yes, John Birt; yes, the BBC Thought Police. They are very effective. I have just come from a session with one of the nicest of the Thought Police, David Hatch, who is responsible for drafting the new regional policy. And he is there to monitor, and to see that not just the letter but the spirit of the policy is being carried out.

There is another dimension. I may talk like somebody who is been on the road to Damascus but having been on a number of BBC Ten Year Strategies in the last week I am a bit punch-drunk. But I think I have seen the future and it came in the shape of a tape of some of the experiments they are doing in America for video on demand. Our house was the last one in our road to get colour television, because my father was convinced it would get better. I think he was right. But I have now seen video on demand and I would buy it tomorrow. I would spend a sizeable proportion of my inconsiderable income on getting this thing whereby you can just come home and decide what programme you are going to have. Say that happens, and I think it will happen faster than the time-scale of ten years. What is that going to do to regionalism? What is it going to do to the concept of channels? What are Michael Jackson and Alan Yentob, as channel controllers, going to do? Well, they are going to become commissioners of software, programmes and software. And what is going to be very important for the BBC is that it maintains its position as a producer of these programmes, as a software provider. I think the only way that it can do that, long-term, is by forgetting about the big structures, forgetting about the big buildings in London and breaking up into much smaller entities — all still part of the BBC, all pulling together with BBC values and BBC grounding but located here in this building or down the road, somewhere where you don't get charged huge rents, making programmes. And that is what the BBC will consist of. It will consist of a whole lot of cells based around the regions making programmes. So I think there is a strong future for regional production at the BBC.

Now the question you have to ask is 'Does regional diversity do any good?' Aside from the economic good of spreading a bit of money around the regions, which is a not insubstantial thing to be doing, what does regional diversity bring? Is it a nation at ease with itself? Is that what regionalism is about? That is probably a bit ambitious. Is it a nation that is starting to talk to itself? People talking to themselves is either the first sign of madness or else a prerequisite of some sort of healthy democracy. I think it is important that we do recognise that there is a diversity of tone. It does not come across all our programming but I think it is particularly good that the area I am working, the Youth Department, is located outside London.

It is hard to measure and there are no key performance indicators or whatever about representation or regionality of programmes, but I think some of the programmes that we have done recently, like *Mrs Merton*, have a non-metropolitan feel to them.

If you do some analysis of those programmes and you ask where do they get most of their audience share, it is curious that they get double their share in this region than they do nationally. What's the hard evidence? Well, that is getting towards some sort of evidence. And I think those shows all share something in common, which is that they are less artificial and less strangulated. Even *Rough Guide* which has got Magenta, the symbol of all things evil in London, at its head, has now also got Simon O'Brian who is from *Brookside* and, again, you look at the figures. It now has a much higher share in this region that it used to have, and a much higher share in this region than it did when it only had Magenta on it.

We have been holding a lot of forums where we have been listening to what young people want from our programming because we are at a crisis in which we don't know which way to take it. But a lot of what they have been saying is that they want programmes that have an attitude, that tell it like it is. Now we have launched this thing called *The Sunday Show,* which is kind of a rag-bag, lunchtime Sunday programme that is meant to have an energy. It feels outside of London. I mean the presenters aren't Northern but the programme itself somehow smells like it comes from outside of London. I don't think it could have been made in London. And, curiously, it happens to be hitting forty-five per cent of the target audience, which is more than *The Word* and is the first BBC youth programme actually to do what has been ordered in *People and Programmes*, the strategy document, which is to talk and get to a youth audience.

Why is that? Most of the stories are American, so what is regional about that? I think it is just this attitude of mind. One of the things that Paul Bonner was talking about was what regional culture means to a young person. Well, you know, they are much more interested in baseball caps ... that *is* their region. Their region is global and half-American. We may not like that. We may think their region should be northern, that it should be rooted in what is happening here. It is not. It is rooted in a much more global sense.

Is that healthy? Should one pander to that or not? I don't know. What I do know is that it is better to have some expression of it on television than to block it and say it should have no expression.

It was interesting that at Programme Review Board, the BBC's forum where it discusses all its programming, the discussion turned to *The Sunday Show* and it was pointed out that it obviously was talking to a youth audience. And somebody at that Programme Review Board said 'Well, if that's all they've got to talk to each other about, then maybe they shouldn't be talking at all.' Now the last time I heard that phrase was at school, and I think there is a really important job for a programme like that to do and it can only do it from being located out of London.

I was listening to what Paul said about the BBC being very English in Scotland. To my father sitting in Edinburgh, who when he lets on votes SNP, the BBC is very Glasgow. He has got this paranoia that it is actually run by a Glasgow mafia that wants to cut Edinburgh out of every sentence. Perhaps what he is getting at the sense that because Scotland is politically adept at putting itself forward in a political agenda, it puts forward a general view of Scotland. Actually Scotland, like England, breaks up into many smaller and many more complex sub-groupings.

I think there is a bit of a paranoia about London, about the idea that London is where the nation thinks and that it is full of people in Agnes B suits who have chosen to enter national life by sitting in London. I think that that is not how it is. Yesterday, we witnessed the failure of *The Late Show* and what has replaced it? Well, *Video Diaries, Video Nation*. That is the sort of freshness that the BBC is looking towards. And, OK, those are national programmes, but there is nothing more regional on British television than those little nuggets.

The other reason why I think the BBC must maintain its regional identity is that every organisation needs new thinking. It is like Bill Gates' opinion which is that the new thinking does not come from the centre, it comes from the margins. That is why I think youth is important because I think youth is a kind of margin.

So where does that leave us? If you look around there is a lot of regionalism hidden in the generality of programming and there are a lot of centres that produce that. Bristol, I think, makes better documentaries than the documentary unit in London because it has a different attitude, it has a more human attitude. I happen to think that we are on the cusp, here in Manchester, of being the next new thing in terms of comedy. We have the best comedy writers. We have the people who write for Steve Coogan and the others. There is a real caucus of them and I think that is going to create a regional voice. I didn't cause that and I only hope that I can ride that particular wave well enough so it furthers my career in some way, but also that it does something to Manchester and for Manchester; it gives and expresses a kind of youthful comic energy that Manchester has and will be the next new thing.

Next time somebody plays an April Fool joke on you and you are lying there recasting your whole world view and your whole view of the broadcasting industry, I think the question to ask is 'Which would you prefer? Would you prefer the current state, the current hope of some movement forward on the regional front, some hope of diversity offered by the words 'the new regionalism,' or would you prefer the old system of benevolent torpor which is what the BBC used to be into? And I think the new, albeit slightly autocratic, regionalism is better than the old-fashioned regionalism that was.

Duncan Dallas: The Conference is about diversity of regions, communities in broadcasting, and I want to say something briefly about each one of those.

I was very interested in Colin Fletcher's talk this afternoon about communities and regions. I have just one story about that. We did a current affairs programme last year from Leeds where we had to get an audience from Leeds which was not blocked out into political groups or pressure groups or anything like that. In a way we had to invent the kind of audience that we thought would say something about modern Leeds. We had a young researcher working in the office and eventually we said, 'Well, look, maybe we needs somebody like architects or town-planners who could sort of tell us what the plans are and so on and so forth. She got on the phone and made some contacts and, you know, you half-hear these things when you are working in the same office. She eventually got on to someone who sounded interesting, 'Oh, yes, really you think that? Would you be able to come? Oh, great,' she said, 'Well, where are you then? Where are you based?' The reply came back 'Well, if you look out the window, across the street, I am waving at you now.'

So that is how communications relates to communities. I agree with Colin that in a way regions are in the middle. The problem with communities just now is that the geographic communities have gone into Neighbourhood Watch and the communities of interest are vanishingly thin. So that is why broadcasting is important and communications are so important because I still think it is important for the nation to talk to itself and for people to decide both how to listen to the nation and what to talk to them about.

When I went up to Leeds in 1968, I had never been to Leeds or Yorkshire at all. I noticed a graffiti on the wall which said 'Leeds today, Paris tomorrow.' And I thought it was a striking symbol. It didn't quite work out the way the graffiti artist meant it, which was that there would be permanent revolution in both Leeds and Paris for the next twenty-five years. But it has worked out in an extraordinary way inasmuch as Leeds which, when I first went there, was sort of a northern industrial city and a bit of an acquired taste for many people, (though I quite liked it) has now developed into a rather modern city on a European model. It happens to model itself on Barcelona and it is not quite there yet. But it is a nice thing to try for. During the period while I have been there while this regeneration has happened in Leeds I have watched a decay in relations between London and Paris. In fact now Paris, which is clearly making a go at being the capital of Europe, is quite a nice, clean, architecturally interesting place to be. London is pretty much as I remember it about twenty-five years ago. And I think that says something about regionalism, which is that the focus of attention for many of the English regions is not London any more; it is Europe or beyond that.

To move on to broadcasting and the enthusiasm for the new regionalism, I am sceptical about it. The cynical nature of it doesn't bother me so much as the rather thoughtless, faultless, nature behind it. In other words there is no real strategy here. It is a reaction to events. In the BBC terms it is a reaction to the Charter. In Channel 4 it is possibly a reaction to having to sell advertising in the regions and it's masquerading as regional policy when, in fact, it's a survival mechanism.

In a way, I don't mind that because I think there is an opportunity. Whether it lasts or not is not, in a sense, up to the BBC or Channel 4 but it is up to people in the regions to make something of it. It is important to address how that could be done and I offer a few thoughts on that.

The first one is that in the past in broadcasting the regions have often been used to represent a continuing and vanishing tradition both of town and country. They have been set against the modernism of intellectual ideas and the cosmopolitan nature of London life, and the regions have often been seen as a useful corrective to keep in mind about the community and traditions of farms and country life and manufacturing, working-class and all those kind of things which were once thought of to be the backbone of England. My feeling about that is that those images have served their purpose, and the problem is that the regions have been associated with a backward-looking picture of England — a world that was, rather a world that might be — and that association is now no longer useful and needs to be re-described.

One of the advantages, however, of being in a region, and where some regeneration might start, is that the failures of all our national institutions in the last five or ten years — government, police, judiciary, monarchy, city banks — have all been associated with London. So, in a sense, London is a good place not to have been, because we can't be blamed for the mess that we are now in. That doesn't mean that there are any specially good ideas in the regions. But it means that at least you start on a par, and it might prove to be a springboard. It also means that the relationship between the regions and the currency of ideas in London is different, that as it were you are not in the gossip — and sometimes that is a good place to be and sometimes it is not. At present I suspect it is not a good place to be.

The next thing is about diversity, because in a way regionality and diversity are not necessarily the same thing. Everybody seems to think that diversity is a good thing now, in spite of the fact you might say that what we want is *less* diversity in Britain, and as some politicians would say more authority. But why do we want to encourage it? What are we groping towards? I think here the hope is that diversity, and the new ideas that might be associated with it, will somehow arrest the decline in our national life which has been such a consistent theme for much of this century. Diversity is really another word for 'national debate', and that is another word in itself for 'national failure'. And so there is a real opportunity: people are on the lookout for new ideas with which to face the next century. If you look at it scientifically, diversity comes about in a species — it comes out genetically in order to survive, and in a sense that's what we are about. We are talking about what kind of Britain will survive into the next century, and who will decide it, and how that debate is constructed. That would be a proper reason for encouraging regionalism, and to give it some sort of focus.

However, there needs to be the right set of conditions. Having lived through the last set of regional enthusiasms for ITV, I think that the road to hell is paved with good intentions, and we now know enough about the economics of high-tech companies and the media and regionalism to know that one essential element for success is clustering. It is no good just spreading the money thinly around a whole huge area and doing it fairly and squarely. Hard decisions have to be made about where the money is going to be spent and who is going to get it and why they are going to get it.

I would just like to make a couple of practical suggestions. One is for Channel Four: if they really want to encourage regionalism, they should not create strands into which individual programmes from the regions would be sited but they should give series to companies or groups of companies in key areas so that we would see different aspects of British life. That would be the brief; that would be something to aim for. It might easily be done in a number of areas, but one would clearly be current affairs. If they were really serious they could commission thirteen half-hours of current affairs from outside London on a particular topic each year, perhaps from a different company each year. Another area might be talks, where the agenda is about different ideas — about ourselves or about Britain. As far as the BBC is concerned, the BBC has worked best in the past as a highly centralised, culturally homogenous organisation. I can't see it going out into the regions and being a cottage industry. I suspect the best way for it to go is to regroup back in Shepherd's Bush and make commissions out in the regions, again in directed ways for specific purposes which are defined by the BBC, not to try and come out from the fortress and be like us.

Sue Caro: Thank you for your suggestions for Channel Four. I would like to point out that *The People's Parliament* is made in Manchester already, but I will take the other suggestions back.

David Keen: I am a producer. I produced hours and hours of network programmes on BBC Manchester up to about ten years ago. Dozens of *Brass Tacks, Great Railway Journeys*, travel shows, lots of it. I can't think of any shows that actually gained anything specifically at all from being in Manchester, but what I can say is that there is a useful *apartheid*. Things develop away from London, away from major centres in ways they could not in the centre. You mention *Rough Guide*. *Rough Guide* is terrific. It is very good travel journalism and would be good from any-where. However, one questions where else it might have come from. I say that as one of the people that turned *The Travel Show* from somebody's hobby into some-thing which had a decent audience on BBC2, and frankly it's eat-your-heart-out time when I watch that, because it's gone on so much further. *The Travel Show* would not have developed in London, but it would have gone down in a contest to the established holiday strand. Ideas would have moved uneasily in the wrong direction, and any originality would simply have drifted away.

And you can see the same models working. There was a distinct difference in programmes that come out of the Kensington House fraternity *vis à vis* the Lime Grove situation, and yet there is an extraordinary similarity now between pro-grammes that come out of Kensington House. We have great strength in being relatively small units away from London, wholly apart from what we may or may not incidentally draw from the region in which we happen to be working. It is that little bit of distance, yet that sense of, as you say, continuity with the network sense of shared values with operators elsewhere. I think it is extraordinarily valu-able, I really do.

Gillian Reynolds: John Whiston has seen the future and interpreted it in a very interesting way. I would love to know in your analysis of future programmes how far you see the BBC continuing as a production centre and how far you are seeing it become a publishing contractor in the future, because I am not quite sure where in your analysis of programmes you see the line dividing.

John Whiston: I think you flatter it by calling it an analysis but thank you. I have in fact written a paper about it for yet another of these ten year strategy groups. This may not be a particularly popular message, but I see the BBC retrenching back into being a production house which may or may not have a strong inde-pendent arm. I think there is danger for the BBC in over-independenting itself. That's not true at the moment. I think that the independent sector is about the healthiest thing that could have happened to the BBC. It has put everybody on their toes and for the next five or seven years until this glorious new future comes around. That is how things should be. But when it does come around, as Duncan hinted, he is my competitor. He is a broadcaster, too. He will have the means of getting his programmes onto the carousel from which they will be chosen. You will get home at night and you will decide you want to watch some documentary. The carousel will come round. There is his programme. There is our programme. We won't own that carousel because as the BBC, unless we go into some pretty strange unholy alliances with people, we just won't have the money that will be needed to bring about that technology. That technology is going to be brought about by somebody else. When you switch it on it will say, 'Murdochvision,' and then somewhere on Murdochvision there will be the BBC product. Now it may be that the BBC will still be licence-funded in which case all those products come to you free and what's going to be important is how different are they from the other products, what are they giving you that the other products can't, so that you know when you are watching a BBC programme that you are getting something special and something unique. Sometimes. I think it will be even more important in the future. It will mean that things will become more stranded so that one-off documentaries will disappear. Everything will become a brand which you know what you are going for. *BBC Timewatch* — that will become a brand and you'll turn on for that. And I think in those scenarios what will happen is that the BBC will need to bring all the means of production back in-house. Why should Hat Trick make a programme for the BBC and then give it to the BBC to call a BBC programme? Why should the BBC have any rights over that? And I think not now but in about five years' time BBC will have to think about whether it wants independents developing long running dramas. Say an independent had come up with *EastEnders*, which will run for another ten, fifteen, twenty years, whatever. But eventually the government will say 'Who thought of that? Whose programme is that?' Maybe it is the independent's. What is the BBC left with if it doesn't own its own product? I think it is left with very little because it isn't going to be able to sell the licence fee on the basis of what you are buying for that amount of money is the judgement of two people — Alan Yentob and Michael Jackson — nice guys, great controllers but you don't want to pay £82 a year to have them decide what progammes you are going to be watching.

Rod Allen (HarperCollins): But you know as well as I do that the physical act of production doesn't constitute ownership. It's investment that constitutes ownership, and the reason the BBC will continue to deal with independent producers is that the BBC will have the funds to invest in their ideas. Although it is an old and honest and respectable idea I can't reconcile the idea of the BBC becoming simply a production house because I know from looking at Hollywood, I know from looking at European film production, that the physical act of production can take place anywhere by anyone but the rights are vested in the investors and, indeed, the underlying rightsholders. And I think that the future is much more complex than that.

I just wanted to go on to one point. I wanted to ask Paul because I have been curious about this for years and years. Well, since 1990. Paul, you were part of the development of the ITV Network Centre policy, the idea of taking peak time scheduling out of the hands of the regional ITV companies which, in my view, has done more to damage or destroy the regional nature of ITV than any other single act. Now clearly that must have been done sensately; people knew that that was happening. Can you describe, in two minutes, what was the underlying thinking?

Paul Bonner: First of all I don't accept the premise that it has destroyed regional output. I think there is a long-term stress. It is to do with the logic of broadcasting. It all goes back to Kensington House in the early 70s. We discovered there — discovered! it was obvious to everybody — what was the biggest fault of the BBC. It didn't recognise the two prime forces, primal forces almost, in broadcasting. One is the people who have to broadcast. They have access to transmitters for whatever reason, charters or their licence or whatever. They must fill that airtime. They are the buyers. Other people, for reasons of money, fame, ideology, artistic aspiration, want to make programmes. There is only one structure and, alas, the BBC has not got it. That is an interface between the buyers — the broadcasters — and the producers. And the natural shape is a circle round the broadcaster of buyers. All right, there has to be specialiast infrastructure for presentation and transmission, there have to be lawyers, there have to be finance people and so on. Outside here you have coherent or incoherent structures; it really does not matter too much because they all present the same, groups of people who want to sell their products and get it on air. Now the structure we set up for Channel 4 was precisely based on that. The structure that we took to the new network centre was made much more sense, I can tell you, than the testosterone-charged arguments of a Monday morning [at the network programme controllers' meetings — *Eds*] that Colin remembers as clearly as I do, and probably with as much horror, in terms of efficient scheduling. It does not lock out regional programming. The fact is that regional programming is perhaps being eased out of peak more as are certain other programmes that are, as it were, programmes that do not appeal to the mass of the whole nation. Then there are the economic effects of competition, and that is what I was talking about. That is the biggest threat and it has nothing to do with either the structure or ITV. It is the same, ultimately, for Channel 4. Channel 4 is riding on a crest of rising revenue now and fighting hard to amplify that by an adjustment of the safety net arrangement. But the fact is that even they are going to be hard pressed by the turn of the century in terms of the new competitors who are taking advertising, remember, as well as subscriptions. And those forces are, I think, pretty intractable.

In relation to the economic forces of pay-per-view, I, too, saw the future in 1977, I think, or 1978 in one of the ancient capitals of Japan, the one with the biggest Buddha in the world. And there Fuji and MITI, the Ministry of Industry and Technology in Japan, funded a real community based pay-per-view and local cable service which was way ahead of its time. But, of course, they were subsidising every household by something like $1500 per year and it is just not economic. What is possible, and maybe this was what you were saying, is that if you have a strong national subscriber based pay-per-view system, it is possible that the BBC could get by supplying either a secondary market or even a primary market to these people, a free slot between high-pay slots for both national and regional public service programmes. But they have to reach an agreement with the operators. The operators would, possibly, think this is a good idea. It might be good to be associated with the BBC. Many commercial operators might see that that way. But actually the subscriber base of any system to be viable needs to be as many people as possible but, certainly, not less than ten to fifteen million.

John Whiston: I wouldn't deny the economics of it. With my sketchy knowledge of accounting I have looked at those graphs and looked at the massive swelling in satellite and cable revenue that is going to be hitting the BBC. It is going to hit it in lots of different ways like putting up the cost of all our rights, all our sports rights. Economically it is going to be a very difficult decision for the BBC to make as to when it decides it can no longer justify or sustain a licence fee. What is the point at which you jump into the new future? Do you jump or do you get pushed? Do you use your economic base at the moment as we have been talking about, to make that jump people say, 'Well, I have got fifty channels so why am I paying £82 for the BBC when I have got 49 other ones that cost me 15 pence per month or whatever?' I think those are very, very difficult decisions.

Now, you know, hopefully and fingers crossed, I will be long gone by the time those decisions have to be made because the predictions are that forty per cent of homes will still have the four or five terrestrial channels and this penetration of this new future because of the costs of the technology won't be that extensive. My only fear is that technology, being that curious thing that it is, always seems to overtake your expectations both in terms of how cheap it is to put in and in terms of the speed with which it comes about. No-one knows. It is quite fun being on ten-year strategies because they should just be called strategies because, you know, no-one knows the difference between ten years, five years, fifteen years.

To wrap up on the point of who owns the means of production: there is the Paramount model whereby you are a studio, you make quite a lot of stuff in-house, you buy the rights to the wilder cards and bring them in-house, bring in independents to make in your studios and that kind of thing.The problem with the new universe is that an independent will have so many different windows to put his programmes on to that he will say, 'Well, the BBC window is only worth an eighth of the budget, so they can't have any of the rights because I am only asking them for an eighth of the budget and I am going to supplement the rest of the income from other windows.' The problem about that for the BBC is that it is very tempting for controllers then to say, 'OK. I can get that programme for an eighth of the budget. Why should I pay full price for a BBC-made production?' And, in a way, without demonising controllers, they become a kind of a barrier to the BBC controlling and owning its own product and therefore being able to survive which is what I think it needs to do in order to survive.

Sue Caro: Thank you very much, everybody, for your contributions.

Session produced by Duncan Dallas

Whose news? To what extent does broadcast news define the region it serves?

Chair: **Ruth Pitt**
Real Life Productions

Brian Hill
Independent producer

Peter Salmon
Channel 4 Television

Richard Whiteley
YTV

RUTH **Pitt:** I have three panellists with me this morning. Peter Salmon is Controller of Factual Programmes at Channel 4. He devised the current *Whose News?* season that is running on Channel 4. He is going to talk very briefly about why he thought that was a good idea and he is going to look at regional news as well.

Brian Hill is currently executive producer of the *Deadline* series, a six-part documentary series running on Channel 4 at the moment as part of that *Whose News?* season. Brian was also the co-director of *Sylvania Waters*; but he is here to defend *Deadline* and what is in it.

Richard Whiteley is presenter of both *Countdown* and *Calendar*. Richard features heavily in the *Deadline* series which was shot entirely in Yorkshire Television's *Calendar* newsroom and he is going to share with us the secrets of what it is like to be in a documentary rather than to make one.

And if I can say a word about my own role, I devised *Deadline* and my company Real Life made it. I was the co-executive producer of *Deadline* with Brian but I also spent many years as a reporter and presenter in the *Calendar* newsroom myself. So I think I qualify to chair this session, if not to sit on the fence.

Peter Salmon: Let me comply with the prophecy of the French commentator who said that the word media is short for mediocre. I take that to be about the general driving down of standards and a narrowing of range and approach, a failure of editorial nerve and a branding out or homogenising of ideas broadcast to viewers.

It is a danger that confronts broadcasting and national culture and a challenge that faces all of us who work in our industry. My theme over the next ten minutes is that it is a threat that regional news needs to take particularly seriously.

My own qualifications to speak to this theme, and also as a general viewer; my home is in Bristol, I watch regional news a lot and I have lived in a half a dozen separate regions throughout Britain — in this one here, I grew up on *Granada Reports* — also as a practitioner, from being a local newspaper reporter to being someone who is so concerned about TV news in general that he decided to devote a whole season of programmes, *Whose News?*, on Channel 4 to this particular theme.

It seemed to me that news was too important to leave to the news managers and that, anyway, there had been some significant changes in ownership, in technology and in intent and they needed closer scrutiny. TV news is a very pervasive technology. Estimates show that we get seventy per cent of all our information from television news and, as a global industry, it is worth somewhere between three and five billion dollars. So this industry is worth looking at. The outcome of the season I don't think is a particularly comforting one either internationally or, in terms of the discussion at this session, regionally either.

For the purposes of my ten minutes, which is not very long, I would like to make three points and show a couple of clips from the season by way of illustration.

Firstly I would like to speak about regional news as political coverage. I want to ask why regional political coverage is quite so insecure that it needs the legitimising approval of Westminster for just about all it covers. I think it is bad enough that all national TV political or coverage looks and feels the same and is served by the same sausage machine at a place called Number 4 Millbank on the Thames which is, for those of you who don't know it, the headquarters of all British parliamentary reporting. I was there just a couple of days ago. Basically it is sort of a posh hotel lobby with lots of offices going off it and restaurants and it is within a stone's throw of Westminster. If only someone *would* throw a few stones, I sometimes think. And, basically, most MPs and political comentators spend their lives yoyoing backwards and forwards between the Houses of Parliament and Number 4 Millbank, which is about a hundred yards away.

My concern is that regional news has, in relation to this building and in relation to the Westminster agenda, allowed itself to play the slave in a sort of master/slave relationship. And I get the feeling that a story isn't a story if a local MP hasn't given it his or her seal of approval down the line from Number 4 Millbank.

I would like to show a clip from the recent *Whose News* edition of *Dispatches*, a little investigation which touched on the dangers of centralised news coverage.

Extract is shown

I ask myself, whenever I see regional political news reporting, whatever happened to bold, fresh, risk-taking, de-centralised local political coverage?

Crime is probably the other defining flavour in regional news. I know it is important. People are concerned about it, too. Each day it is either crime or politics at the top of the bulletin. Now there are some cheap points and obvious points to be scored here to do with fear of crime, the sort of easy, cheap copy that crime affords, stereotypes, all sorts of things. But I should like to touch on what most concerns me about local news and crime. It is another cosy relationship, this time between the police and the regional TV media. We have just lived through a period of the greatest upheaval in national law and order for some decades, with wrongful convictions, forced confessions, mis-judged forensic evidence. I don't think such issues would have arisen if it had been left to regional TV news. I don't think it is just a matter of resources. I think it is distance and I think it is a mutual reliance between these two organisations which could, at times, be unhealthy.

Perhaps if we relied on crime less for our regional news diet and could learn to be more discerning about which stories should and should not be covered, we would probably regain our critical faculties and a distance and a perspective that would allow us to treat the police as just another state agency. I think, sometimes, they become a news agency more than a state agency. I don't think the interest in crime is essentially a British issue. I think that the *Whose News?* season has shown that the fear of and obsession with crime seems as prevalent around the world in the 1990s as fear of and obsession with sex was in the 1890s.

Here's a clip from another programme that we did in the *Whose News?* season. It's from a 'day in the life of the world' programme called *The Daily Planet*.

Extract is shown

Finally, to underline the final point of my little mini-critique, I would like to propose that an originality prize be awarded in regional TV news at one of the many awards junkets that we all attend in our industry. There are originality prizes in factual programmes, in entertainment and why not news? I think news and regional news needs it. It all looks the same, it all sounds the same, it all feels the same — it doesn't matter where you go — the same agenda is largely present from Land's End to John o'Groats. It is the same set, the same colours, the same graphics, the same lighting. I always feel that what I am watching is the result of some rather prolific salesman who sold a kit of parts to every regional TV news franchise in the country and they have all adopted them.

Why no *Big Breakfast* type regional news show? Why no real holiday-style news show with camcorders? Camcorders don't seem to have arrived in regional news yet. Maybe they would make a difference. Why no more interactive news coverage? Clearly, the technology is becoming available. I just think it is time we stood back from regional TVnews and asked if it all needs to look and feel and be exactly the same whether you are in Scunthorpe or Southend.

Some day somewhere in the five hundred channel universe someone, probably a local cable service in Plymouth or Aberdeen or Swansea, will take a big, daring regional news leap. I really think that regional TV news in this country needs to take the leap first and get their hands on that originality prize before they do.
Brian Hill: Ruth introduced me earlier as somebody who was going to defend *Deadline* but as far as I know nobody is actually attacking it, which is curiously pleasant for me because most of the things that I get involved in tend to get attacked quite often. It is going quite well so far.

Last August I walked into the *Calendar* newsroom with Ruth. The series was with Channel 4; it had not been commissioned. We were still talking about it and I had gone up there to have a look. And I walked in and my first thought was 'This is a fantastic location. It's wonderful.' There were people typing away at keyboards. There were monitors going. There was the gallery. There was a live broadcast going out. There were people milling around. And, as a film maker, I thought that this was wonderful, this would be a fantastic location.

And then I met some of the people. I met the urbane presenter, Richard Whiteley. I met his glamorous co-presenter, Christa. I met the hard-nosed news producer and I met the ambitious reporter and then I met the 'been there, seen it all' news crews. And what I was doing was busily slotting all these people into categories. I just thought this was wonderful. I got on the train and went back to London, and on that train journey back I made the series in my head. Up to that point all my information about news and about newsrooms and the people who worked in them — because I had never been in one before — had been gleaned from films like *Broadcast News*, from series like *Drop the Dead Donkey* and from some gruesome but compelling Canadian series set in a newsroom. Though I work in television I have never worked in news, and I had this idea, going back on that train journey, that news was glamorous and exciting. And I thought that this series was going to be a doddle to make. It was going to be easy.

A couple of days later I came back down to work and I realised that, in fact, news isn't glamorous and exciting. The people who work in that newsroom, and in any other newsroom, are just people, and a good documentary series would stand or fall on the strength of those people, whether they work in an engineering factory or a chip shop or a newsroom. So I realised that the series wasn't going to be as easy to make as I thought it would and, in fact, it proved to be very hard work, as all good documentary projects are.

We set about assembling our team and defining what we were going to do and setting our own objectives. I think the buzzword at the time in documentaries was 'docusoap' or 'soapumentary.' This had arisen partly as a result of series like *Sylvania Waters*, and commissioning editors were asking for a soap element to documentaries.

We talked about this and whether we could make it as a soap opera. I don't think that you can make documentaries like soap operas because the defining characteristic of a soap opera is its longevity. I think we tried to borrow some of the conventions of soap opera so that, for example, in each episode we have several stories running at once as you do in soap operas. We tried to make the characters people in whom viewers would be interested and interested in finding out what happened to them so that they would switch on next week. We used music, as soap operas do. We borrowed some of those characteristics and what we wanted to do, what we strove to do right from the start, was to make it a series that would be compelling but would be entertaining, would be amusing and, most importantly, would tell viewers something about the nature of regional news and about how regional news is made and the people who make it. And we were hoping very much that it would throw up some questions that people would talk about.

I am not a great viewer of regional news. So I was coming to it fairly fresh. I think that probably the most important thing that I realised about regional news from making this series was its relentless nature, that it is this hungry beast that has to be fed. *Calendar* goes out every weekday and it must go out at the same time, it must run for a certain period of time because people expect it, it must fill a space whether or not there is news happening, although we could debate whether news is always happening. This team of people must go out every day and they must find news stories and they must come back with them. And it is no good for a reporter to come back saying, 'Well, I didn't think it was newsworthy,' or 'It didn't really work for me,' or 'I didn't really think we should be doing that,' because they must fill that space. They must do it.

Extracts are shown

I don't really have anything else to say except that I think one of the big successes of *Deadline* is that we have made a difficult six-part series with lots of characters in it and we have managed to do it without me having to sit here that much and defend it, although you may think differently.

Ruth Pitt: Richard Whiteley features quite heavily throughout the *Deadline* series and has been kind enough to come along today to share with us what it felt like to be followed around by our cameras. I am going to ask Richard a few questions and then we would all like to have some questions from the audience.

Richard, the thing that I want to know first of all was what was it like being followed around by a camera? It is not an experience that most people ever have to undergo and, certainly perhaps, not one that you have had to experience before.

Richard Whiteley: What strikes me first is that the final image in the film is of me drinking white wine and stuffing some pork pie into my face. We all know how important it is in television to have the last words, so the last word, or the last image of me would be, I suppose, very typical so I can't really complain about that. I suppose, really, that is what the series does get over. It is, I have to tell you, quite typical of what goes on. What's it like to have a camera following you around? I have to say it held no horrors for me because it is my job. I have worked with cameras for twenty-six years so there is no particular horror to me. For other people who got involved, it became less of a horror. When they came to talk to us initially they said, 'Look, you'll find that it will be strange at first but after a while you won't even notice that we are there.' And I think that is fairly true. I think you always sort of knew that they were there because, obviously, there are not many people but there are two people who were reasonably close by. So you know they are there but you sort of didn't really bother about it. In fact when they left, they left about the middle of November just after that Budget programme, then you really missed them. And coming into work every day and them not being there … I have to say that they were missed, not just by the presenters but by the whole of the staff as well. So I think, actually, it was a very pleasant experience. Having said that, they followed us, as it were, warts and all. I never had a wart actually and I see that I have just now got one here which I don't know if anyone noticed, it has almost grown in sympathy. You have created it for me!

Ruth Pitt: But one of the things that I would like to know, Richard, is because you are a known face and wherever you go people recognise you as the presenter of *Countdown* and, indeed, *Calendar*, since the series has been running, have the general public, when they see you, had any views about it? Has it demystified the world of news, do you think, for people, or are people disappointed? What is the response?

Richard Whiteley: Well, the people I have spoken to haven't asked intellectual questions about the making of the news or the process of selection or the moral high ground or any of this type of stuff. They have basically said, 'Wow, that is fascinating. We didn't know what went on.' And it is basically as simple as that. They just didn't know what went on. They know about the paraphernalia of television, that is well recorded, the machinery and the cameras and the links and all that kind of thing. But I don't think they knew actually what went on ... the muttering. Everyone mutters. Have you noticed, everyone mutters? I mean I have seen myself several times now and I didn't know that I muttered so much. Everyone seems to mutter. I suppose if you filmed all our jobs, every day, we would probably mutter a lot. We would all mutter. And a lot of muttering goes on, hanging around, walking around. That is what comes over.

There is a certain amount of rushing. I mean it is called *Deadline,* and, frankly, most days there is at five to six, as in any news programme, tape being rushed up corridors at the last minute. And that is reflected as well. But there is, basically, a lot of nothing happening. I think, in a way, that comes over.

Ruth Pitt: Television, by and large, is not willing to turn the cameras on itself. Do you think that Yorkshire Television were mad to allow us in?

Richard Whiteley: No, I don't think so, no. I don't know why you chose Yorkshire Television, but it was obviously put before the powers that be at Yorkshire TV and I think the decision was very quickly made and that was that. And Yorkshire TV has, over the years, turned the cameras on various sections of society, notably *Jimmy's Hospital,* people in Whitby going about their business, people in an upcoming series, people in Haworth and also a very good one on the election. We followed three candidates, or perhaps four, three I think, round a constituency, a Conservative-held constituency in South Yorkshire.

And so I don't think we could have turned round and said, 'I am very sorry. It is OK for us to do an observational documentary but you are not coming in here.' So the decision was made. Were they mad? I don't think so. It was a corporate video. It is not a PR job. It is difficult to avoid saying the word 'warts,' isn't it? There are warts there. People might think, looking at it, 'That is an exciting place to work. It is very good working there,' or they might think, 'That is drab and dull. What dum-dums they are!' I don't know what the reaction would be in the professional world outside but I don't think they were mad.

Ruth Pitt: That is good to hear. When I was first developing the series I spent quite a lot of time talking to different people in the *Calendar* newsroom to glean their views and opinions and had a couple of long conversations with Richard where we discussed what he thought regional news was and what it should be. Some of Richard's comments, I think, probably informed the way the series finally went more than anything else. And I think one of the more interesting observations that you made was about the nature of a region and whether or not there is such a thing as a region in the way that regional television news programmes tend to reflect them. And I wondered whether you might have any views on that now?

Richard Whiteley: Yes, the word 'region' as applied to television, and I can only speak about the British system, is dictated by a fifty-year old system of electronics, that is to say the terrestrial transmitter system. And that created television regions. When ITV came along post-1955 these regions, or as they became franchise areas, became definite areas of a kind. But they were not related to economic regions or purely geographical regions, at least they were geographic only insofar as that mountains might have stood in the way of a transmission picture.

The Yorkshire Television region is not actually a region — if I can just remind you, it stretches from Scarborough in the north right down the coastline and it goes right round the whole of Lincolnshire, and right up to north Norfolk. And it goes to a place called Wells-next-the-Sea; in fact, Wells-next-the-Sea is thirty-three miles from Kings Lynn. Well, you couldn't be more in the heart of Anglia territory than Kings Lynn. In fact I was very amused by a story. Prince Philip was once going through Leeds in the Lord Mayoral car on a State visit to Leeds. And he saw one of our vans going past with Yorkshire Television painted on it, and he said, 'Yorkshire Television, that is all we can bloody well get at Sandringham!' So there is no region, there is no justification for the region apart from the electronics of the two transmitters.

That having been said, we want to, and have to, and are delighted to 'serve,' as it were in inverted commas, the region. Therefore, believe you me, Wells-next-the-Sea gets pretty good coverage on Yorkshire Television. It probably gets as good coverage as Huddersfield, actually.

We have said, I think, from day one on *Calendar* (and I am very old and I was there on day one) that we recognise that Scarborough is very different from Sheffield, and Sheffield is very different from Scunthorpe. After all when you go to a strange town, a strange city, there is nothing more boring than somebody's else's evening paper, is there? I mean, you look at the *Manchester Evening News* tonight. It is fairly boring if you are used to the *Evening Standard* or if you are used to the *Birmingham Evening Mail*. If you go to Sheffield, the *Sheffield Star* has no interest at all to people who normally get the *Yorkshire Evening Post*, but they are separated by only twenty-six miles. We have to cover the whole region so we have said, 'Look, here we are. We are called *Calendar*. It is called Yorkshire Television,' which, again, is a strange name for a county half of which can't get Yorkshire Television because they get Tyne-Tees. Half of our viewers don't live in Yorkshire but find themselves watching Yorkshire Television.

However the name, as it happens, is not an issue. We have said, 'You are all part of our family between six and half past. We regard you as all with us today for this half hour and therefore if you live in Scunthorpe and there is something terrible happening in Sheffield, we reckon, quite frankly, you should be interested because we are all part of the same family.' And I am not being over-sentimental by using the word 'family.' That, I think, has been the criterion of the region of *Calendar* and Yorkshire Television for all those years — that we are all, as it were, in it together.

Ruth Pitt: I might pick up on a point that Peter Salmon made about the failure of regional television programmes, and news in particular, to be innovative and use all the massive range of options available to programme makers now. Why is it that regional news is always about two presenters sitting on a sofa and the same old one and a half minute or one minute forty-five reports? Why is it like that and are you happy that it is like that? What would you like it to be like if it wasn't?

Richard Whiteley: This is my *bête noire*. There are twenty-seven regional news magazines in this country and I reckon that twenty-six of them are pretty similar. Yes, they are. There are two people, man and woman, sitting behind a curved desk with a logo behind, cut from two shot to single, to single, link-ENG, link-ENG, link-ENG. A friend of mine who does Birmingham Central News, and who has been doing it for many years, says that somebody has been to America and has come back with a good idea that he and the girl presenter sit in a two-shot the whole time. A two-shot! Every time they are on camera!

Now, OK. No report lasts more than a minute and a half. No live interviews. No fun in the studio. I said twenty-six. Now, look. I have only got experience of one news magazine, I have only ever had two employers in my life, ITN and Yorkshire TV. So I can only speak for Yorkshire Television which we are thinking about today.

If you ever do see *Calendar*, it is not actually the same as those twenty-six. It is a bit different. We don't sit behind a desk. We do, as you said, sit on sofas. Very few people in news magazines sit on sofas; they do it at breakfast time. We do, I think, have a sort of *joie de vivre* and a definite junction between part one and part two. In part two we can smile and part one obviously tends to be more serious. And we do, I think, do things that other programmes don't do. I am very happy with the way we do it but I do feel terribly sorry for viewers in other areas who see this endless tedious diet; it is so claustrophobic to see these two at a desk ... cut, cut, cut. Yes, and I agree Peter, and I feel desperately sorry for those regions. The graphics are the same. The only fun in most programmes is the link to the weather man or the weather girl — that is the only time when the presenters are allowed to stray off the Autocue, frankly. You know, what is it going to be like in Wolverhampton, Sally? Honestly, you look at a programme. We have more scope than that, thank goodness!

David Keene (producer): I am a network programme maker, tainted by excessive experience, looking for a regional furrow to plough.

Peter mentioned lack of camcorders and lack of interactive television. That implies he is criticising the accessibility of existing programmes, right? Can I take this in the direction I want to go which is to deal with the treatment of people by regional programmes?

It strikes me that, by and large, they are not at all accessible, even by comparison with network programmes. I can give you a bit of history. There was a Golden Age when everyone was having more fun in television than they are now and I prowled the north of England for *Nationwide*, stealing good stories for the network from under your newsroom, sir, and the local ones on this side of the Pennines. And what we found as we went around was that when you appeared with a trades council or a tenants' group or some particular local campaign, the default assumption was that you were from *Granada Reports* because *Granada Reports* dealt with people like them. When they worked out that you weren't, and you weren't those embarrassing people from the BBC whom they never saw, you were some other bit of the BBC, they then phoned their friend in Granada to check you out. And I was enormously impressed that almost everybody who was engaged in society right across Granadaland knew somebody in Granada by name whom they felt perfectly free to ring up to ask about me and, presumably, to engage their interest in some aspect of their campaign if it was at a point where it was worth Granada's attention.

If you watched the programmes, you saw why they had this relationship. *Granada Reports* used to be extraordinarily accessible. The current programme that has changed its name — it is very glossy, it is very attractive, one quite enjoys it — but it is a different kind of programme. It is actually more like *Calendar*. One has looked a little now about the day by day operations, and I have certainly filmed alongside *Calendar* crews on many occasions. On both programmes their general treatment of people is something out of the dark ages. A London-based indie, even a London-based BBC or mainstream current affairs programme, doesn't treat people in quite the utilitarian way that the regional operations I have been watching do. I would be very interested in what Brian's feelings are after a long period of time alongside it on that particular dimension.

I am interested in the general treatment and what comes out in terms of *Calendar's* relationship with the public. Access is on the other end of that, you know, their accessibility is part of your relationship. It seems to be that they are terribly, terribly utilitarian.

Brian Hall: I think, on the whole, I was unimpressed with the treatment of ordinary people. What I mean by ordinary people are the people who were the subject of news stories and the way they were dealt with. I don't mean that people were horrible to them or were in any way unpleasant but I think the main consideration of those people going out to get stories — and they work to a very tight deadline — is to get their story back and edited and put out that night. When they have finished doing the interview, or whatever filming they are doing, it leaves them very little time to sit down with the person and and just have a chat with them like a normal human being when the camera has gone. That didn't happen very much in my experience of this series.

Helen Hutchinson (Border Television): I am News Editor at Border Television, so I am responsible for these regional news programmes that look exactly the same whether they are in Aberdeen or in Plymouth. Before I get defensive about it, which I am duty-bound to do, I'll just say that regional programmes are not all the same and I can't think of the last time we had an MP at Millbank and it's for the very reason that was put forward that we don't like that kind of treatment, so we don't do it. But I won't go into a slanging match about that.

What I would like to say that worried me about that was the clear formula that was being followed in news and it seemed that as soon as the participants kind of detracted from the accepted formula of news, the searching the lake, the emotional appeal for the witnesses, the reconstruction of the crime, the upset family — 'Has anybody seen my daughter?' — as soon as the whole theatre departed from that, the reporter panicked and phoned up the producer, 'What am I going to do?' I don't mean criticism of the individual reporter because she was clearly under pressure, but that to me exposed what happens. What has happened to us all is that we have got into a formula of the way that we deal with these things. I am not defending it but I am saying murder and missing children are very unpleasant things and, strangely enough, we have all come to accept the formulaic way of doing it. And I would actually argue that regional television does it much better than national television. I mean there was criticism of the way that we do it, but you go to a murder or a missing child where there is national interest and you will really see the way that things work

And we have to meet these people again. We have to bump into them. We'll go to a village fete the next week and they will be there. They will come up to us and they will say, 'What did you do?' I believe that the viewer has come to accept this formula. And it is part of the process now. I think if you look back to the Warrington bombings, the way that Tim Parry's father became part of the reporting of that story, the family's involvement, their public grief, their public appearance on television to engage the whole nation in a private tragedy has now become part of the whole thing. And to knock it and to accuse regional television of exploiting it is rather unfair without thinking how we have all grown up into accepting these formulas.

Just one last thing I would say, going back to the defence of regional news programmes. On a practical level we are certainly the smallest ITV station covering an absolutely huge area. There are very difficult practical reasons why we can't always have an all-singing and all-dancing show of people breaking up that presenter link-ENG kind of duopoly simply because for a lot of our people it would take them two and a half, if not three hours, to get to a place where we can engage them physically in the programme and two and a half hours to get back and search me if I can find people who will spend six hours of their day for a two and a half minute slot on a regional news programme.

Ruth Pitt: May I just pick up one of those points that Helen has made? Peter, when you were putting together the *Whose News* season for Channel 4 you must have watched endless hours of news bulletins and I wonder if Helen's point about the relationship that has to be developed between say, the police and a newsroom or whatever, is quite as unfair as you seem to be suggesting earlier on. Is there a way in which you have to do that and you have to have a certain kind of relationship in the community?

Peter Salmon: Of course you do and you can't criticise local news coverage of things like the missing child type stories or, probably, the Tim Parry stuff; I don't think that is probably the best place to look. I think, by and large, the police/news relationship on those sorts of stories where there is a sort of public service element involved is very important and I commend that.

But I think there is a general cosiness about regional news which I think is discerned on a couple of levels. I think one is that potentially editorially it can lead you to miss an awful lot, or to feel not able to cover certain stories. I think the other thing you need to be worried about, as we all are in broadcasting, is whether you are really keying into people's lives, whether or not what you are saying about the is still ringing true. I think it will be reflected when people get hold of cable and the camcorder revolution really bites in twenty years or in ten years which is hopefully where your business managers are looking, when people have local cable services.

I am wondering whether or not you really tap into the sort of anger, or the emotion, or people who are not media-friendly in your areas. I am somewhat aware when I am watching news that we sort of feel comfortable with most of the people who are served up; I don't know, they are people we are used to seeing every day through a well-worn slipper. I think it needs to bite a bit more and it needs to represent those people who want to bite and who feel disenfranchised or left out. There are in all our families, they are in all our streets, all our neighbourhoods who are all worried and are under-represented. Particularly young people, I think.

I am making a lot of points here, probably unfairly, really, because I am generalising quite a lot. But I think regional news particularly does not speak to young people. I think it is a real problem for you. I think that's why MTV, or even Sky, or Channel 4, are ripping off your audiences. We know you are weak around five or six o'clock for young people. Young people aren't interested in your shows and we are going to take them. Actually it is bad for local democracy in a funny way that they don't feel involved in what you are saying and how you are saying it. They probably aren't reading the newspapers either; I don't know what we do about them quite. But I don't think the vehicles that you have invented, or are using at the moment, are user-friendly for a lot of these groups in your local communities. I think it is a general problem for all of us. What do we do about those people who should be involved who aren't involved? I think you are speaking to the converted too much.

Ruth Pitt: On the one hand you have said that regional news is too cosy and has a cosy relationship with all the comfortable armchair people and the Chief Constables and, on the other hand, what you are suggesting is that we throw all that away and instead go for a youth audience ...

Peter Salmon: I am saying that you should embrace a broader constituency. I think you are too middle-aged and middle-class, generally.

Colin King (University of Exeter): I am not a news editor. I watched the first episode of *Deadline*, and I have to say I found it rather smug and self-satisfied as a reflection of the work that you do. I can imagine that it has got some appeal to your own local audiences but I was watching from further away. I had a different perspective on it. I think what interested me in the programme was its a revelation of how you manufacture your own news, how you set your own agenda during the day, and how you have the confidence, the self-confidence, to manipulate, if necessary, to get the end that you want i.e. the deadline for that programme. That's what came across to me.

I didn't draw much from the thought processes that went into that programme but the other disturbing feature of it is the way I would see it as a piece of television, which I think falls more into the infotainment category rather than hard documentary. The intrusiveness of the whole process, not only you but other news-rooms, in order to get the stories that you want is vividly illustrated.

So I was looking at it from a different perspective and in a sense I would like to add to what Peter Salmon has said about this, that we are looking for a different approach to news rather than the formulaic process that we have all grown rather accustomed to.

I just want to add one other thing. When my students were looking at news programmes a few years back, quite by chance the BBC was making a programme in its own newsroom in London when the news came through that Nigel Lawson had resigned. You may have seen that particular programme. It takes the news-room quite by surprise. They are within minutes of the six o'clock news. They have got to prepare a complete bulletin at nine o'clock. Now that programme only lasts twenty minutes but it is a fascinating programme about the thought proc-esses that go into the building of the blocks of the programme. And I felt more of this was needed in your programme to give it the bite that I was looking for but I think, perhaps, it was in a different slot in the evening and it was more infotainment than hard documentary about news and news values and news processes.

Sue Caro (Channel 4): I am speaking partly in my capacity as an employee of ITN for twelve years where I was the director on *News at Ten* and *Channel 4 News,* and I would just like to say there is no difference. In fact I think national news deci-mates people's lives even more than regional. I would like to give the example of Abby Humphries, the missing baby, I don't know if anybody remembers her. ITN went hell for leather on that story with the rest of the media and, eventually, she was got back. A couple of months later another baby went missing. Only this time he was a black baby, Amos Moses. I don't know if anybody remembers that one. And I questioned our programme editor for that day as to why we weren't run-ning that story at all. And he told me it was because the police had warned him off it because, in their opinion, there was something dodgy about the baby's father. Now, of course, we all might remember that Abby Humphries' father was alleged to be somewhat dodgy, too. But that didn't stop us running the story, and I think that is a very telling point.

And, Brian, I would like to pick you up on what you were saying about how *Calendar* went into people's lives and reflected just certain aspects. I would like to ask you whether there are any other black people in the programme, apart from the family that you showed at great length attacking the camera crew. And did that story appear in *Calendar?* What was the justification for running that in *Dead-line* to the extent that you did? To me that is a perceived image of black people and their position in our society as villains and criminals, and I just think that you reinforced that, maybe unwittingly.

Brian Hall: Sorry, the story about the people coming out of the courtroom?

Sue Caro: Yes, the family whose sixteen-year-old son, we were told, had just been convicted of murder. We were told nothing else about that but it was run, and re-run and re-run — the actual images that your crew filmed of the family attacking the cameraman.

201

Brian Hall: I think it was included because I think it said something again, about regional news. Everything in the *Deadline* series is about regional news. That particular episode showed the news crews talking about the kind of things that they come up against, and talking in a fairly disturbing way, because I think one of them makes the comment 'They are not really getting their case across, if they want to be seen as respectable people, they shouldn't go around doing this kind of thing,' i.e. having a go at the cameraman. So I thought it was quite revealing about the attitudes of people making news. That's why it was in *Deadline*.

Ruth Pitt: Speaking as someone who was involved in the making of *Deadline*, I think it is quite important to point out that one of the things that struck me most about the material that we were getting when we were filming all the time in the newsroom, was that given the racial mix of the Yorkshire Television transmission area and given the fact that almost half the population of Bradford, for instance, is Asian, I was absolutely staggered at how white the subject matter of *Calendar* was. There was only story that cropped up during the whole time that we were filming which in any way involved *Calendar* going into the black community in Chapeltown and that was when there was a riot one Friday night. I was really surprised at the lack of reflection of that racial mix of the area. But it wasn't something we could do anything about. We were reflecting the series.

Dave Rushton (Institute of Local Television): I would like to turn this back a little bit to the theoretical propositions that Peter was starting with. We have had a very interesting and, I think, very typical analysis of the way television addresses itself. We had a theoretical set of propositions from Peter, addressed in an observational way by Brian in a construction or a deconstruction of a television programme *Calendar*, and then we have had, in some ways, a wider justification of why *Calendar* is like it is, and that is that *Calendar* has to deal with an audience that really doesn't associate very much with itself.

The point that I am making, I suppose, is that whilst Richard describes the audience for *Calendar* as a family, I would describe them as a prison, and I think they have been blocked into the unfortunate distribution of Yorkshire Television's signal over forty years. And it is time we released them, looking towards television in the future as a way of releasing them from the blockades of Scottish Television, Yorkshire and so on. I think really people associate with the towns and the cities they are in and have an identity with them. We need to be looking towards an agenda which says, 'Let's look at the news from around the world from our own locality, and let's throw out ITN, let's throw out the BBC from London and let's look at the world from where we are and understand it from where we are. So local, global, national, regional, makes some sense in terms of who we are, where we are and what we can do about it.'

Ruth Pitt: Richard, do you think that *Calendar* has in a sense imprisoned its viewers in a kind of parochialism?

Richard Whiteley: I know *Calendar* is well viewed in Armbridge jail and Wakefield jail so I knew I had a captive audience to a certain extent! But I love your point about all our audience being prisoners. Yes, look, you are talking about city television or even street television. Yes, that's fine. Let's have it! And then we can have the video recorders, then we can have what I think we should have now. It doesn't need any technical trick. It is looser writing. If you listen to the way a news bulletin is written and read, it bears no relation to the way people speak. It does, to a certain extent, on commercial radio. Even then not very much. Those of us old enough to remember a revered gentleman by the name of Sir Geoffrey Cox in his original guidelines to the writers of ITN — and Sir Geoffrey Cox was the most vain and scholarly of people — said 'When you write a story, write it as though you are telling a chap in a pub what's happened'.

Now I think we could have far looser writing on the news which would make it far more colloquial and far more user- and listener-friendly. Yes, and come the day, go down our streets, certainly go to your town and I know at YTV to a certain extent we have it because we are lucky to have a network of transmitters around Sheffield and by linking up these seven or eight we can do a sort of city area for Sheffield which we do, on a regular basis, four or five times a day.

So, yes, I think you are absolutely right. The sooner there is TV for Louth and Wisbech and those little places, the better, I agree with you.

Peter Salmon: Can I just pick up one point that was made earlier about the pressures under which regional television labour and the miles you cover and, therefore, it's difficult to be original and do something a bit different and not to settle into the old formulaic thing because of that? I just don't take that view as an excuse for people not being original. It seems to me that most news, as far as I can tell from my experience, is diaried. I think actually that two-thirds of all stories on any day is known about a month before, or certainly ten days before. The launch of something, the party conference … there is plenty of time to think originally about how you cover those stories, about whose voices you hear, about how we get at constituencies we have never covered before in relation to this story. I think we have got to be very careful we don't use the old logistical argument. Gosh! A hundred miles from Whitby to Bradford, we have got to get the story back therefore we did it the same old two and half minute way. Let's think inventively about how we bring other voices into the news or report that news back to people.

Ruth Pitt: But one thing you can't stick in a dairy in advance is crime coverage. And one of the main accusations made against regional news is that it is too crime-driven these days. What is your view on that?

Peter Salmon: Well, you can't ignore crime. Of course you can't. I am not taking the view that is taken by some papers in London that says that if you report crime you will damage property prices therefore we had better not report crime because otherwise it will drive house prices down. Of course crime is there and it is important to cover it.

My slight concern is — and I am exaggerating to make a point — stolen bicycles aren't news; clearly missing girls and murders are. I am just concerned that news editors and regional news broadcasts are critical enough and questioning enough of the agenda. My point about whether the police are a state agency or a news agency is a proper one. I am really concerned. As somebody who did police calls for the first few years of my life, I know you can just wire yourself up to the intravenous life-line into the local police station and publish what they tell you.

Or you can say, 'Do we need a broader context for this story, is it really relevant? What's the background? What can be done about it? Is the police view the only view about what is going on or do we need to go to the housing estate or village? Is there another story lurking in there?'

We are all guilty of it, of course, at a local and a national level, we are around the corner in Channel 4 from Scotland Yard, as is Number 4 Millbank, as are Sky. You know all these agencies are just a bit too close and a bit too chummy. I think, at a local level, it is even harder to resist that relationship.

Brian Hill: We all know, because we have all seen the statistics, that the battered granny story doesn't mean that granny is at great risk of being battered. It is just that it is an emotional story and in fact young men of about eighteen to twenty-five years are most likely to be violently attacked. And yet I still saw on *Calendar* this lurid reporting of victims of attack. On one occasion a reporter was saying to a couple, 'How do you feel about the attacks on the estate?' And they say, 'Well, we haven't heard about them.' And he says, 'Well, how would you feel if you had heard about them? What would you feel, would you feel frightened?' It is not a criticism of him. I think that is just the agenda in local news. I am surprised that we are still doing that in spite of all the evidence, and we all know that it is not like that, it is still happening.

Laurie Upshon (Central Television): I suppose I run one of the biggest regional news services in Britain and I find myself agreeing quite a lot with Peter, surprisingly. What worries me is not necessarily what we are doing now. It is about the future and the future audiences. I don't think that we are going to get the children's audience. We will be in danger of spreading ourselves too thinly if we try to be all things to all viewers. But what does worry me is will those children who are watching MTV, cartoons or *Startrek*, be an audience to regional news in the future?

I also agree with Peter that news doesn't have an edge. It should be there. And one of the problems is the constraint under which we work within the ITC guidelines. I can remember writing an article about three or four years ago saying that local news ought to be more campaigning. We report campaigns, we don't campaign. By campaigning we are being partisan, and partisanship is in breach of the ITC guidelines. I think we ought to start pushing those methods of reporting a bit until we are rolled back by the ITC.

The main problem with ITV is that it is commercial. We are in business to make money. I am in business to get audiences. We tend to do programmes the way we do at the moment because, by and large, it works. We do have this problem of very large regions. We solve it in one way by splitting into three. I can watch three different programmes every night of the week in my area, and they are different. The three Central programmes have different identities because they are covering different parts of England. The Central region is about a quarter of England. So Monmouth has very little in common with the same Lincolnshire overlap areas that we have with Yorkshire. And if one looks at the most popular programmes in Britain, it is those covering the smallest areas. We have, for years, being trying to chase the coat-tails of Border Television, who regularly get 52 per cent, 53 per cent of the audience. We would love that. I think any ITV head of news would be lying if they said they did not want a large audience.

We want that large audience for a number of reasons. Firstly, it keeps us in work and, secondly, it ensures our funding. ITV news is, by and large, seen as a benefit within the system. We have to be there, though, because the ITC in the last franchise round mandated what was to be provided in terms of minimum hours. By delivering an audience we are earning our place in the schedules and earning funding for live links, for second and third regional services. So I don't think you ought to forget that commercial argument.

Finally, I was one of the judges at the Royal Television Society regional awards this year. I think the judging process was a farce but we did sit through all the ITV and the BBC programmes, and there was, actually, a very wide diversity. It was not just a matter of either sitting on a sofa or sitting behind a desk. And I have to say that the most encouraging thing that I saw, and this might sound patronising although it is not intended to be, was how the BBC had changed from a very structured, almost uniform, look across Britain to taking it on themselves to provide a different look, a different agenda in each region. That was one of the most encouraging things I saw in regional television because if they are going to give us a run for the money, we are going to have to get our act in order.

Jeremy Bower (Ravensbourne College): I have worked for the BBC and I have worked for Yorkshire Television but, in the context of this morning, I think the contribution I want to make is about having worked in Canada, in Vancouver, in the context of cable. The thing that no-one has said directly, though I think Peter Salmon has touched on it, is when you come back from Canada to this part of the world, you are incredibly aware of the attitude of deference which exists broadly in British society. Until that changes, it really does not matter how much you change the technology, how much you change the news protocols; by and large 90 per cent of those who live in the country believe that 10 per cent are running things and they believe they should fit into that agenda. It's very different in Canada. It feels different. There is a natural tendency to feel much more in a position of equivalence with the whole news gathering process.

The other thing I hope is going to change is less to do with camcorders; it's to do with the lower cost of communication links because once more news is live (I have taken Richard's point about the style of writing). Once you are really going live there is that fluency to do with reporting in the present tense. My goodness, it starts to get exciting! And, at the moment, I think there is very little real experience in this country compared to the United States and, to some extent Canada, of the extraordinary things that can happen, and you can start to move maybe, if you wish, into something closer to the *Big Breakfast* feel. Unless local, regional or national news begins to address these issues, there is not going to be an audience interested in news in ten years time.

Charles Lauder: I would like to return to the topic that Sue Caro introduced a little while back and just ask what is believed to be the long-term effect of the continuing disenfranchising of black and ethnic minority groups in terms of the way that news programmes are put together and, indeed, portrayed?

I walked out of here a couple of minutes ago quite simply because I was angry. I was angry, if you look around it, at the constituency of the people who have come to speak at a conference such as this. I was also angry at the fact that, having put my hand up, almost from the end of the speeches from the front, I simply wasn't selected. And I just wonder how much of that is actually symptomatic of what it is that ends up on the screen in the final analysis.

Ruth Pitt: I am sorry if I have only just noticed you. I think, perhaps, one of the best people to answer that question is Ali Rashid.

Charles Lauder: Why?

Ruth Pitt: Because he is the news editor of Yorkshire Television and you are asking about disenfranchisement and the long-term effect of it and it seems to me that if he is the person informing news judgements, then he is a good person to answer it. Unless you have got any other suggestions?

Charles Lauder: I just wonder why the people who are at the front who once were speaking on other things should not speak on this topic, too?

Brian Hill: Speaking for myself, I can only echo what Ruth said earlier, that I also was surprised, given the size of the black population in the Yorkshire TV region, how few stories that concerned the black population are seen on the screen. As she said, in the period of our filming, which was about three or four months, there was only one story, which was a riot in Chapeltown. I found that surprising and rather shocking.

Peter Salmon: I think the point that you make is a good one. It chimes in with some of the themes that I hope I have tried to raise today which is that television news programmes, in general, all look like they come out of the same Kenwood Chef blender, basically. What emerges is this comforting view of Britain which quite honestly to me looks and feels the same as it did when I was watching it in the 1960s. That may be to do with the representation of ethnic minorities, or to do with women decision-makers, or to do with what has happened to young people in the changing job markets of Britain and how they feel about their role in our country. I feel that what we are really doing in a sense is reassuring people. I think news, and television in general, should be slightly more pro-active. Whatever Mrs Thatcher thought and said, we have a society and we have generally to encourage people to understand how it works and what its mechanics are, and to understand and be involved in their community.

Instead of that, we have set up this sort of blend of things and whether we do it with the coverage of black people or young people or other people who are not represented in the news, it sort of comforts them that in twenty or thirty years, in a funny way, nothing has changed. The same deference applies, the same institutions prevail, the same consensus applies. I think we are in for a shock if we don't represent the views of the sort of constituencies that you want.

And it is not just a cultural issue, it is a commercial one. That's the thing that ITV companies have got to get a hold on: they will lose these constituencies to local cable providers, computer games and a lot of other things that people are going to want instead of the stuff that is served up at six or half past six. It's a crying shame because people have a desire to be informed and to be involved. But if it is no satisfied and they don't see themselves reflected back on those news programmes, they won't make an appointment, they won't get involved. And I think the long-term effects, commercially, culturally and politically, are quite severe.

Jackie Harrison (University of Sheffield): I take on board all that has been said about disenfranchisement in the news and so on. I have just completed a content analysis of both national and regional news and what I have found is that in national news and regional news there is a tendency for the ordinary person to be perceived as a victim. But what I have found is that regional news alone, programmes like *Calendar and Look North* actually give ordinary people a chance to portray themselves as proactive. By that I mean community action and campaigns and so on are covered by regional news. They are, usually, neglected by national news. As such we had, for example, things like a Somali demonstration against racism; we had coverage of the campaign of women against pit closures very carefully covered by the regional news.

Now I am not saying that is enough but what I am saying is that national news tends to ignore these issues totally and regional news does make some effort to cover it. And I'll just say that I think that is a very, very important role for regional news and I would like to see more of it.

Louise Bennett (Independent Television Commission): It is just a brief response really to Laurie's point. The requirement for due impartiality comes directly from the 1990 Broadcasting Act and the ITC guidelines flesh that out. It does not stop good investigative journalism.

Ruth Pitt: Or campaigning journalism, you are saying?

Louise Bennett: Good investigative journalism.

Ruth Pitt: There is a difference, though, between investigative journalism and campaigning journalism and I think that is Laurie's point, isn't it? Where would the ITC stand on the issue of campaigning journalism? Say, for instance, Lee Clegg?

Louise Bennett: There is clearly a requirement for due impartiality on things which are not just related to politics but also things which are matters of particular interest and of particular controversy. Broadcasters are not there to take a stand on matters related to politics and matters of particular moment in the national life. They are there to report them, they are there to investigate them but they are not there to push a particular line.

Roy Saatchi (BBC North): *Deadline* was finely observed, and Yorkshire Television should take a lot of credit for allowing the cameras to be turned on itself, but I wonder how typical it was. I certainly don't think it is very typical of regional news programmes. I certainly don't know any regional news programme that celebrates the fact that it starts the day with a blank sheet of paper!

Are we really keying into people's lives? I think Peter is right, maybe not as much as we should but we certainly are. We are making those efforts. In our own case we have made special efforts to build relationships with the community of Liverpool 8, which really does feel quite disenfranchised at the moment. We have appointed an Asian affairs producer to work out at Blackburn. And I do think the BBC's policy of appointing specialist correspondents round the country means we are making something of an effort there.

As for crime coverage, is it true the picture you paint of a relentless portrait of crime just for the sake of it? I don't think it is fair, I don't think it is true. You take the newspapers. I believe that the two that I quote, the Newcastle *Evening Chronicle* and the London *Evening Standard*, have made a conscious decision not to cover crime unless it is absolutely relevant and important that poeple need to know. What has happened? Their circulation has gone up. The same thing is happening in regional news programmes and that is why I do not necessarily believe that *Deadline* is typical of all regional news programmes.

And, finally, is it fair to say that regional television has never been innovative? I don't think it is fair at all. There aren't many ways of presenting a news programme. And even if we stood up at a lectern with all sorts of things happening behind us it would still look like a news programme. But regional news pioneered single camera operation, regional news pioneered multi-skilling and regional news has pioneered giving people video cameras to make their own films. So I think, actually, innovation is alive and well in regional television.

Session produced by Ruth Pitt

Is commerce the enemy of diversity and creativity?

Chair: **Jaci Stephen**
Daily Mirror

John Blake
ITV Network Centre

Steve Clark
Carlton Television

Ray Fitzwalter
Independent producer

Paul Watson
Granada Television

Don Webb
Freelance dramatist

J ACI Stephen: 'Is commerce the enemy of diversity and creativity?'is the title of this session. Or as the driver of a black cab might say, 'Cor blimey, darlin', there's a load of crap on the TV today.' This is basically the question that I think we are going to be asking: is TV getting worse because of the ratings battle or is it getting better? Was there a Golden Age? Are we in the Golden Age now?

Why is it getting worse? Is the ratings battle pushing programme makers down less adventurous routes? The succcess of independents, like Hat Trick Productions, who did the fantastically successful *Have I got News for You?*, and Talkback with Steve Coogan, would suggest that we are living in very good times, at least for entertainment. Is the television world now one in which commercial interests really come higher up than creative ones? Or is it the case that the quality of the audience just isn't what it used to be?

A few weeks ago in America *The Jenny Jones Show*, which is a daytime show, had an item that was supposed to be a ratings winner. They brought on a group of people all of whom were told that there was someone they worked with who had a crush on them. One man who was told that someone he worked with was very keen on him was a rampant heterosexual and, naturally, he thought the person who would be brought on would be a woman. The screen went back and it was, in fact, a gay man. Everyone found this very entertaining. But a short while later the man began to pursue him. Outside work he pestered him and he pestered him. And in the end the victim who had appeared on the show got a shotgun and shot the gay man dead. His lawyer's defence is that *The Jenny Jones Show* drove his client to murder.

That is an extreme case but, in the ratings battle, is the lowest common denominator which makes entertaining viewing what we are heading for? It is also extremely cheap viewing. Or is there now real hope out there from an energy in the independents, in particular, and the new companies who are going to make changes, who are making very successful programmes?

I am going to ask the panellists briefly to introduce themselves in under five minutes and to tell you briefly where they are coming from. Then we are going to open it up to the floor for what we hope will be a very informal discussion where you can address your questions to them individually. So, first of all, we have Paul Watson, producer of factual programmes for Granada.

Paul Watson: I started real life as a painter and then found that a film camera was a much better paintbrush and paid better. So I went into television and joined the BBC where I had a career for some considerable years, too many even to think about, and I left and joined Granada Television last year.

Is commerce the enemy of diversity and creativity? Well, yes, it is and no, it ain't. It depends who you are as a film maker. It depends where you are coming from. If you want to repeat a success because they are going to pay you a lot more money, you will do it and you may just shiver at night when you are on your own, saying 'Perhaps I shouldn't have done that but the money is very handy and it is very comforting in the bank.' Or you can tell people what you want to do and stick to your ground.

It is generally thought that commercial people don't make the important documentaries and they do things, as Jaci has already alluded to, which appeal to the LCD factor — the lowest common denominator is the thing that works.

Over the last few months I have seen lots of different films — crash and bash, flashing lights and coppers arresting and getting their man. I have seen very nice doctors, even nicer nurses and saline drips and close-ups of machines saving very nice children's lives. I have seen wacky entertainers looking after the health of cats, dogs and canaries and oohing and aahing and raising tears. I have seen private detectives luring men to be unfaithful. I have seen women seeking private parts on West African beaches. All of them have some true and some sensationalist elements. All of them would have been, at some time or other, thought to have been on ITV. None of them were. All of them were on the BBC.

Somehow I wonder if the title for this session isn't just that bit old-fashioned. Over the last period I have seen films of insight on Porton Down and Bhopal. I have seen young kids coming to terms with the crimes they have committed. I have seen films on Northern Ireland and how press people responsibly cover that situation. All these films were actually just on one programme on ITV. And that was *Network First*. I would probably part company on how some of those films are made and what they represent. There doesn't seem to be an identity, at the moment, for *Network First*, what it stands for and what it is. I am sure John will address that.

So where is creativity being curtailed, and diversity? I think the diversity is fine. The subjects are responsible, the subjects are wide-ranging and very important subjects. And ITV has being doing them. Whether the call for innovation is being met — that's another question.

Before I left the BBC I did a series called *Sylvania Waters*, and it got a large audience. It turned out, subsequently, three-quarters of the way through, not to be very PC and was suddenly moved to a late time slot on the BBC, for what reasons I have never been quite sure. However when I was approached by Granada, *Sylvania Waters* came up. 'Would you do another *Sylvania Waters*?' I said, 'Well, I'd like to but would we be able to sell one?' Would we be able to sell something that might have some diversity, some originality, some new ideas in it just on the basis of doing a soap about a family? And I think that's where commerce doesn't quite grasp the nettle and come up with new ideas, dangerous ideas in the sense of 'we haven't done it before, let's try it.' However, they do make responsible films.

This happens to be the context of my next series for Granada. It hasn't got police in it, it hasn't got murder in it, it hasn't got mayhem in it. It's about life in a factory. And they have actually financed me to go and look and see what's going on in contemporary Britain, and this is just some of it. So having moved from BBC, the so-called arena for creative and diverse film-making, I don't think that I have been curtailed by going to Granada.

Jaci Stephens: Now Steve Clark, Head of Factual Programmes at Carlton Television.

Steve Clark: Is commerce the enemy of diversity and creativity? It is hardly a title to set the video for!

Jaci Stephens: I didn't set it!

Steve Clark: Well, I got a bit worried when I got a letter from Allan Jewhurst, who persuaded me to take part in this. It said 'Dear Steve, Many thanks for agreeing to take part. Unfortunately I can't be there as I'll be in Hull.' It can't be *that* bad.

I suppose the title means, or implies, if you chase ratings does quality suffer? I think quality always suffers if you don't invest in talent, time and research. Of course it all takes money. I think you can find quality in relatively low-budget regional progammes just as you find it in six and seven figure network shows.

So is commerce the enemy of diversity and creativity? I think the power of commerce was instrumental in setting up the Network Centre two and a half years ago. I think in that time they have had some outstanding successes. I won't trespass too far into drama that Don knows a bit about, but my own company delivers shows like *Kavanagh QC, Peak Practice, Inspector Morse, Soldier, Soldier, Cadfael;* Granada produces the superb *Cracker,* and *Band of Gold.* Now for starters, how's that for creativity and diversity?

But in my own area I believe very fervently that factual programmes on ITV have never had it so good. Output is up by twenty per cent. Audiences are up between twenty-five and thirty per cent. That is all in the last two and a half years. My own company, without giving too much of a party political broadcast, is the biggest single supplier of peak time factual programmes on ITV. The philosophy has always been to deliver the best, most diverse, from in-house and independent companies. That is a philosophy that has delivered *Hollywood Kids, Blues on Twos, Animal Detectives, Big Story.* Most of those shows are capable of delivering audiences of up to ten million and more. Last year we produced I think the biggest documentary of the year which *was Prince Charles: the Private Man, the Public Role*, with thirteen and a half million viewers. We did a one-off on baby Abby for eleven and a half million viewers.

A lot of people would have you believe that the higher the ratings, the more dubious the quality. I think that is a very old-fashioned belief. I am not embarrassed by big audiences. I serve ITV. It is a commercial channel and it has been for more than three decades. Some people would have you believe that some twenty-five or thirty years ago was the real Golden Age of television. I don't think it was. I think it is now. I think the range of slots available for factual programmes, the range and scope of ideas that we are receiving are better than ever. And I think the talent on offer is getting better all the time.

I don't want to say too much but as far as I am concerned the range and diversity is forced on us by commerce, because we are a commercial channel — I am speaking for ITV, not BBC 1 or BBC 2. We have to deliver audiences, we deliver a wide range of programmes to cater for a wide range of audiences. And I don't believe we have suffered for it. So, no, commerce is not the enemy of diversity and creativity.

Jaci Stephen: Of course, talent is one of the big questions. Is it that quality is going down because the talent isn't out there or it is that people aren't utilising the talent? Well, one of the great talents in the writing field is Don Webb. That's what you told me to say, isn't it?

Don Webb: I am a writer, that is all I am. But before I started being a writer I lived another life entirely. I will just tell you a bit about my genesis. I was a salesman and I sold things all around the world for twenty-odd years. I sold soap for Lever Brothers, I sold electricity for Norweb, I sold air conditioning and cookers and space heating for Creda, I sold spices for McCormacks, I sold wood-working machinery for my brother-in-law and when I was sixteen I had a Kleen-Eze bag. And if anyone can remember a Kleen-Eze bag, congratulations!

The thing is that I lost my driver's licence. A dreadful, sad accident. And of course if you haven't got a car and you are a salesman, it is rather like being a cowboy with no horse. There is nothing you can do about it.

I didn't have a car but I found a typewriter and I thought, 'I know, I'll be a writer.' So I wrote this wonderful play about this guy who had this terrible car accident and lost his driving licence, and his wife had left him and he couldn't stop drinking, and I sent it off to the BBC. And they sent it back and they said, 'That's terrible.' I saw in the paper a few days later that the assistant head of scripts at BBC Radio was a guy called Richard. He is dead now, God rest his soul. But I was at Birkenhead School with Richard. I thought, I know, I will send it to him. So I sent it to him and, as a very cunning ploy, on the outside of the envelope, I put the school motto, *Beate mundo corde*, which made sure that he opened it and nobody else did. So he opened it up and a couple of days later the phone rang and he said 'You've got a bloody cheek! This is probably the worse thing that I have read in my life. But I will introduce you to someone who will show you how to write.' So, anyway, I started writing and being incredibly naïve that was the only piece I ever sent off because I had been a salesman, you see. And I thought, 'OK. You can write. It's all you have written. You have got a product. You've written it. There it is. That's your product.' Now, it is useless in the envelope. It is only useful when someone's bought it. And in the first place I took it to theatres and I have had some success there. They couldn't believe it. There was a guy actually arriving there to sell them a play. And then I did the same with television. I used to go to Television House. The point I am making, really, is that it is no matter what you do in this business, if you can't sell it, it's useless.

And, therefore, when you ask if commerce is the enemy of diversity and creativity the answer is no, it's not. If you haven't got commerce, where on earth is your creativity and diversity going to go? Nowhere. That's the short answer. It's not going to go anywhere. That doesn't mean to say that we are the lowest common denominator, that isn't what we are after.

If you are selling clothes, you don't just sell Mao Tse Tung suits to everybody. You don't because unless you say to everyone you have all got to wear a Mao Tse Tung suit — which I believe he did, actually — but if you are selling clothes it is no good. If you are selling soap, it's no good just making Lifebuoy. If you are selling cars, you can't say you have all got to drive a Trabant because it is cheaper than anything else. So the LCD factor doesn't arise here.

What you have to do, with any kind of programme, is make a pyramid, the old Hollywood pyramid. On the bottom level you have got run of the mill stuff and at the top you have got the truly great films. And both ITV and BBC are dedicated to doing good stuff for a wide variety of audiences, through all strata of society. At the top we have got room for stuff that is a little esoteric and at the bottom we have got a solid base load and it is all well done. Most of it. And if it isn't well done, don't forget that people don't set out to make bad programmes. They don't, they set out to make programmes as good as they can within the brackets and the audience they are aiming at. When Alan Bleasdale wrote *GBH*, David Aukin and Michael Grade at Channel 4 were looking for a certain section of ABC1s who would watch that kind of programme. When you do *EastEnders*, that's what you want. When Paul does *Sylvania Waters*, when Ray does *World in Action*, he knows who he wants to hit.

Commerce is not the enemy of diversity. But if you can't sell it, there's no point in making it. So you have got to keep an eye on the customer all the time.

Jaci Stephen: I'll have two Kleen-Eze bags, please, and a box of spices.

Don Webb: Do you know what a Kleen-Eze bag was? We are talking about another culture now. What happened was you had a huge bag and in it was every kind of cleaning material known to man. Every kind. It was a door-knock job. And you would go down and you would knock on the door and you would say, 'Do you want any shoe polish, missus, do you want any tooth brushes, do you want any tooth paste, do you want any floor cloths, dusters?' Your only trick in the business — the only thing that you had to do was, as the door opened, if you could get your bag open and a smile on your face, you had made your first sale. It is all right in the morning but when it gets to about 4.30 in the afternoon in Didsbury or the back of Moss Side, you are finished. That's a Kleen-Eze bag.

Jaci Stephen: Thank you, Don. And next, John Blake, Deputy Controller of Factual Programmes at the ITV Network Centre.

John Blake: These chairs remind me of the sort of thing you see in those family therapy films, those grey documentaries where people own up. OK, I own up. I am a child of the Golden Age of Television. I joined Granada Television in 1973. My real confession, however, is that I really blanch to think of the quality of the programmes that I, as an untrained twenty-five-year-old producer, was allowed to put out on the network and within the region.

Of course, I am incredibly grateful for the opportunity and I regret that there seem to be fewer opportunities to indulge those sort of youthful enthusiasms nowadays. But I am very grateful, too, that VHS technology wasn't invented in those days and that my efforts are not preserved and they are safely locked in the archives of Granada Television in Quay Street.

I rather obviously think there is rather more diversity nowadays and I think there are some fairly obvious reasons why. There is no doubt, or shame, that ITV is about winning audiences and that all the other channels who enjoy various forms of market protection, and the satellite and cable channels, are a competitive threat to ITV.

The answer to the question of whether that competition is a threat to diversity lies in ITV's response. ITV has responded by investing very heavily in quality drama with the result that seventeen out of twenty of the most popular, and rather good, dramas on television are made by ITV. But that is not a question of just pandering to the lowest possible case, LCD programmes (as I learnt for the first time today) is apparently the name. It is because those ITV dramas attract audiences that actually don't watch television. They are capable of bringing in new audiences, so-called light viewers. And so are many factual programmes. The key to the black art of competitive scheduling is not going for the lowest common denominator, it is finding the particular target audience, at a particular time of day, and making a range of programmes that appeals to those people. As Don very eloquently says, 'You don't make your success in business just by selling Chairman Mao suits', and you don't make a success in television by making one sort of programme. You have to find your audience and you have to produce programmes that advertisers know they can sell products round.

There's no getting away from the fact that our business is commercial, but advertisers have a lot of products to sell to a lot of very different people who watch a lot of very different types of programmes. I am not qualified to talk about ITV's drama; I am a factual person. Let's have a look at the range of factual programmes available on ITV last week. Apart from the obvious popular successes during daytime, *The Time, the Place, This Morning,* and *Vanessa,* we had a new campaigning series made by an independent for Carlton, *Animal Detectives.* We have *World in Action* in traditionally robust form revealing the subversion of humanitarian aid in Romania by paedophiles. We have country music on the *South Bank Show.* We have a sensitively observed documentary about foetal surgery in *Network First,* not to mention the enormous strength of ITN News in bulletins throughout the day and in the most popular and most authoritative bulletin at ten o'clock. And we have robust interviews of current politicians like Michael Portillo at Sunday lunchtime. That's not to mention the religious programmes on a Sunday morning. There is a very wide range of very different sorts of programmes available on ITV. And, obviously, there is an equivalent range of different programmes on BBC and Channel 4 as well.

Innovation: is ITV the place for innovation? Have we innovated? Well, any marketing man will tell you you need to be able to sell your products by investigating new markets. We certainly are interested in finding forms that will attract new viewers. We are also — most people who end up running things in television are — essentially creative people and we are interested in new programme forms. So we are proud of the experiments we have had on *Network First* where we have improvised dramatic reconstruction — never before tried — in the *Date Rape* series last year where actors blended with real live people to act out a particular investigation of rape. Equally we are proud of commissioning new styles of programmes for the daytime. We are experimenting with a new documentary soap in a daytime slot this year and we are also commissioning *Network Firsts* that tackle the real issues of popular agendas in a housing estate where people really live.

We are also, and I very much hesitate to say this because it often diverts the discussion, very proud of discovering a new genre of documentary in the *Hollywood* series. It is cut in the style that gave some elder critics a touch of dyspepsia but it communicated to another generation of viewers in a new dialect, if not a new language, of film-making. And we remain proud of it; *Hollywood Kids* was a very worthy successor to *Hollywood Women,* and there will be more in the pipeline.

On ITV there is still an opportunity to shed light in dark places. You will shortly see on *Network First* the product of close collaboration with a dogged investigative producer from an independent and a risk-taking broadcasting licensee with an investigative story in Northern Ireland of a quality and insight and significance to compare with anything to compare with anything the BBC or ITV has done in the last twenty-five years.

We have very concrete evidence week by week that *World in Action* has lost none of its enthusiasm for big targets. As ever, the appetite for tough investigation lies alongside plenty of examples of its reputation for addressing the real agenda of popular concern, rather than the self-regarded pronouncements of politicians.

I agree with Paul that there is a certain danger that in pursuit of audiences, particularly on other channels ironically, the most cost-effective way is a convergence of enthusiasm for a certain sort of slice of life documentary that is now known as the 'shock-doc.' ITV has avoided that and it is because we feel we have other fish to fry. I am not quite as concerned as Paul about it because I think it probably is just a vogue in a way that a certain style of filming was a vogue, and the caravan moves on to something else. I don't think it is here to stay.

Competition has also produced a refinement of talent, and it has produced a lot of disappointment. We are not just competing for audiences, producers are nowadays more intently competing with each other and the industry is, unfortunately, littered with a lot of disappointed people who can't get the programmes they want to make on the air. But the other side of that coin is that commissioning editors now have a far wider range of choice of the sorts of programmes they might be able to put on the air. I think one can look at Channel 4 and the BBC in terms of *Video Nation* and *People's Parliament, The Real Holiday Show,* and see examples of producers and commissioners being very keen to continue to investigate the relationship between the viewer and their lives and the medium. And I would have said, echoing the thoughts of other people so far, that the industry is in a very healthy, creative state.

Jaci Stephen: So why do we open our *Radio Times* so many nights and say 'There's nothing on TV tonight'? We will find that out in a short while, I'm sure. Ray Fitzwalter, ex-editor of *World in Action,* now an independent producer, is a passionate spokesperson for the Golden Age of Television.

Ray Fitzwalter: Let me begin by contradicting you. I don't believe there was a Golden Age of Television, and I don't want to be satisfied with the superficial tosh that we have heard from the other end of this table so far today.

I think we ought to look at this in rather broader terms of evolving trends in television There is no point in picking on particular programmes or series and arguing their ups and downs. We ought, rationally, to look back to what has put its stamp on broadcasting today. And that began to evolve in the mid-1980s with the formulation of the Broadcasting Bill that became the 1990 Act. I imagine everyone in this room, most people in this room, recognise that as a deeply flawed piece of legislation which damaged broadcasting in this country. If it did one thing, it threatened its range and diversity. I rather think that everyone here, with the possible exception of those who are too young, recognise the implications of that Bill and they did so accurately. Many of you spoke up and you said things then that you should remember today.

In fact I am not sure what we can really be disagreeing about, if we are going to be consistent. I would like simply to remind you of one ITV spokesman, Greg Dyke, who put what I thought was an exaggerated position at the Edinburgh Television Festival some years ago when the Bill was in progress and he said, on behalf of London Weekend Television, that they would throw overboard their arts, their children's programmes, some of their documentaries, the expensive end of their drama. And they would concentrate on the safe middle band of production that was commercially sound and relatively free from risk. That was his on-going policy position.

I think it was exaggerated but I think it had some truth in it. Greg Dyke has more recently claimed that his forecast has been seen to come true. That, too, may be exaggerated, but I think that there is some truth in it. And we should, if we are going to be sensible, look at the trends in television — what has happened, what has been the trend, for example, in the production and the slotting of soaps in peak time on television? I would invite you to go back some years and look what did ITV do, what did the BBC do in response, why did they do it? And you will see the expansion of two evening series into three, into five, replies with imported versions and so on. And you have had a build-up of that type of production and an expansion of it. You can see the same with game shows, you can see the same with detective series and there is barely a type of detective series that hasn't somehow or other been expressed.

I won't go into that further but you have to ask, very simply, what is there more of, what is there less of? And this isn't just an argument about quantity, it's also about quality; it's about positioning and, in some case, it's about channels, because things migrate from one channel to another and where sometimes they used to address audiences of eight or ten million they are now migrating to address audiences of something less, maybe much less.

I think if you examine those trends you will see a change in the range and diversity of television if you look at it as a whole. And I would like to put one simple proposition to you. Television is a business, so you should ask yourself 'What is the philosophy behind this business?' And you could compare it with a Japanese philosophy of business, a German philosophy of business or a City of London philosophy of business. I have this proposition for you: Which comes first if you stood, say, in the mid-'80s or the early '90s or the mid '90s, does the making of the programme — the product, as it is now called — come first? Is there an attempt to make a quality product, is there an attempt to get that right and (we mustn't forget it, just as with the Kleen-Eze, you have to be able to sell it, it's useless if you can't) do you try to get that right and make everything else serve that end including the production of profit?

A Japanese businessman would say, 'Get your product right. Make a quality product. Make sure you can sell it and profit will follow.' Or is it the case that the product is not coming first or not coming first as much as it used to? Is it the case that making the profit first is coming first? I would suggest to you that there are people running television today to whom that is an overwhelming preoccupation, and it raises a question mark about the philosophy of its business which goes to the heart of the question of range and diversity.

I want to use a footnote to sum up. I think the BBC were reported last week as commissioning seven new detective series. John Blake has made a very laudable case for ITV as he sees it which is fair in its commercial context, but we have to rise above that context. We see, here, the BBC responding to the same pressures that threaten range and diversity. When did you ever hear of the BBC commissioning seven detective series at one go and making press statements, breathtakingly, arguing the distinction between *Cracker* and another detective series in that they were very different, that there was range, there was diversity? Of course there are differences between *Cracker* and other detective series but there are also things in common, and these are more in common to television programmes today on our screens than they have ever been. There are three common elements that you see coming up like never before and they are basically sex, violence and detection, and if that isn't a narrowing of the range, frankly I don't know what is.

Jaci Stephen: If that is not an impassioned plea for a Golden Age of television, I am not sure what is, perhaps Platinum Age might be better. OK, audience. Were you in agreement that the first four people spoke 'superficial tosh?' and that our last speaker spoke the truth or are we split down the middle?

Rod Allen (HarperCollins): I work at HarperCollins, and I'm even happier every day that I no longer work in television. So as far as everybody else on the panel apart from Ray Fitzwalter is concerned, everything seems more or less all right;

you are fairly happy with the way things are. What are the threats? What could make things go wrong?

John Blake: There is an obvious commercial threat from satellite and cable and undoubtedly, it would be foolish to deny it, there is a threat if those channels which have not got the same sort of commercial freedom of the marketplace that ITV has need to compete too heavily for ratings in order to continue to justify their market privilege.

I think it is a shame that Channel 4, whose role in the television system so far has been laudable, in order to earn its market share has to rely so heavily on imported soap, on movies, on fairly cheap chat shows and middle of the road factual programmes. I regret that those places in the system that are supposed to be there to provide diversity are under the same sort of commercial pressure as we are. But I can understand that it is very hard in Channel 4's position to aim at failure. When they are selling their own advertising space they can't say 'Well, we will only sell to ten per cent.' It is an almost impossible thing to do because if you aim at that you will probably go under, and I have a lot of sympathy for Channel 4's scheduling policy although it does create some problems for those people elsewhere in the system who have to respond to it.

I am also interested that BBC 2 is scrapping its *Late Show* because it wants to open up more late night air time to competitive programming. How do I know that they are not going to replace *The Late Show* with something much more interesting?

There is a particular threat from satellite and cable which is maybe a footnote type of point, but I think it is interesting that the prices that Discovery Channel are prepared to pay for one hour of documentary are so low that they must be getting some subsidy from within the system. That subsidy, effectively, comes from independent companies or through ITV licensees. If, for instance, a one hour documentary is being made for seventeen thousand pounds on Discovery and the same company is making one for ten times that amount for ITV or the BBC, then somewhere there is a cross-subsidy. I think the industry needs to address the questions of the real costs of satellite and cable and it's a long. complicated economic argument which is probably not one we can go into here. But I think that is the place where the real threats lie.

Jaci Stephen: Could I just ask Don, from the point of view of a writer, where the real threats lie?

Don Webb: Well, the real threats lie in opportunities. Where are the opportunities for new writers going to come from? Not only new writers but where are the people going to be trained in television if the profit motive is going to be the only one? Here I side very strongly with Ray's principles. If you introduce a profit motive into anything — this may appear to be contradicting myself and if I am, well, tough — when you introduce a profit motive into anything, no matter what it is, whether it is the National Health Service or any other part of our life today, then it very rapidly becomes the only motive for doing anything at all, very rapidly indeed. And somehow, somewhere, we have to build into our system of television some safeguards which will allow burgeoning talent to be nurtured. I mean talent of all kind. The person who paints with lights and a camera, the person who writes words, the person who wants to make films, the person who wants to learn how to make documentaries.

One of the biggest over-riding threats is that unless the industry devotes some part of its earnings to making sure that there is something for the people that come after us, then that could very quickly see the death of television production in this country as we know it. I see that as the over-riding danger. The only motive will become the profit motive and there won't be anything set aside for training and for opportunity. I see that as a very real problem.

Paul Watson: I would worry about the homogenising of channels, in that retaining individual areas of expertise would be a real worry. I mean we hear of seven BBC detective stories coming on stream. Well, you know, it's a pity. Channel 4 started as selling to two million rose growers because there were only two million rose growers out there, and if they got two million plus x it was a success, and if they got two million minus x, they looked into it but they only sold at the rate of two million and that was a very good deal. People are chasing for more and more.

I would be sorry to see the likes of *Nick Barker, Pandora's Box, A to B of Driving, Signs of the Times,* those sorts of films losing their place because the money had to go into seven detective stories. I would like to see stations aiming at not necessarily the x millions that John is aiming for, but x minus y because there is still a very large number of people out there who don't necessarily want to watch what is on another channel. And there are still many more people watching television than going to the cinema. So it is a very large number of people to go for and there is no shame in having smaller numbers. What's happened is that people have begun to believe that it is a shame not to have the same numbers as someone else.

Jaci Stephen: Can I just come back to a point that Ray made, again, still answering this question? You have talked about people in the industry who really feel their priorities are in the wrong place. Do you think that this is an inevitable part of it, that the industry now attracts a different sort of person from what it did years ago, or do you think active steps should be made to encourage more creative people back into it, with fewer commercial interests?

Ray Fitzwalter: One could quote somebody like Howard Stringer [president of CBS Television — *Eds*] looking at British television. He made a speech saying British television contained a number of people who put programme-making first. I am not attacking the profit motive either. You have to make a profit. But if the programme comes first, even if you were making cars — if you have people who believe in making cars, they make quality ones and they make marketable ones — profits will follow. And British broadcasting used to have a significant number of figures, I needn't name them, who stood for that philosophy. You try to name them today because I find it hard. I don't think they are really there in commanding positions.

If you have a different philosophy which says our first aim and intent is to deliver to the shareholder, you have a different industry and you have a different future. I know that that is the case because I have talked to them and they have told me that is their position. I think it is very honest of them and I don't think that they try to hide it, but it is the nature of the business. If you have an industry that is led purely by businessmen with their quite justifiable business ethics, and there is no philosophy that ever gets above that, well, I would look to your range and diversity and your future.

Steve Clark: What could go wrong? Things could go wrong if the pursuit of profits did lead to a reduction of budget levels down towards cable and satellite. I have seen no evidence of that on our network budgets or on the regional budgets. In our case regional budgets went up by 10 per cent, which is treble the rate of inflation, but I would worry if we had any pressure to reduce them because the four major channels are still by far the most watched channels in cable and satellite homes because we invest the kind of money that you need to produce the quality.

Colin King (University of Exeter): I am wondering if what we are seeing is the passing of institutional broadcasting and it was the institutions, both the BBC and the ITV, who really were patrons of and supportive of a lot of the creative work that went on. And this is something that isn't going to be around for very much longer as I see it. Is Paul Watson, who has a very fine and distinguished record in documentary making, honestly saying that he has no regrets at leaving the institutional base that fostered a lot of what he did? Now, of course, his talent moves with him but, in a sense, he is an individual. Maybe that is the new culture now; he is just taking a product to another broadcasting organisation.

When we talk about the Golden Age, my feeling is that was about institutional broadcasting. If you go right back to ABC and *Armchair Theatre* we can talk about the nurturing of talent there. If you look at the BBC and *Play for Today* and the whole school arising there and how it brought in new writers and nurtured them and supported them, where can young people today turn for that kind of guidance, that sort of continuity which institutional broadcasting is frowned on now but did, in a way, support and nurture that? I wondered if you had any feelings about that, Paul, that you would share with us which might throw more light on this?

Paul Watson: Those are the sort of questions I would ask my subjects but would hate to answer myself. But, as I always said, I only ask questions that I am prepared to ask myself so perhaps I should try. Golden Ages are whenever we were playing in our short trousers and each age has a different Golden Age, I would have thought.

Just to go to the end of your question before going back to the personal part, I think *Cracker* is well written, interesting, unexpected, surprising. Some *Plays for Today* were terrible and some were good. We remember what was good — the Hopkins Quartet, even in black and white, still remains in the mind. But there were probably three plays on either side of that which weren't so good, and we forget those.

I do see, and it is really going back to my last answer on the homogenising of our broadcasters, a timidity, a lack of courage within the organisation called the BBC. I see a number of people, not very good as bureaucrats who, perhaps, are not trained to manage in those areas, abandoning old positions and not prepared to take chances. In the end I fell out with a number of people over a number of decisions over things I would have liked to have made, like to have seen made, certain talents I would like to have seen encouraged, subjects that I would have liked to seen brought on, and the time came when they were better at the politics of survival than I was. At the same time I was being offered a job and being assured that I could make what I wanted to make. Until two hours ago when I stopped work on my script to come here, everything was fine. But then the man who was passing the 79th floor of the Chrysler Building was saying 'so far, so good!' All life is about that and I go back to my very first points that you work for who you work for, you make your rules, they make their rules and, in the end, if you fall out, you go away from it.

I think there are more and more people of, if you like, my sort moving away from the BBC and if that's a bad thing, well, it's flattering but it may not be. It may be that there is a whole new bunch of people to take over the perches that we once proudly sat on. Looking at some of the replacement series recently, I am not sure that that is true. But, you know, everything goes in circles and cycles.

Don Webb: I would just like to add a little bit to what Paul said which has to do with the nurturing of writers. The institutional role in this particular instance is being taken again and again by some of the production companies. In particular the instance that Paul mentioned, *Cracker*, was written by Jimmy McGovern who is a very, very good writer indeed. Well, Phil Redmond of Mersey Television nurtured Jimmy McGovern for eighty episodes of *Brookside* until he felt he was able to release him on to the world, and when he did release him, my word, *Priest*, *Cracker*, that wasn't bad, was it? And that's one of the things that's happening. At the same time, I don't see it as a complete answer by any means. But certainly some of the more well-based independent production companies are taking on that role, particularly so far as the training — no? You don't think so?

Rod Allen: No, I don't think so. I'll tell you why. If Channel 4 , the BBC and ITV are buying a hundred per cent of programme rights from the independent producers and if the BBC, ITV and Channel 4 are failing to let the independent producers build up a capital base, they can't possibly expect them to fund training or development of any kind until the relationship between the programme buyers and the independent suppliers changes and the power reverts to producers, as opposed to commissioners. Of course, Phil Redmond did what he did with McGovern and there are one or two other examples, but, in the generality, that will never happen.

John Blake: Just a quick point, Rod, in that the Network Centre only buys licences. No way, in our purchase of programmes from independents directly, could we possibly take away the capital base of independents.

Sue Caro (Channel 4): I would like to respond to John Blake's deflection of criticism of ITV by loading it onto Channel 4, basically, the smallest channel of the lot. Do I take it from your comments that you will be supporting our campaign to get the funding formula abolished so we don't have to pay you fifty-seven million pounds next year?

John Blake: No, I won't, for the simple reason that I think if you did — I really do hesitate to say this in public for reasons that some people in this room will be very aware of — but if Channel 4 did stick to its remit, it would need the subsidy from ITV that is enshrined in the legislation.

Diane Nelmes (Granada Television): This isn't really a question. I am Controller of Factual Programmes at Granada and I feel I have to speak up. Obviously Granada has a long, distinguished reputation for factual programming of which Ray was a great part. And, obviously, we have been taken over by these businessmen. I would just like to make two points. I have been at Granada for ten years. I am working on a range of programming, including *World in Action,* this morning. Of course the profit motive is there and is important but 'twas ever thus. In the days when I was a researcher there I am sure Ray was never allowed to deliver *World in Action* at a loss. But let me assure you, the programmes are still paramount. Talk to any of our key producers in factuals and they will tell you we talk ideas all the time, because if the idea isn't right, and you don't get the product right, you don't make the programme to the highest possible quality and, in the end, we all fail.

And so you don't just take my word for it, I have a couple of very brief examples. Two years ago we embarked on a drama-documentary called *Fighting for Gemma* which played in peak time on ITV about the Windscale nuclear industry. We set out on that with a forecast showing that it would come in at a loss. Actually, as Ray said, because we followed the Japanese principle and got the product right, the film was good. We eventually sold it abroad and in the end it did show a profit but for the whole time Granada was backing that it did not look as if it would come in at a profit.

Last year I made two documentaries on the downfall of the last Czar of Russia called *Nicholas and Alexandra,* and, again, there was a long period when we were filming in Russia and because we didn't have co-production funds, we just had ITV funding, and because we wanted the highest quality it looked as if we were going to make a loss on those films. As it happens because the films came in at a very high quality, we sold them and they have made a profit. But the idea of the programme is still paramount at Granada and I am sure in most ITV companies because the day it isn't is the day that we all fail.

Steve Clark: I agree with every word that Diane just said. Eighty per cent of our one-hour documentaries made in-house at Carlton are made at an initial loss. It takes us two or three years to recoup that. I think the quality is such that they do sell abroad.

Colin Stanbridge (Carlton UK): I would just like to make a point about training. I agree training is extremely important and relationships with independents who allow training to happen is extremely important ,and that is what Carlton has done from the very start. It has done drama workshops, it has done documentary workshops, it has done comedy workshops and those workshops have borne fruit. Actually, the drama workshops have borne fruit on BBC 2 and Channel 4. That doesn't matter. We are still bringing people in to make the programmes and to learn to make the programmes and that is the most important thing.

Dinah Caine (Skillset): I want to say how much I welcome the comments that have been made in relation to training and the nurturing of talent. And on a point of information in relation to independent production companies, it is important to know that there is now a voluntary levy in place and that independent producers are paying a part of their production fees towards a fund to help subsidise training.

But that is not what I really want to talk about because we are going to be talking about nurturing professionalism in the next session. It is linked, however. One of the challenges that the new commerce has created has been the shift from permanent employment to freelance employment and it is that shift that is creating the problems, partly in terms of the infrastructure and the nurturing of talent. But I would also be interested to know the panel's views in relation to tht shift and how it is affecting the employment of women and black people within the industry and how that then links to notions of diversity in terms of production.

Steve Clark: We have nine in-house producers in Central, at the last count; we don't employ people just because they are women, men or black but it has worked out that six of those nine producers are women. It has never been a problem really. I don't agree with positive discrimination. You should get your position and get your job on your merits. It has never been a problem where I have worked. Maybe I have just been lucky.

Jaci Stephen: Is one of the reasons that documentary audiences have increased partly due to the fact that a lot of the subjects now appeal more to women because the documentaries are being made by women?

Steve Clark: I think it does in regional. I can only speak, again, for Central and Carlton. We have these people in the research department who come down with all kinds of figures that you tend to throw away, but if you bother to study them they tell us that in certain factual categories the female 24-40 audience is improving. Yes, you give people free rein and they come up with ideas that would appeal more to women.

Don Webb: With the vanishing of the institutions what will also vanish is a lot of institutionalised prejudice which exists far more in large patriarchal organisations, so that may be a fortunate spin-off in that the glass ceiling is much more capable of being broken in a production company than in the monoliths that used to exist. You can take it either way. There are advantages in both ways.

John Blake: I am very aware that good work often comes out of institutions and out of teams and I am sometimes nervous about the atomisation of talent. That is one of the reasons that the Network Centre operates a centres of excellence policy as far as some sorts of factual programmes are concerned. We are keen to make sure that ITV doesn't lose those core talents within institutions both as independent companies and in broadcasting licensees, and you can look around and see where those centres are. Obviously Yorkshire and Central are two of them as far as two different sorts of documentary are concerned, and Granada is another in terms of another sort of factual programme. And we are developing certain relationships with some independents who are supplying us regularly with the sort of things we are looking for.

I think the other side of that is that in the past our institutions did sponsor certain indulgence and sometimes that indulgence was very good because it indulged wild creativity which people enjoyed and sometimes it indulged rather boring programmes that were made simply because producers were there and that company, as of right, had a certain number of slots of allotted to it by the controllers' group. I can't but celebrate the fact that we have moved away from the Buggins'-turn system of ITV into the commissioning of programmes on a proposal basis one by one according to the merits of the individual idea.

Paul Watson: But, John, we are in danger from getting rid of that indulgence, of losing those things we never thought might take off, and we will not move forward.

John Blake: It is clearly a balance. There are good indulgences and there are bad indulgences.

Paul Watson: Yes, but all in one hand, aren't they? We are becoming more and more centralised everywhere. This is just not directed just at you. We are becoming more and more centralised. The BBC had a system of warring barons and it was a very good system in many ways because you got behind somebody with a banner and you said, 'I'll support this person,' usually a male in those days but there are more women now, and you vied against other sections. There are only two sections of any importance now inside the BBC. There is only one inside ITV.

John Blake: There are lots in ITV because there are a lot of regional companies with a lot of freedom over their own schedule.

Dmitri Strovsky (Ural State University): Sorry about my English which is not very fluent but I don't know to whom I address this question; it is simply not even a question, but a remark. We very firmly underline now this question with entertainment and advertising but it seems to me that we shouldn't put aside this question from the question how do we cover the political news, how do you prepare the plot of international things? Maybe I simplify this problem but I don't see any difference between the independent television and BBC. Why am I thinking about it? Because quite attentively watching television now and analysing maybe not the British reality which is not familiar to me because I am from abroad, but analysing the reality which is concerned about Eastern Europe and Russia in particular, I think that both televisions, regardless of the fact that they have different economic backgrounds, are very, very similar in analysing these events which are very, very superficial I would say. It is quite a dangerous phenomenon because if people don't understand clearly what the background is of one or another event because their correspondent that covers those events doesn't underline, they go out of this event. I repeat this question which is formulated as the basic question of our discussion should become a question of historical and political background of people who cover these events; without it it's impossible to discuss this question.

Jaci Stephen: Can I just ask, is your question here that you feel that BBC, ITV, Channel 4 are too similar, they are all too superficial and you think that they should be programming from a totally historical perspective?

Dmitri Strovsky: I don't mean that they have to have a totally historical background, and historical perspective. But when they analyse such very critical events as, for example, the situation in Chechnya it is a very live example.

Don Webb: How would you solve it? What would you do to change the system that we have at the moment? We have four channels which because they have the same kind of political history present the same view of events overseas. Can you see a good way of making a proper difference so that events such as the ones you have described, are given their proper validity and reportage. Is there a solution within the framework of the television that we have at the moment or must we rely on the BBC World Service Television and World Service Radio to do that for us because they operate to a different brief?

Dmitri Strovsky: You know it is quite difficult, of course, to give some advice but I think that in particular it is maybe more necessary to attract specialists for even such very short items which Independent Television and BBC show — I mean during these news items. To attract people with different positions not to show views from the one position which are very, very similar regardless of the fact that they have — I underline — a different economic background. It is very surprising for me, it was really surprising, and very painful because the BBC as I see from abroad, the BBC all the time proclaims the ideas of the independents and I am asking the question now, independent of what ?

John Blake: I would just say that you identify an eternal problem of news broadcasting and I think it is one that people who have been involved in news over the years are very aware of. I would like to say, and I think I can say on the whole, and I am not speaking remotely for ITV here but particularly with the role of Channel 4 and *Channel 4 News* and particularly with the expansion of some parts of the BBC's news and current affairs empire, that there is a much greater attention to context in reporting, not necessarily within the news bulletins themselves because there is only so much time but within supporting programmess. I would have thought, it is an entirely personal subjective view based on twenty-five years working in television, that things have got better. They may not be good enough but I do think they have got better. And I think it is also true to say — you may be researching this point particularly — that we did see Chechnya coming. It was reported as a potential flashpoint and I think perhaps we will discuss it later in detail. It is a very interesting example. There were programmes such that, if you had been watching them when the explosions happened, it did not come as a great surprise.

Steve Clark: I speak as a former news editor at ITN. There is a limit to how analytical you can be on foreign stories in British news bulletins. I think such stories are covered outside of news bulletins in documentaries and what have you but you have a home audience to serve as well and, no matter how flippant it might sound, you can easily turn them off going analytical on Chechnya, Rwanda, Bosnia, etc. That's the reality.

Dave Rushton (Institute of Local Television): Do the panellists welcome Channel 5, for the prospect it offers for greater diversity and creativity for viewers and, possibly, for new talent or are they relieved that, for the most part, it's currently the existing TV broadcasters and the former TV broadcasters in ITV that are favoured as the bidders and that it may end up being an ITV 2, a regurgitated repeat of ITV and Channel 4 programmes?

Ray Fitzwalter: It depends on what Channel 5 turns out to be. The first thing that I would ask is where is it going to be based? If it is based out of London then it has a chance of adding to the system and offering something different, being staffed by different people.

The second question will be who owns and runs it, and who has the licence. I think there are two declared bidders, and two other possible bidders. The appearance of them has been that they are very heavily London-dominated consortiums who are interested, I suspect, not just in Channel 5 but in the digital opportunities that may go with it, and they may be very interested in using it as an outlet for off-loading production from existing production houses, repeats and so on. They will need a lot of very low budget high volume production but those questions haven't been answered.

John Blake: I wouldn't be optimistic that Channel 5 is going to be that life-enhancing experience we would all like.

Don Webb: We don't know what it is going to be. We don't know how much they are going to pay for it. How much it is going to be worth to anyone or even what area, particularly, it is going to cover nor how much it is going to cost people to retune video recorders which will necessarily have to be retuned. In short, it is a pig in a poke. It would be really nice to think that it could be innovative. I have deep cynicism about it, I really do. I don't think it will and I think the word 'regurgitate' you used was absolutely precise.

Steve Clark: At the risk of talking superficial tosh, I just hope it is going to create some new jobs in broadcasting.

Paul Watson: Ray said no-one has answered the questions. I am not sure anyone is asking the questions, that is what is worrying me. Those who are doing the selecting are the same lot that gave us all the other channels and, frankly, I would welcome it going down the pan because I have a hard enough time watching four, let alone five.

Colin Young (European Film Studio, Paris): I am a French resident and I watch French television where we have six channels if you buy the decoder from Canal Plus. I could speak for about half an hour about the differences between those channels which are much more diverse than I had ever expected them to be from hearing that Britain had the best television in the world before I could sample French television. It is not all that bad. But that is really beside the point. What occurs to me in a meeting about regionalism and diversity is that there is the law of the market, and there is a thing called broadcasting policy. At one moment there used to be a difference between these two, now they seem to be more and more the same thing. Isn't it the law of the market that there should only be five major Channel 3 companies rather than the number we have now? Isn't that what the inside industry analysts are all telling us? That a more rational, more profitable, more coherent Channel 3 would be one which was dominated and run by five companies rather than the number that we have now and, if that were the case, if these analysts are correct, what would the effect be on diversity?

Ray Fitzwalter: Given that the broadcasting industry lost the battle of the Broadcasting Bill and lost it so ignominiously, it would have been better to recognise what you just articulated, and the ITC, in my view, were crazy to advertise fifteen new licences on a map that was basically thirty years old and reflected other times and had no reflection of the business climate that had arrived. It would have been better to have recognised defeat and to have advertised a small number of strong viable licences with strong regional commitments, but fewer of them. Instead, they went into bat again with fifteen licences in utterly changed conditions, and what we have seen is the haphazard pattern that has inevitably followed where there are takeovers, there are surreptitious changes going on all the time and the thing is moving, if you like, in a disorganised market system. There is no effective public policy there.

It is almost pointless to offer a view about it — all you can say is it is just a pity, frankly. And to follow it to its logical conclusion, there will obviously be another round of rationalisation in the same haphazard fashion. The odds on that must be very high. There are a small number of ITV companies that are like a rump, who are really scarcely at terms with the modern world, as it were, and there are three big players and there are two sitting in between — one in grave danger of take-over and the other one looking to be taken over, actually looking for a partner. And, of course, the regional structure is going, piece by piece, with it.

Unidentified speaker: Getting back to the original theme of this afternoon, I don't think commerce, in itself, is deleterious, but I think it does change the relationship between the make of the programme and the recipient. Instead of being a viewer and a listener, you are becoming a customer, and this fundamentally changes the whole idea. Sir Alan Peacock spoke of 'paying the piper'. I am wondering to what extent members of the panel agree that the relationship between them, as programme makers, and the viewer and listener has been changed by the increasing of market forces.

Steve Clark: It has never occurred to me at all like that. I still think that practically every viewer in Christendom looks at the television and thinks of themselves as a viewer. If they don't like it they turn over, as a viewer.

Don Webb: I think the notion of the viewer as a customer has about as much validity as the notion of a bedridden cancer patient waiting in Barts for a bed as a customer. To call him or her a customer has just about as much validity. But I do take your point that some people would like us to. I think the viewers will always remain viewers and should so remain.

Kim Peat (BBC): Firstly on satellite. I don't think we need to feel quite so negative about satellite. Discovery Europe in this country are doing some quite interesting things with new programme makers. That is also true, of course, of the ITVcompanies, it is also true of the BBC. But I think, increasingly, we will begin to look towards some of the better satellite companies for new talent. I think for people coming into the industry, it is a very good way of cutting their teeth, producing a show, being able to tout that around the more established broadcasters.

And on the subject of budgets, it is well worth saying that their budgets are, I think, pretty much in line with what the ITV companies are paying for their new-comers' strands. So I don't think we should be led too far astray on that one.

Secondly, in terms of access and the issues about diversity into the BBC: I have come from Channel 4; I have beeen in the BBC for a year and I have been amazed at the difference between the two organisations. The BBC has a tremendous number of routes in for independent producers, which is the area that we work in, and tremendous competitive rivalry still I think, Paul, both between departments internally, between the regions and with the new independent commissioning executives providing another element of competition. So I think, certainly, diversity with money being pushed out to the regions in the BBC is very much still alive and well.

Jaci Stephen: It seems to me that there is lots of ground for enthusiasm and optimism. If you look at the good popular dramas that we have been talking about, like *Peak Practice* and *Heartbeat*, that is, obviously a very healthy area. What worries me is when ITV has the courage to let go of them when they have really run their course. Anyone currently watching *Peak Practice* must surely think that it is time for that one to be put down.

On the documentary side of things, I think there is a range of diversity. There's diversity, there's creativity and there are new styles of programmes being made. I think the most worrying thing, and certainly the most interesting thing that has come out of this afternoon, is to do with people in the industry. I have been a TV critic for ten years and years ago everyone seemed to be much more supportive of each other's creative talents; it seems to me that we are losing our love of each other in the industry, to put it in an Americanised way, and I think that if commerce is the enemy of anything, it is the enemy of our relationship with each other in the industry.

Session produced by Allan Jewhurst

Nurturing professionalism in the post-broadcasting age

Chair: **Colin Shaw**
Broadcasting Standards Council

Professor Colin Young
European Film Studio, Paris

A S I wrote these notes, I was not sure how to pitch my contribution. Marshall McLuhan used to argue that if you sized up the audience perfectly, and prepared yourself for that, you probably would end up telling them nothing new. There is the same danger when parachuting into the Symposium half way through. So I lean on experience. I am an enthusiastic, passionate, committed supporter of training at all levels. This is not an obsession which I share with all my professional colleagues. But I have learned from experience — in talking about training it's better to assume nothing than to assume too much. So, in order to look at the present, and look into the future, I think some history is necessary. You are all totally reconstructed, deregulated, free-market entrepreneurs (or want to be), but it was not always so — and it certainly was not like that when I came back to Britain from California in 1970 to start the National Film School.

I knew roughly what the job was then — to set up the school from scratch and, as soon as possible, save the film industry from destruction. At least I did the first.

Even that was not easy.

Basically, people had mislead me into thinking that the arrival on the scene of a national film school was the one thing which everyone had been working towards, everyone wanted, and which had brought together in cosy harmony the unions and the employers.

Maybe it had been, but I suspect that the story told to each warring party may have differed in small but significant ways so that, in the perfectly decent search for consensus on the project, the Lloyd Committee had persuaded itself that the differences of opinion which did exist were a price they were prepared to pay, since they were certainly persuaded that a school of the sort proposed was a good idea.

As it happens, I agreed with them. Dennis Lloyd's blueprint for the school remains the best prospectus for professional training in our industry which I have ever read, here or in any other country. His understanding of what was needed was surprisingly profound for a layman — complex, sophisticated, thoroughly professional but at the same time genuinely innovative — and set quite outside the usual academic framework in which he had made his own reputation.

I think the arguments he adduced then *for* the school are pretty well known and are, anyway, not the point of this discussion.

What is perhaps relevant are some of the concerns which were expressed then, and subsequently. They are relevant because it might be useful to define what I mean by 'professional training'.

The objections to a professional school can be summarised as coming under two headings:

- you can't really learn anything useful at a place like the NFS — learning on the job is much better;
- and secondly (when that proved manifestly absurd) graduates of the NFS had an unfair advantage over everyone else trying to get ahead in the industry — most of whom had never received any formal training.

Those who voiced the first of these criticisms were convinced not only that a post-graduate professional school was irrelevant to industry's real needs, but could almost certainly be a bad influence — developing attitudes which would get in the way of fitting into the industry.

This really was a crunch issue. The model being proposed by these critics was that of an existing industry which was a good and effective one, which needed, from time to time, some new blood. These newcomers would be apprenticed into the industry by their elders. Too much 'school learning' would impede this process of assimilation. The whole thrust of the Lloyd Report, however, was that the model was flawed — a stagnating production sector, increasing casualisation of the work force, a film economy too dependent on Hollywood. If there was a training policy then it amounted to — 'The BBC trains the people they need, and ITV steals them later on'. The Lloyd Report sought to modify this 'policy' with proposals for systematic training, across the board, of at least a small number of people who could enter the industry somewhat more on their terms than as junior apprentices. We had the leadership of the ACTT (as it then was) solidly behind us. But the Union membership was split down the middle on the question, as time was to show.

There may have been a genuine misunderstanding about the level of training that a school like the NFS could offer. The model *we* had in our heads was that of the great conservatories of film in Poland, France, Czechoslovakia and Hungary. The model some supporters may have had was that of a technical school. They were therefore surprised by the ambition of our first graduates which only seemed to confirm that they were jumped up tea-boys and tea-girls with ideas way beyond their station.

Of course, in that first group of graduates in 1974, we had some who failed to make their mark. But it did include Chris King, Jonathan Lewis, Michael Radford, Nicholas Broomfield and Steve Morrison. Among those who came the next year were Diane Tammes, Jana Bokova, Roger Deakins, Jeff Perks, Malcolm Mowbray, and Bill Diver.

So the argument shifted. We were now seriously disadvantaging those who had not received this level of training, and our graduates' wings needed to be clipped. Resentment gradually built up inside the union — and elsewhere, and the joke around Beaconsfield soon became that the School would remain extremely popular as long as it was not too successful. When people asked Jeff Perks where he'd been for the last three years he found it easier to say that he'd been in jail than to say he had been at the NFS.

We were soon facing belligerent motions at the annual conferences of ACTT which came from some of the technical sections of the union — camera section, editing and sound. They had one thing in common — frustration with an industry which was so badly organised that the rank and file had to dislike and distrust a training programme which seemed to create a privileged elite. No matter that our graduates, many of them married, some with children, had put up with a minuscule grant for three years to get the qualification which was now to be derided. The annual conference motions tried to limit their access to work, reducing their status to trainees who had to spend a number of years in each grade before being allowed to practise the profession for which they had been trained. This restriction was to be reserved for NFS graduates.

General Secretary Alan Sapper came to the rescue. He proposed that NFS graduates should have the same status as unemployed members of the union, and that it was up to employers to determine what they were capable of doing by offering them appropriate employment. This policy was installed, but it was not until about ten years later that the opposition in the grass roots died down and an annual conference could be enjoyed for reasons other than NFS-bashing.

Thus ended a sad episode, made sadder because ACTT's first general secretary, George Elvin, had supported the school from the beginning. Remembering it all now, it is hard to believe. But I wonder if all the suspicion about formal, professional training has evaporated, or just shifted from the union to some other place.

In any case, what about this model of 'learning on the job'? What's wrong with it? Among other things, the following:

1. There's the Catch 22 of 'No job, no learning, and no learning, no job'.
2. There is a strong likelihood that people will imitate their 'elders' rather than challenge them (that's called self-preservation).
3. The view from the shop floor is very restricted.
4. There is a lack of opportunity, or time, to experiment — on other people's money.

These were serious limitations in the days of closed-shop, highly regulated industries. Has the position changed for the better — for new entrants and for the industry in general?

1. It sometimes seems as if almost anyone these days can get a job, somewhere in our industry, so long as they are fit, will work long hours and won't worry about union minimums. Is this an improvement?
2. It is possible that innovation is more highly prized in new entrants than imitation, at least in some sectors, but *generally* I doubt it.
3. Everyone who has ever come to a short course at Beaconsfield has said how restricted their view is of the totality of production, and how refreshing it is to be able to see around the corners, even if only in a small way — because it

helps their understanding of how their contribution fits in. How often does the workplace allow for this?

4. I don't believe that there is any more time now to experiment on the company's money than there ever was.

And, in any case, the issue is not one of how do we maintain the existing state of play. It is: how do we survive within a changing environment, where the competition for spectators is increasingly fierce, where the structure of the market into which we are placing our goods is changing all the time, when new media and new technologies are making new demands, where multi-skilling — which used to be seen as a capitalist/fascist plot — is more than ever necessary and where the state itself is no longer sure of the service it wants from the domestic audio-visual industry and has (almost) no policy for it? And in all of that, what is the role of training in an increasingly deregulated industry? And who will pay for it?

Assumption no 1. There will always be larger or smaller companies in television with core staff who devise their own means of working to produce the programmes which are a staple part of their licence commitments. This core activity will need updating and renewal, but most of this will be taken care of in-house. Those companies will be best able to do so, if the staff is encouraged to be innovative, multi-skilled and multi-capable, not fitting into pre-determined slots, but able to range across different programme strands, with differing and changing levels of responsibility. The model for a television company can no longer be that of an ocean liner, or a ferry, sailing to a known destination on a reliable schedule — the Network Centre and the different and changing demands of the regions have made certain of that.

This should make television more interesting for the people who work in it, but it will probably be more risky.

Assumption no 2. There will always be more people already working in television than people entering the industry. So companies have to develop training policies for the majority, already employed, as well as for the minority whom they will employ. But what sets the tone?

Small companies may be better placed than the larger companies to introduce the flexibility in working that is increasingly necessary. But the former idea of career structures within tightly organised specialisations may have to give way to structures which accept more diversity and less specialisation if the company is going to be quick enough on its feet to meet changing conditions without having to lay off large numbers of staff each time the corporate ship changes direction or changes owners. This calls for great skill, and perhaps new skills, in administration, and in personnel management, as well as in the programme and technical areas.

Scottish Television recently ran a post-graduate trainee scheme in which six graduates were turned loose inside the company — most of them in programme areas. I don't think there is any doubt that they learned a lot, but from my own observation the greatest value of that scheme may have been the demands it placed on the existing staff to accommodate these fresh implants. They had to articulate their needs in ways which are not thought to be necessary in an established company — people just 'get on with things'. And in doing so, they opened themselves up to the possibility of self-doubt and renewal. Not a bad thing.

Assumption no 3. Professional training, outside the companies, has real value, both for short courses and for longer, full-time training. There's not much need be said about short courses — they are subject and population specific — how to do this or that. There should be more of them, but that is another story. The question of longer-term training is more complex. There are certain basic necessities in such programmes.

The training must have a real professional base. The trainers must themselves be professionals, and they must combine teaching ability with a clear knowledge of what the industry needs. [For this to happen, professionals should not look for a permanent career in teaching. It should be *one* of the things they do in t h e i r professional lives]. The training must be independent — listening to what the industry thinks is needed, but not slavishly tied to that. And, although the training has to be organised, to be effective, it should leave maximum room for individual development, free from methodological dogma.

Students must be chosen for their independence of mind as much as for their talent.

The training must prepare people for an enterprise based culture, as members of a team, but as independents, not employees. After they are established a bit, they will be as likely to create employment as to require it.

And, most importantly, the training must be based on the three Ns — *nature, nurture, and knowledge*. They must have *natural talent*. This must be *nurtured*. And they must acquire the *knowledge* which they will need to make their way professionally. Any training programme must work out how these concepts should be applied in specific cases.

In the beginning years at the NFS we had some simple slogans. We said it was a place for learning as much as for teaching. We had an open curriculum rather than a closed one. Students, not teachers, were our main resource. I had various pragmatic reasons for issuing these rallying cries. One was that there was a real shortage of good teachers, and another was the lack of consensus in the industry about what the school should be teaching. So the School became a place where the students could use the staff, the facilities, the money, to learn what they were capable of. They were not limited by the 'system', but set on their own paths. The curriculum was *à la carte*, rather than *set menu*. Far more than people realised, an educational experiment was going on at Beaconsfield which applied a radical interpretation of the Lloyd Report. Since it worked, no-one seemed to worry about the details. Later on, as the number of students increased, and the industry's demand for more specialist training took hold, the School had to adjust. But the underlying benefit of the system was that nurturing was an effective teaching method. We were, after all, dealing with adults.

Assumption no 4. Companies must meet independent schemes (at least) half way:
1. They must invest in them.
2. They must seek to influence but not to control them.

3. They must distinguish between short term training which they can buy for their own staff and long-term training in which they must invest for their (and the industry's) future development.
4. They must create space in their programmes for internships and in their schedules for the use of new talent.

What is actually happening?

1. I am sorry to say that it is proving harder, not easier, as time goes on, to find money for training. We may look at why this is, during the discussion.
2. Although the industry would weaken the school if it tried to control it, it can still interact, intimately, with the School at all levels to provoke discussion of the industry's long-term and short-term needs, and to help guide students to prepare for that future. This happens to some extent already but it could, in effect, 'go with the money'. If the School is thought in any way to be irrelevant to the industry's needs, who is to blame?
3. There is also evidence that companies who pay for training are much more secure with paying for short courses — where the result is immediately measurable and the benefit to the company (and therefore the shareholders) can easily be described — than they are with the idea of a longer term investment in professional training as such. One person who is influential in such matters asked the question the other day — why don't we take a look at the students accepted for Beaconsfield in a given year, and compare their subsequent careers with those of the people whom the NFTS rejected in that year. Behind this question can only be real scepticism for the basic exercise. (In Britain, by the way, companies paying for the NFTS are still getting a bargain, since the DNH puts up roughly half the total cost).
4. One way for the companies to get immediate benefit back from the NFTS would be to programme their films. The quality is not that bad. The fiction regularly wins festival awards in competition with television material, animation is often nominated for BAFTA or the Oscars and even wins, while a lot of the documentary is already sold to television. In a documentary festival in Paris last month, there were four UK films in competition — three were from the NFTS.

But an even better decision by companies would be to commission work from new graduates of the School — either by developing new strands, or by creating slots within existing formats. That would seem to make perfectly good business sense.

It is by heeding these various things that I believe the industry can best prepare to provide for diversity — encouraging innovation at all levels, inside and outside the companies, investing in independent training, and having an active policy of recruitment among the graduates of this training.

I should also mention NVQs — National Vocational Qualifications. These were introduced across all but a few industries some years ago, and were brought into our industry in the teeth of great scepticism. At the time, I was sure myself that NVQs would help new entrants by allowing them to build up qualifications which then may make it easier for them to get a job — especially when we consider that 'the employer' is changing all the time. If, by ducking and diving a bit, training programmes can qualify the trainees for a nationally recognised qualification, they would be wise to conform.

But we should be careful. Are they relevant to advanced professional training? What is the NVQ for a Director of Photography, a director, a producer, a documentary film maker, a writer, a composer, an animation director, an art director? Those are just some of the career titles for which training is available at the NFTS, for example.

In the rush to make things more systematic, room must still be left for individual talent, because it is that talent, in the end, properly trained, which will save us from the competition, and from ourselves. This is as true in regional development as it is in the centre, and how that might work out in practice should perhaps be examined.

Session arranged by Colin Shaw

Face the Symposium

Chair: **Rod Allen**
HarperCollins Interactive

Steve Morrison
LWT Broadcasting

ROD Allen: Steve and I were once on a trip to Hollywood together. We were invited to go and watch KNBC-TV in Burbank transmit the news one evening. We pitched up in the studio at about five to six and it was absolutely deserted; there was nobody there. And there were some cameras, and there were some scripts lying around. We said 'Have we come at the wrong time? Is it the wrong place?' And at 5.58 we were looking at the vision mixer and we were saying, 'We could work this if we really had to,' and at 5.59:30 the crew and the presenters walked in and started the news at six. Steve obviously took inspiration from that and has perfected that kind of just-in-time entrance here.

Steve Morrison: Whoever upstairs invented the word irony would have to smile when looking down at me here today. Born in Scotland. Weaned in Granada on a diet of anti-metropolitan fervour. Buys out London. Triumph of regionalism! End of story. End of speech. Great. We can all go home. But to paraphrase Jane Austen, never judge a person's character without an intimate knowledge of their new situation.

I arrived in London last September to join the ranks of the London Scottish, and what did I find? Well of course I didn't just *arrive*. I had been coming to London for 20 years, two days a week, to fight my network corner and retire bruised for the rest of the week. (As John Birt said to me when I first joined the ITV Controllers' Group, don't forget you got up at 5.30 in Manchester and we all got up at 8 o'clock in London. When you arrive you're dead).

Anyway last autumn, like a faded pop star, I pretended I was re-entering the metropolis, claiming I knew nothing about London. So I formed the LWT London Lunch Club. Every month I ask my distinguished guests from the capital's artistic, business and public institutions the same question. What should their local television station (or at least the one with 'London' in its title) do for the region?

At first they are perplexed. But London doesn't exist, they cry: we have no city government, no single identity, no single culture. We all race home at night and leave town at weekends if we can afford it. Our problems are manifest: transport, health, crime, education, ethnic unemployment, but as the cross-roads of Britain we are too culturally diverse to cohere into anything as practical or manageable as a *region*.

But I persist and I call on Aristotle for help. Surely 'men came to cities to live — and stayed to live a better life'. Why are we so defeatist about London? Why don't we make it work for us all within the capital and without?

After all, we still have to our surprise the greatest financial centre in the world. It has more American banks than New York and more Japanese banks than Tokyo. And even the feared German Deutschesbank has moved its European HQ from Frankfurt to London. London accounts for approaching 50% of the world's foreign exchange market.

And it has tourism, Britain's fourth largest source of revenue, contributing £10bn in foreign exchange to our economy. And London is the tourist's gateway to the rest of the country. Tourists spend 20% of Oxford Street's turnover, 25% of all taxi fares, 40% of all theatre tickets. (I owe these facts to David Puttnam, who gathered them for his 1994 LWT London Lecture.) And as one of my lunch guests, the Chief Executive of London Underground, said: 'Every time you create a job in London, you create another one somewhere else — to create the goods that the London population needs to consume.'

And of course tourism feeds off the arts. The arts in London are the flagship of a major British industry, estimated to employ half a million people and to be worth £10 billion a year. In the arts we excel and London is our yardstick, the largest concentration of theatres in the world, the market for many of those tourists. But what are we, not just those of us living in London, but all over the country, making of these riches?

We are constantly told that tomorrow's media explosion is now today's. The value of American and Australian multi-media companies multiplies on the promise of this future media cornucopia.

But he who controls the software controls the future. It is the mixing of creative skills: from live theatre, graphics, music, design, television, film and computing, the convergence that we hear so much about, that will be the fuel for new media expansion. The challenge is to harness it, not to complain about others doing it. In ITV, we still have access to the skills and the talent to produce the software that will be in such demand. But we will have to look far beyond our regions for inspiration and for business.

When I was at Granada we never thought we were just a regional television company. We thought we were a national and international company which happened to be based in Manchester. But we also *believed* in the Northwest — its people, its commerce, its enterprise and its culture, whether played on a pitch or a stage. The region repaid the compliment by sometimes calling itself Granadaland.

And that's what I believe LWT should be to London. Not only its reporter and entertainer but also its animator and its champion. In *The London Programme's* 20th year we increased our audience by 50% for no less challenging journalism. But we also argue, entertain and celebrate the best of the capital. London belongs to all of us, not just those who can afford to live there.

I know it's not politically correct to say these things. The BBC intends to increase its quota of programmes from the regions. I don't believe in quotas. I believe in simply the best. I don't believe television take-overs will squash regional production. Ask Yorkshire whether a secure financial base will underpin or undermine its regional budgets. Ask the ITV Network Centre whether the well-funded companies are more or less likely to invest in the network programme budget when Channel 5 begins to compete.

Good regional programmes won't die in this competitive future. LWT makes almost two hours a week more than we are obliged to by our licence and most ITV companies show considerably more than the minimum. But regional programmes will have to compete for audiences against national and international programmes on other channels. Channel 4 aimed its American imports quite deliberately at ITV's home-made regional programmes. This meant that regional programmes had to change. They had to become more competitive and more attractive to viewers. Competition may mean that the ITC's attitudes will need to change too. I believe they are wrong to disqualify Granada's *The Motor Show* on the grounds that it isn't local enough, just because it films rally cars being tested on the salt flats of Utah, not on the beaches of Fleetwood. The test of a good regional programme is whether it serves local tastes and interests, not whether it pays lip service to regionalism by being shot in irrelevant regional locations.

LWT is currently trying out a new series about a new fast-moving snooker game, *Tenball*. It's a regional programme about a regional craze but half the ITV network have bought it. That doesn't make it any the less regional. The idea started here and LWT as the local ITV company took it up. That demonstrates one of the benefits of our regional base.

Regional production gives ITV a great potential laboratory for developing new formats, ideas and talent; where risks can be taken and new partnerships tried out. There are no nursery slopes on the ITV Network. Regional productions offer the scope for innovation and risk-taking that the Network rarely provides. Another recent development, co-productions between ITV companies under the same ownership, has been viewed sceptically by some — including the ITC. But if they are led by good strong ideas with relevance to the regional audience and where combined resources will make for a more ambitious and high quality programme, I see this as a positive outcome of take-overs and a creative interpretation of our regional role in an intensely competitive environment.

In the end every channel has to be *about* something and I believe the best and brightest regional programmes — whether made for the local transmission area or the network — will continue to be one of the defining characteristics of ITV.

Rod Allen: While the audience is formulating its questions I want to ask you one question that directly stems from what you have said. You paint a rosy picture and it is difficult to argue with a lot of what you say. What, however, could go wrong? What are the threats to that picture? What would stop a company like LWT investing the way it does in regional programming?

Steve Morrison: Loss of revenue, mainly. Channel 5 will be the first mainstream commercial competitor that ITV, or indeed any other channel in Britain, has faced because Channel 4 has its remit and the satellites only get to 20 per cent of the country. So Channel 5 will be the first seventy per cent coverage mass commercial competitor, and because of the difficulties of its revenue base and the cost of its retuning and other elements, its programme budget will be very small. And, therefore, the vast majority of its programmes, probably about sixty per cent, will be foreign. This will be the first time on mainstream British television that we have had, essentially, an acquired channel. The tragedy will be if the viewers prefer these acquired programmes to British programmes. But no amount of legislation or rules will stop the viewers going where they want to go and, therefore, ITV's programmes will have to be as attractive whether they are regional or network. That is the big dilemma, which is as more and more channels compete, and there is less and less revenue, the danger will be that more and more programming is bought in and not made, and that bought-in programming could prove more attractive than regional programming unless, as I said earlier, regional programming gets as competitive as national programming.

Rod Allen: What do we know about what makes regional programming attractive now? What is the core of that?

Steve Morrison: There are many different elements to it. For a long time Granada ran what you might call 'life-style' programmes against *EastEnders*, which is the BBC's most successful show, on a Tuesday night, in peak time, at half past seven. Granada got the highest audience of any ITV company for these programmes. They were programmes like *House Style, The Green Life Guide, The Main Ingredient, Traveller's Check,* — programmes about what people could do in the region in leisure activity. They got thirty-five to forty per cent of the audience while other companies were playing all sorts of other programmes, including acquired progammes, and not doing as well. So there was obviously an alternative audience there to the *EastEnders* audience. But that was a very interesting example, there are many other examples.

Rod Allen: It certainly doesn't happen in London, though. You can't play that kind of thing in London against *EastEnders*.

Steve Morrison: On Tuesday at 7.30, which is not in my air time, the local programmes don't fare very well audience-wise and it is being treated as a safe haven for minority programmes rather than a competitive haven. I suppose what I am saying is as more and more channels compete there will be less and less safe havens and more and more programmes will have to be competitive.

Rod Allen: I didn't want to let *Tenball* slip past. Can you just say a bit more about how that is really a regional progamme?

Steve Morrison: That is a very interesting question. What is a regional programme? In my view a regional programme is a programme of interest to viewers in the region, not necessarily a programme about a geographical element of the region. *Tenball* has just recently grown up. It hardly exists but the entertainment department have got on to it. It's, I suppose, attempting to do for pool what yellow tee-shirts and one-day matches did for cricket. So everybody will be very colourfully dressed. They will all rush at the table and within less than ten minutes they have to finish the game.

We started this as purely an LWT programme because the players came to LWT and asked if we would make a progamme about this because, obviously, they want this fad to catch on. And it is catching on before it has gone out, because half the network have taken it. Now I think there is a problem. A regional programme should not be disqualified from being a regional programme just because it becomes too successful.

Rod Allen: Absolutely not, but what you are talking about at some point becomes a technical definition of a regional programme rather than a description of a regional programme in the sense that it represents the region to its viewers or to the rest of the network.

Steve Morrison: Well, of course there are so many dimensions. Regional programme policy is rather like the balance of payments. It has many different objectives all of which are contradictory. One is to serve the interests of the region. One is to attract viewers in the region. One is to honour your franchise promises. One is to serve minorities. One is to develop and nurture new talent and creative people in your own region on a kind of nursery slope. There you have at least five competing objectives. But, given that it is the one bit of your air time which a local television company can control, we do try and experiment within all these five.

Louise Bennett, whom I complimented, but not by name, for banning the local *Motor Show*, step forward!

Louise Bennett (Independent Television Commission): Indeed, I am the ITC representative in the north-west and, perhaps, at this stage, it might be actually be helpful to give some idea of the ITC's definition of the regional programme. What we look for is something which is of particular interest to the viewers in the region and displays a distinctive regional character.

Steve has raised the issue of *The Motor Show*. What we felt there was that yes, it was a perfectly well-made programme but it had stepped beyond the boundaries of actually displaying a distinctive regional character and of being of particular interest to the viewers in this region. It is an interesting programme but it is of general interest, not of particular interest. It does not necessarily mean that you are confined to the geographical boundaries of the region. For instance, I am afraid I wasn't there last night but I understand that Mike Spence of Granada mentioned a programme which looked at a Stockport man returning to the Bridge on the River Kwai which we had helped build. That brought a particular distinctive perspective to that subject and, as far as I am concerned, that will count towards the regional quota. But, with something like *The Motor Show*, what you are not able to do is to dilute the regional character of those eight hours forty-six minutes, which Granada pledged on average per week. You have got to keep the character strong and you have got to make it of particular interest to your audience, not of general interest.

Rod Allen: Do you have a view on *Tenball*?

Louise Bennett: I am afraid that I have never seen it so I couldn't give you a view on that at all.

Steve Morrison: I think Louise's attitude is consistent and well thought out and, if followed to the letter, would expel regional programmes to the most marginal reaches of the television schedule. The real problem here is that traditionally regional programmes were boring. They were very worthy but they were boring. That was the traditional position. You had very entertaining programmes and you had boring programmes and, on the whole, regional programmes were boring. They were put in places where they were relatively safe commercially. So you would have programmes about politics — about three MPs sitting in a studio. That's the old-fashioned view of a regional programme.

Nowadays there is no place to hide. So you have to find more and more interesting ways to make programmes, as we said before in the *EastEnders* example. One of those programmes, *House Style*, really worried the ITC. They said 'God, this programme is just too interesting. It is too attractive. It is about houses in general. It is not about houses in Stockport.' And we said 'Well, people in Stockport are interested in houses in general and doing up houses.'

I think this is a really interesting debate because if the ITC freezes its attiitudes, regional programmes are going to go further and further away from the mass audience and what we have to do is find ways of making regional programmes more and more attractive. Since Channel 4 came in regional programmes have changed quite dramatically on ITV because Channel 4 went out at ten o'clock with American drama, *ER, NYPD Blue,* movies which were made for millions of dollars against these little regional programmes about these three MPs sitting in the studio. Well, not surprisingly, people preferred to watch the movies. So suddenly ITV had to react. Scotland was the most interesting example because they had offered something like twenty hours a week of regional programmes in Scotland and were playing regional programmes right across the week at 10.30 and the viewers in Scotland preferred American programmes. So here you have a programme which might be of particular interest and relevance to the viewer in the mind of the ITC, but not in the mind of the viewer.

Rod Allen: So we have regulation which requires you to continue to deliver particular numbers of hours, and a marketplace which requires you to do something different inside those hours.

Steve Morrison: That's it. It is interesting that most ITV companies still do more than they promised. LWT promised, I think, three and a half hours a week and does nearly two hours a week more which is quite astonishing for a two and a half day franchise. I think they will go on doing it and changing it to make it work.

Rod Allen: Just tell me what exactly you mean by 'making it work.'

Steve Morrison: Getting an audience. That doesn't mean the programmes have to be any less good; in fact, you might have to invest more in them to make it work. We have to continue to find ways to make regional programmes attractive to their viewers, and that means the old-fashioned ideas of four people in a studio arguing about some local political matter just ain't good enough.

Louise Bennett: I am sorry but it is to use your own argument back at you, in a way, Steve, in that you quoted *The Main Ingredient* which was one of the life-style programmes that went out on Granada last year at seven thirty against *EastEnders,* with an audience share of thirty-three to thirty-six, which is perfectly creditable at that sort of time. If you will pardon the pun given that it was a food programme, it gave a very strong flavour of the region and it was good, watchable programming. I don't see that the ITC's definition means that you have to make boring, mundane programmes.

Steve Morrison: But I think that we are coming together there. It is just that we are apart on *The Motor Show.*

Helen Hutchinson (Border Television): I am not in the business of ITC bashing; I can't afford to be. I know you said that it doesn't have to be geographically based, but I find it astonishingly patronising to say that a programme must have a regional flavour. I mean what is a distinct regional flavour? Surely you just said yourself that we are caught between a rock and a hard place in terms of a very fearsome market in which we have to operate at the same time as being the most highly regulated broadcasting industry anywhere. We are operating under those guidelines as well. And surely what we are looking for is programmes that viewers want to see, and if they want to see programmes that are well made in Penzance or in Fife, does that programme necessarily have to reflect whatever this Cornish flavour is or this Fife flavour is? I mean, to me, a good programme is a good programme. I don't care where it is made. I would love more programmes to be made in our region and we are quite capable as Borderers, as the people of the debatable lands, of making programmes which are of interest. Full stop. They are of interest to our viewers, they are of interest to Granada's viewers or London's viewers. If they are good programmes, they are good programmes and I am just horrified by the regulatory bodies who deem what is interesting.

Rod Allen: But wait a minute. In the debate that led up to the 1990 Act, there was a lot of powerful argument — some of it from the companies, some of it from outside the companies — about preserving the essential regional character of ITV. And, indeed, the Commission decided not to change the map and not to change the clock because of the strength of that argument. At the same time peak time was handed over to the Centre to provide a homogenous, unified schedule which, although it drew from production outside London, was and is the place where national and international standard programming wherever made is shown on ITV. The companies then said 'And we will do regional programming,' and there is surely a difference between those two kinds of programming.

Helen Hutchinson: Yes, I accept that. You can't say exactly what kinds of programmes you are meaning. But there is still a place for the kind of programme which is geographically based and which does tie in the viewers geographically to the region, of course there is. And it is doesn't have to be dull. But I do question the notion that these strong regional flavours are decided upon by a very few number of people.

Steve Morrison: There is another ITC problem which is not of the ITC's making. In the old system the ITC — the IBA before it became the ITC — were prefects, and now they are mon-itors. They were the prefects — you can talk to the prefect beforehand. With a monitor there comes a point where they say, 'We can't really give an opinion on this. We can only tell you after the fact.' So they become more legalistic. This has meant that there are absolutely wedded to the bible and the bible is the licence application. But, unfortunately, the licence application is only the Old Testament. It was written in 1991. We are now in 1995. Viewers' tastes change, and you have ITC officials saying to you, 'Well, you said here on page 43 of the application that you would do precisely this and now you seem to be doing that.' The answer to this is that all television is piece work; it changes all the time. I don't think this is of the ITC's own doing but I think, as I said earlier, situations or circumstances create people to suit them and I think there is a huge danger in British television, which hasn't yet been properly publicly debated, that the gap between the programme makers and the regulators is getting wider. And what we had in America, which was a standards and practices mentality, is building up. So the programme maker now takes his programme to the standards and practices, or what we call now in England the Compliance Officer.

Before this new system the programme makers were their own compliance officers. There was a sort of unwritten agreement that we and the regulators would settle and agree on the code. Now the gap, in my opinion, is widening not because the individuals want it to widen but because the system has become much more legalistic. And the Old Testament rules until somebody, Jesus, comes — and you know what happened to Him!

Rod Allen: Of course, that is true. I committed HTV to all kinds of things in our 1990 application that they can't come after me for. But I want to go through some of the points that have arisen over the past couple of days. You don't have to answer, of course, for your colleagues who are now absent. But the issue of the Network Centre and the unified schedule has some inexorable logic in it about the regional pattern of ownership and I would like you to talk a little, if you could, about the possibility of further combination and merging within the ITV companies. What are the arguments for and what are the arguments against fewer companies?

Steve Morrison: Well, the main argument for companies joining up is that as the market splinters, there will be less relative revenue into each channel, no matter how well that channel does. If there are fifteen commercial channels, each channel will end up with less revenue. This means that the pressure on the programme budget of a collective channel, like ITV, will increase. At the moment the budget increases by the rate of inflation which is, in our case, about twenty million a year. Now next year, because of its different cost base, Channel 4's budget is going to go up by more than ITV's budget. That really is not sensible. It is not sensible for a mass commercial channel, with forty per cent of the audience, not to be investing more in its programme output.

ITV invests five hundred and fifty million in its programme budget, Channel 4 only invests two hundred million. So we are starting from very different positions. But when Channel 5 comes along it will take audience share from ITV which will reduce ITV's revenue at exactly the point when ITV should be increasing the investment because we are now in direct competition. But most stations with little money, high bidders, smaller companies don't want to increase their investment at the time when their revenue is going down. Most people in business increase their investment when their revenue is going up and cut their costs when their revenue is going down. So there is going to be a huge tension inside the system when at the very point that we should be investing more, the revenue is at most threat. And, therefore, the more channels there are, the more financially secure or firmly based the ITV companies will have to be.

Rod Allen: Can I just be clear? You are talking there about combining to take costs out? And freeing them into programme investment?

Steve Morrison: And having the ability to invest in the schedule. Now some people say there should be a limit to combination and that is what the debate is about;

the most popular limit that is expressed is twenty-five per cent of British terrestrial television advertising. If you don't want one company to control too much television so you have to find a limit.

Then we move on to the second category which is cross-media ownership where, ironically, I take the opposite view, which is that if you let television companies and newspapers own each other, you are, in effect, reducing the plurality of the news agenda or the editorial agenda in the country. So, for example, if the *Daily Mirror* owns Scottish Television, the most sensible thing would be to combine the Scottish television newsroom with the *Daily Record* newsroom and they become one newsroom. And, thus, you now have one agenda.

Rod Allen: You haven't done that with Granada and LWT. Carlton hasn't done that with Carlton and Central.

Steve Morrison: They haven't because they are in different parts of the country. I think that a newspaper based in the same town as the television station would find it very difficult to persuade David Montgomery [chief executive of Mirror Group Newspapers — Eds] not to combine them. So my view is that it would reduce the democracy of views in the marketplace if *The Telegraph* owned Carlton or vice versa or *The Guardian* owned Granada or vice versa whereas I don't see that problem inside one channel's television companies because the regional programmes and the plurality of output is still the same.

Rod Allen: So it doesn't matter that London News Network supplies both Carlton and LWT?

Steve Morrison: Well, it's an interesting point. I looked at this when I came. I think it is a better news service for being combined and the London viewer probably doesn't notice the join between Thursday and Friday. The only debit that I notice is that it doesn't make the arrival of London Weekend as distinct as it used to be. Now this is a commercial issue, not really a viewer's question. What I want to say to the viewer is, 'Thank God, it's Friday! This is London Weekend. This is different. This is fun. This is more relaxing, more entertaining than it was during the week.' It is very difficult to do that if you are putting on the same programme. But this is just an aspiration. I think weekdays are different from weekends and you have good programmes, very good programmes in both, but each television station wants to have its own identity and that is the downside of having a joint news service. But I think it is outweighed by the upside of having a better news service and I don't think the viewers lose anything.

Rod Allen: You don't think there is an issue of plurality there?

Steve Morrison: No. I think the news on Friday coming from a different organisation from the news Monday to Thursday is not a huge gain. I think the better resourcing of it probably outweighs that plurality. But I do think newspapers and television is a difficulty; I don't mind cross-media investment but I wouldn't be for cross-media control.

Rod Allen: I have deflected you a little from trying to arrive at an optimum size channel three, an optimum company.

Steve Morrison: I'm not, and this is another disagreement I think we might have with Carlton, for one company owning ITV. I am a little bit more moderate but I may be wrong eventually if there are a hundred channels but, for the moment, the twenty-five per cent rule would mean that there would have to be a number of companies in ITV. I think that is good. It is always good to have competing centres of finance, production, excellence. And if you look round ITV in the network as well as the regional schedule, you see programmes from all round the country. In fact you see many more programmes from outside London than you do from inside London. London is not particularly well reflected on the national screen. You get *EastEnders, The Bill, London's Burning*. But you have said it. You don't get a great deal of London culture on the screen. Basically ITV has always been dominated by the north to the betterment of it, actually, because that culture, as expressed on ITV, made it the most popular channel. Had it been a London-based channel, it probably would have settled at a lower audience.

Rod Allen: Though is has always weakened it in the south.

Steve Morrison: It has weakened it in the south, particularly more south than London. One of the problems has been that the south-east contractor has never, in the history of ITV, been a large enough contributor to the range of material on the ITV screen. Let's say we have ended up with four or five companies which is more or less where ITV began, I don't think that would do any harm but I wouldn't think that one company, for the moment, would be a good thing.

Rod Allen: Would you regret the loss of Westcountry, Border?

Steve Morrison: Well, the other interesting thing about this is that when the rules were relaxed, it wasn't the smallest companies that were taken over because if you can grow your business, and you have got one or two chances to do it, you don't add Border, you don't add Channel, you don't add Westcountry because it doesn't make that much difference financially. And it may be that we end up, again, with what ITV began with, which is major companies and affiliates and the affiliates gain from their association with the larger companies. If we take the Border example, Granada transmits Border but has no influence whatsoever on Border's programme production so Border has just saved transmission, which is not really vital in its personality, and gained the money to put on the screen. I can't see anything wrong with that and I would predict that more and more companies will begin to combine on these engine-room elements. For example with Carlton we already transmit together and it doesn't do either station, really, any damage whatsoever.

Rod Allen: Does anyone disagree with this unifying vision of the originally regional ITV structure? Or does it sound like a really terrific idea?

Unidentified speaker: I think as long as Scotland stays separate because the experience of the last years with Scottish Television has been — I am not sure of the figures, at 10.30 they might be as bleak as Steve mentioned they were — but at 6.30 they regularly get thirty-five per cent of the audience by doing programmes which, if anybody had any sense elsewhere in the network, they would also buy. But they meet the ITC definition of regional. They are all in that totally incomprehensible dialect of Central Scotland and they are bloody good programmes made for what is, relatively speaking in network terms, very small sums of money. By being innovative and by being daring, they have taken the Scottish audience away from BBC

Scotland at those times of the day when they are broadcasting regional programmes.
Steve Morrison: That is a very good example, actually. Because of this competitive problem which was ironically brought about by this minority channel, Channel 4, playing all its American progammes at ten o'clock, Scottish moved its regional programmes away from ten thirty and into the seven o'clock areas, which is even more risky and adventurous because seven o'clock is right bang in the middle of the prime time schedule. So across the week at seven o'clock, Scotland plays its own half hour regional progammes which are generally factual programmes and they are very, very good programmes. This comes back to the point we made earlier that regional programmes are changing in response to competitive pressures and that doesn't mean they are getting any worse.
Rod Allen: If you were running BBC1, how would you stuff them at seven?
Steve Morrison: At seven, in Scotland? I think I would play a soap, a Scottish soap, five days a week.
Rod Allen: So that would be an expensive solution but it would be a do-able solution?
Steve Morrison: This is a BBC point, but the national regions in the BBC are allowed to make many different kinds of programmes which the English regions are not allowed to make, although that may alter with what is going on. So in the north-west of England the BBC viewer gets a half-hour news magazine and one half-hour opt-out a week, at least it did when I was there. Now that is really pretty ridiculous when in Scotland there is a much wider range, in Ulster there is a much wider range, in Wales there is a much wider range which makes it all the more creditable that Scottish Television beats them hollow.
Rod Allen: Let's go back, briefly, to the short-term future environment. Is there a programme strategy that allows one broadcaster to dominate in the range from five to fifteen competing channels?
Steve Morrison: Yes, there is. I can't really tell you what it is because that will be giving the game away but I have no fears that as the channels begin to increase, ITV will be able to hold its dominant position mainly because — and this, again, I'm afraid, comes back to money — ITV can afford to generate its own hits. That sounds simple but it is really one of the few commercial channels in the world of which that is so. Most commercial channels rely a lot on foreign programming made by other people and on third-party relationships. Sky relies on buying sports rights and buying films, that's how it gains audience. ITV generates its own hits and people don't really wonder any more that ITV progammes come on to the screen and get ten million or more people. They just take it for granted. But it is very difficult to pull off, which is why you need these very strong production centres. It is all the more reason why it is good for some of these companies to combine. Carlton combining with Central, for example, will make Carlton a lot stronger because it has now got a production centre which it didn't have before.
Rod Allen: Which it said it wasn't going to have in its licence application. 'We are not going to do any of that stuff. We will be a publisher-contractor.'
Steve Morrison: Well, I think as time goes they will be very grateful for that because if you have a problem on a Monday night at nine o'clock, it is very useful to

be able to go into your own production centre and say, 'Look, how do we solve this problem?' Whereas if you're just buying third-party programmes you are in a bidding war where everybody bids the price up to such a point that the cost of it is so expensive that there is hardly any point in buying it. So I think that capacity could well be ITV's saviour as long as — and this, I am afraid, is the condition — the companies' revenues are robust enough to continue investment in high cost production.

Rod Allen: And, presumably, in high risk production as well. When I was at LWT and our finance director was the great Peter McNally anything that was the slightest bit risky was very, very difficult to deal with. Do you think, with the Network Centre system, ITV is better at taking programme risks now?

Steve Morrison: It goes in phases. When they started they were incredibly conservative because they didn't know what would work and they didn't want to make a mistake. Also about eighty per cent of ITV, because it is a mainstream channel, is continuing. So you are only really only refreshing twenty per cent of the schedule. That means that there is a hell of a lot of competition for very few slots and the competition is very intense. There was a phase when they were more reliant on proven actors, shall we say, and good scripts from proven writers than doing something very unusual. However one does usually find, and I think the BBC may find this, that if you imitate success too formulaicly the audience has already gone past you and the programme won't, necessarily, work. For example, we tried a programme on ITV called *Under the Hammer* which had Richard Wilson in a John Mortimer script about an auctioneering family, and it didn't work. The audience had moved on. If you take the programmes that have worked, that have been more innovative like *Cracker* or recently *Band of Gold*, they are accessible, but they are unusual enough for the audience to think 'This is different.' It is the old British thing of taking invention to innovation without going so far that it is inaccessible but going far enough for it to be unusual.

Rod Allen: Is the pitch system appropriate to developing that kind of programme strategy?

Steve Morrison: There is a feeling amongst the creative community that, in the old days, they could be nurtured and guaranteed their creative development by going to a variety of ITV companies and forming relationships with them. I think that still goes on and, again, there is an argument for having solid companies, so the Paul Knights and the Brian Eastmans still feel very comfortable with LWT and somebody else feels very comfortable with Carlton. That still goes on. The difference now is that it is only in development; the bigger companies are taking risks by spending money on development before it is commissioned. As long as we are able to do that, as long as we are able to fund development, I think there won't be a problem.

Rod Allen: How many times can you do that? It is an expensive hobby, isn't it?

Steve Morrison: Well, it is probably costing the system quite a few millions per annum but there is no other way of doing it.

Rod Allen: If you reduce to four companies, do you still have a Network Centre?

Steve Morrison: Well, there was a big argument, when the so-called Big Three emerged, that they would dominate the Network Centre and it hasn't. These big companies are very competitive with each other and the reason why the companies themselves created the Network Centre was to find a more objective mechanism for selecting the best on merit and to get away from programme guarantees or programme quotas which produced very good programmes but wasn't competitive enough. I think that logic still stands. Therefore if the Network Centre wasn't there, you would have to invent it.

Rod Allen: I want to be absolutely sure that everybody has had a chance to ask questions. Steve is the most senior representative of the system we will see in these two days.

Jeremy Barr (Ravensbourne College): Just a very brief thought. There has been a lot of discussion during the last day about regional programming being an area of nurturing new talent, nursery slopes, all those sorts of phrases. In the light of what's been said in the last half hour, I have been wondering whether regional programming should also be there for the sharpest, not necessarily the newest, talent and is there any way in which you would say your own company, or others, are actually encouraging people not to think that regional means less demanding in terms of their own creativity?

Steve Morrison: There is a very good example on the air at the moment. *Lily from the Lilydrome* is a co-venture between Granada and LWT. It is basically putting alternative comedians, sharper comedians, on the screen. It has always been very difficult to do this on ITV because you had to get a very large audience and, by their very nature, they weren't yet at that point. So these comics started on Channel 4 and then BBC 2 and then, gradually, when they made it they came to ITV. It seemed to us very sensible to start programmes that gave a vehicle to those kind of artists that couldn't go straight on to the network. I think we will see more of that in these collaborations.

Rod Allen: Is that sex, violence or detection? We were told earlier that all new programming was either sex, violence or detection.

Steve Morrison: Well, it's more like the funny bone side but comedy has become very successful amongst that audience and, for as long as that goes on, I think we will be making those kind of programmes.

Rod Allen: Steve, thank you very much indeed for taking the time to come and visit us, and for letting yourself be questioned.

Steve Morrison: Any excuse to get back to the heart of the country. Thank you very much.

Select Committee: the participatory exercise

The 1995 Symposium's participatory exercise described by
John Gray
Honorary President, University of Manchester Broadcasting Symposium

T HE by-now traditional participatory exercise at the 1995 Symposium was not traditional in its form. It was less competitive in certain aspects. It was not concerned with the financial or economic aspects of the industry, and only marginally with the technical aspects. An old cynic could say it appealed more to the literate than to the numerate.

It was, nevertheless, designed to reflect the themes of the Symposium — Diversity, Regions and Communities in Broadcasting, and in the words of the briefing notes 'to make participants more aware of many of the potentially contradictory aspects of the problems which form the theme'.

The exercise was based on the premise that the government had set up yet another Select Committee to reconsider what it should do about broadcasting — this was eight months before the Bill actually appeared. The Select Committee had itself established sub-committees of three members to consider various aspects of broadcasting and this particular sub-committee was concerned with regional and community identity in broadcasting.

The participants grouped themselves into six teams, notionally corresponding to

- a major ITV company
- a small ITV company
- a BBC National Region
- BBC centrally/English Region
- a radio consortium and
- a cable/satellite consortium

The Select Committee warned these organisations that they would be required to give evidence, and that the questions which would concern the Committee were likely to be whether the present ITV Regions were appropriate, the extent and importance of productions for their own regions for network, and for sale, their views on inter-media ownership, whether networks should be centred outside London, the responsibility of cable systems for programme initiation and whether there was an optimum size for a local radio station.

Some background material was available both in briefing notes and in general literature. The teams gathered themselves together, went in to huddles, and then submitted their representatives for gruelling examination by the members of the Select Committee.

So much for the exercise as designed. It says much for the theories of group dynamics that to a great extent each team did take on something of the nature of what it represented. As it was a 'game' there was inevitably certain amount of irreverent *joie de vivre*. It may also reflect something; of the BBC today that perhaps the teams representing the BBC were the least successful in coming to grips with the questions before them. It also reflected reality in that the cable/satellite consortium took a very detached and almost uninterested view of the questions.

It is not, therefore, very surprising that the two teams which both appreciated what they were supposed to do, and did it, were the one representing small scale ITV — largely basing itself on Border Television — and the team considering the problems from the angle of radio. As stated, the exercise was non-competitive, but the Select Committee praised both these organisation for the manner in which they presented their case, to which it stated 'they would give serious consideration'. The 'Border' small ITV presentation effectively combined gamesmanship, levity and serious thought, and the radio group showed that in many respects there was a greater concern with purpose and identity in radio than in television — which hardly surprised the wiseacres.

Those taking part seemed to enjoy the exercise. Two things arise from it in retrospect, both of which may be of interest to, or lessons for, the future, The first is that within limited time and in the setting of an event such as the Manchester Symposium an exercise which requires informed discussion rather than problem-solving may be the more efficacious. The other point of interest is the revelation how deeply ingrained parliamentary type democracy is entrenched. As at the 'House of Commons' debate in the Granada set some years ago, almost instinctively participants adopted the styles and usages of parliamentary procedure. Can something be learned from this? Especially at a time when the broadcast industry is often at the mercy of uncomprehending politicians, it might be well to increase our understanding of politicians by playing their own games and having more such exercises.

'Select Committee' was devised by John Gray

If you would like to be kept in touch with plans for future University of Manchester Broadcasting Symposia, please write to:

Marjorie Burton
University of Manchester Broadcasting Symposium
School of Education
Oxford Road
Manchester M13 9PL